Journey of the Software Professional

A Sociology of Software Development

Luke Hohmann

To join a Prentice Hall PTR internet mailing list
point to http://www.prenhall.com/register

Prentice Hall PTR
Upper Saddle River, New Jersey 07458
http://www.prenhall.com

Library of Congress Cataloging-in-Publication Data

Hohmann, Luke.
  Journey of the Software Professional / Luke Hohmann
      p.   cm.
  Includes bibliographical references and index.
  ISBN 0-13-236613-4
  1. Computer software--Development. I. Title.
QA76.76.D47H64 1997
005.1'068--dc20   96-30560
                                         CIP

Editorial/production supervision: *Nicholas Radhuber*
Manufacturing manager: *Alexis Heydt*
Acquisitions editor: *Paul Becker*
Cover design: *Design Source*
Cover concept: *Luke Hohmann and Miko Yamaguchi*
Cover illustration: *Brent Rosenquist and Rhett Guthrie*
Cover design director: *Jerry Votta*

© 1997 by Luke Hohmann
Published by Prentice Hall PTR
Prentice-Hall, Inc.
A Pearson Education Company
Upper Saddle River, NJ 07458

The publisher offers discounts on this book when ordered in bulk quantities.
For more information, contact:
        Corporate Sales Department
        PTR Prentice Hall
        One Lake Street
        Upper Saddle River, NJ 07458
        Phone: 800-382-3419, Fax: 201-236-7141
        E-mail: dan_rush@prenhall.com

Printed in the United States of America
10 9 8 7 6 5 4 3 2 1

ISBN 0-13-236613-4

Prentice-Hall International (UK) Limited,London
Prentice-Hall of Australia Pty. Limited, Sydney
Prentice-Hall Canada Inc., Toronto
Prentice-Hall Hispanoamericana, S.A., Mexico
Prentice-Hall of India Private Limited, New Delhi
Prentice-Hall of Japan, Inc., Tokyo
Pearson Education Asia Pte. Ltd., Singapore
Editora Prentice-Hall do Brasil, Ltda., Rio de Janeiro

For Noura
with love

CONTENTS

LIST OF FIGURES

FOREWORD

by Gerald M. Weinberg

It's customary, when writing a foreword, to say, "I couldn't put the book down." I can't say that about *Journey of the Software Professional.* I not only could put it down, I had to put it down, and often.

This book is not, as its title might imply, a biography. Nor is it a pleasant fiction furnishing an evening's entertainment. Instead, *Journey* is a compendium of ideas—ideas derived from a comprehensive model of software development as problem solving. The "Journey" in the title is the acquisition of hundreds or thousands of ideas accumulating in the mind of any person who is to be an effective software developer. It's this massive accumulation of ideas that makes it impossible to read this impressive book without setting it down.

As I read, I would find an idea that would force me to stop and ask, "Do I agree with this? How does it relate to other ideas? How could I apply this with my clients?" Sometimes I didn't agree (although not often), so I had to depart from the journey onto a long side trip ending in confirmation or conversion. Sometimes I couldn't relate this idea to others in the book, so I would detour back and forth among the various sections. Sometimes, I couldn't think of a way to apply the idea to my own clients, so I had to discuss the idea with some of them.

Eventually, I came to understand the "Journey" in a different way. It is not the career journey of some sociological average software professional. It is, rather, the journey of one particular software professional—me, the reader. It is a journey through the book and through the labyrinth of ideas that I've accumulated in the forty-odd years of my life as a software professional. Thus, for each new reader, it will be a new journey.

To complete a journey through a labyrinth, you need a model—either a map or an algorithm to guide your escape. To navigate a particularly rich labyrinth, such as the accumulation of ideas that form the sum total of learning in a professional lifetime, most of us need more than one map. Although I have several models of my own to map my way, Luke Hohmann guided me through my personal labyrinth using yet another—his model of problem solving. This model made it possible for me to take a fresh, pleasurable, and productive journey through what I thought was familiar territory.

In many ways, it opened my eyes. If you are a software professional, I think it will open yours as well.

Gerald M. Weinberg

PREFACE

It was my first managerial assignment. I was ready. I had worked as a developer for several years on many different projects. Some were successful. From these I learned what to do. Some were failures. From these I learned what *not* to do. I was armed with a *masters* degree in Computer Science and Engineering from a prestigious University. I had *studied* software engineering and was ready to *apply* it. I read *a lot* of books on managing people and projects, from *Peopleware* to *The Mythical Man-Month*. Their advice and insights from the trenches of software development made sense. I was going to follow *all* of it.

The cold truth slowly sank in. My first job as a manager was less than a stellar success. Yes, the project was completed, the system was implemented, but I could have done a *far* better job. Since then I've led other projects and in the process learned many things. Past project experiences don't always apply in new projects. In fact, what *brings* success in one context *causes* failure in another. *Learning* about software engineering is far different from *doing* software engineering. And, while all the advice given in "Peopleware" books is definitely useful, I found myself continually asking "What are the underlying principles of software development? What might guide or drive the advice and insight of people like Gerald Weinberg, Frederick Brooks, Larry Constantine, and Tom DeMarco[1]?"

This book was written for three reasons. First, it explores the underlying principles of software development through a simple but comprehensive theoretical framework. Second, it shows how to put this framework to good use through practical

---

[1] Test yourself: do you know these names? Give yourself a C+ if you know them but have not yet read something they've written. Give yourself a B+ if you've read two or more of their books. Give yourself an A+ if you are frustrated with me for not listing your personal favorite author!

advice built on top of the theory. Third, it contains specific advice for both developers and managers in a clear and understandable format.

Why include practical advice and the theoretical framework supporting it in the same book? If a book gives practical advice but lacks a theoretical foundation you are left wondering from what credible principles the "advice" is drawn and how to successfully apply the "advice" in your environment. If a book provides only theory, you are left wondering about its practicality. Even the most elegant theory requires examples of how it is used to provide value. Theory is important for providing a way of thinking about a topic, but theory without practice is a car with no engine[2]. While the majority of the book consists of practical advice, it contains the theory necessary to support it.

One advantage to practical advice is that it can provide a ready response to a tough situation. But, what happens when you are faced with a situation *not* described in this book? Alternatively, what happens when you disagree with my advice? Once again the theoretical foundation of this book becomes essential, for it provides you with the tools you need to *create your own advice* and respond effectively to novel situations.

Finally, you may have wondered why I've included specific advice to developers and managers in the same book. Their jobs are decidedly different and often antagonistic, right? A book certainly cannot give advice to both at the same time, right? Wrong. Certainly the jobs of developers and managers are different. So what? Take any difficult problem faced by a group of developers and their management. Unless each member of the group understands what they can do to improve the situation and does it, things are not likely to improve. Isn't the *real* job of *every* person involved with the development effort to ship the best system possible? Instead of emphasizing *differences*, perhaps we should emphasize the ways developers and managers can work *together*. This book was not written for the intersection of the population of developers and managers. It was written for the union.

"WHAT'S IN IT FOR ME?"

Here is what this book will do for you:

- ♦ It provides a simple and comprehensive theory of how developers and teams of developers create software.
- ♦ It shows how advice found in other books makes more sense when applied in the context of this theory. After reading this book, you will never think of a data model or a coding standard in the same way again!
- ♦ It will introduce you to several new strategies and techniques on improving your and your team's effectiveness.
- ♦ It makes understanding and implementing these strategies and techniques easier by giving explicit advice to both managers and developers. I don't want

[2] Unless you're Fred Flintstone, this is likely to be a problem!

you to waste any time trying to determine if the practical advice in this book is intended for a manager or a developer. Instead, I want you to put these ideas into practice as quickly as possible.

♦ It addresses a broad range of topics and issues not usually addressed in most books on software development you *will* encounter over the course of your career. While you may not have an *immediate* need for every chapter, owning this book means you will be prepared to address these issues when they do arise. And they will.

Finally, it seeks to entertain you with personal stories and anecdotes that illustrate, expand, or otherwise bring to life the ideas in the book. These are offset from the main text in an italicized font.

CONTENT AND ORGANIZATION

This book is organized in five parts:

Part I   Describes the mental processes of software development. It integrates cognitive models (models of how we think) with software methods (specifications of the activities we should undertake when developing software).

Part II Explores a wide variety of topics on how individuals and their managers can improve performance using the SPO framework presented in Part One. My goal is twofold. First, I hope to show how some of the traditional advice found in other books on such topics as code reviews makes better sense when applied in the context of the SPO framework. Second, I hope to introduce you to some new ideas such as future perfect thinking and how (and when) to make pancakes!

Part III Applies the SPO framework to teams. It moves from cognitive models (which describe the individual) to organizational models (which describe interactions between individuals). Integrating organizational models with methods shows how the SPO framework provides a single, cohesive framework helping us to understand, predict, and guide both individual and collective behavior.

Part IV Mirrors Part Two by using the SPO framework as the foundation for practical advice designed to enhance the effectiveness of teams. Again, I hope to show how traditional advice on such topics as the importance of standards make better sense when discussed in the context of the SPO framework. Of course, I also hope to introduce you to some fresh approaches to common problems such as building trust between developers, creating appropriate system architectures and structuring teams to support them, and writing useful status reports.

Part V   Concludes with a discussion of issues related to context—such as learning how to avoid poor working environments. It also deals with creating (or finding) the right context in which to apply the advice contained in parts two and four and serves to round out the book.

The structure of the book is as follows:

The Individual	Chapters
Part One: Theory	1 – 2
Part Two: Practice	3 – 6

The Team	
Part Three: Theory	7 – 8
Part Four: Practice	9 – 14

Context	
Part Five	15 – 17

AUDIENCE

There are three distinct paths in the journey of the software professional. In the first, effort is focused inward, and the goal is improving personal performance. In the second, effort is directed outward, and the goal is improving both self and others. In the third, effort is directed upward, and the goal is to create an environment whereby others can be most effective. This book was written to address the needs of a developer on each stage of the journey.

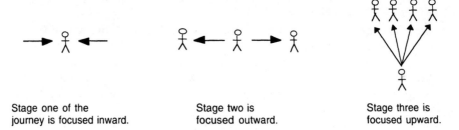

Stage one of the journey is focused inward.

Stage two is focused outward.

Stage three is focused upward.

Here are some ways specific populations can benefit from this book.

If you are a student or developer with less than three years' working experience you are likely to be concentrating your efforts on stage one of the journey. If this is true then reading this book will provide you with the theoretical foundation necessary to *understand* how to improve your effectiveness. At times the book may be a bit challenging, but rest assured the effort you put into reading it will be worthwhile.

If you are an experienced developer (e.g., a senior architect or lead designer), then you are probably in the second stage of the journey. In other words, your primary job is to help others be effective by capitalizing on your experience. Such a job is uniquely demanding: you've got to marry technical *and* social demands. But how do technical and social issues really interact? Reading this book provides the foundation for discussing the answer. Of special interest to you are parts three and four that concentrate on teams, especially chapters seven and twelve.

Finally, managers of all levels of experience can derive several benefits from reading this book. First, an understanding of how developers work both individually and in teams as they create software is a necessary prerequisite for the establishment of effective managerial practices. To see why, just read any Dilbert™ cartoon! Second, the practical advice serves as a managerial handbook and provides specific answers to difficult questions in the context of a strong theoretical framework. Third, as a manager you have the responsibility for creating an effective work environment. A strong theoretical framework enables you to accomplish this effectively (see especially chapters nine, ten, and eleven).

HOW TO READ THIS BOOK

First, *read Chapter One*. The primary constructs of the SPO framework are established in chapter one. Reading this chapter first will provide a background in the primary terms as used in the remainder of the book.

Second, *feel free to skip chapters in Parts Two and Four*. This book can be read quite satisfactorily in a nonlinear fashion. Be forewarned, some of the practical advice may seem a little out of place without the theoretical foundation in place to support it. Because of this, I do recommend you read part one before any chapter in part two, and part three before any chapter of part four.

Finally, read aggressively. Highlight or underline passages you think are important. Make notes to yourself in the margin. Dog-ear important pages for quick reference. Do whatever you need to do to make the most of it!

ONE FINAL WORD

The writing of this book, like the creation of a large software system, is a strange journey, one never quite finished. To further my own personal journey, I ask you to write me concerning the material presented herein. What did you like? What is useful? What benefits have you derived from reading this book? How can I improve the material in either form, content, or presentation?

I wish you a long and interesting journey, filled with an appreciation for our chosen profession. Thank you, and enjoy what follows.

Luke Hohmann
lhohmann@acm.org

ACKNOWLEDGMENTS

Although it is common to thank your spouse at the end of your acknowledgments, I feel I must begin this brief section with a special acknowledgment of the role my wife, Noura Bashshur, has had in helping me create this book. Although I had no time to write this book, she nonetheless encouraged me to pursue my dream. She patiently listened to my ideas, suggested new ways of solving tough problems, pointed out inconsistencies in my arguments, and showed me how to incorporate other disciplines into the ideas presented in this book. She has been a constant inspiration, friend, and critic. Without her insight, support, and considerable experience this book would have been far less than what it is today, and would probably not have been written at all.

To my former colleagues at EDS, I especially thank Vern Olson, who gave an eagle wings; Jeff Heller, who taught him to fly; and Jim Young, who not always seems to do the right thing but also manages to do things right. Also, to Glynn Spangenberg, John Steele, Bob Mabry, Katherine Goodwin, and Coty Smith, each of whom taught me something about structures, processes, and outcomes in general and management in particular.

To my friends and colleagues from the University of Michigan Highly Interactive Computing Environments (Hi-CE) research group, I'd like to thank Mark Guzdial, Sara Staebler, Iris Roth-Tabak, and Yasmin Kafai. Special thanks goes to Elliot Soloway who challenged me in so many ways, all the time, and whose theories continue to profoundly affect my thinking. From the University of Michigan School of Business Administration I am grateful for the opportunity to have worked with Karl Weick, Robert Quinn, Dan Denision, and Joel Kahn.

I am indebted to my colleagues at ObjectSpace, who collectively represent the singularly *best* collection of software developers devoted to object technology. Special thanks to those who took the time to review this work (many of them reviewing the same section multiple times!): Kevin Lehnert, Craig Harrington, Wayne Parrott, Tom Cook, Georgia McNamara, Adam Shackleford, Walter Bodwell, Jef Newsom, Craig Larman, Chis Thomas, Michael Klobe, Paul Johnson, Graham Glass, and David Norris. *Very* special thanks go to Todd Girvin, Jack Carter, and Raj Wall who provided valuable encouragement from the very beginning, and whose friendship is a source of continuing inspiration.

I'd also like to thank my friends, students, and clients, many of whom have tried the ideas presented in this book. I'd especially like to thank Ramona Dunn, Dan O'Leary, Eric Adams, George Heyworth, and Russ McClelland. A very special thanks go to Miko Yamaguchi for helping transform my ideas for a cover into reality.

I've often wondered why authors thank their editors and reviewers. After writing this book it is *obvious* why authors thank these very special people. From Prentice-Hall, I'd like to thank Paul Becker, Maureen Diana, and Nick Radhuber for working so hard in making certain the book met all production deadlines. I'd like to thank my reviewers who included Robert Glass and two anonymous reviewers. Your criticisms pointed out the weakest parts of the manuscript and showed me where to improve. Any mistakes, of course, remain my own. I would also like to thank Martha Williams for her excellent copyediting of the manuscript. A very special thanks to Brent Rosenquist and Rhett Guthrie who prepared the final version of the cover art on very short notice and helped keep the book on schedule.

I have undoubtedly forgotten to mention one or more individuals who have helped in the creation of this book. This was, by no means, intentional, but yet another manifestation of the limits of my own cognitive abilities.

It is not the critic who counts, not the man who points out how the strongman stumbled, or where the doer of deeds could have done them better. The credit belongs to the man who is actually in the arena; whose face is marred by dust and sweat and blood; who strives valiantly; who errs and comes short again and again; who knows the great enthusiasms, the great devotions; who spends himself in a worthy cause; who, at the best, knows in the end the triumph of high achievement, and who, at the worst, if he fails, at least fails while daring greatly; so that his place shall never be with those cold and timid souls who know neither victory nor defeat.

— Theodore Roosevelt

Part One

How does an individual developer develop software? That is, how does a developer take a problem statement and generate a working system? Is there a relationship between how a developer works and the method selected for the development of the software system? If so, what is it? And what about our basic personality? How does it influence the way we solve problems? These questions, and more like them, are fundamental in understanding how we create software. Answering them is the primary goal of Part One.

Chapter 1 begins by describing the mental processes of a developer writing software. To do this, it integrates cognitive models (models of how we think) with methods (specifications of the activities we should undertake when developing software). The result is the Structure–Process–Outcome (SPO) framework, a simple theory that can describe problem solving. Several examples of the SPO framework are shown, and the critical role of feedback between components of the framework is discussed.

The SPO framework is insufficient to account for all problem-solving behavior. Many times we must make decisions that are *not* dictated by the structures, processes, or outcomes defined by a method. By incorporating values, personality, and goals into the SPO framework Chapter 2 creates the integrated SPO framework, which can be used to explain all problem-solving behavior. It concludes with an exploration of the conflict and tension that can arise as different components of the integrated framework compete for importance.

1

SETTING THE FOUNDATION

Suppose I ask you to help me solve a problem (e.g., write a program to perform some function). How would you do it? Would you begin by asking me questions to make certain you understand my request? I hope so. Part of the problem-solving process is making certain you understand the problem you've been asked to solve. What will you do next?

That depends on a variety of factors. Consider experience, or how well you know the problem. If you're an expert, you can quickly harness your broad and extensive array of experience to solve the problem directly with simplicity, speed, and elegance. If you're a complete novice, you will have to try and think of something—anything—and try it as best you can. Creating a solution will take longer, as you'll probably experience one or more false starts. More testing will be needed along the way to verify the proposed solution is correct. When finished, the solution is likely to be less optimal than an expert's (but that's often OK—you did solve the problem, didn't you?).

Is expertise the only factor to consider? No. There are many others, including

♦ the preferred and actual processes we use when problem solving, which aren't always the same thing;
♦ the degree to which the desired outcome is known;
♦ the perceived complexity of the problem, which changes our process;
♦ the structures supporting and/or otherwise influencing our processes (e.g., we're likely to use a slightly different process when using C++ versus COBOL);

- ◆ the time given to solve the problem;
- ◆ and many more!

The purpose of this chapter is to create a framework for thinking about problem solving in terms of structures, processes, and outcomes. It does this by integrating cognitive models, which are descriptions of how we solve problems, with methods, which are descriptions of disciplined processes to use when we solve a problem.

Chapter Overview

The chapter begins by exploring problem solving from two perspectives: cognitive models and software methods. These are compared and contrasted in Section 1.1. Section 1.2 provides a brief overview of the concepts associated with structures, processes, and outcomes.

Sections 1.3 through 1.5 discuss each aspect of structure, process, and outcome in greater detail. Section 1.3 begins by discussing *process* first, because process is the link between descriptive cognitive models and prescriptive methods. Section 1.4 addresses outcomes, the end result of mental or physical processes. Section 1.5 discusses structure, focusing on the absolutely essential role structure plays in problem solving. Structures, processes, and outcomes are again united in Section 1.6, which further elaborates on the relationships between the three.

Section 1.7 provides examples of the framework and shows how the concepts of structures, processes, and outcomes can describe a wide range of human problem-solving behavior. Section 1.8 discusses the critical role of feedback between the various components of the framework. Section 1.9 reviews and summarizes the chapter.

1.1 PROBLEM SOLVING: DESCRIPTIONS
AND PRESCRIPTIONS

Ultimately, every team of developers boils down to individual developers working on specific problems—subsystems, modules, programs, objects, and the like. As such, part of unraveling the mystery of how software is created begins with an understanding of how we solve problems. This does not mean we solve problems in the best possible way: We could use a bad process, or produce irrelevant outcomes. Methods to the rescue! By providing a consistent, reasoned, and thorough approach to problem solving, methods enable us to solve problems more efficiently, quickly, and correctly.

1.1.1 Cognitive Models

A *cognitive model* is a description of how we solve problems. Developed as researchers study developers (and other people) engaged in complex analysis, design, and maintenance activities, cognitive models provide a way of thinking about how

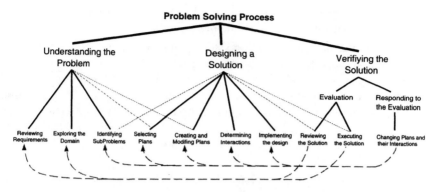

Figure 1-1   A Cognitive Model of Software Development

we think. The model used to guide the rest of this book is presented in presented in Figure 1–1. It draws from research on expert developers [Soloway 1984, 1983], [Shneiderman 1980], novice developers [Hohmann 1992], [Miller 1982], mathematicians [Poyla 1956], and executives in large organizations [Wood 1990].

The top half of Figure 1–1 represents major activities in problem solving with subactivities beneath them. These activities proceed from left to right (i.e., we start with Understanding the Problem and then move to Designing a Solution). The model implicitly assumes a goal-directed approach in which the goal is the resolution of the problem, although the presence of a goal is not a requirement. As you review this model, think about two things. First, think about your own approach to problem solving. Is the model consistent with this approach? Second, if you have used a method, compare the steps prescribed in the method with the steps described in this model. Are they consistent? Does the method support the activities described in this model?

Each major activity is described below. In reading these descriptions, it is important to keep in mind I am describing *mental* processes. Physical things, ranging from sketches on a piece of paper to actual source code are only *optionally* created in one subactivity, *Implementing the Design*.

♦ *Understanding the Problem.* The first step of solving any problem is trying to understand it by creating a mental model. A *mental model* is your internal representation of the problem. It is formed as you review requirements, explore the problem domain, and attempt to reduce the complexity of the original problem by partitioning it into smaller, more easily solved subproblems. Strategies for improving this activity include trying to examine the problem from different angles by varying the requirements (e.g., you might emphasize different words in the requirements, or try changing the constraints described by the requirements). It is also common to compare the current problem with past problems, noting where and how they differ.

Ideally, Understanding the Problem continues until you are comfortable that you do indeed understand the problem. But when is that? There is no universal answer to this question: Each of us takes our own amount of time. But what if we are taking too much time?

Fortunately, there is a good strategy for determining how much time to use. It is called the law of diminishing returns. The *law of diminishing returns* states you should stop trying to understand a problem when spending more time on understanding will not substantially increase understanding. Asking the same questions or continually revisiting the same issues are two strong indications you need to move toward designing a solution. Usually, your best bet is to try to understand a less complex version of the original problem.

To illustrate, suppose I asked you to build the air traffic control system for Chicago O'Hare airport, all very nicely documented in 1,500 pages of requirements. I don't know about you, but I wouldn't try to understand all 1,500 pages at one time. Instead, I'd first try to understand the issues associated with a much smaller problem, such as an air traffic control system for an airport with a single runway and only one plane. Once I understood the issues and complexities associated with this much simpler problem, I would gradually add complexity in specific steps. For example, my next step might be to try to build a control system for two airplanes. Or, I might try and solve the problem for two runways instead of one. The point is that I would continually look for a problem whose complexity I can understand.

♦ *Designing a Solution.* Once the problem appears to be understood (or, at least, understood well enough), our mental processes switch to designing a solution by examining previously solved problems to determine if one or more of these solutions may be appropriate in the context of the new problem. If so, the solutions are used as is. If not, which is generally the case, our old solutions must be *tailored* to meet the new problem. If and when I'm successful, I can remember the new solution, a process we call learning.

Solutions to problems reside in a "cognitive library." The library metaphor library is intentional. First, it nicely explains the role of experience: More experienced developers have larger and more varied cognitive libraries.

Second, it explains what kind of experience is best. The best experience enables us to increase the number and complexity of the plans within our library. As Maguire [1994] points out, spending five years writing the same kind of program is not five years of experience. It is one year of experience five times over.

Third, it provides some ideas on how we might provide external organization so we can solve problems more effectively. Some people even go so far as proposing that we "catalog" every solution and how to apply it. This catalog would then be used to solve new problems quickly and effectively. In practice, this is problematic, and even counter productive, as shown in this and later chapters.

The design process draws upon several different kinds of knowledge.

♦ *Semantic-Syntactic.* Semantic knowledge describes the general strategies we have learned about problem solving and programming paradigms (e.g., "What is objected-oriented programming?"). Syntactic knowledge is knowledge of a specific programming language or development environment. It is easier for humans to learn a second syntactic structure when it is based on another known semantic structure [Shneiderman 1980]. This helps to explain, for example, why it is easier to learn a second language (such as C) when you know a different language based on the same semantic paradigm (such as Pascal).

♦ *Plans.* A *plan* is a stereotypic solution to a problem. We develop plans as we solve problems and add them to our cognitive libraries where they can be reused. Plans are *private*. To illustrate, consider how you drive to work each morning. Do you take a new route each day? Or, do you settle on one route, with one alternate in case of bad traffic? Each route is a plan for driving to work.

Quite recently, there has been a large amount of theoretical research and practical application to the externalization of commonly used (and useful) plans. A *pattern* is an externalized and generalized plan. Patterns are important because they can be used to rapidly increase the size and effectiveness of our cognitive library. Instead of reinventing known solutions, I can simply look them up in a catalog. Unlike plans, which are tailored through mental processes, the descriptions of patterns usually include specific advice on *how* to tailor the pattern to solve a problem. The best patterns include additional advice on when a pattern should not be applied to a specific problem. Finally, patterns also provide a key mechanism for facilitating communication among a group of developers [Gamma 1995].

Although patterns have great value, not every plan should be elevated to pattern status. First, many plans are idiosyncratic to a problem domain or specific solution. The true value in a pattern lies in its applicability *across* many problems. Second, many plans represent simple semantic-syntactic knowledge and should thus be considered a part of the core knowledge about the domain of software development *all* developers should share. The concept of a subroutine is not a "pattern" for solving a range of problems. It is instead a core piece of knowledge required for effective use of almost any programming language. Third, it does not make economic sense to expend the effort to "patternize" every plan inside our head; the payback is simply not there. Finally, the existence of a pattern solving a problem only has value if you know it! I'm not yet convinced the best strategy for problem solving is searching through hundreds or thousands of patterns in search of *the* pattern meeting the exact requirements of the problem.

To illustrate the difference between a plan and a pattern, consider the following example [Johnson 1995]. Suppose you and I work in a small company, and we have to move our offices. Assuming we had never moved our office before, we may be somewhat unsure of what furniture to move first, and what shortcuts can be taken (e.g., do we have to empty the drawers of the desk into a box, or can we just move the desk with the drawers intact?). The plan I develop for moving my office would be different from the one you develop for moving yours, but both would reflect our general experience in moving things. Once we had completed our respective moves we could compare our efforts, identify which activities worked well—and did not work so well—and create a more general, reusable pattern of the best way to move an office. This, in turn, can be shared with other members of the team. Of course, if only I was to move my office, it would not make sense to go through the effort of creating a pattern.

♦ *Rules of Discourse.* These specify guidelines for the implementation of programs shared among developers. These may be formal (all variables will be named according to the Hungarian naming convention[1]) or informal (a variable should be named according to its purpose). The best formal and informal rules are mutually supportive (i.e., a variable named `lpszPhoneNumber`[2]). Rules are developed and refined over time, with experts possessing more varied and complex rules than novices. Like the other kinds of knowledge described above, rules of discourse may not be explicitly taught.

A key idea in this model of the problem-solving process is *search.* Specifically, a person engaged in problem solving is actively engaged in searching for the best plan meeting the criteria of the problem. When does search stop? Precisely when the problem can be solved based on past experience. An important influence on this search process is the effect of time pressure. An individual under severe time constraints will likely do four things, all of them contributing to an incorrect solution.

First, their search behavior will focus on the most obvious aspects of the problem. Unfortunately, the "hard part" of most problems is *rarely* what is obvious; it is what is hidden! Second, judgments will be made to simplify the problem, inappropriately reducing its complexity. Third, the search process will stop on the first plan seeming to fit the problem. Virtually no time will be spent exploring alternatives, even when it is felt an alternative solution is likely to be superior. Finally, the verification phase is spent generating plausible justifications as to why the plan selected is appropriate instead of verifying the plan as actually solving the problem. It is often faster to justify why the selected plan is correct than to write a detailed test case actually demonstrating the plan is correct.

[1] The Hungarian naming convention is a set of detailed guidelines for naming variables and functions in the C programming language invented by Charles Simonyi.

[2] `lpszPhoneNumber` is a variable name corresponding to the Hungarian naming convention reference above. It can be "decoded" as follows: "lp" = long pointer; "sz" = NULL terminated ASCII string. Thus, `lpszPhoneNumber` is a long pointer to a NULL terminated ASCII string, presumably containing a phone number.

Only in rare circumstances can time pressure lead to improved performance. How rare? Increased performance under time pressure requires us to identify the problem correctly and already possess a plan for solving it. In other words, we have to be an expert in the problem and its solution, a rare occurrence in any environment. And, even experts cannot quickly and accurately respond to every problem, for any single cognitive library is necessarily limited in scope.

Researchers have also studied what happens when "too" much time is given to developers. Their results indicate too much time actually reduces performance because developers experience dissatisfaction (e.g., boredom, listlessness) with the overall process [Abdel-Hamid 1990; Vinton 1992]. Of course, I don't think I have ever been given "too much time" to solve a problem! Nonetheless, it does appears time pressure is not necessarily negative, although putting pressure on developers to complete their work faster is rarely an effective strategy for increasing effectiveness.

Finally, it should be noted that design plays the key "linking" role in the overall process, as shown in Figure 1–1 by the dashed lines linking design to some of the subactivities in understanding the problem and verifying the solution. To get from the beginning to the end, one must pass through design.

♦ *Verifying the Solution.* When the design process is complete, the developer has formed a mental model of both the problem and a potential solution. The first step of verification happens mentally as the model is executed. Does the solution solve the problem? The important point here is that this kind of verification takes place *in the mind* of the developer before the system is actually implemented. Although all developers engage in some kind of mental verification before they implement their solution, most don't spend enough [Humphrey 1995]. More specifically, *thinking through your solution* before you implement it usually results in improved perfomance.

If the human brain had infinite processing capacity, all we would have to do is this mental verification and then simply translate our ideas to a working system. However, our minds are limited in capacity. While we may be satisfied our mental model of the problem *and* solution are correct, there is only one way to tell for certain: The solution must be implemented and formally verified through execution. Because verification occurs both before implementation (mentally) and after (testing), it serves as the only component in the process providing the feedback necessary to reinforce and/or correct the mental model.

The dotted lines in Figure 1–1 indicate the presence of feedback loops. Feedback loops are an important component of human behavior, as they provide information on how well we are moving to a resolution of the problem. If the feedback is positive (i.e., the proposed solution is thought to be correct), then there is motivation to continue the pursuit of a particular course of action. If the feedback is negative, indicating an undesirable outcome, there is motivation to return to some prior activity and try an alternative approach.

Most complex human activity includes some aspect of feedback. For example, tightening a nut with a wrench provides direct physical feedback: You know the nut is more securely fastened as it becomes harder and harder to turn the wrench. Fortunately, because a natural aspect of software development is the creation and execution of a program, software developers have an advantage in problem solving. Our feedback is a "built-in" and expected part of the process.

Like all other models, the model presented in Figure 1–1 suffers from overgeneralization, abstraction, and presentation. Each of us has our own problem-solving process. It can (and does) change based on the kind of problem we are solving. It is dynamic in a way no static representation can ever hope to capture. Accordingly, countless models could be created for each of us as we tackle new projects or undertake new activities.

One way to address the shortcomings of this model is to take a few moments and reflect on your own approach to problem solving—your own cognitive processes. Do you perform more or less of the subactivities listed above in analysis? Design? Why? One developer I interviewed for this book noted there are times when his "comfort level" seems to increase dramatically, his sign that he not only understood the problem but also had a good "feel" for the solution. A central theme of this book is that increasing your understanding of your own mental processes will enable you to be a more effective developer. Don't worry if this seems a little hard right now. You will be able to use the framework described later in this chapter to help guide you in this understanding.

1.1.2 Benefits of Cognitive Models

Cognitive models enable us to understand how individuals solve problems. The research data they have generated and the theories they have created provide the following benefits:

♦ *Explanation of behavior.* Cognitive models help explain the complex behaviors associated with learning (i.e., adding a new plan), forgetting (i.e., losing the index to a plan in our library), and the impact of experience (i.e., a larger cognitive library).

♦ *More efficient processes.* An understanding of how we solve problems enables us to determine which modifications to existing processes are likely to have a positive impact.

♦ *Improved education procedures.* The bulk of my research was concerned with trying to devise more effective means for teaching programming. The first step in this process was to examine expert developers and develop a cognitive model of how they worked. The second step was to compare how experts actually solve problems with how we teach novices to solve problems. As you can guess, there was a wide gap between how experts create software and how it is normally taught. To correct this, we created a special curriculum and programming environment explicitly designed to teach an expert model of problem solving to novices [Hohmann 1992; Guzdial 1993]. In general, our results were very encouraging. Our students were able to become more effective programmers using our teaching techniques as compared with traditional techniques. Marcia Linn [1992] and her colleagues at the University of Berkeley have also achieved impressive results with a similar approach.

♦ *Understanding of creativity.* It is not clear how an individual can create a "creative" or "novel" solution within the confines of the precise problem-solving steps prescribed in a method. Cognitive models, on the other hand, don't present us with any preconceived or predefined notions of the exact right way to solve a problem. Indeed, cognitive models provide an explanation of how creativity occurs. Creativity occurs when we apply a plan from one domain to another. The more "creative" the solution, the greater the difference in plans combined [Hanks 1991]. Thus, there is an easy way to systematically promote creativity: Combine more plans!

♦ *Development of methods.* Methods are created to help improve problem-solving effectiveness. The best methods support the cognitive model described above. Understanding this cognitive model, in turn, helps create effective methods.

♦ *Improvement of methods.* If all cognitive models provided were a description of problem solving, they would be of dubious value. Software developers are busy! We don't have time to waste thinking about how we think about problems. Or do we? Just because a method says we should engage in a particular activity *does not* necessarily mean it is the *right* activity. There is always a difference—a gap—between what a method tells you to do and what you actually do. This difference is referred to as the difference between espoused theory and actual practice. Cognitive models can help to explain these differences. When they are great, cognitive models provide insight into how the method (or its use) should be changed.

1.1.3 Method

Software methods[3] attempt to improve software quality by providing a systematic approach to software production. A method prescribes a precise sequence of processes, together with outcomes produced by each process. Usually these outcomes are models representing a specific aspect of the problem, and concentrate on the analysis and design phases of a system. Preparing all the models (i.e., following all the processes defined in the method) contributes to our understanding of the problem.

---

[3] My use of the word method is consistent with Booch [1994], who defines a *method* as "a disciplined process for generating a set of models that describe various aspects of a software system under development, using some well-defined notation." A methodology is "a collection of methods applied across the software development life cycle and unified by some general, philosophical approach." Not all authors use the same definition. Yourdon [1992] considers a methodology a synonym for a life cycle. This book concentrates on the use of a method as a disciplined and rigorous approach to problem solving.

There is no single universal method, as different methods are optimized for solving different problems. The Booch method, for example, is optimized for developing object-oriented software systems, while Structured Analysis/Structured Design (SA/SD) is optimized for building more traditional systems (e.g., COBOL or C). However, abstracting away the details of these methods reveals they are focused on essentially the same processes and outcomes. It's not that I think the details of a method are unimportant—they are. However, the details of a method are not important for a broad conceptual understanding of methods. As you review the following list, ask yourself if the processes map easily into the cognitive model presented earlier. In other words, do *method* processes effectively support *cognitive* processes?

♦ *Requirements determination* is the process of determining the problem that must be solved. Paraphrasing Gause and Weinberg [1990], it is the process of documenting the difference between "things as perceived and things as desired." While not every method addresses requirements determination, every method agrees on the importance of accurately stated requirements.

The most common outcome produced by the requirements determination process is a textual description of the proposed system supplemented by one or more additional outcomes. Textual descriptions are often problematic in many kinds of systems, so we often supplement this textual description with additional outcomes. For example, a system making extensive use of a graphical user interface may use a *prototype* as the model of how the system will look and feel.

♦ *Requirements analysis* is concerned with defining *what* a system does rather than how it does it [Coleman 1994]. During analysis we attempt to document the manner in which the system interacts with external systems and agents; the underlying truths and constraints of the problem domain; the entities or objects within the problem domain; the specific state of the system at any time during its operation; and the pre- and postconditions specifying legal state transitions. All of this is done without regard for the specific implementation of the internal components comprising the system.

The subprocesses of analysis are supported by appropriate outcomes. *Use cases* and *scenarios* describe how the system interacts with external systems and agents; *entity relationship diagrams, class diagrams,* or *object models* document the entities or objects within a domain and their relationships; *state transition diagrams* show the legal states of the system (or any single entity); and *extended use cases* or *operation schemas* show the specific pre- and postconditions of every operation the system supports along with the results of the operation (usually stated in a declarative form). Additional outcomes often produced in analysis include the *system architecture,* which shows the structure of the overall system.

♦ *Design* specifies how to create interactions between the components discovered in analysis so as to correctly meet the requirements. In this manner, design specifies the *how* of the system. Unlike analysis, the design phase usually focuses on outcomes showing the dynamic behavior of the system. Such outcomes include *structure charts* and *data flow diagrams* for nonobject-oriented systems and *object interaction graphs* or *message trace diagrams* for object-oriented systems; *state transition diagrams* for specific entities or objects; *design object models* showing how the relationships among objects are to be realized; and *module* or *class* descriptions detailing the implementation attributes and functions (behaviors) of a module or class.

♦ *Implementation* is the act of translating the analysis and design models into a software system (e.g., executable source code) in such a fashion as to solve the problem specified by the requirements. The outcome from implementation *is* the system. Ideally, all prior outcomes directly contribute to this outcome.

♦ *Verification* is the process of comparing what was implemented with what was desired. Outcomes produced by verification validate the correctness, appropriateness, and usefulness of the system. Examination of these outcomes often results in modifications to any or all of the outcomes produced in requirements determination, analysis, design, or implementation.

♦ *Maintenance* is the on-going activity associated with the modification and enhancements of the software system after it has been placed into production. One outcome associated with maintenance is a change request. A *change request* is a written description of the specific modifications desired in an existing system. Change requests are usually submitted for review to a *change control board* who prioritizes change requests. They represent the heart of a formal change control process and are used throughout maintenance.

Specific methods differ in many dimensions, including the manner in which these processes are organized, the notations used in documenting the outcomes of each process, and the automated tools that may exist to assist the developer in employing the method. The greatest differences lie in notation, but even these differences are immaterial for achieving a conceptual understanding of methods. What is most important in any method is the degree to which it facilitates problem solving by providing a precise structure for problem-solving processes.

Included in the structure of a method and not described above are the definitions of how outcomes produced by one process (or subprocess) are used as input to the next. For example, most object-oriented methods recommend the preparation of a class diagram before the operation schema because the operation schema refers to objects within the problem domain. Failing to produce the class diagram first makes it nearly impossible to create an accurate operation schema. More generally, skipping steps in any method is usually counterproductive as method processes are carefully organized.

Following every step defined by the method really saved me in one consulting assignment. I was asked to build a route planning system, and the initial requirements were so well-written I was tempted to skip the step of describing in detail the results of each system operation. Such a decision would have been fatal, because in documenting the post-conditions and results of one of the system operations I realized the requirements had masked the client's true wishes. As it turned out, the system desired by the client was reducible to the traveling salesman problem, which is known to be NP-complete! An NP-complete problem is intractable, because it cannot be solved in a reasonable amount of time for even small numbers of input by any computer, no matter how powerful. [Wilf 1986]

Methods differ in the degree of structure they provide to control processes and outcomes. Some methods are more *formal* in the manner in which they control processes by providing more "tests" to determine if an outcome is complete. If the test fails, you haven't prepared the outcome completely and should not move to the next process. Other methods are less formal, as the movement between process steps are less strictly controlled by the method.

There are times when any given set of method defined processes can seem nearly identical in focus, and it can be tempting to blur distinctions between them. To illustrate why this blurring is ill-advised, consider the differences between requirements determination and analysis, two activities with unusually strong relationships. First, requirements are generally written for or by the customer and tend to use native language. Analysis models, on the other hand, are created by developers for developers using precisely defined technical notation. Certainly customers can be trained to read and validate such models, but this activity must be undertaken with care.

Second, although the documentation generated from analysis does allow for precise communication, it is not a panacea. Facets of the system such as specific performance requirements can be difficult, if not impossible, to express in most analysis models and are instead more effectively stated in requirements documents. Many invariants of the system cannot be expressed easily in analysis models and find a natural home in requirements documents. Requirements documents can also serve as a repository of preferences [Gause 1990]. Requirements documents can admit ambiguity, while analysis models cannot. This ambiguity can be an advantage, for it allows us to defer certain decisions as necessary or incorporate changes caused by external factors.

1.1.4 Benefits of Methods

The following list presents some benefits associated with methods (adapted from [Coleman et al. 1994]).

- ◆ *Process Automation:* Tools can be created to provide automated support for the processes and outcomes associated with the method, significantly enhancing it. (Such tools are often referred to as *Computer-Aided Software Engineering* or *CASE* tools.) In fact, a CASE tool cannot be created without a well-defined set of processes and associated outcomes. In other words, a CASE tool must have a method.

- ◆ *Requirements verification:* The models prepared during analysis and design usually uncover inconsistencies and/or ambiguities in the requirements. Detecting such problems early in the process is the most cost-effective way to build systems. Boehm [1981] reports the cost of fixing an error in design is three to six times that of fixing it in requirements. The cost ratio continues to rise from there.

♦ *Clearer conceptual understanding:* Each activity of the method should lead to a better understanding of the problem by capturing one specific facet of the system.

♦ *Less implementation rework:* The models and notations used in analysis and design allow the problem to be explored at different levels of abstraction before implementation. This enables the developer to concentrate on gaining a correct conceptual understanding of the problem before committing to any solution.

♦ *Better factoring of work:* Large problems require team development. Efficient teamwork requires decomposing the problem into independent subproblems. Doing analysis and design makes problem decomposition across teams easier.

♦ *Improved communication:* The models of a method provide the foundation for precise, efficient, and effective communication among developers. In addition, certain models are more easily shared with customers, increasing the breadth of communication.

♦ *Improved maintenance:* Software is often maintained by someone other than the original developer. Analysis and design documents can help maintainers understand underlying assumptions, broad strategies, and intentions. Of course, improper maintenance of analysis and design documents decreases maintenance effectiveness.

♦ *Reference materials:* Widely practiced methods have numerous books and reference materials describing how they can be used to solve many different kinds of problems. These reference materials provide excellent opportunities to learn and practice the method. They can even provide direct insight into current problems.

1.1.5 Comparing Methods and Cognitive Models

Methods provide a systematic approach to software development by prescribing the processes and rules by which we create the outcomes associated with a software system. Cognitive models, on the other hand, seek to describe *how* we solve problems. The relationship between methods and cognitive models is summarized in Table 1–1.

1.2 STRUCTURES, PROCESSES, AND OUTCOMES: AN OVERVIEW

Problem solving can be described using three simple concepts: structure, process, and outcome. Structure defines the form and content of outcomes and prescribes and supports the processes we use to create them. Process refers to the mental and

TABLE 1–1   Comparing Methods and Cognitive Models

	Cognitive Models *descriptive—heuristic*	Methods *prescriptive—rules & procedures*
Primary Purpose	Describe how developers work.	Improve the effectiveness of software developers by organizing their activities.
Area of Focus	Internal, mental processes employed by developers as they generate outcomes.	The precise definition of the form and content of the outcomes created in software development.
		The kind of processes and how they should be ordered as outcomes are created.
Intended Result	Improvement of the formal and actual processes of software developers.	Repeatable and sustainable software development through defined processes and outcomes.
		Improvement of methods.

physical activities we use to produce outcomes. Outcomes are the things produced. Together, these three components form the Structure–Process–Outcome (SPO) framework. The remainder of this chapter will explore each of these aspects of the framework in greater detail. Process will be discussed first, as it plays the key linking role between cognitive models and methods. Outcomes will be discussed second, as they are the result of processes. Structure will be discussed last.

1.3 PROCESS

Although methods and cognitive models are used for different purposes, they can be integrated through the idea of process. By examining the process of problem solving (e.g., writing software) in greater detail, we can see where this link occurs.

1.3.1 Linking Methods to Cognitive Models

Methods prescribe both a specific process to use when writing software along with specific outcomes associated with each process. The link between methods and the thought processes described by cognitive models occurs as outcomes are generated. We use cognitive processes to create the outcomes defined by the method and then create physical outcomes based on our thoughts (see Figure 1–2).

To illustrate how this linking occurs in actual practice, consider a developer who is using the Fusion method to develop an object-oriented system [Coleman 1994]. During the analysis phase, Fusion specifies the generation of an object model. As described above, an object model defines the primary objects within the system and the relationships between them. (For readers who are unfamiliar with object-oriented programming, an object model is basically a traditional entity-relationship

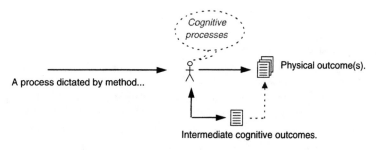

Figure 1–2   Linking Methods and Cognitive Models

model, with appropriate extensions for object-oriented programming.) At this stage, Fusion is *prescriptive*.

But *how* do we generate the object model? The Fusion process recommends examining the problem domain, looking for candidate objects and the relationships between them. It is precisely here process changes from the prescriptive focus of methods to the descriptive focus of cognitive models. *How* we determine what objects exist within a problem domain is based on several interrelated plans within our cognitive library. These include our familiarity with the problem domain (domain-specific plans), our understanding of "what" constitutes a "good object" (semantic-syntactic plans), and our general experience with object-oriented analysis (plans enabling experts to create more complete and correct object models when compared with novices).

Through the application of our mental processes we produce one or more physical outcomes. At this step the method once again becomes critically important. We can compare our outcomes with the outcomes defined by the method and determine if these outcomes are appropriate. Thus, we can take our analysis model and compare it with the Fusion-defined notation for analysis models to ensure it was created in a proper manner.

1.3.2 Process Leveling and Experience

Take any method. Review its prescription of the problem-solving process. Sounds easy, doesn't it? Simply follow the steps in the right order, prepare all the outcomes, and presto! Your problem is solved. Yet, as many of us know from experience, it is rarely easy. No matter how well we might try to follow the dictates of the method, our processes just don't always seem to go by the book. We do a little analysis, then maybe some design. More generally, when problem solving "crosses over" from the prescriptive processes of the method to actual thought (which is most of the time), we lose the ability to precisely specify the activities of the developer. Although a method can completely prescribe a set of processes that may or may not be followed, a cognitive model cannot.

Why can't a cognitive model precisely prescribe a specific set of mental processes? The answer lies in two parts. The first part is simple: Cognitive models are created to describe mental processes, not prescribe how we should solve problems.

The second part of the answer lies in how cognitive models are created. In general, cognitive models are developed by observing subjects solve complex problems. Such observations, which are almost always videotaped for further review, are usually referred to as "think-aloud" protocols. During the problem-solving episode, researchers interrupt the subject and ask: "What are you thinking? Why?" By encouraging the subject to "think aloud" we have a reasonably good understanding of what they are actually doing. Over time, careful examination of hundreds of such sessions have enabled the creation of the cognitive model described in Figure 1–1 (and others like it).

It may seem easy to review a transcript of a subject and place a label on an activity. *"There! She is engaged in analysis."* And then, somewhat later, *"Design. Now she is doing design."* Yet, anyone who has reviewed such transcripts knows the reality is *much* different. Sometimes the subject seems to be doing analysis. Barely a moment later, they seem to be doing design. Their focus shifts and shifts rapidly. What appears to be an analysis activity may in fact be solving a vexing implementation question. Alternatively, a prototype may be created to solve a difficult design problem. Taking a slightly cavalier approach, you pick the "stage" of problem solving, and I'll justify why the developer is "in" that stage! But wait! Did they shift again?

Shifting among the different mental processes described in the cognitive model is the hallmark of the problem-solving process. This shifting occurs as a developer reviews their cognitive library of previously solved problems, looking for those matching the characteristics of the current problem. If a match is found, the developer can work at a more general (or abstract) level, perhaps even solving the problem directly. If, on the other hand, no match is found, the developer must work at less general (less abstract) levels. More time must be spent tailoring existing plans to fit the new problem, as understanding of the larger problem is facilitated by solving the details.

Tailoring a plan can take many forms. A developer engaged in analysis in an unfamiliar problem domain may try implementing a simple model of the domain. Working through the details of a simplified problem helps the developer make certain the tentative plan has been tailored correctly. The developer is working at a "lower" level—closer to the machine. Conversely, a developer with a plan directly matching the problem domain need not resort to an "implementation test" of the plan to know it works. They can solve the problem completely in their mind.

Leveling describes the shifting among different levels of generality or abstraction during problem solving. In general, leveling is not subject to external control, cannot be predicted, and does not proceed in a simple linear progression.

What determines the amount and degree of leveling? Experience, as realized by the breadth and depth of the developer's cognitive library. One way to characterize experience is to imagine tracing the cognitive process of a person solving a problem as they search their cognitive library. What we would find is a path that sometimes explores a proposed plan superficially (it matches) and at other times explores it in great detail. The path correlates to experience in the following way. When experience is low, more potential plans need to be explored in greater detail, because there are fewer plans that can verify a proposed solution as correct. Of course, this is paradoxical, because low experience means there are fewer plans to explore in the first place!

Another way to contrast experience is to think of the path to a correct solution of the problem as being either messy or clean. A novice's path will appear to be messy. There are more false starts. The same topic may be revisited multiple times. At times, it may be so messy the novice will have extreme difficulties explaining it. Experienced developers, on the other hand, have larger and more sophisticated cognitive libraries. Their process appears to be unusually clean, primarily because the messy part was already done once. The solution—the clean part—has been stored as a plan. This does not mean experts find it any easier to explain their processes. Trying to explain richly encoded plans is difficult and potentially frustrating. When asked to explain how they solved a problem, an expert may reply, "I don't know how I got the solution. I just know it is correct!"

Deep experience in a problem domain (e.g., on-line transaction processing, network management) tends to equate to more effective problem solving within that domain. This is not to say deep experience alone is needed for effective problem solving. Experience can be a drawback if you spend more time trying to fit old plans to new problems instead of working to create new plans more appropriate to the problem at hand.

Choosing the right set of plans to place into our cognitive library is a tough decision as it involves trying to balance two competing forces. Becoming an expert in any single domain (i.e., having the ability to quickly and easily solve problems in that domain) *means* we have a large number of domain-specific plans [Chase 1973]. Developing such plans means spending a fair amount of time in a specific domain.

However, experience in multiple domains as defined by having many different kinds of plans means we can solve new problems effectively. Consider a developer with experience in writing software in many different paradigms: expert systems, object-oriented programming, and more traditional functional decomposition. Each paradigm provides a different set of plans for solving problems. When presented with a novel problem, such a developer could select the plans most appropriate for it, instead of trying to fit old plans onto the new problem. The ideal situation, of course, is a combination of deep and broad experience.

Unfortunately, these conclusions present a paradox. It is desirable to increase the size of our cognitive library as much as possible. However, every plan we add is added in a particular *context*. This context includes the technology used by the solution. Over time, technological progress and subtle changes in the problem domain render these plans less relevant. Our tendency to reuse plans eventually proves harmful and our effectiveness begins to decrease. This is not to say successful solutions should not be repeated or failure is something to avoid at all costs. Success should be repeated for reasons obvious to anyone who has ever had the joy of experiencing it. But failure can be beneficial *if* we use it to grow our cognitive library. Failure is one of the mechanisms by which we learn. When we fail, we gain important knowledge something is wrong about how we are solving a problem. We can use this knowledge to modify and correct faulty plans as well as add ones.

The point is that a finite set of static plans rigidly applied to every problem will not lead to sustained high performance. Instead, we must continually modify our cognitive library, searching for ways to add both deep and broad experience. I am reminded of the growth of our bones. Even after they have reached their adult shapes and sizes, they are constantly changing. Old bone is destroyed and new bone is formed in its place. If new bone were not continually reformed the old bone would quickly become brittle and snap under the pressures we place on our body. In a similar manner, we must work to avoid rigidity in our cognitive library. One way rigidity can be avoided and appropriate new plans created is to spend more time forgetting and relearning, rather than remembering. Others will be discussed later in this book in Part Two.

Sometimes technological changes can invalidate numerous plans at once. A few years ago I made the decision to switch from C to C++. I still remember many of the difficulties I encountered learning C++: The syntax is considerably more complex than C, the notation for references is confusing, structs aren't structs anymore, and trying to remember all the different combinations of inheritance caused me real grief! Not only did I have to learn the language (syntactic-semantic plans), I had to learn several new implementation plans—such as throwing an exception instead of using an assertion. The decision to move from C to C++ made several years of accumulated plans regarding design, implementation, testing, invalid or obsolete.

Was I somewhat surprised by this? On one hand, yes, for I expected more of the plans associated with C to apply to C++. On the other, no, for I had enough experience in other object-oriented programming languages to realize the most effective approaches for developing solutions in object-oriented languages and nonobject-oriented languages are substantially different. In the long run, my semantic plans related to object technology enabled me to learn C++ rapidly. In a way, I was lucky, for without such experience, I am certain the move to C++ would have been considerably more difficult.

1.3.3 The Descriptive Benefits of Process Leveling

Leveling helps to explain much of the behavior associated with problem solving in software development. Consider what might happen should an expert prepare a design for implementation by a novice. Such a design is likely to rely on many of the plans stored in the cognitive library of the expert, many of which the novice is not likely to possess. The result? The novice will likely be at best confused and will be forced to ask the expert for clarification. At worst, the novice will incorrectly implement the design. Of course, this doesn't mean experts cannot communicate with novices effectively. It simply means the potential for miscommunication is greater, especially when they are relying on different plans to solve the problem.

Both novice and expert programmers exhibit leveling when solving a problem, but experts differ from novices in several aspects. First, experts know more plans and patterns from which to draw and have more experience in tailoring and composing these solutions into working systems. It is quite difficult to gauge the appropriateness of a linear programming strategy when you *don't know* linear programming!

Second, experts tend to have more domain experience, allowing them to quickly determine what aspects of the problem exhibit the most complexity. In other words, experts not only know to solve the "hard part" of the problem first, but they can also correctly identify what the "hard part" is. Novices, on the other hand, not knowing what the "hard part" is, tend to focus on the wrong aspects of the problem, thereby generating inferior and/or incorrect designs [Adelson 1985].

Finally, and most importantly, experts have more refined problem-solving strategies and more refined processes for applying these strategies. These can be thought of as metaplans. Such plans are used, for example, when determining which paradigm (e.g., object oriented or rule based) to use when solving a problem. Novices do not have well-defined strategies and usually fail in solving complex problems beyond what have been taught [Guzdial 1993].

Leveling also provides clues on how we can teach effective problem-solving skills. The basic idea is to study what experts do and teach this to novices. For example, experts prefer working at more general (or abstract) levels, avoiding the movement to specific (or concrete) levels until necessary. Novices, on the other hand, tend to move into lower levels more quickly than experts, and once at a lower level, they are less adept at returning to higher levels or examining alternative solutions to the problem. By teaching the concept of leveling, and explaining how movement occurs between levels, novices can quickly learn expert-level problem-solving processes, even if their cognitive libraries are not as sufficiently rich.

A very effective technique for accomplishing this goal is mentoring, in which an expert guides the novice in problem solving and provides expert-level plans to help the novice solve difficult problems. As an analogy, consider driving a car with a standard transmission. An expert can talk on their cellular phone or change the radio station while shifting smoothly. A novice is usually overwhelmed with remembering when to change gears and how to use the clutch and usually drives more effectively when an expert is in the passenger seat helping.

Leveling also describes why it is important for developers—both expert and novice—to at times build parts of the system (or even a full prototype) before the system is completely defined. Sometimes the only way to understand a complex problem is to solve part of it [Rittel 1973]. This solution, which is likely to be less than perfect, provides the information necessary to solve the real problem the right way. Of key importance here is the self-discipline the designer exhibits when generating such solutions, a topic discussed further later in this chapter.

1.3.4 Process Leveling, Stepwise Refinement, and Opportunistic Design

Wirth [1971] published a paper describing in detail how to solve the eight-queens and n-queens problems.[4] The foundation of the design approach used in the paper is stepwise refinement. *Stepwise refinement* is a top-down problem-solving technique whereby solutions to a problem are constructed from a high-level specification through a series of refinement steps.

Each refinement step further decomposes and refines the problem into smaller and more manageable subproblems. Ideally, this decomposition is accomplished through a specific set of uniformly and rigorously applied design decisions. Data and algorithms are refined in parallel due to their interdependent nature, although it is preferable to defer exact representations of data as long as possible. Wirth also cautions that stepwise refinement may cause us to "back up" a step and try a different alternative when a problem is found with an earlier decision. The process terminates when the problem can be directly specified in an implementation language.

In one sense, leveling mimics stepwise refinement. Leveling encourages us to try and solve problems at the most abstract level possible, deferring specifics where possible. In this manner leveling can be thought of as a *kind* of stepwise refinement.

Did you notice how nice and clean the stepwise refinement approach sounds? Starting with a high-level description of the problem, the solution is created through a series of specific steps. Each step is the result of a rational decision-making process. Unfortunately, there is a problem with stepwise refinement: Real experts don't solve problems using purely top-down techniques. Bill Curtis and his colleagues [1987] found expert designers solve pieces of a problem in apparent contradiction of stepwise refinement. Solutions to subproblems seem to "magically" appear. Over time, these solutions are integrated to solve the larger problem. There is no top-down, stepwise refinement process being rigorously applied.

Curtis and his colleagues have characterized this approach as "opportunistic design." The basic idea in opportunistic design is not that developers solve a problem in an uncontrolled manner, but that developers can rarely follow a top-down process. Robert Glass [1995] suggests the "opportunistic design" approach described by Curtis is based on a developer's idiosyncratic view of the hard part of the problem.

Both Curtis and Glass are correct, but the idea of process leveling provides a better explanation of behavior. Opportunistic design occurs when a developer is scanning his or her cognitive library for plans matching the current problem. When a match is found, it is "opportunistically" pursued. The reason problem solving appears to happen in pieces is because each of our cognitive libraries contains a unique set of plans. You find a match for one aspect of a problem, while I find a match for another.

---

[4] "Given are an 8 × 8 chessboard and eight queens which are hostile to each other. Find a position for each queen such that no queen may be taken by any other queen."

This is not to say stepwise refinement is an ineffective technique. Stepwise refinement can be quite effective provided there are enough plans closely matching the problem. However, when there are few plans in the library, opportunistic design (i.e., "find a match as best you can and pursue it") is the best apparent approach. Leveling improves on opportunistic design by borrowing some of the best ideas from stepwise refinement. Specifically, leveling encourages us to work at the most abstract level of the problem as possible. Yes, we can move into a lower level as necessary, but we should strive to return to the more abstract level as soon as possible.

Finally, Glass's assertion is correct: *Expert* developer's do tend to work on what is perceived to be the hard part of the problem first because their cognitive libraries are sufficiently well developed to know that solving the "hard part first" is critical to future success. Moreover, they have sufficient plans to help them identify what the hard part is. Novices, as noted, often fail to work on the hard-part-first for two reasons. First, they may not know the effectiveness of the hard part first strategy. Second, even if they attempt to solve the hard part first, they are likely to miss it.

1.4 OUTCOME

The end result of a process, either mental or physical, is an outcome. There are numerous outcomes associated with software development. Many are prescribed and defined by a method. We create other outcomes to help govern, guide, and otherwise control our work. A method may require requirements documents, data models, structure charts, and so forth. Additional outcomes can include project plans, meeting notes, sketches of a proposed user interface, and the like. Each outcome serves to document, predict, explain, communicate, track changes, and verify the overall solution to the problem. Abstracting, simplifying, and generalizing the cognitive processes shown in Figure 1–2 results in Figure 1–3.

Figure 1–3   Relationship of Process to Outcome

1.4.1 Preparing Outcomes for Understanding

It is a mistake to think outcomes are generated once, without need for modification or correction. Developers create countless intermediate outcomes, such as sketches on a whiteboard or small exploratory programs. Such outcomes are raw and unrefined, but they assist us in the process. Generally private to the developer, they continue to exist in this state until additional effort is undertaken to transform them to a form that is suitable for sharing with others. This can be a considerable undertaking for the experienced developer, because more of the information needed to explain the outcome is contained within their mind and is thus not necessarily in a form easily transmitted to others.

Parnas [1986] provides great insight into exactly how we should prepare outcomes for understanding. The basis of his argument is this: While experts don't use a rational, top-down design process, they should nonetheless generate outcomes *as if* they had used a rational, top-down design process. The advantage to this approach is quite apparent: We find it easier to understand the work of others when we are shielded from the messy details of how the work was created.

1.4.2 Lessons from Architecture

Examining the outcomes produced by other fields is one way to better understand the outcomes associated with software development. Architecture is one field with many parallels to software development. Both software developers and architects must often accommodate many different stakeholders. They must deal with uncertainty: The final solution is usually different than the proposed solution. Moreover, until that solution is finalized in steel and brick or source code, both are in a perpetual state of discovery. Both fields regularly create many different outcomes to try to reduce uncertainty and increase understanding. Architects create blueprints, scale models, and even computer-based simulations of the proposed building. Software developers create requirements documents, data models, prototypes, state charts, and the like.

There are two broad areas where software professionals can learn to create and use outcomes more effectively by studying architecture. The first lies in the selection of outcomes. Outcomes should be always be chosen with an understanding of *who* is going to use the outcome for *what* purpose. Put another way, it is not possible to share our mental processes. The *only* way we can communicate is through outcomes (e.g., gestures, language, models, and so forth), a point elaborated on in Chapter 7. Choosing the right outcome and preparing it in the appropriate manner is essential for effective communication.

This approach is evident in architecture. The customer is rarely shown all models associated with the planned building in all their glorious detail. Instead, the customer is shown a relevant subset of models, each designed to give the customer a more complete understanding of the building (how it will look, how it will work, and so forth) before the building is built. For example, floor plans or external elevation might be shown to the customer, but not detailed foundation or framing plans. Moreover, when a customer is reviewing these outcomes an architect is usually present to ensure they are properly interpreted.

Unfortunately, such care is not always taken in software development. Customers are often shown every outcome when in reality a relevant subset will suffice. Customers are sometimes asked to review technical outcomes (e.g., data models or data flow diagrams) without training or guidance. I do not mean to imply customers are incapable of correctly understanding technical outcomes. I do mean miscommunication can easily happen unless care is taken when technical outcomes are shared with them.

The second area concerns the management of reviewer expectations. When a senior architect obtains approval from his or her client based on a few sketches, the next step is to build a scale model. The natural analogy to software development is the creation of a working prototype once the customer has approved the initial screen designs. Unfortunately, customers often have trouble distinguishing a prototype from a real system. After all, a prototype—a software scale model—*looks* and *feels* like the real system: Why doesn't it *perform* like one? Here is where an architect has an advantage over a software developer. Since a scale model is *obviously* not a real building, we do not expect it to perform like one. One way developers can address this problem is by making certain the customer understands how much of the "real" or "complete" system the prototype represents *before* the review.

1.5 STRUCTURE

The previous sections have discussed the processes of the developer as they build software systems and introduced the idea that outcomes are generated by these processes. These two concepts explain much of the development process, but there are still many unanswered questions. What is the form and content of the outcome? How can I determine when the process has produced a valid outcome? How should processes be organized? The answer to these questions lies in structure.

Structure defines the form and content of outcomes and supports the processes we use to create them (see Figure 1–4). It is an axiom of this book that all human activity takes place in the context of some structure. I cannot write this book—or even think about the words I am about to write—without the structure of the English language. Without an understanding of that same structure you cannot read it.

This axiom is partly derived from the linguistic theories of Edward Sapir and Benjamin Whorf. The Sapir-Whorf hypothesis states that language structures thought, a concept known as *linguistic determinism*. Associated with this concept is *linguistic relativism*, which states that people who speak different languages perceive and think about the world quite differently [Whorf 1956]. Although the hypothesis cannot be proven, most linguists accept the idea language strongly influences, if not completely structures, thought [Whitman 1983; Chandler 1994]. You can see the effects of linguistic relativity if you know more than one programming language. Given the same problem, I would expect different solutions from

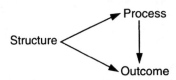

Figure 1–4   The Structure–Process–Outcome Framework

one developer using Smalltalk and another using C++. Although both languages are based on the object-oriented paradigm, each structures thought in very different ways. The Sapir-Whorf hypothesis also predicts that translating from one language is difficult, at best. This concept can also be illustrated by computer languages. Try taking an expert system written in LISP and converting it to COBOL. Certainly it can be done, but the process is likely to be so extraordinarily difficult few of us would bother to try.

A good structure promotes the best possible practices in process and defines outcomes promoting effective communication and problem-solving strategies. A pOoR STRUCTURE makes achieving the outcome DIFFICULT, at best.

All methods strive to create a structure for effective work. They do this by prescribing a sequence of processes that together produce a well-defined set of outcomes. "Structure" is a more abstract term than method. We may not always follow the processes prescribed by a method, but we *always* work according to some structure. Moreover, the structure provided by a method does not necessarily apply to our mental processes, even though our mental processes are always governed by structure.

The impact of structure is pervasive. The moment you have diagrammed process, you have structured it in a particular way. An example of this came earlier in this chapter. The only way I could explain the cognitive *process* associated with problem solving was by *structuring* it in Figure 1–1. This structure, in turn, predisposes us to think of problem solving according to the activities outlined in the model.

How much structure is needed? This answer lies in two dimensions. The first is related to the problem, while the second is related to our cognitive processes. From a system perspective, as problem complexity increases, the need for structure in solving the problem also increases. To illustrate, let's say your brother-in-law owns a small bagel shop and needs an inventory/cash management program. Instead of purchasing such software, you decide to write it from scratch because it would provide a great avenue for learning Visual Basic™ and Access™. How much structure is needed to solve this problem? Do you need a formal requirements document? How about a change control board for approving changes to the requirements? Will you use formal or informal test plans? Will you use any test plans at all? How will you manage maintenance releases and bug fixes? Now, suppose your brother-in-law manufactured equipment that automatically dispenses chemotherapy drugs to cancer patients. If he asked you to write the software controlling the flow of drugs, would your answers to these questions be the same?

The second aspect of structure that differs greatly among individuals is the amount of structure each of us needs when solving a problem. Some of us can get along fine with very little external structure, while others need quite a bit more. The question is "Why?" The answer lies in our *cognitive style,* which is the interaction of our preferred cognitive processes with structure used to solve the problem. Some of us are *adaptors,* preferring to solve problems within existing and/or mutually agreed upon structures. Others are *innovators,* instead preferring to work without a substantial amount of external structure or in structures we invent [Kirton 1994].

As an analogy, consider a car engine. The size and sophistication of our cognitive library is the size of our engine. How we like to run it is our cognitive style. Neither adaptors nor innovators are *inherently* better than the other at solving problems. The need for structure (and for people with a particular style) is often dependent on the problem. Some problems are more suited to adaptors, while others are more suited to innovators. No matter what our cognitive style, *everyone* needs structure—enough to help them define the problem, enough to keep them on track, enough and no more than to allow them to work in reasonable mental comfort. This recognition is another area in which experts differ from novices. Experts are more adept at determining how much structure is needed to assist them in solving the problem and are more experienced in creating this structure.

As an undergraduate and graduate student at the University of Michigan, I had the good fortune to work with Elliot Soloway for over five years. A prominent researcher in cognitive psychology, education, computer science, and artificial intelligence, Elliot taught me many things about creating appropriate structures. I remember one conversation vividly, because it continues to shape my thoughts. Our research was concerned with developing more effective ways of teaching programming skills to novice programmers. I was convinced the right way to solve this problem was to define a new language novices could more easily understand. Elliot, on the other hand, was convinced we needed to develop a programming environment to provide "cognitive scaffolding" for students engaged in the design process. The goal of this scaffolding was to assist students in managing the complexities associated with programming and problem solving. Like real scaffolding, the goal of cognitive scaffolding was to help the students gain access to solving problems beyond their current abilities.

The "artificial intelligence" part of the project was our goal to have the amount of scaffolding provided to the students fade over time as the students internalized effective problem-solving techniques. This is similar to a building, whose scaffolding fades over time as workers no longer need it. Although I didn't realize it at the time, this was the first time I was exposed to the powerful impact the right kind of structure can have in the problem-solving process.

How effectively a developer uses structures is not a matter of style, but discipline. The most effective kind of discipline—self-discipline—is motivated from personal values. Self-discipline is what motivates me to review my analysis before I charge forward with design. A stronger form of self-discipline motivates me to modify my analysis when, through design, I uncover some previously unknown aspect of the problem. Similarly, self-discipline is what motivates us to reject a computationally correct, "tricky" implementation and replace it with something more understandable, more straightforward, and ultimately, more maintainable.

While your working environment can require you to update your analysis, my experience as a manager is that the worst developers are those without self-discipline. No rule or procedure I ever put into place has forced a developer to "have" self-discipline. I can promote this as a manager, but I can't create it. It comes from within. Brooks [1995] talks extensively about self-discipline, especially in the design of the "second system."

His words are as true today as when they were first written. As Parnas [1972a] aptly stated: "Formal testing of the specification isn't essential—self-discipline is!"

1.6 THE STRUCTURE–PROCESS–OUTCOME FRAMEWORK

The Structure–Process–Outcome (SPO) model presented in Figure 1–4 links methods and cognitive models into a consistent framework. The value of the SPO framework is that it provides a tool to organize our understanding of both methods and cognitive models. From this understanding, specific, concrete steps can be taken to improve our effectiveness independent of any given method. The SPO framework presented here draws heavily from the work of Avedis Donabedian [1981], who developed a similar framework for understanding and determining the quality of health care delivery systems and organizations. While Donabedian's area of focus was considerably different, the framework has great power in describing behavior.

Which component of the framework is more important? Structure? Process? Outcome? No one component is more important than another. If structure is emphasized, problem solving becomes too rigid, unable to change in response to environmental conditions or cognitive style. An extreme focus on structure means there is only *one way* to solve the problem. As discussed earlier, there is no *single* way to solve a problem.

If process is too strongly emphasized, outcomes will be produced, but it is not at all clear if these outcomes will actually contribute to the solution. Without the controlling mechanism provided by structure, outcomes can be prepared in any order, even randomly. At a general level, the processes prescribed by a method *do* match our internal mental processes quite well. In other words, method prescribed process helps us solve problems more effectively.

If outcomes are overemphasized we will be motivated to use *any* process to produce the outcome. This approach may not be optimal and could even be quite bad. The ultimate outcome of any software system is the system itself. Focusing solely on this outcome means an acceptable process is to simply sit down and hack and slash the system together. In the extreme, focusing solely on outcomes can motivate individuals to engage in unethical practices—who cares how the job was done, as long as it was done? Thus, a balance is needed among structure, process, and outcome.

If each component of the framework is important, which comes first? This question is much easier to answer. *Structure must always come first.* All human activity, mental or otherwise, takes place in the context of a structure. Without structure there can be no process. Without process there can be no outcome. The natural consequence of this is that for work to be most effective we must focus on creating the right structure for that work.

The need for structure before process can be illustrated by an individual performing a bench press. If she loads one side of the bar with a 45-pound plate, and another with a 5-pound plate, it does not matter how perfectly she controls her form when performing the exercise. The poor structure will prevent her from engaging in a successful process, resulting in an undesirable outcome. Of course, once the structural problems have been corrected, process and outcome become critically important. Similarly, consider a developer who is currently using C and has been asked to adopt C++. If they do not also adopt new structures, they will not be successful [Bashshur 1995].

The need for structure before process implies you know in advance the appropriate structures for the problem. More specifically, you know the desired outcomes and the processes necessary to create them. This is not necessarily the case. Quite often you may not know which process will promote the creation of the desired outcome. Indeed, the desired outcome may not even be known. In this case, you may define (imagine) the desired (assumed) outcome, and create (imagine) the processes necessary to achieve the outcome. Once this is done you should define (imagine) the structures necessary to support the processes. This approach is most effective when the result is organized into an SPO framework. This sequence of activities, presented in Figure 1–5, is discussed at length in Section 3.2.

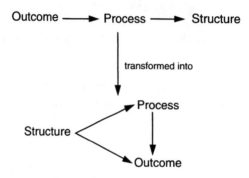

Figure 1–5   Creating an SPO Framework

1.7 THE SPO FRAMEWORK IN ACTION

This section provides several examples of how methods and cognitive models are linked through the SPO framework. My goal is to show the generality of the framework. I'll begin with the Fusion method for developing object-oriented systems. Figure 1–6 presents the structures, outcomes, and processes defined within Fusion.

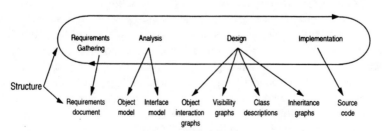

Figure 1–6   Fusion and the SPO Framework

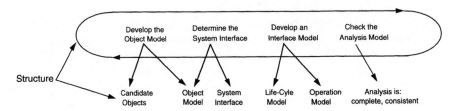

Figure 1–7   Fusion Analysis and the SPO Framework

Applying the framework in a recursive manner, the Fusion activities related to analysis can be organized as shown in Figure 1–7.

Figure 1–7 represents the end point of Fusion with respect to analysis. The specific outcomes detailed in Figure 1–7 are the result of cognitive processes. It is here where the trade-off between method-defined process and cognitive process occurs. The Fusion-defined processes of *Determine the System Interface* and its associated outcomes of *Object Model* and *System Interface* are based heavily on the abilities of the programmer. A method can provide advice on how this might be accomplished but cannot strictly define the processes or intermediate forms of outcome produced by the developer.

An important benefit of the SPO framework is the ease with which it can be applied to all of the activities associated with software development. We can, for example, characterize configuration management through structures, processes, and outcomes. *Configuration management* is an ongoing activity enabling developers to identify appropriate outcomes (e.g., data models, source code, requirements documents, and so forth) so they can review, compare, extend, or otherwise modify these outcomes in a coordinated manner. A configuration management system provides a structure and prescribes a process for engaging in these activities. Outcomes associated with configuration management are a controlled development process, revision histories, and the like.

The SPO framework can be applied to a broad range of systems organizing or supporting human activity. To illustrate, consider the Franklin Day Planner™, a personal time management system. In the Franklin system, structure is provided in the form of calendars for recording appointments, prioritized daily task lists to record tasks that must be accomplished, and a separate note page for recording daily events. Additional structures can be purchased, such as meeting planning or project tracking guides.

The process of using the system begins by setting aside a few minutes each morning to review the tasks that must be accomplished that day, prioritizing each task in order of importance. The process includes periodic review of long-term tasks. Additional tasks or appointments can be scheduled based on this review. One ongoing process is taking notes of important events during the day directly within the Planner.

Outcomes include a daily log of tasks accomplished and a history of notes that can be referenced at a later date. Outcomes also include increased satisfaction with our personal and professional lives, as we experience improved performance and control over our activities (although I think "increased satisfaction" could be more associated with the marketing literature than with our actual performance!).

I've been using the Franklin system for several years. Recently, I missed an important meeting because I forgot to review my Franklin that morning. As in most problem-solving frameworks, adhering to the structure established and following the processes it prescribes become critically important once an appropriate structure has been established. While structure can prescribe a process, it is up to us to follow it.

My training and accomplishments in figure skating provide another example of the relationships between structure, process, and outcome. One form of structure was provided by my coach, Johnny, in the form of a precise schedule of on-ice and off-ice training sessions. With Johnny as your coach, adhering to this schedule precisely was without question. A good manager operates in much the same manner, making certain we adhere to the structures prescribed by the method.

Throughout my 14-year career I had numerous outcomes: some terrific (winning the National Junior Championship), some not so great (recovering from one of a number of injuries). Yet, structure didn't force me to train up to eight hours a day, and outcomes were never the primary motivator. Above all else, what kept me going was a sheer love of the process. Skating so fast you can feel your hair being pushed back by the stale cold air, performing a complicated lift with your partner, returning home each day exhausted and content but not quite satisfied. Because of these experiences, I feel an individual is most successful in any field, including software development, if they understand, adhere to, and respect structure, derive enjoyment from and reflect upon outcomes, but most of all, have a passion for process.

1.8 THE CRITICAL ROLE OF FEEDBACK

The elements of structure, process, and outcome do not exist in a static relationship. Instead, they are linked together through a complex set of feedback loops. The concept of a feedback loop can be easily illustrated by any number of human activities. For example, consider a musician tuning a piano. A key is struck, a note is sounded, and the musician adjusts the tension in the piano wire to obtain the desired pitch. This process is repeated until the desired pitch is obtained. The "feel" of the wheel provides important feedback on the stability of the car when making a turn. The cognitive model presented earlier was described as having feedback loops: Reviewing a proposed solution provides the feedback necessary to modify it to solve the problem correctly. More generally, a feedback loop links the output of some transformation process with its input, in a potentially complex, interdependent nature, as shown in Figure 1–8. For a significantly more detailed discussion of feedback, see Weinberg [1992].

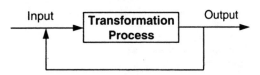

Figure 1–8   Feedback Loops

Feedback loops exist among each of the components of the SPO framework, as illustrated by dotted lines in Figure 1–9. The impact of these feedback loops is described below.

◆ *Outcome ⇒ Process*

Outcomes influences process in two ways. First, as we become adept in producing certain outcomes our problem-solving processes begin to skew toward processes requiring the use of these outcomes. Second, we modify processes to produce the same outcomes using more efficient processes.

◆ *Outcome ⇒ Structure*

Even though structure may define a certain outcome, practical experience with *actually* creating the outcome may show the structural definition of the outcome does not meet your needs. You may, for example, decide not to produce a specific outcome on the current project (thereby altering structure). Alternatively, the method-defined outcome may be incomplete or ambiguous. In this case, you will have to extend or otherwise modify the structure to suit your needs.

◆ *Process ⇒ Structure*

The impact of process on structure can be characterized by tension. In general, how we *actually* solve the problem is often at odds with how we are *supposed* to solve the problem. To illustrate how strong this tension can be, try explaining to your manager the reason you need to implement part of the system is so you can complete your analysis! Without an understanding of mental processes, such a statement doesn't make sense.

This feedback loop exists as the descriptions of how we *should* solve problems become more advanced. Sure, top-down stepwise refinement of a problem is fine technique, but so is bottom-up, sideways, inside-out, outside-in, and a whole host of others! In this manner, experience with processes improves structure by changing structure.[5]

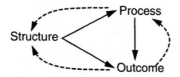

Figure 1–9   Feedback Loops in the SPO Framework

---

[5] Some readers may note that there can be no real feedback loop from process to structure, for the realization that a process and a structure are at odds is itself an outcome. Thus, a more rigorous and sophisticated analysis of feedback in terms of the SPO framework would state that the feedback loop from process to structure can occur only through the examination of outcomes. While this is true, thinking of a feedback loop between process and structure is a reasonable simplification and helps reinforce the interrelated nature of the components of the framework.

One additional aspect of feedback deserves mentioning. Unless there is some structure in place to capture feedback it will be lost. The musician described earlier was *expecting* to hear the feedback necessary to tune the piano further. Unless we are looking for similar feedback as we solve problems, it is likely to go unnoticed. Thus, feedback-motivated changes may happen quickly, slowly, or even not at all.

1.9 REVIEW

Software development is a complex problem-solving behavior. Cognitive models, which are descriptive in nature, provide insight into the mental processes used by developers engaged in software development. The foundation of these mental processes are plans, stereotypic solutions to problems. Problem solving is the act of applying and tailoring plans to fit a new problem. Generalized and externalized plans are referred to as patterns.

Software methods provide a structure for mental processes by prescribing a specific set of processes and associated outcomes. This sequence of processes usually includes requirements determination, requirements analysis, design, implementation, verification, and maintenance along with one or more outcomes appropriate for each activity.

More generally, software development can be described in terms of structures, processes, and outcomes. Structure defines the form and content of outcomes and supports the processes we use to create them. Process refers to the mental and physical activities we use to produce outcomes. Key to understanding mental processes is the concept of leveling, which captures how the behavior of more experienced developers differs from less experienced developers. Outcomes are the things produced. A software method is a complete structure–process–outcome framework. Many such frameworks are needed to support all the activities associated with software development.

Our actual process does not have to match the process prescribed by the method. We may choose to use method-prescribed processes poorly, ignore them entirely, or augment them based on our experience. The degree of structure needed during problem solving is based on two variables. The first is the problem itself. More complex problems need greater structure to solve them correctly. The second is based on our cognitive style, or the amount of structure each of us prefers when solving a problem. Adaptors prefer more structure. Innovators prefer less. Neither style is inherently better at problem solving.

Structures, processes, and outcomes do not exist as independent entities but instead are tightly linked via complex feedback loops. These feedback loops provide the mechanism by which software development practices can improve.

2

THE INTEGRATED FRAMEWORK

Certain aspects of problem-solving behavior are difficult to describe solely in terms of structures, processes, and outcomes. Humans are complex beings, and our behavior is motivated and influenced by more than structures, processes, and outcomes. Our values, personality, and goals also govern much of our behavior. By weaving these concepts into the SPO framework, this chapter provides a more complete understanding of behavior.

Chapter Overview

Values, personality, and goals are discussed in turn in Sections 2.1 through 2.3. These three aspects of behavior are integrated with structures, processes, and outcomes to create the integrated SPO framework in Section 2.4. The "soft" aspects of values, personality, and goals can conflict with the "hard" aspects of structures, processes, and outcomes. Sources of conflict and tension are discussed in Section 2.5. The chapter is reviewed in Section 2.6.

2.1 VALUES

Developers make countless numbers of decisions during development. Some of these decisions are made according to our experience base (as explained by cognitive models) as well as problem-solving structures (as dictated by methods). Ideally, all of these decisions are made according to objective criteria provided by such things as requirements documents. In reality, many decisions are not prescribed by structure, nor can they be justified on purely objective grounds.

Consider a developer faced with choosing between two equally promising plans. Which plan will be chosen? Why? When faced with such a situation, the SPO framework begins to break down. It cannot provide a reasonable answer as to why a specific plan was chosen, nor can it help to predict or shape that decision. Values provide a missing link in understanding how we make key decisions during the development process.

A *value* is a concept deemed worthy or important. When something is valued (e.g., friendship) it guides our decision making. You may not realize you have values associated with software development, but you do. In fact, you probably have several. Do you favor correctness of code? ease of maintenance? time or space efficiency? consistently formatted source code? Values are intimately tied to rules of programming discourse, personal beliefs about the development process, and experiences both good and bad. In a sense, values provide a kind of structure, for they help us make decisions in a consistent manner. This kind of structure, of course, is far different from a method-defined structure or the structure provided by a specific language.

Values help guide us in making decisions when explicit or objective requirements do not exist. They are related to, but distinct from, cognitive style. Recall that our cognitive style describes how much structure we prefer during problem solving. Values describe the unconscious priorities each of us brings to the decisions we make. Not surprisingly, developers will try to follow values if they are explicitly stated (e.g., "Easily understood variable names are important"), a topic discussed extensively in Chapters 3, 8, and 11.

We often fail to explicitly state our personal values, which can detract from performance in solving complex problems in new domains. Why? Explicitly knowing your values can help in making consistent decisions and serve as a very high-level plan for solving problems.

> *The impact of a set of values cannot be understated. I was recently sent an e-mail from a client describing how he changed the development practices of his organization by constantly pursuing an iterative-incremental process model. By letting his upper management know how strongly he valued this approach, he was able to convince them to give it a try on a medium project. Even though it took several months, numerous setbacks, and some risk to his own career, his value system allowed him continue promoting change in face of conflict.*

2.2 PERSONALITY

A *personality* is a complex set of relatively stable behavioral and emotional characteristics that can be used to uniquely identify a person. Several authors have discussed the relationship of personality to programming [Shneiderman 1980; Weinberg 1971] and problem solving [Wood 1990]. Our personality affects everything we do (Figure 2–1).

One aspect of our personality, cognitive style, and how it affects the SPO framework, was discussed in Chapter one. Here are other personality factors that impact the SPO framework.

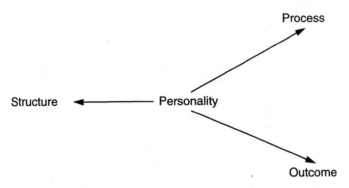

Figure 2–1   Impact of Personality on the SPO Framework

Mental set. The *mental set* of an individual is the implicit expectations or beliefs they bring to a problem-solving task. It "frames" how we approach the solution to a problem. For example, if we have found using a method (or any specific structure, process, or outcome) to be helpful in the past we will be predisposed to use it again in the future. Alternatively, we will avoid using a method if we think it will slow down the overall problem-solving process. As you may have already guessed, my "mental set" includes the beliefs "using the right structure aids in problem solving" and "methods provide a good structure for software development." As such, I'm favorably predisposed to using a method!

Self-efficacy. At times, software development can be a long, slow process. You think you have the correct solution, the code debugged, and the system ready for delivery. And then you test it, only to realize a new error has occurred. Over time, this can take a toll on even the most confident people. *Self-efficacy* refers to a person's beliefs about their capacity to continually engage in problem solving processes [Wood 1990]. A strong sense of self-efficacy is required to keep going when our initial attempts to solve the problem fail. Self-efficacy can help us continue to search for the right plan and can help us in our efforts to tailor plans to meet the problem.

Assertive/Passive. The assertive individuals are confident in their abilities and their work, take the initiative, and are generally known for "getting the job done." They are more likely to question both the need for and content of structure. Assertive people may exhibit a more chaotic process, because they are more confident that no matter what process is used they will be able to generate the final outcome. Alternatively, a passive individual is more likely to work within the confines of established structures, and his process may appear to be more in control.

Tolerance of anxiety. Anxiety can be characterized by apprehension about the future state of an outcome. It can be caused by many factors: an unfamiliar problem domain, a tight schedule, office politics, and so forth. Individuals who have a low tolerance for anxiety will create poor outcomes when operating in a high anxiety environment, usually by failing to follow a good process when creating outcomes. When these outcomes are evaluated and found unacceptable, anxiety increases. Ultimately, this results in a negative feedback loop, in which anxiety produces poor outcomes which produce more anxiety in an endless cycle [Weick 1979; Weinberg 1992].

High/Low tolerance for ambiguity. Every outcome associated with a complex system is a potential source of ambiguity. Requirements documents are often incomplete; analysis models may conflict with or contradict the requirements; it may not be entirely clear how a design is intended to be translated into source code, and so forth. The fact that actually constructing a program requires zero tolerance for ambiguity makes the situation even more difficult. A computer will only execute the program as we have designed it. Developers must constantly play the role of the middle man, translating ambiguous problems into unambiguous solutions. Clearly, staying sane as a developer requires more than a little tolerance of ambiguity.

These personality factors are certainly not all-inclusive. It is possible to identify additional factors and assess their impact on the framework. And, we all have each of the characteristics described above to some degree. Moreover, personality is not fixed: Our personality changes based on environmental conditions and current experiences. What is most important is to realize personality has a strong impact on how an individual operates within the SPO framework.

2.3 GOALS

Values help explain the motivation for certain kinds of decisions during software development. Personality provides us with an understanding of how we operate within the framework. Yet, how do we organize our long-term behavior?

Goals provide the answer. A *goal* is a special kind of outcome guiding and controlling behavior generated by an individual for their own personal satisfaction. Like values, goals provide a certain amount of structure to decision making, as we usually try to make decisions that help us achieve our long-term goals. Goals direct long-term processes and spur the creation of intermediate outcomes that can be measured for progress against the goal.

A goal can be a want, an expressed need, a desired experience. Goals capture our imagination and provide us with inspiration. For example, my goal might be to become proficient in Java™. This goal in turn, might motivate me to find a project using Java, read magazine articles or books describing how to program in Java, or take a class in Java. The nature in which goals impact the SPO framework is illustrated in Figure 2–2.

Goals are distinct and independent from the outcomes defined in a method, although we *may* choose to align our goals with method-defined outcomes. Differentiating between goals and method-defined outcomes is fairly easy. Goals are what *I*

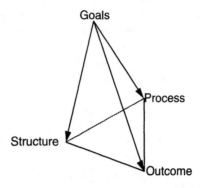

Figure 2–2   Goals in the SPO Framework

generate, not what some other party generates and gives to me. In general, goals transcend work and serve to impact our entire life in ways work cannot. For example, our work can be a component of a goal (e.g., financial security) but does not serve to define it.

2.4 THE INTEGRATED FRAMEWORK

Integrating values, personality, and goals into the SPO framework produces a three-dimensional figure presenting a complete model for understanding problem-solving behavior (see Figure 2–3). While not shown as such, it should be noted that personality retains a link between the other components in the integrated framework.

What are the differences between structures, processes, and outcomes and values, personality, and goals? Structures, processes, and outcomes are more concerned

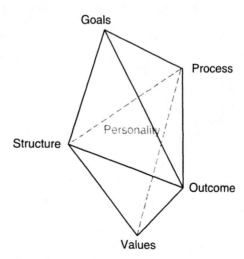

Figure 2–3   The Integrated SPO Framework

with controlling, guiding, supporting, and defining problem-solving behavior. Values, personality, and goals represent the "human" aspects of problem solving and capture the means by which we make decisions that are not dictated by structure. As such, they are not often discussed or addressed by methods. Because they profoundly influence our behavior, they are important components of the integrated framework.

2.5 CONFLICT AND TENSION AMONG COMPONENTS OF THE FRAMEWORK

Like other engineering disciplines, software development has inherent conflict and tensions [Petroski 1985]. Should the application be small or fast? Both are desirable, but in general making an application small conflicts with making it fast, as many optimization techniques that increase the speed of the system also increase the size of the source code. Should parts of the application be redesigned before implementation is finished when a better algorithm is discovered? How much time, if any, should be allocated to the schedule to allow programmers to rework their code?

In a similar manner, each component of the integrated framework can be the source of conflict and tension in software development. To illustrate, consider the potential for conflict or tension between goals and values. The goal of obtaining a bonus by working extra hours conflicts with the value of spending time with our families.

Such tension may not be as readily apparent in the structures, processes, and outcomes defined in a method, but they are there. Methods are not perfect. Tension surfaces when developers attempt to apply the method in a context not foreseen by its designers. To illustrate, the original Fusion method had little support for concurrency, contributing to tension among developers using it to build concurrent systems (e.g., disagreements in how concurrency should be displayed). Even though methods are generally designed to be applied to a wide variety of problem-solving situations, they can't be applied equally well in every conceivable situation. Errors and ambiguities are bound to exist in their definition, producing variation in their application.

Finally, although a method may give us guidelines for determining when a given outcome is complete, in practice there are very few absolutes that can be applied in translating requirements statements into a working system. A method may tell us analysis is complete when all requirements (as known) are captured, but how do we know in an objective and certain manner this has been accomplished? The same can be said of design: When is design "complete"? Answering these questions requires experience, judgment, and sometimes just plain good luck.

Conflict and tension will always remain a part of human problem-solving behavior. By embracing the premise that conflict and tension will always be one aspect of software development, finding ways to reduce and control them is that much easier.

2.6 REVIEW

Certain aspects of human problem-solving behavior are difficult to describe solely in terms of structures, processes, and outcomes. By adding values, personality, and goals to these concepts, we can improve the SPO framework, using it as the foundation for a more complete understanding of problem-solving behavior.

Values are concepts deemed important. They provide an internal structure helping us solve problems consistently and completely. Our personality is a complex set of relatively stable behavioral and emotional characteristics that uniquely identifies us. Different aspects of personality (e.g., cognitive style, mental set, and so forth) impact structures, processes, and outcomes in different ways. Goals are very special kinds of outcomes that provide additional structure in problem solving.

Part Two

The integrated framework provides a complete theory of human problem solving. It is a tool for thinking about and discussing problem solving. Unfortunately, theory can only take you so far, and an understanding of the framework alone does little to improve our skills as software developers. As a theory, the framework is admittedly a bit abstract to be useful for the day-to-day questions that arise when developing software. How can the SPO framework impact my decision to use a CASE tool? If values are important in the integrated framework, should I try to identify mine? How?

My goal in Part Two is to provide you with strategies, techniques, and advice (lots of advice!) for improving your abilities as a software professional. As stated in the preface, specific advice will be given to both developers and managers. Here is an overview of Part Two.

Much of the real work in developing software happens inside the head of the developer as they are thinking about the problem. Therefore, what is needed to improve software development *are not* methods per se, but ways to use any method more effectively. Chapter 3 presents several such ideas.

Chapter 4 continues to focus on what is inside your head, but this time concentrates on the "soft" parts of problem solving—values, personality, and goals. A significant aspect of understanding yourself means identifying how these shape and frame your approach to software development.

Chapter 5 addresses the right way to use tools and support staff to enhance your effectiveness as a developer. Chapter 6 finishes Part Two by showing that developing a lifelong training plan is *your* responsibility. It concludes with a set of structures for self-managing this process.

3

FORTIFYING THE FOUNDATION

The "universal" approach to problem solving goes something like this:

Step 1: Define the problem to be solved.
Step 2: Decompose the problem into more easily solved subproblems.
Step 3: Repeat step 2 until the subproblems can be solved directly.
Step 4: Integrate the solutions to solve the larger problem.

While the steps seem simple enough, doing them well requires a substantial amount of knowledge (e.g., plans) on both the problem domain and problem-solving strategies and techniques. The purpose of this chapter is to provide you with several proven strategies and techniques that can supplement and enhance any method. Some of these techniques are derived from the SPO framework and its description of problem solving. Others are derived from studying expert software developers as they work. By learning the structures experts have created to guide their work, the processes they follow, and the outcomes they generate, we can improve our own abilities. And some are just good ideas borrowed from other fields and recast in a manner appropriate for software development.

Chapter Overview

Existing structures, including those provided by a method, are often insufficient to solve complex new problems. Section 3.1 begins by showing you how to create structures and processes as necessary to achieve desired outcomes.

Of course, it isn't always easy to know beforehand which structure or process is best. Sometimes it is easier to focus on the outcome first! This technique can provide value; Section 3.2 shows you how.

Obtaining feedback is an essential part of problem solving. Section 3.3 shows why this is so and presents several structures and processes for achieving it.

An extremely simple summarization of Chapter 1 is this: Experts solve problems more effectively than novices. To become an expert, add more plans to your cognitive library. What kinds of plans? And in what order? Read Section 3.3 for the answer.

As described in Chapter 1, the outcomes associated with a method consist of multiple models of the problem. Section 3.5 shows why multiple models are important and presents several strategies for building them quickly and effectively.

Most problems can be solved more than one way. Generating and selecting among alternative solutions is the subject of Section 3.6. Section 3.7 concludes the chapter by discussing the benefits of differentiating between kinds and styles of thought and focus in problem solving.

3.1 CREATE STRUCTURES AND PROCESSES TO ACHIEVE OUTCOMES

What is an expert? An expert is an individual who has mastered a particular problem domain. Their large cognitive library contains many plans enabling them to quickly and easily solve problems. Included in these plans are the structures, processes, and outcomes needed to solve the problem. An expert works in a deceptive manner. Because they "know" what to do, they seem to solve problems without the need for external structures. Yet, even the most experienced software developer can be faced with an unfamiliar problem. How then should the problem be solved? Answering this question well is important no matter what your experience, for none of us is an expert in every aspect of software development.

All developers work within some structure, following some process and generating one or more outcomes as they work to create the system. The best developers use a formally defined method, with carefully prescribed processes and well-known outcomes. Expert developers know how to use this method to their best advantage. Furthermore, they've also learned which problems the method solves well, which problems the method solves poorly and are able to modify the method-defined structures as necessary to fit their needs and the problem. Alternatively, they create their own structure by defining processes and/or outcomes to help them solve the problem.

The need for creating our own structures, processes, and outcomes goes beyond any single method, for no single method can define *every* aspect of work. As I read *Programmers at Work* [Lammers 1989], a series of interviews with 19 of the most famous and influential developers of all time, I was struck at the number of times these individuals created their own structures and processes to achieve outcomes. Charles Simonyi invented the Hungarian naming convention to provide a structure for naming variables. Butler Lampson details how he structures his design process and the discipline by which he follows his own dictates. Jonathan Sachs proudly gives an example of his own C coding standard (a structure) and proceeds to show how all his source code (an outcome) follows it. In these, and numerous other examples, we learn expert developers regularly create structures—and then follow the processes they prescribe—in order to achieve desirable outcomes. Becoming an expert developer means developing the skills necessary to create appropriate structures when needed. Once created you must then have the discipline necessary to follow them.

The creation of structures and processes is not an expression of our personality or goals. Each of the developers in *Programmers at Work* has a unique personality and was working for very different goals. The creation of structures and processes is instead an expression of a commonly held value: The belief that software development is more effective when appropriate structures are in place to support it. If these structures do not exist, one should create them as necessary to support the development process. Adopt this value as your own.

ADVICE TO DEVELOPERS

Creating structures and processes to help you in the development process may seem like a daunting task, but it isn't. I'm not asking or suggesting you create your own method or programming language. Instead, I am asking you to examine your work habits and current work environment, looking for ways to add structure or modify process in order to achieve more desirable outcomes. If no coding standard exists, invent your own. Create a formal test plan even if it is not part of your method. By thinking about what structures and processes you need *before* you begin, you establish a simple habit for continually improving your performance.

Know your existing structures before creating new ones.

Define what is wrong with the old before creating a new structure.

Adopt a structure before creating a new one.

Do not confuse creating structure with solving the problem.

Keep it simple.

Do not impose your structure on others.

Know your existing structures before creating new ones.   Before you expend energy creating a new structure, make certain your current structure can't do the job. Suppose you are building a data model for a small bookstore and discover that a customer cannot be deleted if they have an outstanding book order. This is known as a restricted deletion, and most data modeling notations define a special symbol to express it. What happens if you cannot remember the symbol? Rather than invent your own symbol, review the reference materials associated with the method and use those defined by the method.

More generally, before inventing a new structure, review the current structure. Consider asking other members of your team for help—have they faced this problem in the past? The last thing you want to try and justify to your manager is why you spent three days inventing your own notation for a data model instead of using the one defined by the method.

Define what is wrong with the old before creating a new. If you are certain you must create a new structure, begin by defining what is wrong with the current structure. Use this definition to ensure your new structure will meet your needs.

Adopt a structure before creating a new one. Using the definition of what is wrong with your current structure, take time to review other existing structures before creating a new structure. Why? When a new structure is created, it tends to stand alone. There is little experience with the structure, few or no tools, and no other mechanisms available to support its use. Thus, it is preferable to adopt the use of a structure rather than invent an entirely new structure.

How much time should you spend reviewing other structures? You should attempt to examine at least two other structures addressing a similar problem. If you fail to find the structure you seek, create your own.

Do not confuse creating structure with solving the problem. It is easy to get caught up in the idea of creating a new structure or process. Remember, your job is to solve the problem, not devise new structures.

I think every developer has made this mistake at least once in their career. I know I have. For example, when I was trying to build the programming environment designed to help students learn programming (described in Chapter 1) it was easy to get carried away into building more and more elaborate forms of structure. Not all of my ideas contributed to solving the real problem, which was helping students learn how to write programs by supporting them as they engage in an expert form of work. I've witnessed this problem countless times in my consulting work. Once the decision is made to invent a new structure, teams easily become enamored with creating these structures instead of focusing on the problem. Resist the temptation and define only the structures you need.

Keep it simple. It is a mistake to define an elaborate structure when a simple structure will solve the problem. You can see this happen by watching methods evolve. When first created, methods are often quite lean. They are focused on solving a specific set of problems. Over time, additions are made to solve problems not originally foreseen by the creators. Eventually, the method often becomes so big reference aids (a form of structure) are created to help determine what parts of the method are needed for a particular kind of problem! Resist this temptation. Be a minimalist. Keep whatever structures you create to their bare essential.

Do not impose your structure on others. Although creating a structure can be an effective mechanism to govern your work, it is a mistake to think others will immediately adopt it for three reasons. First, your structure may not match their cognitive style. Second, unless your structure is "sanctioned" by management others may avoid using it. Third, there may not be sufficient incentive to work on sharing your structure with others. In general, you should think of a structure you create as exactly that: a structure *you* have defined to help *you* perform your job. Imposing its use on others is inappropriate and can even cause feelings of ill-will.

ADVICE TO MANAGERS

Inevitably, your developers will find themselves faced with creating their own structures because of ill-defined requests, new problems that resist solutions using old structures, and new technologies that cannot be effectively employed using old structures. As a manager, your primary concern is making certain developer-created structures are appropriate and necessary. Ideally, you should remain aware of the structures used by each developer so that you can encourage them to use existing structures where appropriate. Alternatively, when you find a developer has created a good new structure, you will want to identify it and support its use within the team.

Avoid changing developer structures.

Look for and promote good structures.

Resist too much diversity.

Avoid creating emergency structures and processes.

Avoid changing developer structures.   Unless fundamentally flawed or redundant with existing structures, avoid changing structures created by your staff. Doing so will instill a healthy "self-reliant" attitude among your developers.

If you must modify a developer-created structure, try doing it by asking questions rather than issuing specific commands. Approaching the modification this way encourages developers to *think* about their structure. Of course, you can always resort to a command if needed.

Look for and promote good structures.   If a structure or process generated by a developer is sound, consider promoting its use to the rest of the team.

Resist too much diversity.   If every developer is following his own idiosyncratic structure, teamwork is made overly difficult. Typically, developers will operate under different structures if no standard operating procedures exist for accomplishing a task. Solve this by making certain your staff knows proper procedures. Adopt a method and follow its prescriptions faithfully.

Avoid creating emergency structures and processes.   A common mistake is to create a structure or process to compensate for a nearly random or highly unlikely or undesirable outcome. For example, suppose your organization has a policy of performing full backups on Tuesdays and Fridays and incremental backups on other workdays. Your team has been working on an important system for three months. Two developers have worked all weekend long to implement a particularly complex part of the system. On Monday morning, the server crashes, an undesirable outcome by any measure. Normally, this would not be a cause for too much concern, but in this case two of your developers lost two days of work—and they are not at all certain they can re-create the solution! One natural reaction of the team members who lost their work is a request for an extended backup policy (i.e., one including weekends).

While this is a possible solution to the problem, it should be resisted. Structures and processes created in response to unusual or undesirable outcomes are often inappropriate for normal day-to-day operation. Furthermore, there are three hidden costs associated with such structures. First, there is the cost to establish the structures and educate team members on the processes. Second, there is the ongoing negative impact on resources (more backups require more energy expended in managing them, and so forth). Third, most structures are surprisingly resilient to change. Once a structure is established, we tend to resist dismantling it, even when we agree the structure (or process) *negatively* impacts productivity! In this case, a more appropriate solution would be to educate the team on the existing backup policies and ask them to create their own private backups of work done on a weekend. In this way, the responsibility and organizational impact of backups for exceptional working conditions (working on the weekend) are placed where they are most appropriate.

3.2 PRACTICE FUTURE PERFECT THINKING

Much of the activity associated with software development is specifying precisely that which does not yet exist. Software developers must constantly imagine the future, describing and detailing the system yet to be realized. We find ourselves trying to answer the question, "What should the system do?" Answering this question well has a significant impact on performance. The more detailed the answer, the greater the chance the system will operate in the desired manner.

Unfortunately, we are asking the wrong question! Instead of using the simple future tense and asking "What *should* the system do?" we should use the future perfect tense and ask "What *will* the system have done?"[1] Why? By changing the tense of the verb, we change the way we think about the future. Our frame of reference changes from thinking about what *might* occur to thinking about what *did* occur.

---

[1]Using future perfect thinking is as valid for maintenance activities as it is for new development, for even maintenance requires us to think about the *future* state of the system. However, be careful when asking this question. Since most development activity centers upon maintenance, it is easy to think this question applies to the current system. It doesn't. The question is being asked about the system which does not yet exist.

Why is this shift in tense so important? Studies have demonstrated we develop significantly more detailed descriptions of future events when we describe such events as if they have already occurred. Bavelas [1973] divided a group of subjects in half and told the first group: "A professor *will* take a six-week sabbatical trip in Europe. Write out his itinerary." The second group was told: "A professor *took* a six-week sabbatical trip in Europe. Write out his itinerary." The only difference in these statements is the tense of the verb: Has the trip been taken? Bavelas found the descriptions of the second group were significantly more fanciful, richly detailed, sensible, and longer, presumably because it is easier to understand and describe a trip that has been taken over one that has not yet been taken, even if *neither* trip has been taken.

Weick [1979] outlines research asking subjects to predict the outcome of a future Superbowl game from two perspectives. The first from the future tense (i.e., "Image today is Saturday. Detroit and Miami will play in the Superbowl tomorrow. Write down the score and describe what will happen during the game."). The second from the future perfect tense (i.e., "Imagine today is Monday and Detroit and Miami played in the Superbowl yesterday. Write down the score of yesterday's game and describe what happened during the game."). Neither group of subjects were able to predict the winner more accurately than the other. However, subjects who described the game from the future perfect tense wrote more detailed and fanciful descriptions of the game.

The key result of these and other studies is that the descriptions generated by the subjects using future perfect thinking were significantly more detailed than those who engaged in mere future thinking. This notion of detail is important, for no other engineering discipline requires the constant precision and attention to detail as software development. Programming a computer requires absolute perfection if the program is to execute correctly. For this reason alone, future perfect thinking should be considered a major strategy for systems development: By helping to create detail, it helps us solve thorny problems *as early as possible* in the development of the system.

Future perfect thinking has other important ramifications. By thinking of a future event as one that has already occurred, you can imagine at least one sequence of processes that can be taken to generate the event. If you ask "What *should* the system do?" you are left wondering about not only what the system will do, but also how the system could possibly do it. If instead you ask: "What will the system have done" (or, more simply, in the future tense, "What *did* the system do?"), you not only have an idea of what the system did, but you can also begin to answer the question "How did the system do it?" Thinking of the system as already completed enables us to make more effective use of our cognitive libraries by directing our search processes and reducing the possible set of outcomes to consider before a suitable plan is selected.

While future perfect thinking can help us generate a plausible outcome, it should not be the only technique we use in thinking about the future system. Practicing extreme forms of future perfect thinking means we think of *one* outcome and then work hard to achieve *that single* outcome. By asking "What should the system do" in conjunction with "What will the system have done" we remain conscious of the fact that iterative refinement of the problem is ongoing. The planned activities generated through this use of future perfect thinking represent starting points for development efforts. It is quite likely these will change over time once these activities are engaged. The greatest freedom for defining a correct solution lies in the interplay between simple future thinking and future perfect thinking. Simple future thinking encourages us to imagine any potential outcome. Future perfect thinking provides a powerful tool for imagining how to create a specific outcome.

In terms of the SPO framework, future perfect thinking consists of first defining an outcome appropriate to the problem. The second step is to define a set of processes to achieve the outcome. The final step is to create a structure supporting these processes. Before activity begins, the elements are organized into the shape of the SPO framework. This is an important step. By arranging the elements *before* activity begins, you have another opportunity to reflect on the linkages between these elements. Once process is initiated to achieve the outcome, the proposed structure becomes more real. The proposed steps of the process gain more importance, and the possible outcome becomes a desired outcome due to our investment in making it real. When finished, the proposed structure is known, the imaged process becomes reality, and the possible outcome (or something close to it) is produced. This sequence of events, diagrammed in Figure 3–1, also describes a kind of learning function. When finished, the structures, processes, and outcomes can be reused to solve new problems.

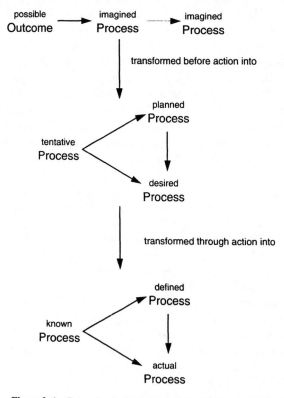

Figure 3–1   Future Perfect Thinking and the SPO Framework

The idea of using future perfect thinking in the development of computer systems is not entirely new. The growing awareness of the importance of creating highly usable systems has increased the focus on the field of study known as Human-Computer Interaction (HCI). One way the HCI literature has encouraged future perfect thinking is by urging developers to create a comprehensive and detailed user manual before the actual construction of the system [Gould 1988]. Less well known are the psychological reasons why this approach is effective. Future perfect thinking provides one reason for the answer. When you are in the process of developing the system, a myriad of details must be resolved in the operation and definition of the user interface. Writing the user manual first, a kind of future perfect thinking, forces you to resolve numerous problems in the operation of the system *before* the system is built. Similarly, writing thorough test plans encourages you to move from future thinking to future perfect thinking. By specifying how the system did behave, you have the opportunity to engage in more detailed thought.

When I first learned about future perfect thinking, I decided to test it informally in classes I teach on building graphical user interfaces. In one assignment students are faced with the problem of coordinating the interaction between a check box and an input field. The correct solution requires the student to enable the input field only if the check box is checked and the data being edited meet certain criteria. When I ask students "How should the check box control the input field," they usually have great difficulty in designing and implementing the correct solution. When I ask "How did the check box control the input field," they usually generate the answer much more readily.

I'm so convinced future perfect thinking helps build systems I now try to incorporate its use into all my classes. When teaching project managers, I ask them to visualize their current system as successfully implemented . What steps did they take to ensure success? How were these steps organized? What problems did they encounter, and how did they solve them? I've found project managers are able to create far better plans, anticipate risks more completely, and do the right activities far more easily when asked these questions.

ADVICE TO DEVELOPERS

Because future perfect thinking can have such a significant impact in the development process, it is important to find ways to incorporate it into your daily routine. Fortunately, this is much easier than you might think!

> Examine your method for opportunities to use future perfect thinking.
>
> Write the user manual and test plans first.
>
> Use future perfect thinking to prevent thrashing.
>
> Use a storyboard in graphical user interfaces.
>
> Use explicit time references to encourage the shift to future perfect thinking.

Examine your method for opportunities to use future perfect thinking. The best place to start using future perfect thinking is your current method. Look at the outcomes it defines. Which of these lend themselves to future perfect thinking? Although the shift in verb tense can be used for any outcome, future perfect thinking is best used by trying to find those outcomes naturally lending themselves to the technique.

For example, an entity-relationship diagram (or object model) does not lend itself to future perfect thinking because such models are designed to accurately capture the existing problem domain. They are not designed to predict or shape the future system.

Data flow diagrams (DFDs) are different, for they are used to predict and shape the processing of information in the future system. By creating this diagram from the perspective of how the system *did* transform data rather than how the system *will* transform data, we can use future perfect thinking in the development of a DFD.

Object-oriented systems are often described through use cases. Each use case describes a specific interaction between some outside agent and the system in an implementation independent manner [Jacobsen 1992]. Future perfect thinking can be used to develop more detailed use cases by imagining how the system *responded* to an input event instead of wondering how the system *could* respond to an input event.

Write the user manual and your test plans first. This is so important, I thought I should write about it twice. Maybe you have heard about this before. Come on! Try it! None of this advice is any good unless you use it!

Use future perfect thinking to prevent thrashing. Anytime you ask "What should the system do?" during implementation, you are in trouble. Why? Asking this question means you don't know what you want the system to do. You are engaged in a form of exploration (simple future thinking) to find the answer.

This often happens when you begin translating a high-level design you think you understand into source code and things don't go quite as smoothly as planned. You begin to repeatedly compile the program, making small modifications each time, in the hope one of the changes will work. I call this behavior "thrashing," because it is similar to what happens when an operating system repeatedly swaps the same pages to try to fulfill a memory request. A lot of work is done, but no real progress is made. When this occurs, immediately stop and use future perfect thinking to define what you should do next. Instead of trying to describe (and then implement) what you think the system *should do*, describe (and then implement) what the system *did*.

Of course, preventing thrashing means you must first detect it. How can you do this? The only way to do this is by monitoring your own behavior. Experience can help, as developers with more experience are often more skilled in self-monitoring. Discipline also plays a role, as detecting (and then correcting thrashing) can require strong discipline. Perhaps the best way to detect thrashing is to periodically assess your progress in completing a well-defined outcome. If you cannot demonstrate good progress, examine your process to see if you are thrashing. If you are, see if future perfect thinking can get you out of a jam.

Use a storyboard in graphical user interfaces.   The interaction between the user and a graphical user interface can become extraordinarily complex. Sometimes it can be difficult to clearly define the best sequence of activities to accomplish a goal. Use future perfect thinking to create a storyboard to manage this complexity by clearly defining the steps necessary to achieve a goal.

Imagine each possible state of the user interface in terms of a "snapshot" of what is shown to the user. If these snapshots are ordered, 1, 2, 3 . . . , $n-1$, n, you can create a storyboard showing how actions made by the user are reflected in the user interface. The application of future perfect thinking is not to start with screen 1 and imagine what actions are needed to get to screen n, but to instead *start* with screen n and work backwards to screen 1.

Use explicit time references to encourage the shift.   Learning to use it can be somewhat problematic to use future perfect thinking because we have a tendency to shift from future perfect thinking to simple future thinking when recalling an event [Harris 1973]. To help you in using future perfect thinking, use explicit adverbs or time references when constructing sentences [Bransford 1972; Morrow 1985]. To make it even easier, add as much contextual information as possible. Thus, the question "What will the system have done?" is not nearly as effective as "Imagine it is next Thursday. Sam, a member of the marketing department, has been using your system to search for a customer. How did he do this?"

ADVICE TO MANAGERS

Encouraging your staff to use future perfect is a simple, proven technique for developing more detailed descriptions of systems. It is a mistake, however, to think of future perfect thinking as a tool only appropriate for your staff.

> Not everyone can use future perfect thinking.
> Use future perfect thinking for any planning activity.
> Develop the system from the impact it *had* on the business.

Not everyone can use future perfect thinking.   You may encounter some difficulty in encouraging your staff to use future perfect thinking if you have any members of your team from a Far Eastern country. Why? Many of the languages used in the Far East (e.g., Indonesian or Vietnamese) do not have the future perfect tense of the verb. Because they have no experience in using this tense of the verb, people who speak these languages often find using the technique difficult.

Use future perfect thinking for any planning activity.   Perhaps the most enduring example of future perfect thinking for planning purposes comes from

Weick, when he describes a manager trying to write a five-year budget plan who is experiencing writer's block.

One way to handle that block about the five-year plan is to imagine that it is six *years later. Now, write yourself a letter from your boss, congratulating you in great detail on how well your five-year plan worked. Be as specific as possible in the congratulatory letter. Although you are writing a letter of congratulations for a set of activities that have not yet occurred, in doing so you may clarify things you want to accomplish in those five years in a way that thinking in the simple future tense won't. [From Weick, K.E.* The Social Psychology of Organizing, *2nd edition. New York, NY: Random House, 1979. Reprinted with permission.*

Elite athletes practice visualization—a form of future perfect thinking—all the time. Most begin by thinking about a successful performance and then think backwards about all the activities and actions required to achieve the performance. As a pair skater, my partner and I would think first about the ending of a successfully completed lift and then think backwards about all the movements required for a successful lift. Once this was completed we would move forward, working on each movement leading to future success. Visualization is like building a storyboard: You start with the end and work backwards. As a manager, thinking first about the completion of a project and second about the activities needed to make the project successful will help you develop more detailed plans.

Develop the system from the impact it *had* on the business. Describe, in detail, this impact in the requirements document and encourage your users to think about these effects in the context of their current work. Such a perspective will help your users to understand and plan for the impact of the future system and will help to ensure you are planning the right system.

If you are willing to be a little radical, you might consider postponing the development of a detailed data/object model until the customer has approved the system prototype. Once the prototype has been approved, "reverse engineer" the data/object model from the system. Such an approach forces future perfect thinking, because to show a prototype to the user you must have specified the behavior of the system.

3.3 REVIEW EARLY AND OFTEN

It is rare to understand the requirements well enough to accurately build a system in one pass through the method. The variables involved are simply too complex! It requires our cognitive library to contain all the plans necessary to solve the problem. It requires a precisely stated, unambiguous, and completely stable set of requirements. For all practical purposes, this is an unattainable goal! Most problems are so complex we cannot accurately specify them in advance. Furthermore, customers do not have complete control over their environment. They—and the problem they are asking *you* to help them solve—are subject to external constraints and pressures. Even if they have given you stable requirements in the beginning of the project, they might change them due to any number of legitimate business reasons. It is best to approach each problem with the *expectation* that we do not have the all the necessary plans in our cognitive library and that requirements are somewhat unstable. In other words, our process will be a little messy, we will have to work on it, and we will have to try to achieve stability as quickly as possible.

Given this, what is a good strategy for increasing our understanding and achieving stable requirements? One of the best is to review outcomes early and often throughout the development of the system. A *review* is a controlled examination of a specific outcome by a group of people to assess the appropriateness of an outcome for its intended purpose. Any outcome can be effectively reviewed, from a simple hand-drawn user interface to a complex algorithm. Reviews provide critically needed feedback to the entire development process, and provide both managers and developers with the information necessary to modify outcomes to ensure they meet stated requirements. The goal is to obtain feedback as early as possible in order to minimize total effort as illustrated in Figure 3–2.

Development would be easy if we perfectly understood the problem and the knew the right way to solve it. It would be like walking to a perfectly known destination along a well-travelled path.

Because it is rare that we understand the problem or its solution perfectly, we lay out the best possible path and begin the journey. As we inevitably veer off track our total distance increases, representing increased effort and/or wasted work.

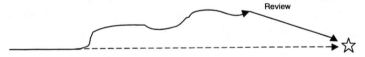

When our work is reviewed the problems are identified and we lay out a new course for our destination.

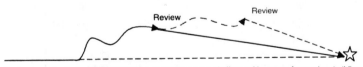

Reviewing earlier instead of later reduces the total amount of effort and keeps us focused on building the right system as quickly as possible. Reveiwing earlier minimizes the total distance traveled.

Ultimately, development is like a series of curved paths and straight lines. The straight lines represent the best way to build the system. The curved paths represent our actual efforts.

Figure 3–2   Impact of Review in Development

There are several benefits derived from early reviews. First, you will learn about the problem and the right way to solve it in smaller, easier-to-manage chunks. Second, early review allows your customer to prepare more effectively for the changes to their business processes as a result of the new system. This is especially important if the system represents a substantially new or different way of doing things. Third, early review by your users enables them to learn the system gradually over time instead of all at once. Users are more willing to support the system, especially when you make the enhancements they suggest during the review. Most importantly of all, early review reduces the magnitude of mistakes and the time you will spend correcting them.

3.3.1 Kinds of Reviews

There are many kinds of reviews that can be used to gain feedback. The most common of these are outlined below. For details, I suggest *Handbook of Walkthroughs, Inspections, and Technical Reviews* by Freedman and Weinberg [1990].

Informal discussions. An informal discussion held at lunch regarding specific aspects of the system is a form of review.

Walkthroughs. Walkthroughs are informal reviews of outcomes in which participants examine an outcome to look for specific errors. Participants plan for the review, but the actual review has little structure.

Fagan-style inspections. A Fagan-style inspection is a structured examination of an outcome designed to assess the appropriateness of the outcome. Fagan-style inspections are named after their inventor M.E. Fagan [1976]. Specific roles exist in the review team to ensure the review is executed completely. Although this chapter is devoted to improving individual performance, Fagan-style inspections are included here because of their demonstrable effect on improving all forms of outcomes. They are arguably the most important technique known for ensuring software quality.

Simulated prototype. This kind of review is popular for testing the usability of a specific user interface by having users test a simulated version of the real system. Like a Fagan-style inspection, a simulated prototype is a structured form of review.

While informal discussions and walkthroughs can provide valuable feedback, they are less effective than Fagan-style inspections and simulated prototypes. However, the real point is that each type of review has a place in the development process.

3.3.2 Formal Review Structures

The last two reviews described above are based on formal structures. This section outlines these structures, beginning with their commonalities and then focusing on their differences.

Both Fagan-style inspections (hereafter referred to as inspections) and simulated prototypes are based on a team of three to five reviewers. Each review is led by a *review leader*, whose primary responsibility is to ensure the overall quality of the review (i.e., a good review of an inappropriate outcome identifies accurately what is inappropriate). Thus, the review leader has responsibility for collecting and distributing materials, securing an appropriate environment, organizing reviewers (and users, in the case of a simulated prototype), and preparing the review report.

Both inspections and simulated prototypes generate a *review report*, a specific outcome detailing the results of the review. This outcome must include the following three items. First, it must be clearly identified for tracking purposes. Second, it must identify who participated in the review (subjects in a simulated prototype are not identified by name, but by an anonymous tracking number). Third, it must clearly summarize the results of the review. Freedman and Weinberg [1990] suggest the following summary:

Accepted:	❑ as is	❑ with minor modifications
Rejected:	❑ major revision	❑ minor revision
Review not completed:	❑ (explanation follows)	

Any modifications or revisions are listed on an *issues list*. The issues list details the specific problems identified by the review team. In general, the issues list should not contain solutions to these problems, as the primary purpose of the review is to assess the quality of the outcome being reviewed.

Both kinds of reviews work best when the following general guidelines are followed. First, focus on the outcome being reviewed, not the person who produced it. Second, set an agenda and stick to it. Any review longer than two hours is probably trying to review far too much. Third, identify problems but don't solve them. Fourth, take *written notes*, preferably directly in a word processor. It is far easier to generate an issues list when the notes begin in this manner.

Inspections and simulated prototypes differ in the roles assigned within the review team. In addition to the review leader, an inspection team assigns the role of *recorder* to take the notes forming the foundation of the issues list generated during the review process. The *producer* of the outcome being reviewed is also present to answer questions. The remaining members of the team are designated as *review participants*. They are responsible for reviewing the outcome before the meeting to assess its appropriateness. During the review they discuss any concerns or issues they have with the outcome. This discussion is often more important than the review report, for during the discussion the producer has the opportunity to obtain feedback from multiple sources.

Simulated prototypes are a bit more complex than inspections. The purpose of this review is to test the usability (e.g., ease of use, learnability, enjoyability) of the system. It does so by *simulating* the operation of the user interface. In effect, you

TABLE 3–1   Roles in a Simulated Prototype Review

Role	Responsibilities
Greeter	Greets people, explains test, handles any forms associated with test.
Facilitator	Runs test—only person allowed to speak.
	Performs three essential functions:
	1. Gives the user instructions.
	2. Encourages users to "think-aloud" during the test so observers can record their reactions to the user interface.
	3. Makes certain test is finished on time.
Computer	Simulates the operation of the interface by physically manipulating objects representing the interface. Thus, the "computer" rearranges windows, presents dialogs, simulates typing, and so forth. This means they *must* know application logic.
Observer	Takes notes on 5 × 8 cards, one note per card.

"play computer" and observe the user's reaction. In addition to the review leader, a simulated prototype relies on the roles defined in Table 3–1.

Because of the special nature of simulated prototypes, a very special structural rule applies to the selection of users. *Users selected for the test must be representative of the target population.* If the system is for nurses, test with nurses. If the system is for data entry personnel, test with data entry personnel. Avoid testing with friends or co-workers unless you are practicing "playing" computer.

ADVICE TO DEVELOPERS

Engaging in a review with your customer is more than simply handing them a partially completed system and asking "What do you think about this?" Following a few, simple techniques and strategies will help you obtain the greatest benefit.

Review when ready.

Create appropriate review structures.

Use a parallel review process for technical reviews.

Beware of repeated reviews of the same outcome.

Your fellow team member is not your customer.

Review in the implementation domain, not the development domain.

Use reviews to help apply the law of diminishing returns.

Leave your ego at the door.

Provide a "Jacuzzi."

Review when ready.   To what degree should an outcome be considered "complete" or "perfect" before it is submitted for review? For example, source code that is about to be put into a production environment should be as perfect as possible before being submitted to review. More specifically, if you and I are working on the same team, I would be offended (and possibly downright angry) if you submitted source code not adhering to our coding standards.

Alternatively, if you were designing a new graphical user interface as a replacement for a current mainframe system I would be dismayed if the very first thing you submitted for review was a highly detailed and operational prototype. Why? First, you probably spent far too much time on getting the details right before making certain the "big-picture" was correct. Second, you are less likely to change your system based on my feedback precisely because you spent so much time on the details.

The trick, of course, is to find the right balance in preparing an outcome for review. If your intent is to obtain feedback early in the process it is acceptable to submit high-level and potentially incomplete outcomes. If your intent is to finalize an outcome for production then the outcome should be production quality.

Create the appropriate review structures.   The structures, processes and outcomes you need are dependent on your motivation. First, state clearly and precisely the outcome you seek. Do you want to know if the requirements are correct? Do you want to know if the initial screen designs are usable? Future perfect thinking can help.

Second, create a structure supporting the review process. For example, suppose you are developing an interactive voice response system for a bank. The goal of the system is to allow clients of the bank to perform simple banking transactions over the phone, such as obtaining their account balance or transferring funds between accounts. Before coding begins, you decide to review the script with the customer to ensure that it is acceptable (a good idea). An improper structure is to ask your customer to simply "read" the script, because reading a script doesn't properly simulate production conditions. A far more effective structure is to use the simulated prototype process described above with appropriate modifications for this style of a user interface.

Simulate the system by having your customer call you on the phone. You, in turn, respond as the system would respond. You can schedule observers to watch the customer, looking for clues indicating that usability problems exist. By responding as if you were the system, your customer will be able to assess the effectiveness and correctness of the script. Depending on the kind of review, you may want to furnish the reviewer with additional structure to help them understand the outcome before the review, such as user manuals. You may want to create additional structures for helping you conduct the review, such as video cameras for taping the subject. Once you are prepared, conduct the review, making certain review outcomes are accurately recorded.

Use a parallel review process for technical reviews.   There are three ways to organize the individuals or groups engaged in a technical review process:

1. as a single team who review in one pass;
2. as multiple teams who review in parallel;
3. as multiple teams who review in succession, with modifications to the outcome between successive reviews.

Research has shown the most commonly used technique is the first. This is unfortunate, because that same research demonstrated the second technique is more effective at finding defects [Martin 1990; Schneider 1992]. The third technique is rarely used because it is too time intensive. Why is the second technique so effective? Once again, the answer lies in our cognitive library. Each reviewer brings their idiosyncratic set of plans to the review process. Thus, each reviewer or review team focuses on different aspects of the outcome being reviewed. The overall effect is that more errors are found.

Beware of repeated reviews of the same outcome.   The intent of a review is to provide feedback into how the outcome should be changed. Repeated reviews of essentially the same outcome are a symptom of a poor overall process. If you are going to review the same outcome, make certain you have either addressed the results of a prior review or you have incorporated changes to justify the additional review.

Your fellow team member is not your customer.   Beware of letting other members of your team review your system in lieu of your customer. While this technique can be effective in shaking out initial problems, only your customer can determine what is acceptable.

Review in the implementation domain, not the development domain.   Developers often have access to more powerful hardware than their customers. One common mistake is to show the customer a prototype of the system using the development environment. This is dangerous because it skews the results of the review, especially in terms of response time.

Use reviews to help apply the law of diminishing returns.   The stereotypical image of a developer is a person who wants to just begin coding as quickly as possible. While this may be true in certain cases, like most other stereotypes this one is also a gross oversimplification. As a manager, I've found some developers suffer from the exact opposite affliction: They want to analyze a system endlessly! They almost seem to forget that you actually have to *implement* a system to know if your analysis is correct. But, how do you know when an outcome is complete? Apply the diminishing returns described in Chapter 1, which (slightly reformulated here) states an outcome is considered complete when further work on the outcome doesn't materially improve it.

How do you determine completeness? Through reviews! If you are unsure if an outcome is finished, show it briefly to another member of the team for their opinion. If they say "Yeah, that looks pretty complete to me," then you know you have at least one other opinion for moving on. Conversely, if they ask questions that you can't answer, or can easily poke holes in your proposed outcome, then you have a strong indication that you *are not* ready to move on.

Leave your ego at the door.   It is certainly acceptable to put your heart and soul into creating the best possible outcome. But, to get the most out of a review, leave your ego at the door. The inevitable error *does not* mean *you* are defective [Weinberg 1971]. An analysis model or program is not a reflection of your worth as a person.

Learning to put all of these ideas into practice can be more difficult than it seems. Each outcome we create is in some way an expression of our identity. Reviewing an outcome before we think it is perfect can be difficult, for our feelings cloud the overall process. Writing this book demonstrated in a very real way just how strong these feelings can be.

After I had worked on the book a few months I had a fair amount of material, including an outline of the overall book with some of the chapters filled in. At this time I started talking to friends about the book (Chapter 4 explains why this is important). I was surprised when one of my friends asked to review what I had written thus far. At first I was reluctant, because the book was far from complete. But, then I remembered the advice of Gerald Weinberg [1971], and decided to try and remove my ego from my book (as much as I could) and give it to my friend for review. Fortunately, this process was made much easier by the facts I had a great deal of trust in him and highly valued his opinion. Lesson number one: Although separating our ego from the outcomes we produce can help us evaluate these outcomes objectively, there are times when the very first review needs to be performed by a friend.

Once that initial review had been completed I found subsequent reviews much easier. Lesson number two: The earlier you start, the easier it is to incorporate reviews as part of the overall process.

Later, after more of the book had been written, I decided to try and employ a parallel review process. At first this worked well, because reviewing the first few chapters and outline for the rest of the book was small enough that I was able to obtain rapid feedback. As the book grew in length, the review process took longer, feedback was delayed, and the overall result was starting to become satisfactory. In the long run, I adopted a partially sequential, partially parallel approach. A sequential process was used when I wanted feedback on major portions of the book. A parallel process was used when I wanted quick feedback on a much smaller section, such as a single chapter or section. Lesson number three: There is no perfect process, and very large outcomes need a combination of serial and parallel review.

As can be expected, when a parallel process was used, certain of the reviewers provided feedback more quickly than others. When this happened I had to fight the urge to immediately change and/or correct what I had written based on this early feedback. This was especially important as I learned each reviewer had a different opinion, and what one reviewer liked another disliked. Lesson number four: If you are using a parallel review process, defer making any substantial changes to the outcome reviewed until the majority of the reviewers have completed their work (of course, obvious errors should be corrected immediately).

The next technique is rather advanced. Using it at the right time, and in the right circumstances, will help you create systems that truly exceed the requirements and delight your customer. Using it at the wrong time, or in the wrong way, will alienate your customer, and may even cause them to lose trust in your abilities.

Provide a "Jacuzzi."   There are wonderful moments in the development of a software system where everything "clicks." Through effort and inspiration, you have found a way to solve the problem in a unique and novel way. If your solution meets the *stated* requirements, so much the better. But, what happens if your solution does not meet the requirements as stated by the user, but you are *convinced* it is what the customer needs? In this case, a slight sense of dread may cloud a review: What if the customer makes changes to a system I know is what they need, even if it is not what they want?

There are two answers to this question. The first is you haven't really understood the customer as well as you thought you have. During the review process, your customer will then request changes to the system. While I know this is painful—I have been through this process numerous times—listen to your customer. Always *try* to leave your ego at the door, and make the changes as necessary.

The second is you really have produced a fantastic outcome and have exceeded the requirements as stated by your customer. In this case, your sense of dread is well founded, because it is human nature to change *something* when we are given the opportunity to do so. To ensure your solution is adopted, *give your customer something to change.*

As I was preparing for a presentation of a prototype system I had designed, my manager noticed how worried and concerned I was about the review. It was very important to me that this prototype prove successful, because it incorporated several somewhat radical concepts for my customer: a distributed client-server architecture with connections to legacy systems built on top of a graphical user interface. More importantly, I was convinced the metaphor I chose for the user interface was the correct metaphor and absolutely essential to the success of the system. He took me into his office and told me the following story.

A certain architect was commissioned to design a new church for the local parish. Something about this church inspired him, and he buried himself in his work. He attended meetings of the elders, the softball team, the Sunday school. He attended church, and watched the ebb and flow of the congregation, trying to understand both their stated and unstated requirements. This is not to say it was an easy process, for the church elders (his chief customers) wanted to review preliminary sketches. Unfortunately, every review invariably produced many things to change. One elder was especially contentious and could always find something wrong.

One Friday night, while the architect was taking a walk outside and looking at the trees lining his street, a new design for a truly awe-inspiring church suddenly appeared in his mind's eye. Hurrying back to his studio, he worked late into the night drawing sketches. The next day, he returned to his studio, confident enough in his sketches to create a scale model of the new church. This was quite a big step, for although he was confident in his design, building a scale model is expensive, and he was concerned about the elders. Nevertheless, he charged ahead and completed his model by working late into the night. On Sunday morning, he announced he had created a new design and asked for a meeting that night with the elders.

Without a word, he faced the elders and unveiled his design. The room fell silent. Truly, this was an inspired work, fitting for the new parish. The elders rose from their seats, and proceeded to review the model. The architect waited for someone to speak, hoping that everyone would approve the design. Finally, the most contentious of the elders broke the silence.

"Your design is truly elegant," began the elder, "and will certainly make a most impressive place of worship. However, there is a problem. It is unacceptable and must be changed before any further work is done." As if on cue, the other elders murmured agreement.

Feigning a hurt look, the architect replied "What is that?"

"The outdoor Jacuzzi must go."

ADVICE TO MANAGERS

Managing a development process based on early and frequent reviews is as challenging for you as your staff. You will have to balance the need for stable requirements with the need for change as feedback from reviews drives the development process. The best way to achieve this is to create an environment where reviewing early and often is considered a normal part of the overall process.

> Provide the necessary training.
>
> Burn some pancakes.
>
> Maximize the economic benefits.
>
> Beware of feature creep when reviewing with the customer.

Provide the necessary training.   The roles and responsibilities associated with Fagan-style review require some training and experience to execute well. If your staff is new to such formal reviews, expect initial reviews to take longer and be less concise. To help compensate for this effect, consider asking more experienced reviewers from other organizations to participate in early reviews.

Burn some pancakes.   There are four primary reasons developers avoid seeking feedback. Here are ways to identify each along with suggested solutions.

1. *Tools making it difficult to obtain feedback.* Certain tools, such as compiled languages, make obtaining reviews on completed portions of the system difficult. Consider C++ versus Smalltalk. A Smalltalk developer can make the slightest modification just about anywhere in the system and immediately ask others to review it. A C++ developer runs the risk of making a change that forces an extensive and expensive recompilation of the entire system. One easy solution is to use tools, such as interpreted languages, that support small changes and quick reviews.

2. *Lack of access to the customer.* Many developers avoid reviewing early and often because they don't have access to the customer. This is easy to fix: Give them access!

3. *Educational Baggage.* Most educational experiences implicitly and explicitly support the idea that in order to "hand in your assignment" it had to be "correct the first time." In other words, how often were you encouraged to hand in a partial solution to an algebra proof for some feedback from your teacher? The answer, of course, is not ever. Instead, we were given an assignment, told when it was due, and graded on our ability to complete it without any expert feedback.

   Not surprisingly, our educational baggage permeates our adult working life. Old habits die hard. Learning to submit partially complete outcomes for review (as appropriate) takes time and energy. As a manager, you can minimize the effect of educational baggage by making certain reviews are incorporated throughout the development process.

4. *Bad management.* The biggest reason developers avoid seeking early feedback is bad management. No one wants to be judged or evaluated on an outcome that is obviously "work-in-progress." To combat this trend, make certain your developers know that you support an iterative development process and will not pass final judgment on incomplete results or first attempts.

In one assignment I had to find a way to change the development process of a team of developers whose prior management had enforced an extremely strict waterfall approach. In a waterfall process, you are expected to create complete outcomes from each process before moving to the next. The only problem was that my predecessor had elevated the practice of waterfall development to an anal-retentive art: Developers were expected to produce nearly perfect outcomes! As I tried to change their overall development process from waterfall to an iterative one, I encountered extreme resistance. In the past, the staff had learned that if they did not practice waterfall they would be punished. How could I change their attitude? The only thing I could think of was to introduce them to the burned pancake process model. Burned pancakes?

I am not the best cook in the world, but every now and then I like to make pancakes. The trouble is, I always seem to make the skillet too hot for the first pancake. By now I have accepted the fact that I will, with a high degree of probability, burn the first pancake, throw it out, fix the temperature, and start again. To encourage my staff to get an initial system completed, I would ask them to "burn some pancakes" (i.e., create an initial system), with the assurance I wouldn't "eat" (i.e., judge) the first pancake. At first, they responded tentatively. The idea became quickly adopted when they learned I meant what I said I would not judge them on incomplete outcomes.

Within a few weeks they had fully adopted the approach, making it a part of the culture of the group. When asked for an outcome, staff members would respond: "How edible does it have to be?" If I responded with: "fairly edible," they knew I was looking for a rather complete outcome. On the other hand, if I responded with "completely burned," they knew I just wanted to assess their activity briefly to ensure they were headed in the right direction. In no way would they be judged on the outcome. Soon, the entire team was talking about pancakes, and productivity started to improve.

Maximize the economic benefits.   In general, reviews lead to reduced development costs by detecting errors earlier in the programming process where they are most easily and cheaply corrected. Fagan [1976] found in his classic study the systematic use of formal inspections resulted in a net productivity increase of 23 percent! Freedman and Weinberg [1990] report:

"In larger systems, where accurate records have been kept, projects with a full system of reviews report a ten times reduction in the number of errors reaching each stage of testing. The concomitant cost reduction for testing efforts runs between 50 and 80 percent, even when the cost of reviewing is added to testing costs.

Reviews also have a very favorable effect on maintenance costs. A typical program that has been thoroughly reviewed during development and for which maintenance changes are also reviewed shows a five to one reduction in maintenance costs.

In the long run, reviews have a remarkable effect on staff competence, a difficult effect to quantify." [From Daniel P. Freedman and Gerald M. Weinberg's *Handbook of Walkthroughs, Inspections, and Technical Reviews*, 3rd ed., pp. 12–13, Copyright © 1990 by Daniel P. Freedman and Gerald M. Weinberg. Reprinted by permission of Dorset Publishing, 353 West 12th St. New York, NY 10014. All rights reserved.]

Beware of feature creep when reviewing with the customer.   Of course, reviewing early and often is not without some risks. The biggest risk is *feature creep*, or the tendency of the customer to request the addition of a substantial number of new features during every review. Even worse, your customer may begin to ask for substantial changes *during* development. This is perhaps the greatest danger, because your staff needs some stability in features in order to create a system! Both of these problems are often symptoms of deeper problems, as the requested number of features of a system should stabilize over time (see Figure 3–3).

To prevent feature creep, adopt an iterative process model, where the system is built through a controlled sequence of iterations. Each iteration produces a system with a specific set of features that are frozen before development begins. At the end of each iteration, a formal review takes place. It is during this review your customer can add or remove features. The advantage to this approach is twofold. First, your staff knows they can work from a stable set of requirements during a iteration. Second, your customer knows they will have the opportunity to change the requirements during development, albeit in a controlled manner. Both walking on water and developing a system from requirements are easier when they are frozen.

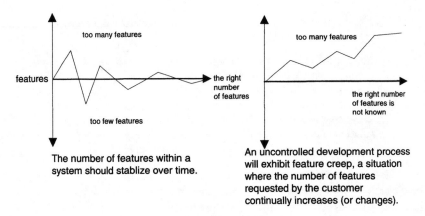

The number of features within a
system should stablize over time.

An uncontrolled development process
will exhibit feature creep, a situation
where the number of features
requested by the customer
continually increases (or changes).

Figure 3–3   Feature Creep

3.4 GROW YOUR EXPERIENCE

Much of the research into cognitive models described in Chapter 1 indicates prior experience may be the single most important determinant of success when building a software system [Adelson 1985]. But, what kind of experience is important? Is detailed knowledge of C++ more important than experience with your method? Is experience in the problem domain (e.g., the stock market or the telecommunications industry) more important than knowing your database management system? The purpose of this section is to try and answer these questions and to provide some ideas on the experience (as represented by plans) we should seek to add to our cognitive library.

The most important kind of experience is domain experience (i.e., knowledge of the rules, procedures, nomenclature, and other aspects of the problem domain). Without it, how can we be certain the correct problem is being solved? Indeed, why bother working on a problem at all if you are working on the *wrong* problem? The most striking example of this came in a study led by Curtis [1988] that tried to determine what factors contributed to the success of a software project. The striking finding of this study was that regardless of project size each successful system was lead by *one* or *two* technical experts with *extensive* domain knowledge.

The importance of domain experience was realized early in artificial intelligence research. For example, a program called the General Problem Solver was designed to solve a wide range of problems. Although the program created many innovative programming techniques, it could not solve many problems. Why? It lacked the domain knowledge necessary to make effective decisions when searching for solutions to problems [Barr 1981].

Once you've identified the right problem to solve, the next most important kind of experience is in solving the problem the right way. This is experience in using a given method and/or implementation technology—experience following the processes prescribed by a method to generate the right kinds of outcomes and experience in using the implementation technology to clearly express your solution.

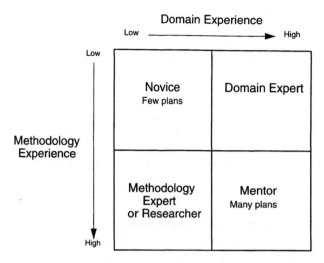

Figure 3–4   Effect of Experience

But even this description is somewhat overly simplistic. First, I am explicitly concentrating on only two broad kinds of experience. Second, what good does it do to be a domain expert if you cannot implement your solution? Alternatively, what benefit is it to be a guru in C++ unless you can apply this knowledge to solve real problems? The right way to solve these problems is to first learn a small subset of your method and/or implementation technology so that you can solve simplified domain problems in a realistic manner. As you solve these problems you will increase domain knowledge. Over time, you will increase your need for greater knowledge in the method or implementation technology and can learn these as necessary. Thus, even though domain experience is the most important kind of experience, we must start with method and implementation technology first.

The relationship between domain and method experience is presented in Figure 3–4, which shows the kinds of plans that exist in the cognitive libraries of developers with varying experiences. This diagram can be used to predict your chances for success at solving a problem in a given domain using a given method. The greatest chance for success is when you are familiar with both the domain and the method. You have many plans and can draw from them easily. The lowest degree of success is when you know little about either the problem domain or the method. In this case, solutions tend to be incorrect or incomplete because there are few plans to draw from.

ADVICE TO DEVELOPERS

It is difficult to separate the experience enabling you to solve the right problem versus the experience helping you solve that problem the right way. However, they are different, and by describing them separately I hope to provide a structure for acquiring each kind. Let's begin with domain experience.

> Structure your knowledge.
>
> Look for invariants and constraints early.
>
> Use your method in a disciplined manner.
>
> Spend as much time as possible with domain experts.

Structure your knowledge.   Structuring your knowledge will help in two ways. First, it will help you learn what is important. Second, it will help you locate relevant information quickly. Begin by clearing a small section of a filing cabinet or your desk. Put inside it articles, books, notes and anything else that you can find about your problem domain. Use this information to make certain you are solving the right problem.

Look for invariants and constraints early.   An *invariant* is some aspect of a problem that must always be true. A *constraint* is a requirement that cannot change. *Both* provide structure to the problem domain. Invariants help determine if the solution is correct, while constraints limit the way we can solve the problem. Identifying them early prevents wasted effort.

Use your method in a disciplined manner.   A method prescribes a specific set of processes and outcomes. Using a method in a disciplined manner means following all of the processes and generating all the outcomes. It doesn't mean skipping any steps.

Why is discipline important? Each process and outcome defined by the method is carefully designed to increase our understanding of the problem (and therefore) our ability to solve it. Skipping a step means skipping the benefits gained from doing that step. Being disciplined means being aware of and using the tests that control the movement between method processes.

Spend as much time as possible with domain experts.   The best way to determine if you're headed in the right direction is to ask an expert (and save their answer).

The second area to address is a lack of experience with a method or implementation technology.

> Learn your method.
>
> Read how experts use the method.
>
> Treat outcomes with skepticism when learning a method.
>
> Practice, practice, practice.
>
> Avoid using complex or advanced features.

Learn your method.   Most methods are usually defined by a single, seminal book. Purchase it. Read it. If it has exercises, do them.

Read how experts use the method.   Many of the creators of the popular methods are also prolific authors, constantly publishing examples of how to solve problems using their method. While the authors may not solve a problem exactly like yours, reading such articles provides three clear benefits. First, these articles demonstrate correct use of the method. Second, such articles often introduce extensions to the method. Such extensions increase the usefulness of the method or correct any known deficiencies or ambiguities. Methods evolve through use, and reading articles keeps you current. Third, there is always the chance the author will use an example drawn from your problem domain, providing you with another perspective. If you are especially lucky, they might even address *your* problem, giving you an outline of a solution you can grow and change or alerting you to some as-yet unforeseen problem.

Treat outcomes with skepticism when learning a method.   What makes you think the outcomes you create are correct if you have little experience with the processes used in their creation?

Practice, practice, practice.   There is an old vaudeville joke that goes like this. A tourist walking down 5th Avenue in New York City stops a pedestrian and asks: "Excuse me sir, how do you get to Carnegie Hall?" The pedestrian replies: "Practice, practice, practice." What can get you to Carnegie Hall can also help you learn a method. Quite literally, practice solving problems using your method.

But not just any kind of practice. The secret is *how* you practice. For practice to be most effective, you need three things. First, you must be prepared. This means finding a quiet place where you can concentrate and pick a somewhat challenging sample problem. Inventing a sample problem from thin air can take some practice. Alternatively, you might purchase a book such as Peter Coad's *Object Models: Strategies, Patterns, and Applications* [1995]. It shows how to develop object-oriented analysis and design models by solving six specific case studies. In addition, most of the books describing a method include case studies. Second, it takes effort. You must practice as if you mean it: Try to use all the processes to generate all the outcomes prescribed by the method. Perfect practice equates to perfect performance. Third, you should have some means of comparing your outcomes to what are considered correct (e.g., sample solutions or access to a mentor who can review your work).

Avoid using complex or advanced features.   Don't use complex or advanced features of the underlying implementation technology unless these features are absolutely needed. While it is great fun to explore, and exploration *should* be encouraged because it helps you learn your tools, such exploration *must* be grounded in solving the problem at hand. Your implementation technology is no different than your word processor. It is quite rare for a single project to require the use of every available feature. Just as you would never install a word processor and try *every* single feature simply because they are there, neither should you immediately try to use every possible aspect of your implementation technology.

The previous sections focused on the attainment of experience as experience relates to the problem domain and the method. One aspect of solving the problem the right way is "street smarts," or getting the job done. This is experience in putting all the pieces together and getting the system not only built but shipped. It is, in many ways, the most important kind of experience of all.

> Grow domain experience in the context of a method.
>
> Look for solutions in other computer-related fields.
>
> Find a Fred.
>
> Strive for balance between deep and broad experience.
>
> Go end-to-end at least once.
>
> Finish.

Grow domain experience in the context of a method.   What should you do if you find yourself working in new domain using a new method? Which kind of experience should you grow first? Ideally, of course, you would like to grow your experience in both at the same time. In reality, this is too difficult, and you should instead take a zigzag approach (see Figure 3–5). First, learn how to prepare the most important outcomes defined in the method. Although modern methods can define dozens of unique outcomes, you can often accomplish quite a lot with just a few. Learning these few provides you with the tools you need to concentrate on learning your problem domain by solving problems in the context of these outcomes.

The best way to grow experience is to use a zig-zag approach,
growing method experience first and domain experience second.

Figure 3–5   Growing Experience

Look for solutions in other computer-related fields.   It is tempting to think every problem we face is completely new and that our solution must be invented from scratch. Of course, this is wrong. Many branches of computer science have identified and solved problems that are either directly applicable within your domain or can provide insight (and even inspiration) on how to solve your problem. Table 3–2 presents a small number of examples of the kinds of solutions you can find if you take the time to look. It doesn't take much time—an easy way to start is to reference an introductory textbook on any of these areas.

TABLE 3–2   **Problems Addressed by Fields in Computer Science**

Branch	Some Problems Addressed by This Field
Operating systems	Multiprocessing, concurrent programming, fault tolerant systems
Database design and implementation	Transaction management, distributed data management, database performance tuning
Artificial intelligence	Knowledge representation, advanced search techniques, reflective programming
Computational theory	Computational complexity, algorithmic efficiency, graph algorithms

Find a Fred.   During a class on user interface design I was illustrating the concept of hypertext-based help systems when I asked the class: "What do you do when you have a problem with your present system?" Collectively, they replied "Ask Fred." It turns out "Fred" was the recognized expert on this system. Apparently, he knew "everything" about the operation of the system. Certainly, a Fred is better than any help system—if you can find him (or her)!

You can put this strategy to work by taking the time to learn a little about the skills and experiences of your fellow team members. As a manager, I found the best way to do this was to read the resume of every member of my staff. You can do this too. If you do find an expert, periodically ask to review their work, for one of the best ways to improve your own skills is to review the properly annotated work of an expert [Linn 1992]. Alternatively, why not ask Fred for a presentation? Most experts enjoy sharing their knowledge, and the presentation provides a valuable forum for asking questions and sharing knowledge with other people. If your "Fred" does agree to such a presentation, make certain you videotape it for future reference.

Strive for balance between deep and broad experience.   Deep experience can help you select plans more likely to be initially correct. However, deep experience in a single domain has two drawbacks. First, deep experience tends to make us desensitized to our environment as we become increasingly used to familiar stimulus. The result is that we lose the ability to detect subtle changes in our environment, much as a frog, when placed in a pot of water whose heat is slowly increased, does not detect the change until it is too late. Following method-prescribed processes in a disciplined way can compensate for this effect, for these processes are designed to help us understand the problem such that even small changes are noticed and understood.

Second, deep experience in one domain does not necessarily equate to deep experience in others. If we are asked to solve a problem in a slightly different domain deep experience may not be all that helpful. One study by Adelson and Soloway [1985] demonstrated this quite convincingly: Experts asked to design an application in a domain similar to their field of expertise performed quite well. However, when asked to solve a problem in an unfamiliar problem domain, they were far less effective, often performing barely better than a novice.

Broad experience, on the other hand, tends to make developers more receptive to their environment and provides different kinds of plans for problem solving.

These observations are supported by research which demonstrates that broad experience in multiple programming languages and paradigms is usually better than deep experience in a single language.

This is not to say one should seek broad experience over deep experience. In fact, the opposite is true: One should first seek deep experience and then extend it to other domains for three reasons. First, developers are frequently associated with a specific project and problem domain for quite some time (roughly two to three years). To be maximally productive requires knowledge of this domain. Second, it is easier to learn a second domain when a first is well known, as described in Chapter 1. Think of this kind of learning as a "mapping" process: You map a plan formed in one domain and context into a new domain and a new context. More plans means the mapping process is easier. The third reason is entirely practical: Being a recognized expert can often be more rewarding (both mentally and materially) than being a generalist.

Go end-to-end at least once.   At least once in your career you should go through every single aspect of a software project. I mean *every* activity: requirements gathering, analysis, design, coding, verification, maintenance. Yes, even maintenance. Is this hard? Sure. Is it worth it? You bet! Going end-to-end provides three benefits.

First, individual differences in cognitive style and personality mean we are likely to be better at some aspects of development than others. How will you know what processes you are good at until you give them a try?

Second, having the experience of producing every outcome will make you more aware of the importance of preparing outcomes that are both complete and correct. I never learned to document code well until I had to maintain the code I wrote. I thought I knew, but I didn't. The experience of reading my own comments during maintenance showed me how to write much better comments during design and implementation.

Third, unless you stick around to witness the delivery of the system, you'll never know if your early solutions resulted in an effective solution.

> *I do not mean to imply every developer should be involved in every activity on every project. Such an approach would be counterproductive, because it would prevent necessary specialization in different techniques and technologies. However, going end-to-end at least once in your career is critical to the development of several different kinds of experience. I never fully appreciated what it meant to solve a complex problem until my first consulting assignment, where I had to start with requirements and stick with the project through completion.*

Finish.   During a long development process, it can be easy to lose sight of current activities and instead begin thinking about a new project. Soon, idle thoughts turn into a yearning to move to a new project. Resist this temptation to leave your current project and instead concentrate on finishing. There are at least three benefits to finishing. First, completing a project is immensely satisfying. Leaving, or attempting to leave, a project before it is finished robs you of this satisfaction. Second, working on the project until it is finished will improve the quality of the plans stored in your cognitive library. How will you know what works if you leave before it is finished? Third, and most important, by concentrating on finishing you will differentiate yourself from the hordes of developers who cannot seem to finish what they start. People who can finish are special. They are rare. They can make the difference between success and failure on the project, and smart managers will always try to have one or two finishers on their team. Finishers will always be in high demand.

Of course, the desire to finish must be tempered with the reality of your current situation. I'm certainly *not* advocating hanging out against all odds. A project doomed to failure because of impossible schedules, wildly fluctuating requirements, inadequate tools or controls, or any other number of reasons is a project you should leave as quickly as possible. Such a project is not likely to ever "finish."

ADVICE TO MANAGERS

In the ideal world your team has all the experience it needs to correctly solve the problem. Of course, this is not likely to happen, so managing the growth of experience is an important ongoing activity. The most important area to concentrate on first is the needs of the business. Thus, the first aspect of experience to manage is domain experience.

Provide domain experts.
Put a developer on the requirements team.
Give them an opportunity to rework their code.

Provide domain experts.   Ensure your staff has ready access to domain experts who can guide them as needed through the problem domain.

Put a developer on the requirements team.   Even a small system requires your team to make hundreds of decisions during analysis, design, and implementation that are not directly addressed in the requirements. Placing a developer on the requirements gathering team will help ensure these decisions are made in a manner consistent with the needs and desires of the customer. In a similar manner, you may want to place a customer representative on the development team to quickly answer any questions about ambiguous requirements. In this manner, the team can follow the "spirit" as well as the "law" of the requirements.

Give them an opportunity to rework their code.   Every developer has had the experience of looking at some old code and immediately thinking of a better solution. What happened? Did the developer become suddenly smarter? Did the problem become easier? Is it magic? It's not magic, but there is a good answer. Developers are *constantly* learning about their problem domain and this learning is often reflected in realizing there are far better ways to solve a problem. Second, our subconscious mind continues to work on a problem long after we have created a solution. Thus, even though the problem may be "solved," it is quite common for a developer to look at his solution and "immediately" think of a better one.

What should you do? One response is to simply ignore the new solution. As the old saying goes, "If it ain't broke, don't fix it." Alternatively, you could explicitly schedule for the implementation of the new solution. Is such an approach cost-effective? In general, yes. Lehman and Belady [1976] found changes made to a system tend to make it less maintainable unless special efforts were made to keep it under control. In other words, changes made to a system increase entropy (the state of disorder) unless the change is specifically designed to reduce entropy. Compensate for this by scheduling "entropy reduction episodes," where developers can maintain the maintainability of your system *and* take advantage of the growth of their experience in the problem domain.

How often should such entropy reduction episodes be scheduled? This depends on several factors: the size of the current system, the rate of change within the system, time pressures associated with the project, implementation technology, and the like. Preparing detailed descriptions of exactly when to schedule entropy reductions is beyond the scope of this book, but the following approaches have worked well. At a minimum schedule one entropy reduction phase between each release of the system or every three to four months, whichever comes first. It is best to schedule entropy sessions immediately *after* the release of the system. Doing so will give your developers a chance to make the necessary changes while they are still fresh and will prepare the system for further development.

Inexperience in the method or implementation technology requires a related set of managerial responses. It also implies the trickiest form of experience management: discipline.

Demand discipline.

Use a mentor.

Provide good reference materials.

Encourage your developers to form study groups.

Be aware of the impact of time.

Demand discipline.   If one or more developers on your team has little experience, demanding discipline from them in the preparation of outcomes will help to provide them with the experience they need to solve the problem. By adhering more strongly to structure, you create an environment helping them be most effective.

Use a mentor.   A mentor has what your team needs: experience! As experts, mentors prevent small mistakes from growing into huge setbacks and guide the efforts of the team. This experience can be domain experience, but more often consists of experience using the method and/or implementation technology. An essential goal in using a mentor is experience transfer. Ideally, your team will gain experience through apprenticeship learning, where the mentor *guides* your team in learning the skills necessary for success. This form of learning is especially effective because the apprentice can take advantage of the cognitive library of the mentor [Guzdial 1993]. If the project is substantial or mission critical, the mentor should be allocated for the duration of the project.

If one expert is good, how about two? or three? or an entire team of experts? Wouldn't that be the best way to solve the problem? Actually, no. A team comprised of experts is rarely the best way to solve a problem. First, experts are expensive, and most projects can't afford the cost.

Second, it can be more difficult to achieve consensus in a group of experts: If everyone is a leader, who are the followers? If everyone is equally right who decides? Objective requirements can help, but experts are adept at demonstrating why *their* particular solution just happens to be the *right* solution.

Third, although experts can be quite adept at applying plans within their cognitive library to a tough problem, there is a certain aspect of creativity in the interaction between a novice and an expert. Why? Experts are expert because they can quickly generate one or two good ways to solve a problem. To a novice, any way is just about as good as any other, which is one reason why novices spend more time searching for the right solution. Which is precisely the point. Novices may stumble across a novel solution, one an expert can help shape to meet the needs of the business.

Fourth, novices will ask "simple" questions. Answering these questions motivates an expert to review their solution. This review will provide another opportunity for feedback. Finally, if you use only experts, you disallow one of the most important sources of learning for novices: working with an expert.

Using mentors can create problems. How should they be selected? How can you be certain you are getting what you pay for? First, make certain they have the experience and credentials needed for your project. Review their resume, questioning them on those experiences especially relevant to your situation. *Check* references. While you are likely to find only positive references, reviewing references is an excellent way to make certain they will be a good fit within your environment. Second, make certain you are clear on the deliverables: Why are you hiring them? what will they do? what will they deliver? Finally, ask mentors how they plan to exit the project. The best mentors strive to literally work themselves out of a job. Becoming dependent on a single mentor can be a costly mistake.

Provide good reference materials.   At a minimum, this should include the following: the formal definition of the method, language, or technology; one or two books describing the practical use of the method; one magazine subscription devoted to the method or technology.

If your development organization is making the move to object technology, I strongly recommend subscriptions to magazines and journals specializing in object-oriented technology. Four of the best are *Object Magazine* (more of a manager focus), the *Journal of Object-Oriented Programming* (academic), the *C++ Report* (developers), and the *Smalltalk Report* (developers).

Encourage your developers to form study groups.   In study groups developers can review the method and its use together. This form of encouragement must be visible and obvious. One way to achieve both is to formally schedule the review process. Better yet, schedule the study group on Thursdays at noon, and buy them lunch every week. This small investment will more than pay for itself. Another is to track the progress of the study group in reviewing the method as part of the overall project plan. For example, the study group might formally review one method-defined outcome per week.

Be aware of the impact of time.   If you press your developers to use new technology too rapidly, you will force them to apply the new technology using cognitive plans created in the context of an old technology. Like it or not, developers need some time to develop the skills required to use a new technology effectively. Yes, a new technology *can* improve the quality of work or reduce the amount of time required to generate a system, but a new technology should never be used to justify a schedule reduction on the *first* project using it.

While knowledge of the domain and the method are important, knowledge of how to get the job done is even more important. As a manager, you can have a direct hand in helping developers acquire this experience. The first step is identifying when experience is low.

Watch for behaviors indicating inexperience.

Create end-to-end experiences.

Share finishers.

Watch for behaviors indicating inexperience.   Experience, or the lack thereof, is neither good nor bad. It just is. However, as a manager you should watch for behaviors indicating inexperience so you can make appropriate adjustments. Ultimately, the root cause of inexperience is the absence of the appropriate plans in the cognitive library of the developer. The basic compensation technique is to provide structure helping the novice solve the problem. Some behaviors and appropriate adjustments are as follows.

Rework. Inexperience means there will be more rework before the final solution is implemented. Compensate for this by reviewing initial outcomes more frequently. In addition, try to adopt an iterative-incremental development process, where the system is built in successive stages.

Rushing to implementation. Inexperience motivates us to focus on the concrete activities associated with development. In other words, there is a tendency to rush into the implementation phase even when the analysis and design are incomplete. Compensate by following the process steps and checks defined by your method. The tendency to rush to complete certain outcomes (i.e., moving too fast to implementation) can also occur when the method is new but the developer has quite a lot of domain experience. In this case, the tendency is to revert to what is known.

Failing to identify constraints. Complex problem domains have many interrelated and hidden constraints and invariants. Inexperienced developers often fail to locate, document, and subsequently solve problems within these constraints. Compensate for this by periodically including customers, users, and domain experts in the review process.

Forcing the solution. Inexperienced developers often spend substantial amounts of time trying to force fit their solution to the problem rather than trying a different approach entirely. Such behavior can indicate inexperience in both the problem domain and general problem-solving skills. Compensate by asking developers to generate and evaluate alternative tentative solutions to complex problems before one is chosen for further development.

Create end-to-end experiences.   Perhaps the only way to gain an appreciation for the impact of analysis and design decisions is to live through the ramifications of these decisions at least once. By having your developers take a project from requirements, through analysis and design, and finally to implementation, they will gain an experiential appreciation for the importance of making sound decisions that cannot be attained through any other mechanism.

This may seem like an impractical piece of advice, especially in a very large project. A very large project, however, will consist of smaller subsystems, each of which can be taken by a team of developers through multiple stages of development. You can, in turn, assign specific tasks to developers so they engage each major phase of development on these subsystems.

Share finishers.   Once you have found that real gem of a developer, the one you know you can count on to get the project finished, your natural tendency will be to hoard him, keeping him or her under your control for as long as possible. Resist this temptation, and instead share these individuals with other managers. Doing so will provide three clear advantages. First, the overall organization will benefit: *Your* project isn't always the *most* important project in the organization. Second, once you have identified a finisher, you will naturally structure tasks so they are the ones who continue to grow in "finishing" experience. This, in turn, will prevent other members of the team from gaining this experience. By moving them on, you will force yourself to nurture the ability to finish in other members of the team. Third, it is not fair to ask one person to shoulder the responsibility for finishing. He needs a rest. Give it to him.

3.5 USE MULTIPLE MODELS

A *model* is a representation of a problem or solution that emphasizes certain kinds of information by forgetting others. The physical models (outcomes) prescribed and defined by methods assist us in creating mental models of the system. Thus, physical models are the primary tools we use to understand and solve complex problems in manageable pieces rather than all at once. However, because a model means we are abstracting (i.e., selectively forgetting) certain aspects of the problem it also means no single model is sufficient to understand the total problem. Instead, multiple models are required, each addressing a different aspect of the planned solution.

Tom DeMarco asserts information systems require *at least* three different physical models to generate a complete mental model [1982: 75]. The first is the *function model*, "the partitioning of the system into constituent functions and inter-function interfaces." The second is the *information model*, the data the system is expected to store and maintain in some external storage medium. The third is the *state model*, a description of the system's legal state transitions. While not every model is required for every system, (e.g., systems that simply transform data but do not store it externally may not need an information model) together these three cover a vast range of systems.

More recent methods define many more than three models. The Unified Modeling Language [Booch 1995] defines eight specific models. Is the Unified Modeling Language designed to inundate you with needless work by forcing you to prepare every model for every project? Of course not! The intent of the Unified Modeling Language is far better: Provide a consistent and standard notation enabling developers to deal with varying degrees of problem complexity accurately and completely. The trick, of course, is choosing the right models.

The use of multiple models in the SPO framework is shown in an abstract manner in Figure 3–6. Each process produces (or contributes to the production of) one or more models. Models produced by one process are used as an input to a subsequent process (e.g., data and process models produced during analysis feed the design process). The overall process is iterative, which means models are not static. Once created, a model can be revisited and extended throughout development. Finally, the presence of feedback loops means that a model used as input to a subsequent process

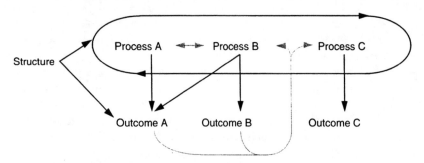

Figure 3–6   Multiple Models in the SPO Framework

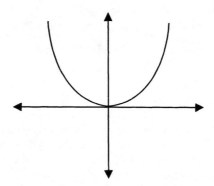

Figure 3–7   One Model of a Function

may in fact be modified or extended by that process. However, an excessive amount of modification is an indication that the model used as input was not properly prepared.

> *What can you tell about the function displayed in Figure 3–7? You can probably remember it is a parabola. But, can you tell me its degree? Is it $y = x^2$? $y = x^{4.4}$? $y = x^{12}$? You cannot determine the degree because the axes are not labeled. Even if they were labeled, it might still be difficult to precisely determine the degree. By providing another model, namely, the equation, we can more easily and quickly understand the function under study. Together, the equation and its graph provide us with a much deeper understanding than either does alone.*

ADVICE TO DEVELOPERS

Among the most effective tools for understanding your system are the models defined by your method. Learn them. Use them as your tool. Invest the energy required to produce them.

Believe in the value of multiple models.

Beware of the dogmatic creation of every model.

Use any model that helps you understand the problem.

Remember models are only representations of reality.

Take care in reviewing models with customers.

Believe in the value of multiple models.   Expert developers routinely use multiple models in the solution of problems. Some of these models are idiosyncratic; most are defined by the method the expert knows best. By working on multiple models, *often at the same time*, experts can quickly develop an accurate mental model of the problem and proposed solutions.

Resist the temptation to try and choose a single "best" representation of the system. It simply cannot be done. If you use only one model, you must, by definition, selectively forget some other aspect of the system. This, in turn, will encourage you to form an incorrect mental model and will eventually lead to an incomplete or invalid implementation.

> *One of the methods we use at ObjectSpace is the Fusion method. Recently, we had a series of e-mail exchanges on the use of visibility graphs, a model of the system that can be fairly time-consuming to develop and usually appears obvious from prior models. The focus of the discussion was to try and determine if visibility graphs provided enough benefit in the development of the system to justify the time and effort spent in their production. The discussion was summarized well by a colleague, who stated "even though they seem obvious, I think preparing visibility graphs is important. They are another model of the system, and usually this model helps increase understanding of the problem from an entirely new perspective."*

Beware of the dogmatic creation of *every* model.   While multiple models help understand the system, it is equally foolish to dogmatically pursue the creation of *every* model defined by the method for *every* system. Models are tools for understanding, no more, no less. Your method should clearly state what the model is intended to show and when it is needed. If your method does not provide such guidance, you can use the following questions to help you select the right models. What aspect of the problem is the focus of this model? Is this relevant to my problem? What does this model help me forget? What other model(s) are needed to help me understand what this model helps me forget?

Use any model that helps you understand the problem.   Remain open to the use of models not defined within your method, for something difficult to describe in one model can be easy to show in another. For example, decision tables have a distinct advantage over data flow diagrams for showing complex transaction processing logic, such as approving or rejecting a credit card authorization request. Alternatively, many times it is appropriate to augment a method with additional models that increase understanding. For example, I regularly recommend augmenting the Fusion method with the design object model of OMT or the use cases of objectory.

Remember models are only *representations* of reality.   Waterman, Peters, and Phillips begin their famous article "Structure Is Not Organization," [1980] with the following:

> *The Belgian surrealist René Magritte painted a series of pipes and titled the series* Ceci n'est pas une pipe: *this is not a pipe. The picture of the thing is not the thing.*

The same holds true for your models. They are not the system. They are abstractions. Always remember the difference.

Take care in reviewing models with customers.   A model is usually a precise representation of a system prepared using a formally defined notation. Asking your customer to review and/or approve a model can be problematic. Unless they are properly trained in how to read the model they may not understand what the model represents.

Many organizations mandate customer approval of data or object models before development. To achieve this goal, developers often ask customers to review these models. Because the customer has trouble viewing the model directly, they ask developers to explain the model. This is precisely the problem, because the customer is no longer approving the model. Instead, they are approving your *description* of the model, an entirely different thing. Problems will arise *anytime* your description deviates from the actual model. Such deviations can wreak havoc in software development ("I thought that was what you wanted! Didn't you *approve* the model?" No, they didn't.).

This situation is similar to the one I faced when reviewing the architectural plans for building my home. The external elevations and interior sketches made good sense, but the electrical, plumbing, and framing plans didn't. I had to ask the builder for assistance in interpreting the symbols defining specific electrical outlets. Even through I did approve of the plan, I'm not entirely satisfied with the outcome: Some of the switches are not placed in the best location. Of course had I greater experience in reading such models I'm sure I would have requested some changes.

How can you rectify this situation? If you're lucky and the customer *does* understand the notation, have *them* explain the model to you. Another technique is to generate multiple models, some of which are simple abstractions of more complex models. The simple models are used for review while the more detailed and complete models are used for development. (This approach creates another problem: It forces you to maintain multiple versions of the same thing.) If you must explain your model, the best approach is to be careful, thorough, and deliberate. Take time to ensure that your reviewer accurately understands the model. A final technique is to use a method that generates outcomes that are accessible to customers while supporting the needs of the developer. For example, most object-oriented methods use scenarios or use cases, both of which are easily understood by a customer and also provide great value to the developer.

ADVICE TO MANAGERS

You are probably more familiar with the use of multiple models than you realize. Budget projections and project plans are two models we use for estimation, one for expenditures and the other for project development activities. The goal is to take your experience with multiple models and apply it to the models your staff creates during systems development.

> Take the time to generate multiple models.
>
> Use appropriate models.
>
> Define a core set of models to use on every project.

Take the time to generate multiple models.   The biggest complaint I hear when suggesting the use of multiple models is that they take "too much time" to create. Unfortunately, both managers and developers routinely voice this complaint. Developers do this because they lack self-discipline or naively think that writing code is the most important aspect of development. Managers make the mistake of thinking only one or at most two models are needed, underestimating the complexity of the problem or overestimating the experience of the staff. Even more dangerous, some managers do not think models are important at all, and instead prefer their staff to begin implementation as soon as possible.

Thinking that multiple models are not needed, or they take too much time to create, is flawed for at least three reasons. First, one model cannot accurately portray all aspects of the system. When you leave out a model, you risk creating an incorrect system because of faulty assumptions created by your developers. Second, method defined models are mutually reinforcing. Skipping one model takes away a substantial amount of the information required by others. Third, by far the easiest part of building a system is writing the source code when the hard part of understanding the problem is finished. Developing multiple models makes certain the system is well understood before the source code is actually written.

Use appropriate models.   Of course, I am not recommending you mandate creating *all* models prescribed by in your method on *every* project. Some methods define more than 15 models! Creating all 15 models is probably overkill if the project is only expected to take six months. The best approach is to select the most important models of your system in the earliest phases of the project. Of course, this does require some experience with your method and problem domain. If you don't have such experience, then the next best thing is to develop preliminary versions of your models and then make a decision as to which are most important.

The first step to fixing problems created by prior poor management is to understand what transpired to create the mess in the first place. One group I inherited had worked for a terribly incompetent manager. When she assumed control, one of her first decisions was to adopt a method for developing systems. So far, so good. The problems started when the team tried to apply the method. As it turns out, this method defined roughly a dozen interrelated models, but did not require any single model. Instead, each project was expected to select the models germane to the problem. Because her staff was relatively inexperienced in using the method, they were unable to decide on their own which models should be used. Because she did not understand the method or the models within it, she was unable to help her staff make these decisions. Not so good. As you can guess, everyone was disappointed with the performance of the first projects using this method. Why wasn't it helping as much as it should have? The answer, of course, is that the wrong models were being used for the project. The fatal mistake came when she decided to require that every project prepare every model.

This decision was about as successful as a lead balloon. Developers despised producing every model—as well they should, because preparing most of these models was a waste of time. Projects continued to spiral out of control, only at a faster pace. Why?

When a developer was late, the response was simple: "I'm working on model ABC, which is the third model defined by the method. I can't begin doing anything else until I'm finished."

Fixing this situation required three actions. First, I educated the staff on the core models of this method. Second, I outlined the purpose and potential usefulness of each of the other models in the method. Third, and most importantly, I met with each project team to review the method and select the models that team would use on their project. We took a minimalist approach, only adding additional models when needed. Taking this approach helped to ensure developer buyin, which allowed me to make certain a model would be used once it was selected. The result? An overall process that was more demanding, because the developers had to think about their selection of a model, but, ultimately, significantly more satisfying, because there was no stupid work.

Define a core set of models to use on every project.   Using a different set of models for every project raises a different problem: consistency. How can you make certain your team is consistent across projects? The best way to achieve this goal is to define a core set of models that must be used on every project. Using this core set of models as your guide, you can review your method and add additional models as appropriate.

But which core set of models should be used? Recall that DeMarco [1982] defines the core set of models to include the *function model*, the *information model*, and the *state model*. For object-oriented systems, I require the following equivalents:

1. A class diagram, which shows the classes within the system and their relationships

2. An object interaction diagram, which shows the dynamic interactions of these objects

3. A state model that defines the legal and illegal states of the system

4. A set of use cases that define how the system interacts with external agents

In addition to these models, I also require that every project create and maintain a glossary of terms (often known as a *data dictionary*). The glossary of terms is a shared repository of definitions of terms and concepts. It is a powerful tool: New team members can use it to learn the problem domain more quickly; customers can review it to make certain domain-specific information is correct; developers can use it to resolve disputes, especially when things are remembered differently. Best of all, such glossaries are relatively easy and inexpensive to create and maintain—any word processor will do. Once created, they can be easily put on the Web.

3.6 GENERATE ALTERNATIVES

The use of alternative designs is a long established tradition in almost all forms of engineering [Petroski 1985], and software development is no exception. Cognitive models encourage the use of alternatives for a simple reason: There are often many ways to solve a problem, and it is only through the examination of alternatives one can select the best. Methods encourage this for two reasons. The first is that unless alternatives are documented, subsequent developers will not have a complete history of the system. Without this history, they are likely to waste efforts by trying solutions that were previously rejected. Alternatively, you might *want* to review rejected solutions that are now appropriate because of changing requirements or hardware specifications [Mathis 1986]. The second is an educational goal. Learning a method is often easier when alternative solutions are presented for the same problem, as each solution provides practice in using the method.

ADVICE TO DEVELOPERS

Being advised to generate alternatives is one thing; generating and recording them for future use is another. First, generating alternatives is not necessarily easy. Sometimes it can feel impossible to generate a single solution to a problem, let alone several! Second, suppose you have some alternatives. How do you select the right one? Third, is generating and reviewing alternatives practical?

> Work at generating alternatives.
> Save alternative solutions.
> Establish criteria to help you evaluate alternatives.

Work at generating alternatives.   Generating alternative solutions doesn't require genius or divine inspiration. It does require a bit of work. When I have trouble thinking of a solution (or an alternative), I find three approaches effective. The first approach is to simplify the problem until I can create one solution. By simplifying different aspects of the problem, alternative solutions come to mind. For example, you might assume the program will run on a computer with infinite memory, removing the need for complex error processing. Then, you might assume all input will be perfectly formatted, removing the need for edit checks. Once I have a few simple solutions, I "complicate" each alternative until it matches the complexity of the problem. Usually one of the alternatives is quickly established as being superior to the others.

The second approach is to use a metaphor. A *metaphor* is a figure of speech that substitutes one thing for another. Using a metaphor, try and transform your problem into a different problem like the original but easier to solve. On a workflow system I designed we thought of the problem of routing workflow objects like a mail system sending messages. We then explored mail systems to see how they solved the problems of handling mail messages sent but not delivered, sent but not read, and so on. Borrowing the solutions of another system helped us solve problems in a different system.

The third approach is the most important of all. Have fun! What is the *craziest* possible solution you can imagine? Many practical solutions are derived from "crazy" ones. (For additional ideas on how you can take this approach, see Hanks [1991] or Glass [1995].

> *As an aerobics instructor, generating alternatives is absolutely essential to teaching the same group of students year after year. If I don't generate alternatives—new variations of the same movement—students will become bored and stop coming to my class. Who wants to do the same move every class? Generating alternatives—new choreography— is no easier in aerobics than in software development. It takes work. Over the years I have found several techniques to help. I take classes from other instructors. Sometimes, I will find choreography I can adapt to my teaching style or directly incorporate into my own class. You can do this through code reviews. As you review a solution, see if you can apply it in your own work. I attend conferences specifically geared toward the teaching of the latest choreography from around the world. You can also attend conferences, learning the latest techniques in software development. Finally, I experiment. I go to the gym and play with movement. How do I know if a new move will work until I try it? You can engage in experimentation by writing small programs that explore various aspects of your problem, language, or programming environment.*

Save alternative solutions.   Don't immediately reject an alternative solution. Instead, write it in your project notebook (project notebooks are discussed in Section 5.2), and keep it around long enough to explore its advantages and disadvantages.

Establish criteria to help you evaluate alternatives.   Having alternative solutions is great, but how do you select which one is the best? The best way is to use objective criteria, preferably the requirements document. What if you don't have objective criteria? Don Gause and Gerald Weinberg [1990] provide an answer: Think of three things that are wrong with your solution. Then, solve these three problems. Continue this process until you can't really think of anything wrong— you'll have your solution!

Alternatively, you can use a simple structure my mom has advocated for years. Write down each alternative on a piece of paper, separating each by five or six blank lines. Next, draw two columns. Label the first column "Advantages" and the second "Disadvantages." Write down in each column the relative advantages and disadvantages of the decision. It is surprising how often the best decision seems "obvious" once you write it down on paper. When finished, save the result in your project notebook (see Section 5.2).

ADVICE TO MANAGERS

The wrong way to obtain alternatives is to mandate them. Saying "Show me several different solutions, and explain why the one you have chosen is the best" is a recipe for disaster (or mutiny)! It is far better to encourage your staff to generate alternatives by creating a supportive environment and maintaining a practical perspective on the value—and cost—of alternatives.

> Add some toys.
>
> Avoid preparing detailed descriptions of each alternative.
>
> Pick one and get on with it.

Add some toys.   A key aspect of generating alternatives is the number of different ways in which a developer can think about the problem. In the advice given to developers, I recommend they have some fun as they generate alternatives. One way you can help this process is to provide some toys in the office. Yes, toys. Toys help unlock the creative genius of the subconscious mind when working on a problem. Juggling bean bags, Nerf guns, small robots, hacky sacks, and other toys are actually cognitive tools that can help your staff become more effective problem solvers [Hanks 1991].

This can be a very tough piece of advice to implement, especially if the prevailing culture of the company discourages "toys." In my experience, however, developers don't abuse this privilege. Instead, they use toys when they are really stuck and *need* to blow off some steam. When they are finished, they can attack the problem from a fresh perspective.

Avoid preparing detailed descriptions of each alternative.   While it may sound great to record every alternative, this doesn't always work well in practice. At an abstract level, alternatives are easy to record. However, as detailed outcomes are produced, the complexity of the documentation task increases and quickly becomes impossible to manage. Instead of trying to prepare detailed outcomes— which won't happen anyway—simply record only enough information to accurately remember the alternative and why it was deemed appropriate or inappropriate. This allows you to gain the value of alternatives without spending a great deal of time working on trivial details.

Pick one and get on with it.   When a creative team gets on a roll the ideas just don't stop. This too can be a problem! Make certain you manage the amount of time allocated to the generation of alternatives. Too much is just as bad as too little. Eventually, you will have to stop creating alternatives, pick one, and get on with building the system!

But when is "eventually"? The following heuristic can help determine that. When three apparently equally good alternatives exist it makes sense to stop generating more alternatives and pick one of the three. If this idea works, then you have no need to go further in either generating or evaluating other alternatives. If the idea does not work, try the other two candidates. If neither of these proves suitable, then return to the alternative generation process. Working in batches of three makes certain you are not spending too much time on generating alternatives while also making certain you have enough alternatives to evaluate.

3.7 DIFFERENTIATE

Nearly all methods encourage us to begin with requirements and proceed through a logical series of processes (i.e., analysis, design, implementation, and verification) to generate the system. Implicit in this approach is differentiating between each of these process steps. In analysis we explicitly concentrate on *what* the system does and avoid as much as possible specifying *how* the system will work. This can be difficult, because as described in Chapter 1, we do not solve problems in a compartmentalized manner. Because of process leveling, we cannot help but think at least a little about how a design could be created solving the problem identified and documented during analysis. We are left with a paradox: Methods assume differentiation, but our natural problem-solving process finds such differentiation difficult, if not impossible. What should we do?

Before answering that question, perhaps we should determine if differentiation is useful. Why *should* we differentiate between different process steps? Does differentiation provide any benefits? Yes, for at least three reasons. First, as discussed in Chapter 1, a solution is easier to understand when it is documented *as if* it were created in a differentiated way. Second, differentiating helps us focus on specific aspects of the problem. This focus, helps us understand and solve the problem in more manageable pieces rather than all at once. This, in turn, helps reduce complexity. It also helps us generate alternative solutions. Third, and most importantly, by focusing on *what* the system should do rather than *how* it does it, differentiation helps ensure the right problem is solved the right way.

> *Some classes at ObjectSpace have students build object-oriented simulations of the game of Monopoly™ as a means of helping them learn object-oriented analysis and design. Not only is it fun, but Monopoly is also a rich problem domain for understanding objects, and the near universal appeal of the game means almost every student has played the game at least once. The first phase of the assignment focuses on creating the basic objects that comprise the game and having two players move around the board. Most student teams read the initial requirements, skip analysis, and design a solution storing the squares on the board in an array. These teams require coaching to learn what the rare student has discovered through a proper analysis: The best way to represent the squares is a circularly linked list. But how did the student derive this answer? By first focusing on what the system needs to do, they were able to generate several alternatives as to how it could be done. By focusing on the relationships between objects, they discovered a square has a relationship with another square. These analysis discoveries make it easy to pick a design solution implementing linking each square one to another.*

ADVICE TO DEVELOPERS

Here are some ideas you can use to help you ensure you are maintaining a good degree of differentiation among the activities of software development.

> Choose objective or subjective modes of thinking to help differentiate.
>
> Differentiate outcomes from one phase by generating alternatives in the next.
>
> Use the right approach for subjective thought.
>
> Use your method to help differentiate.

Choose objective or subjective modes of thinking to help differentiate.   We know we are supposed to differentiate between analysis and design. In other words, we *know* that analysis is concerned with "what" and that design is concerned with "how." Ideally, this means that somehow during analysis we should put our minds into a mode of thought that encourages close attention to those thoughts that are closely related to "what." It means we should strive for differentiated *thinking*.

Can this be done? I think so. Recall that one influence on our problem solving is our mental set which "frames" how we approach the solution to a problem. By establishing a mental set that encourages a specific mode of thought we are more likely to differentiate between method-defined processes. One way to establish a mental set is to specifically try and think in an objective or subjective manner. When we are objective, we are looking for and/or applying constraints without bias or prejudice. We are concerned with facts, not opinions. When we are subjective we think in largely the opposite manner. We focus on ideas, emotions, opinions. We don't always follow constraints, and instead ask: "What if...?" We follow our "intuition," and "go with out gut."

The next step is to examine specific method activities to see which are more objective and which are more subjective, as shown in Figure 3-8. By knowing which kind of thinking is most appropriate for the activity, we can choose the style that fits our needs best. Requirements gathering, for example, is largely subjective (e.g., "what should the system do?" or, in the style of future perfect thinking, "what will the system have done?"). Analysis, on the other hand, is objective (e.g. "what are the

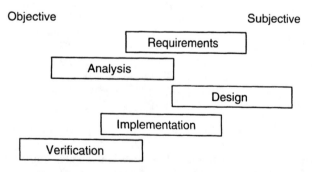

Figure 3–8   Objective and Subjective Method Activities

constraints?"). Design is subjective, while implementation seems to fit best somewhere in the middle. Finally, verification is the most objective of all!

The most striking aspect of Figure 3–8 is the gulf between analysis modes of thought and design modes of thought. In general, any outcome of a method can be used in an analytical (objective) or design (subjective) perspective. Thus, when reviewing and/or using an outcome, first decide which perspective will help the most. If your goal deals more with analysis, choose an objective mode of thought. If your goal is more oriented towards design, choose subjective.

The Monopoly example also illustrates the movement between objective and subjective ways of thinking. During the analysis phase, the best performing students are objective. During design, they become more subjective. Finally, they return to objective thought to evaluate which design alternative is the best candidate. When students finish the first phase of the project, I tell them this story to further reinforce the need for objective versus subjective thinking.

Suppose an architect in the process of creating a building prepares a floor plan for the northwest corner looking something like the one portrayed in Figure 3–9. When shown to the client, the architect is perceived to be the designer, because it is his idea that defines the shape of the building. (In this case, design refers to the creation of the external appearance of the building, and not the internal details of construction.)

Figure 3–9   An Architect's View of a Corner

When the plans are given to the builder, however, the perspective changes dramatically. The architect is no longer the designer, but instead, the analyst. The builder, in turn, becomes the designer, because the builder should be free to implement the architect-analyst's specification any number of ways. Figure 3–10 shows four possible ways the builder could accurately implement the specification of the architect. It is here the skill of the builder shines, for D outperforms any of the other choices. D is not only easier to manufacture and assemble, it will also resist sheering forces more effectively than A, B,

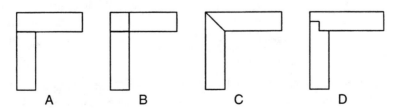

Figure 3–10   A Builder's View of a Corner

*or C. If, on the other hand, the architect had specified A, B, or C, he would have not re-
alized the benefits of differentiation.*

Differentiate outcomes from one phase by generating alternatives in the next.   Can your analysis allow you to generate two or more designs? If not, then the analysis might be incorrect. Analysis should focus on *what*, not *how*. A proper analysis should allow you to generate multiple designs. If there is only one reasonable design for a given analysis, chances are the analysis is not really an analysis at all, but merely one specific design described in analysis terms. This approach is most beneficial for differentiating between analysis and design, but it can be generalized and applied to any outcome feeding a subsequent process. For example, if there is only one possible source code implementation of a given design (i.e., the design is *completely* isomorphic with the source implementation), then the design may be overspecified.

Use the right approach for subjective thought.   Let's say you are working on a project to replace an existing order entry system with an entirely new system. The old system is mainframe based and is very difficult to use. The new system will be based on a client/server architecture, where the clients are Intel-based personal computers running Windows '95™. You have completed a preliminary analysis of the system and are now just about to start an initial design of the user interface. At this stage, you want to be as subjective as possible.

The *wrong* approach is to use a PC to draw the initial windows for at least four reasons. First, no matter how easily your tool can create a screen, you will be inexorably drawn to connecting those screens together to make the system "work." Doing this means your mode of thought has moved from subjective to objective. Second, subjective thought requires freedom. A window design tool provides a structure for drawing the screen. This structure, in turn, constrains our thought. Paper and pencil, on the other hand, are the most flexible screen design tools (structures) at your disposal. Third, it is nearly impossible for any single tool to contain all currently available user interface widgets. For example, some tools don't include a spreadsheet widget. What happens to your design if you think a spreadsheet is appropriate? Finally, the general idea of a graphic image is far easier to convey using paper and pencil than a screen painting tool.

The *right* approach is to create your preliminary design using good old paper and pencil. Your initial design can be created quickly and easily using readily accessible tools whose outcomes are easy to change. Moreover, paper and pencil designs can be tested as effectively as computer-based prototypes (through simulated prototyping).

Use your method to help differentiate.   Many methods control the movement between different processes through a series of tests designed to determine when an outcome is "complete." Use these tests to help differentiate between different activities by reviewing these tests *before* you prepare outcomes.

ADVICE TO MANAGERS

The management of differentiation is a form of control: You want to put structures and processes in place to encourage differentiation by controlling the formal, external processes of your staff. Such control is usually easier to put into place for the team instead of the individual. Still, there are some things you can do to assist individual developers gain the benefits of differentiation.

> Examine outcomes for differentiation.

Examine outcomes for differentiation.   To assist developers in generating differentiated outcomes, ask them to explain how an outcome produced in one process can be used to generate alternatives in another. For example, an analysis model showing the state transitions of the system can be implemented in a wide variety of ways (e.g., as a state machine or as individual objects). If you are concerned about a lack of differentiation, ask the developer to list those aspects of the outcome overly constraining the production of subsequent outcomes. Examine this list and change as appropriate.

4

UNDERSTANDING YOURSELF

The integrated framework identifies values, personality, and goals as three key components of software development not often discussed in traditional books on software engineering. Understanding yourself means identifying how these three things shape and frame your approach to software development and using this understanding to enhance your abilities as a software developer.

Chapter Overview

The first three sections of this chapter parallel the first three sections of chapter two. Section 4.1 begins by showing how to clarify values and then use them to enhance decision making. Section 4.2 discusses two important aspects of our personality as they relate to problem solving, our cognitive style and our temperament. Section 4.3 discusses goals: how to set them and how to achieve them. Section 4.4 concludes by providing a structure and process for determining your talents. By understanding your strong and weak points you can know the best manner to contribute and craft specific strategies for worthwhile improvement.

4.1 CLARIFY VALUES

As described in Chapter 2, values provide an internal structure guiding us during decisions. By making this structure explicit, you can make tough decisions easier and improve the consistency of each decision made.

ADVICE TO DEVELOPERS

Functional values guide us in our daily actions with respect to how we perform our job duties. There are two categories of functional values important to most developers. The first are process values, or values related to solving the problem the right way. The second are outcome values, which describe or govern aspects of the outcome. The first step to understanding either set of values is to write them down.

Clarify your coding values.
Do not impose your values over your customers.
Expect your values to change.
State your process values.
Learn your manager's values.

Clarify your coding values.   Begin by reviewing the list of items listed in Table 4–1, adding or removing items as necessary. Next, rank these items in order of importance. For example, if writing highly efficient programs is something you consider very important (perhaps you are writing a computer game) then it would be ranked number one. (If you get stuck you might want to review [Maguire 1993]). Once you have determined your coding values, use them to consistently guide implementation decisions (i.e., "Given two ways of coding a function, one emphasizing efficiency and the other portability, which do I choose?").

This exercise can be repeated for any aspect of software development, especially those dealing with activities related to design. Consider the design of a graphical user interface. Typically, the desire to make the system easy for novices to learn

TABLE 4–1   **Value System Ranking Chart**

———— Correctness
———— Efficiency
———— Understandability
———— Maintainability
———— Clarity
———— Small memory size
———— Personal expression
———— Personal convenience
———— Adherence to standards
———— Testability
———— Portability
————
————
————
————
————

conflicts with the desire to make the system fast and efficient for experts. By establishing your values with respect to important design activities, you will make every design activity easier.

Do not impose your values over your customers.   Once you have clarified your coding values, you *should* use them to help guide you making decisions. However, if you place your values above your customer, you are taking this too far. If the customer requests that the system be as efficient as possible, you have an obligation to *value* efficiency. Our personal coding values are always subservient to stated requirements.

Expect your values to change.   While most values influencing our behavior are relatively static, the values associated with software development tend to change slightly given your experience, the problem, the requirements, and the context of the working environment. Because of this you should consider creating a new ranking of values for each project.

State your process values.   Do you believe in a method? On what aspects of the method are you willing to compromise? Forget the method. Do you at least believe in engaging in a rigorous analysis before design? How strongly do you hold these values? Are you willing to do what Ed Yourdon suggests in *Decline and Fall of the American Programmer* [1992] and change jobs to find a company who values good development practices as much as you?

Learn your manager's values.   Your manager is constantly evaluating the decisions you make. One criterion used both consciously and unconsciously in these decisions is your manager's values. Learning your manager's values will help you in making decisions consistent with those values, contributing to an overall image of effectiveness.

ADVICE TO MANAGERS

Values have great impact on how groups of developers interact. Because of this, the majority of advice for you regarding values will be deferred until later in this book. However, there are some specific managerial actions you can take to clarify your staff's values and your own.

> Clarify value-based decisions.

Clarify value-based decisions.   We've all had the same problem: Value-based decisions become misinterpreted by our staff. They wonder what crazy things we have done now, especially when our values differ from theirs. Unfortunately, differences between your values and a subordinate's *can* cause problems. If you suspect such a problem exists, explain your actions and listen to their responses. The goal is not for you to change your decision (although this is a possibility). Instead, the goal is to clarify value-based decisions.

4.2 UNDERSTAND YOUR PERSONALITY

Chapter 2 defined *personality* as "a complex set of relatively stable behavioral and emotional characteristics that can be used to uniquely identify a person." In trying to understand personality, there are two broad lines of research. The first concerns how situational variables affect our behavior despite our personality. This section focuses on the second major area of personality research, individual personality traits. Two major theories will be described here, the Kirton Adaption-Innovation Inventory (KAI) and the Myers-Briggs Type Indicator (MBTI). The KAI is valuable because it is a measure of cognitive style—how one likes to solve problems in the context of a given structure. The MBTI is equally valuable, for it gives us a means by which we can describe our preferences for sociality, obtaining data, making decisions, and taking action. Understanding these traits allows us to use structure more effectively, improve our abilities in engaging process, and understand our preferences in creating and using outcomes.

4.2.1 The Kirton Adaption-Innovation Inventory

The idea of cognitive style—how we like to run our engine—was introduced in Chapter 1. One of the main theories describing cognitive style is the KAI. The KAI attempts to measure the amount of structure a person needs to solve a problem and the amount of structure that must be consensually agreed upon when working with others. The two ends of the KAI scale are the adaptors and the innovators. *Adaptors* prefer to solve problems within existing and/or mutually agreed upon structures. *Innovators* prefer working in few or invented structures [Kirton 1994].

As an example of these differences, consider two developers who have been asked to increase transaction processing times of a system by 10 percent. An adaptor might solve the problem by making a series of minor adjustments to every system module, keeping the basic data structures and processing algorithms of the main module intact. An innovator, on the other hand, might achieve the target by replacing the data structures and algorithms of the main module with entirely new ones. Put another way, adaptors have a preference for "doing things better" while innovators have a preference for "doing things differently."

One important result of the KAI theory is the interdependence of adaptors and innovators. Without the groundbreaking, new way of doing things created by the innovator, the adaptor wouldn't have much to improve! Similarly, without the stability and optimizations provided by the adaptor, the innovator would have no foundation to work from and their innovations would go unnoticed.

Our preferred style can be quite different than our actual behavior. For example, an innovative person can use coping behavior to operate effectively when placed in an adaptive environment. The need for coping behavior should be minimized, as it drains energy from the individual and contributes to cognitive dissonance. One study, for example, found employee turnover was highly correlated with KAI scores. Although the organization wanted to become more innovative and was successful at hiring innovators (as measured by the KAI), the prevailing adaptive climate was so strong most of the new hires ended up leaving in less than three years [Hayward 1983].

> *I became interested in the KAI when I tried to understand some of the abnormally high turnover rates of some of my clients who are in the midst of adopting object technology. The problem was perplexing because this client had worked very hard to prepare the organization for the change, including extensive training, reasonably defined projects, and good consultants. The KAI provides one answer: Adopting a new technology requires innovative people, because there is precious little structure associated with the technology. Unfortunately, big organizations tend to be adaptive, having optimized structures enabling them to be effective in known environments. The nature of the problem sets up a clash between the existing adaptors and the new hired innovators. I am convinced much of the turnover associated with this organization is due to differences in cognitive style and could be substantially reduced through application of KAI theory.*

4.2.2 The Myers-Briggs Type Indicator

One of the most well established measurements of personality is the Myers-Briggs Type Indicator, which measures preferences of Jungian personality types. A Jungian personality type is a cluster of typical behaviors an individual exhibits in a generally stable way over a number of years. The four preferences measured by the MBTI are summarized below.

1. Preference for sociability: Extrovert (E) or Introvert (I)
   Extroverts are social, tend to feel energized around other people, and may even feel lonely when not around others. Introverts are more territorial and tend to prefer quiet and/or private activities.
2. Preference for obtaining data: Sensation (S) or Intuition (N)
   Sensation-dominant people prefer precise, specific data in making what they would consider to be realistic and practical decisions. Intuitives seek holistic information describing possibilities and tend to see themselves making innovative decisions based on relatively general data (trends).
3. Preference for reaching decisions: Thinking (T) or Feeling (F)

Thinkers stress logic and formal modes of reasoning; they generalize and abstract and seem to base their choices on impersonal factors. Feeling-dominant people form personalistic value judgments; they individuate, explain things in human terms, and emphasize affective and personal processes in decision making.

4. Preference for taking action: Judging (J) or Perceiving (P)

   Judging-dominative people approach their life with a sense of urgency. Making decisions, planning ahead, and reaching closure are all viewed as extremely important. In this sense, judging-dominative people are outcome oriented. Perceiving-dominative people, on the other hand, tend to prefer process to outcome: Reaching closure is not deemed as important as keeping options open, and adapting is viewed as more desirable than planning. Thus, perceiving-dominative individuals are process oriented.

It is important to stress that Jung viewed personality types as *dominant,* and not as *absolute* modes of expression. All people exhibit the preferences described above, but most people have distinct preferences. This is similar to the KAI, where adaptiveness and innovativeness are two ends of the same continuum. In addition, Jung's theory allows for changes to occur over time. Thus, while abrupt shifts are rare, an individual can change a preference (e.g., an extrovert can become more introverted) based on sociocultural and environmental conditions. For example, although an introvert would not ordinarily prefer to work on a team of extroverts, over time they can become more at ease as they establish friendships or create a special role for themselves within the group.

Single dimensions of personality are interesting, but it is the complex interactions of different personality types that are most fascinating. These interactions are called *temperaments.* Temperaments are important because they provide "anchoring" points on the dimensional scales represented by the personality types. Although there is some slight disagreement on the exact pairings, the most common information-processing temperaments related to problem solving are Sensing-Thinking (ST; left-brained, emphasizing analytical techniques); Intuition-Feeling (NF; right-brained, emphasizing intuition and judgment); Intuition-Thinking and Sensing-Feeling (NT and SF, respectively, neither predominantly right- or left-brained).

Another useful way to view temperament types is to place them on a two-dimensional scale (Figure 4–1). Organizing temperament types in this way helps reinforce the view that preferences represent ranges and helps increase our understanding of how another type may make a decision different from our own given the same data [Williams 1989; Nutt 1979].

4.2.3 Relationship between the KAI and MBTI

There appears to be little direct correlation between the KAI and the MBTI, although there is some evidence the KAI integrates several personality types

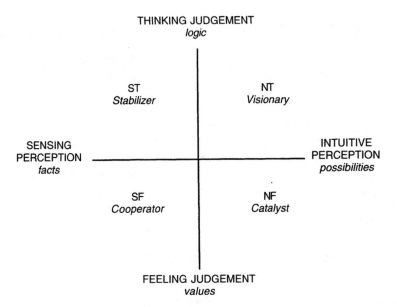

Figure 4–1   Two-Dimensional View of Temperament Types

[Goldsmith 1994]. For example, innovators tend to be more intuitive than adapters, but there is no preference among either adaptors or innovators for thinking versus feeling. In addition, it is not at all clear how much any personality trait of either the KAI or the MBTI is a result of genetic predisposition and/or environment stimuli. As a result, it is best to think of the KAI and the MBTI as measuring five distinctly different dimensions of our personality (one for KAI; four for MBTI).

4.2.4 The Intersection of Personality and Values

Which comes first? Values or personality? Do I write source code *adhering* to the coding standard because I value standards or because I am an adaptive person who prefers to work within structures? Alternatively, do I write source code *ignoring* the coding standard because I value personal expression or because I am an innovator who prefers working in little or no structure?

I don't know of any research that attempts to establish a link between coding values and personality. I've seen both introverts and extroverts value the disciplined use of a method, just as I've seen them eschew the use of a method. Some of the most innovative people I know value structure and use it even though they don't need much of it. Yet, it seems there must be some link between values and personality.

And I think there is. Values are related to personality in that our personality reflects our values. Quite literally, we behave in a certain stable and predictable manner way because we value certain things.

ADVICE TO DEVELOPERS

While it is beyond the scope of this book to give you the tools to measure your cognitive style (as measured by the KAI) or personality type (as measured by the MBTI), it is nonetheless a useful exercise to review the descriptions provided earlier and try to assess your personality. While not as precise as a full measurement, self-assessments have been shown to be reasonably accurate (e.g., we are pretty good at determining if we are adaptive or innovative, introverted or extroverted, and the like). Once we have an understanding of our personality, we can use it to improve how we might operate within the SPO framework and with each other.

Be tolerant of KAI differences.

Choose projects complementing your KAI style.

Use knowledge of personality types to facilitate communication.

Beware of decision-making biases in MBTI temperaments.

Be tolerant of KAI differences.   Unfortunately, one consistent finding in KAI research is that adaptors and innovators tend to view each other pejoratively. An adaptor describing a fellow adaptor might use phrases like "sound, stable, precise, reliable, working within the organization." An innovator describing that same person might instead say "stodgy, boring, uncreative, never challenges the status quo, always wants to do the same thing." *Neither* adapters or innovators are inherently better than the other. By understanding KAI differences, we can work together to ensure problem solving is most effective, as shown in Table 4–2.

TABLE 4–2   **Adaptors and Innovators Working Together**

An	adaptor	adaptor	innovator	innovator
colloborating with an	adaptor	innovator	adaptor	innovator
supplies	additional stability and harmony	a stable structure from which to work	new and alternative structures for producing outcomes	support for alternative ideas and fuel for their collective creativity
and should watch out for	holding on to existing structures too rigidly.	unnecessarily dampening the creation of new structures suggested by the innovator.	overloading the adaptor with too many untried ideas.	spending too much time exploring ideas without getting real work done or failing to reach an agreement on a specific structure.

Choose projects complimenting your KAI style.   I'm a big fan of the KAI because it has helped me understand so much of my own behavior. For starters, it helps explain why I prefer to work on relatively unstructured assignments or in groups where each individual is given tremendous autonomy. Now, I explicitly *seek* these assignments and working environments and am much happier for it. I suggest you do the same.

Use knowledge of personality to communicate effectively.   An MBTI preference for thinking versus feeling means the person wants facts, not opinions. Give them to him. Similarly, during a meeting some developers may be more quiet than others simply because they are more introverted.

Beware of decision-making biases in MBTI temperaments.   Both Jungian personality types and the information-processing temperaments based on these types exhibit distinct cognitive and behavioral preferences when making decisions. These preferences lead to *input biases*, in which certain forms of data are incorrectly preferred when making a decision. Input biases lead, in turn, to process-related errors and ultimately to incorrect outcomes [Haley 1989]. For example, when given identical information, people with different personality types will process this information differently, reaching different conclusions [Nutt 1979]. By remaining aware of your input biases (see Table 4–3) in a complex decision task, you can select a wider range of input data on which to base your decision. Alternatively, you can try to imagine how a different temperament would approach the problem: What would they think is important? How would they engage in the process? Would their outcome be more suitable? You could also find someone who has a distinctly different temperament and confirm your outcome (and the input on which it was based) with them.

ADVICE TO MANAGERS

Why take the time to learn about your personality and those of your subordinates? Any team is a mixing pot of different personalities. Some combinations, as shown above, can be volatile! By understanding personality, you can defuse problem situations before they arise. Perhaps even more importantly, an understanding of your own personality can facilitate interactions with subordinates of a different type.

Do not use personality factors as the sole basis for hiring decisions.
Do not force others to fit your personality.
Support differences in "environmental" factors.

Do not use personality factors as the sole basis for hiring decisions.   At one time, people thought personality tests could predict programming

TABLE 4–3   Cognitive Biases of Information-Processing Temperament Types

Temperament	Input Bias	Process Bias	Outcome Bias
ST	Oversimplification of complex data Reluctance to use qualitative information	Excessive reliance on standard operating procedures Reluctance to try new and/or different approaches	Rejection of novel solutions Preference to keep initial outcomes, even in the face of changing data
NT	Discounting of data inconsistent to their preferred mode of abstract thinking In extreme cases, throwing away contradictory evidence	Preference for longer-term, open-ended processes Too much process	Difficulty in generating outcomes in unstructured environments
SF	Preference for people-oriented data as opposed to problem-oriented data	Preference for consultative, group-process solutions Lack of detailed exploration of any single premise	Belief that outcomes representing group decisions are most important due to strong needs for acceptance by others
NF	Generalized data is ignored; high-impact outliers are preferred	Excessive reliance on analogy in generating solutions Oversimplification	Outcomes may not be subjected to rigorous testing Failure to generate outcomes that can effectively handle complex data

performance. In general, this has not been the case, and you should never base hiring decisions solely on personality traits. This is not to say there is absolutely no correlation between personality types and developer performance. All other things being equal, I would much prefer to have an extrovert as part of my requirements gathering team as opposed to an introvert. However, I wouldn't make any hiring decision solely on personality traits.

Do not force others to fit your personality.   We often tend to try to mold others into our personality. Avoid this at all costs. People are different, and these differences are good.

Support differences in "environmental" factors.   The Facility Management Institute of the University of Michigan has measured how temperament types utilize their workplace. Over 70 attributes were considered, including such things as number and type of conference tables and chairs, extent of personalization, extent of storage capacity, and so forth. A summarization of these results are presented in Figure 4–2 [Williams 1989].

You can make use of Figure 4–2 in two ways. First, because different temperament types prefer different work areas, everyone should recognize their colleagues (including managers and subordinates) will prefer different customizations of their working environment. This is most easily accomplished if an individual has a personal office [DeMarco 1987]. Because this is unlikely in most corporations, where offices are usually reserved for managers, an acceptance of individual differences is especially important in "cubeland."

Second, many software engineers tend to be STs or NTs, both of which prefer easy access to reference materials, and lots of them! Thus, while you can't necessarily control whether each developer has a separate office, you can strive to provide them with adequate filing and library space. Finally, when engaging in space planning, consider how individuals are situated with respect to each other. Putting

THINKING JUDGMENT

A work area geared toward action.	Ample storage for historical and reference material.
Easy access to procedure manuals, charts, and gaphics used in daily work.	Relatively high degree of privacy.
Desk and table tops used for work, not filing.	Plenty of shelf space for books and documents.
Evidence of electronic devices for analyzing and storing relevent data.	Work surface usually filled with work-in-process.
Very little evidence of personal effects or momentos.	Relatively few space constraints.

SENSING PERCEPTION   INTUITIVE PERCEPTION

Chairs, tables, countertops for frequent use by visitors to the work area.	Presence of many personal items.
Less privacy required so may be located near center of activity.	Intermixing of work and personal items on bulletin boards and work surfaces.
	Chairs and tables for use with visitors.
Evidence of receipt and transfer of information such as "in" and "out" boxes.	Cluttered in appearance because desk and table tops used for "filing."
Work area neat and orderly in appearance.	Evidence of much unfiled but not used information.
Evidence of working electronic devices.	

FEELING JUDGMENT

Figure 4–2   Workplace Preferences of Different Temperament Types

disparate personality types adjacent to each other may cause unnecessary problems (e.g., imagine an introvert-adaptor sitting next to an extrovert-innovator).

4.3 GOALS

The motivation for identifying goals is simple: They help focus efforts in daily work. More importantly, an unidentified goal is impossible to achieve! Of course, once a goal has been identified, it is possible to create and/or modify structures, processes, and outcomes to achieve it. Although this is primarily a book on software development, the goal-setting and achieving techniques described in this section can be applied in all areas of your life.

> *A major portion of my research at the University of Michigan involved developing a programming environment to assist novice programmers learning software design skills. Goal setting was considered to be such an important part of the process it was a required step: The environment did not allow students to generate any source code until they had first defined the goal the source code was designed to achieve. The process of setting goals and then selecting plans to achieve them was even reflected in the name of the environment, the Goal-Plan-Code Editor (GPCeditor).*

4.3.1 Setting Goals

Grab a sheet of paper. List all the things you would like to accomplish. Aim high. Brainstorm. Vary your time frame: What do you think of your life in three months? one year? three years? ten years? Do you want to learn a new programming language? What about moving from one aspect of development, such as database administration, to another, such as distributed computing?

It is not reasonable to try and achieve all your goals at the same time. Some will be more important; some be easier to achieve; and others still might be prerequisites. Therefore, the next step is to review your list, and select those goals that are truly most important.

To help you in selecting goals keep the following points in mind. First, any goal you wish to pursue must be consistent with your values and your personality. For example, it is not reasonable to try to fundamentally change basic attributes of your personality.

Second, distinguish between a "high" goal and an immediate goal. A "high" goal focuses our efforts over a very long period of time and consists of numerous intermediate goals. Let's say you are having trouble finding a comprehensive reference book on performance optimization techniques in Visual Basic. An intermediate goal would be to learn how to identify which aspects of the application require performance tuning and how to fix these. A high goal would be to write the reference book you seek.

Third, make certain any goal you select is sufficiently motivating. If it really is a high goal, you will expend a lot of time and energy achieving it. You should also make certain you share a high goal with others, such as your spouse, because achieving it will take time away from them.

Fourth, make certain the goal is reasonable given your current environment. This includes your personal life, your career, and your abilities. Learning Smalltalk is a wonderful goal, but it may be inappropriate if you are not using object-oriented programming at work or don't have a personal computer at home.

4.3.2 Organizing Goals

Once you have selected a goal, the next step is to establish intermediate goals to help you achieve it. Use Figure 4–3 to help. Begin by writing your goal in the box at the top of the triangle, along with the date you wish to achieve this goal. Then, record intermediate goals and their dates in the layers underneath the triangle, beginning with those that must be achieved first. If this chart sounds like a project plan, it is, although in a different format. Metaphorically, the format resembles climbing a mountain, where each intermediate goal is a well-defined step towards the peak [Noe 1984].

Once you have completed this chart, photocopy it and place it on your wall. This will serve two purposes. First, when others ask about the chart, you can tell them about it, which will further reinforce your desire to achieve it. Second, you can mark your progress toward your long-term goal in a visible manner, helping you maintain the momentum necessary to achieve the long-term goal.

ADVICE TO DEVELOPERS

Some of us are intensely goal driven: Everything we do must be somehow related to a long-term goal. Others are not so intense—life is a bit more relaxed. Still, each of us has goals. They may or may not be big. They may or may not change the world. But they are there, waiting for us to write them down and achieve them.

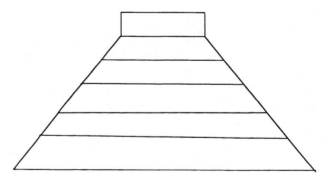

Figure 4–3   Goal Planning Guide

> Ask for help.
> Enjoy your achievements.
> Help others.
> Let *your* mentors know how you are doing.

Ask for help.   If you set your goal high enough, you will find it cannot be achieved without the help of others. Don't be afraid to ask for such help! I could never have written this book without the help of my reviewers, my friends, and the students in my classes who listened to the theories contained within this book or provided feedback on some of the writing. Most of all, I could never have finished this book without the support of my wife, who freely gave of her time so I could achieve this goal.

Enjoy your achievements.   Achieving any goal should be an opportunity for enjoying the fruits of your labor. You've earned it! More importantly, achieving one goal gives you the confidence to do it again, producing a positive feedback loop of goal-setting and goal-achieving success!

Help others.   Everyone should make it a constant, long-term goal to help someone else. It is immensely satisfying, helps you grow as a person, and solidifies friendships.

Let *your* mentors know how you are doing.   The people who are helping you achieve your goal want to know how you are doing. Share with them your successes *and* failures. They will share in the happiness of your successes and console and support you in failure.

ADVICE TO MANAGERS

Your staff cannot achieve many of the goals they set without your help. By focusing on their goals, you help the overall team succeed.

> Maintain an awareness of the goals of your subordinates.
> Do not coerce subordinates into revealing their goals.
> Encourage the setting of task-related goals.
> Provide feedback.
> Consider experience when setting goals.

Maintain an awareness of the goals of your subordinates.   Helping your subordinates achieve their goals should be a primary goal of your own. For example, suppose one of your developers who knows COBOL wants to learn C++—a pretty common occurrence! If at all possible, you should try to provide opportunities to help him achieve this goal. For example, you might provide him with a book on the language or include him in code reviews.

You should approach this carefully. What happens if you have a staff of ten COBOL developers who all want to learn C++? In this case, it would be reasonable to provide each of them with a book but restrict future efforts to those developers who demonstrate the most commitment to the goal. In general, you should restrict your efforts to professional goals, but helping individuals achieve goals in nonwork-related areas of their life is certainly worthwhile. This kind of help binds the individuals to the organization, creating extreme amounts of loyalty and increasing overall job satisfaction.

> *Over the years I have had some terrific managers who really helped me to achieve my personal goals. For example, I started working at EDS just after I had won the National championship in pairs figure skating. Because of my intense training schedule, I needed a flexible work schedule with a fair amount of time off for competitions. Because I could only work part time, I was ineligible for vacation. Yet, every single EDS manager allowed me extreme flexibility in my work schedule, and always gave me the time off I needed to attend a competition. I could not have achieved my skating and work success had I not had a manager who was willing to bend the rules in my favor. This is not to say EDS did not benefit from this support, for it instilled in me an extreme sense of loyalty to the organization.*

Do not coerce subordinates into revealing their goals.   Goals can be highly personal, and your staff may feel uncomfortable sharing them with you. Don't force it.

Encourage the setting of task-related goals.   Motivation for work can be exceptionally high when it is organized as a goal to be attained *provided* it meets three critical criteria. First, the goal should be challenging—not too hard but not too easy. Creating the right amount of difficulty is hard, because between the difficulty of a goal and motivation is nonlinear. It is almost a step function. Specifically, when a goal is perceived as too simple there is little motivation to work to achieve it. Motivation is also low when a goal is perceived as so difficult as to be unattainable. Why expend energy on the impossible?

Second, the goal must be within the current abilities of the developer. It is at best inappropriate to ask a developer to achieve a goal clearly outside the scope of their current abilities *unless* the goal is to develop these abilities. Third, there must be sufficient resources necessary to achieve the goal.

> *All three items must be present in order for the goal to be an effective motivator for improving performance. If one of them is missing, performance may suffer because of frustration, anxiety, or confusion. One subordinate of mine wished to attain a promo-*

tion to the rank of advanced system engineer. While he possessed all the required technical skills, I felt he lacked the necessary communication skills. Working together, we defined the goal of writing a paper on his current project as a suitable goal for demonstrating his ability to communicate technical ideas clearly. Over the next few weeks I was mystified: Instead of actively pursuing this goal, he become increasingly frustrated. Finally, I called him into my office to discover what was wrong. It was actually quite simple. Because he had never written a technical paper before, he did not know how to conduct the research necessary to support his implementation. The goal was challenging, within his ability, but not within his resources. To correct the situation, I provided him with a few papers, enabling him to get started on achieving his goal. I also provided him with an outline of how to do a literature search at the library. Given the proper resources and training, he began to make rapid progress toward the promotion.

Provide feedback.   Once a goal has been established, feedback which indicates progress in relation to the goal is essential for the goal to lead to higher performance.

Consider experience when setting goals.   A novice requires simpler goals that are more fully decomposed into attainable subgoals than an expert. The best approach is to create a series of goals that increase in complexity over time [Wood 1990].

4.4 KNOW WHAT YOU ARE GOOD AT

In a landmark study comparing developer performance, Sackman, Erickson, and Grant [1968] found there is an order of magnitude difference between the best and worst developer. Incredibly, there are some areas of programming performance in which the best performers were 28 times better than the worst! Wait. It gets even worse. Sackman and his colleagues found experience has little correlation with ability: Novices were able to outperform experts in several situations. They summarized their study in the following way:

> *When a programmer is good,*
> *He is very, very good,*
> *But when he is bad,*
> *He is horrid.*

Some have pointed out the design of the study may have impacted the data obtained [Weinberg 1971], but there is general agreement the data are significant (i.e., there may not be a 28:1 difference, but there can easily be an order of magnitude in difference). In general, it is best to assume that for any given activity there will be a 10:1 difference in ability between the best and the worst.

How can a novice with little experience perform better than an expert with many years of experience? To answer this question, you must examine the kinds of experience. If you are solving the same kinds of problem year after year, you *are not* substantially increasing the size and/or complexity of the plans within your cognitive library. This does not mean we should never specialize in a given aspect of software development. It means we should avoid overspecialization.

Perhaps the most underutilized results of research in programmer productivity is that each of us is particularly good at one or two aspects of the development process. Productivity is measured through outcomes (e.g., fully debugged lines of source, implemented and tested function points, objects, and so forth), not processes. However, processes generate outcomes, and processes are heavily influenced by our experience, values, and personality. Somewhere in the interaction between all these things lie your talents, or those process-outcome combinations particularly suited to your style. If you value clarity, are generally a neat person, and perhaps are a bit extroverted, then your talent may lie in writing requirements. Alternatively, if you have a high tolerance for stress, prefer working in short, intense bursts of energy, are slightly more adaptive than innovative, and like to work on many different things at the same time, then your talent may lie in maintenance.

ADVICE TO DEVELOPERS

Learning your talents enables you to select the activities you like the most and can do the best.

Learn your talents.
Use training to improve and balance your talents.

Learn your talents.   Here is a four-step technique you can use to help discover your talents. First, carefully review Table 4–4, adding additional entries as necessary. Next, order these activities according to what you like to do in column a. Thus, place a 1 in column a next to "Implementing complex algorithms" if this is your favorite activity. Now, repeat this exercise, but this time order the list according to the activities you think you are good at. You may want to have a few team members generate this list. Select team members that are close to you, as this is a more private kind of exercise. Thus, if you are very good at "Writing test plans," place a 1 next to this activity. Record these results in column b. Add the two numbers together, and order the list one more time according to the total column. The activities receiving the *lowest* points are likely to be your talents.

Use training to improve and balance your talents.   Compare the numbers in column a with column b. Identify any disparities and place them in the

TABLE 4–4   Determining Your Talents

a	b	Total	
————	————	————	Writing requirements
————	————	————	Testing source
————	————	————	Fixing maintenance problems
————	————	————	Developing project plans
————	————	————	Designing user interfaces
————	————	————	Implementing complex algorithms
————	————	————	Working with hardware
————	————	————	Optimizing programs for size and/or speed
————	————	————	Applying new technologies
————	————	————	Writing test plans
————	————	————	————————————
————	————	————	————————————
————	————	————	————————————
————	————	————	————————————
————	————	————	————————————
————	————	————	————————————

competency framework developed in Chapter 6. Consider obtaining additional education in these areas.

ADVICE TO MANAGERS

You have two talents to manage: the collective talents of your team and your own individual talents.

> Use knowledge of developer talents to help create a balanced team.
>
> Increase understanding of your managerial talents.
>
> Support changes in preferences.

Use knowledge of developer talents to help create a balanced team.   Determining the talents of your team (see above—and keep the results confidential) can provide direct benefit in two ways. First, it will assist you in assigning tasks. You could, for example, assign tasks to the most capable developer. Alternatively, you can direct assignments to develop or improve desired skills. Second, you can identify weak areas in the team and provide training where appropriate.

Increase understanding of your managerial talents.   While beyond the scope of this book, an understanding of your managerial talents—your strengths and weaknesses—will help you become a more effective manager. For more information on this topic, see *Becoming a Master Manager* by Robert Quinn [1988].

Support changes in preferences. It is tempting to keep a developer who is good at one thing doing the same thing for a very long period of time. In the long run, this is counterproductive. Keeping a developer in the same job for too long encourages overspecialization and prevents other developers from learning the skills associated with that job.

While many of us have an intuitive "feel" for what we are good at, this feeling is almost always based on what we "like" to do. When this feeling is correct, it can be a wonderful experience for everyone involved: The individual and the team benefit. I once had an employee whose high tolerance for stress made him perfect for the team leader position over the production support team. I was especially fortunate because this individual liked this position and was interested in improving his skills as a maintenance programmer. Similarly, the best requirements I've ever read were produced by a woman who had several years experience in writing requirements. They were exceptionally clear and straightforward. Unfortunately, she was no longer interested in writing requirements and wished to move onto other tasks, a common managerial dilemma. I'd much rather have kept her writing requirements, but she had earned the right to explore other activities. To resolve the situation, I assigned her to a new project but retained her as a reviewer of the requirements written by other members of the team.

5

WORKING SMARTER

Previous chapters have focused primarily on the ways we think about problem solving and how these can be improved. This chapter takes a different approach. Our effectiveness is not based solely on how we think or the size of our cognitive library. Sometimes, we need the structure of an automated testing tool to track down and find errors we just wouldn't think of otherwise. And, even the smartest and most capable person needs support staff to help them get their job done. Working "smarter" *means* using all the tools available in our environment to get the job done. This chapter discusses the use of such tools and how each can improve our performance.

Chapter Overview

Developers use many specialized tools to create software systems. Section 5.1 provides a conceptual foundation for understanding and using tools effectively. One particularly effective and simple tool for structuring our efforts in problem solving is a project notebook. Section 5.2 is devoted to explaining how to use it effectively. The primary goal of time management in software development is to create blocks of time for focused effort. Achieving this objective is the focus of Section 5.3. This chapter concludes with a discussion on working with support staff in Section 5.4.

5.1 USE TOOLS WISELY

Anthropologists have long argued what separates man from other creatures is our ability to make tools. In a sense, the essence of what it means to be a human lies here. Yet, just because a tool exists does not mean it will solve the problem for us!

We must learn which tool to use for what problem and how to use that tool effectively. Given the wide range of available tools, ranging from simple paper and pencil to sophisticated Integrated Development Environments, selecting the right tool can be a problem in and of itself!

There is no "tool-independent" way to solve a problem, for all tools provide some form of structure. What is of critical importance is the appropriateness of this structure relative to the problem we face.

5.1.1 What Is a Tool?

A *tool* is a device that extends our abilities. Some tools extend our physical abilities. A sewing machine stitches fabric more precisely, with greater speed, and with more regularity than sewing by hand. Antilock brakes not only stop our car; they also prevent us from skidding out of control by automatically adjusting the amount of force applied to the brake pads. A crane enables us to lift heavy objects, and so forth.

As developers, we need different kinds of tools. We need tools that can extend our *mental* abilities. A metric tool can analyze far greater volumes of code faster and with more accuracy than reviewing the same volume of code by hand. A configuration management tool helps manage the ripple effects of changing a component. An Integrated Development Environment (IDE) supports our *mental* problem-solving processes by enabling us to work with a minimum of disruptions. The following list presents a categorization of tools.

- ◆ *Productivity* tools enhance our productivity by helping us accomplish a tedious task faster and/or with less effort.
- ◆ *Educational* tools assist us in learning new skills (e.g., multimedia computer-based training).
- ◆ *Modeling* tools assist us in generating models of the problem and/or our solution.
- ◆ *Planning* tools assist us in generating, evaluating, and monitoring plans.
- ◆ *Coordination* tools assist us in working effectively with ourselves and others by mediating interactions.
- ◆ *Visualization* tools help us visualize the problem by simulating one or more components.

A single tool can be viewed under multiple categories depending on how it is used. A drawing tool such as Visio® is a modeling tool if we use it to generate models, a planning tool if we use it to generate a timeline, and a visualization tool if we use it to assist in creating a user interface prototype. In general, we think of a tool being focused on a specific task because it provides more explicit structure for the processes and outcomes associated with that task. Thus, Microsoft Project is a more effective project management tool than Visio® because it is highly specialized to generate, evaluate, and monitor project plans.

5.1.2 Impact of Tools in the SPO Framework

In the SPO framework, structure defines the form and content of outcomes and orders the processes necessary to achieve those outcomes. The impact of a tool in the SPO framework lies in the interaction between processes and outcomes. When using the right tool, the creation of outcomes is easier precisely *because* the tool provides structural support for the processes necessary to achieve those outcomes. For example, using a good data modeling tool will enable me to generate a data model faster, with greater ease and with more precision than using paper and pencil. Why? Two reasons come to mind (there are probably more). First, a tool makes changing the model easier once it has been created. Second, a tool provides direct support for the notation used in the model.

In all cases use of a tool significantly changes the process. Consider the effects of a really easy-to-use modeling tool on process. An easy-to-use tool is enjoyable, so much so I am likely to look forward to using the tool to generate models. An easy-to-use tool makes changing the model easy. Thus, I'm likely to generate more alternatives if I perceive the cost of making changes is low. And, I'm delighted when the tool provides support for managing alternatives! Table 5–1 describes the impact of tools in the SPO framework.

5.1.3 Limitations and Dangers of Tools

Outcomes generated through the use of a tool are not guaranteed to be correct. A tool doesn't even mean the process will be any easier—tools based on poor structures impose elaborate and wasteful processes on our work, making them difficult (if not impossible) to use! Tools are not panaceas. The following list presents some limitations and dangers associated with tools.

♦ *Cost.* Acquiring the tool, learning how to use the tool, and learning how to apply the tool all require investments in time and money.

♦ *Limitations and/or deficiencies.* All tools have inherent limitations that must be accounted for by the skill and know-how of the user.

♦ *Expectations.* In general, tools cannot be easily molded to our purpose. The maker of a tool creates the tool with a certain philosophy or expectation of how the tool is to be used. This expectation imposes a set of restraints which limit our ability to use the tool in novel ways.

♦ *Power.* Tools with great power for good can also provide great potential for harm if not properly managed. VisualWorks, the Smalltalk implementation from ParcPlace-Digitalk is a great example. In VisualWorks, a developer can redefine virtually any aspect of the system—from the compiler to the memory manager! Unless such modifications are undertaken with extreme care the entire system is likely to come to a crashing halt.

♦ *Management.* Losing the centralized repository of source code managed by a configuration management system would have serious repercussions among a team of developers. Management, in this sense, is not a limitation or a danger, but a responsibility.

♦ *Dependency.* As we become familiar with our tools, we come to depend on them and become less capable of working without them.

5.1.4 Tools for Software Development

There are two ways to characterize the tools we use in software development. *Essential* tools are required to support your task. If you are programming in C++, an essential tool is a C++ compiler. *Supplemental* tools expand our abilities but are not necessarily required for the task. Thus, a static code analyzer is a *supplemental* tool for C++ development. It makes our job easier, but we can get along without it.

We tend to focus on only the essential tools. This is unfortunate, because focusing only on essential tools unnecessarily limits your abilities as a developer. You should approach tools for software development like a carpenter, who has several

TABLE 5–1   Tools and the SPO Framework

Type	Impact	Examples
Productivity	Shortens the time needed to generate outcomes. Assists in creating more complete and/or correct outcomes.	Testing tools can automatically perform regression tests after changes have been made to the system. Source code analyzers can examine large amounts of code for questionable coding practices.
Educational	Increases understanding of structure defined processes and outcomes. Improves our ability to engage in process.	On-line help systems assist in acquiring tool-specific knowledge. Tutorials help us learn the best way to engage in a process to achieve an outcome.
Modeling	Supports more efficient and complete processes, primarily by increasing our knowledge of the problem domain.	CASE tools providing assistance in generating and/or evaluation data models.
Planning	Helps create outcomes by managing the sequence(s) of processes producing the outcomes.	Time management systems.
Coordination	Supports processes and outcomes by coordinating current processes with previously produced outcomes.	Configuration management tools coordinate the interactions among developers for software components.
Visualization	Supports feedback loop from outcome to process.	Animation tools provide understanding of our problem and/or our solution by providing visualizations of complex phenomena.

TABLE 5–2   Tools for the Developer

Tool	Motivation for Use
Customizable Editors	While most development systems provide an editor, it is often not customizable to the individual preferences of a developer. A good editor can make programming a much more enjoyable experience.
Source Code Control System	While normally thought of in conjunction with team development, a source code control system is equally important for the individual developer.
Reference Materials	The ever-increasing complexity of programming languages and software development environments requires that developers have several reference books in a shared library available for consultation.
Pretty Printers	The default printed output associated with most programming environments is quite poor. Specialized printing programs are needed to produce source code listings in formats suitable for developers.
Static and Dynamic Analysis Tools	Ensuring a language is used properly or tracking down a memory leak are tough tasks. Static and dynamic analysis tools can provide tremendous value. Another kind of analysis tool is a coverage tool that assists in systems testing by ensuring all lines of code in the system have been tested. Fortunately, the most commonly used languages have numerous static and dynamic tools that perform a wide range of valuable services
Whiteboards	Developers are constantly drawing diagrams and exploring concepts. This process usually requires a lot of real estate, the ability to make quick and easy changes, and the ability to share work with other developers. Whiteboards meet all three constraints elegantly. Electronic or printing whiteboards further enhance all these characteristics.

kinds of hammers, as opposed to a handyman, who may have just one. To assist you, Table 5–2 lists several different kinds of tools and provides motivation for their use.

ADVICE TO DEVELOPERS

Using tools effectively is not always simple. Many development tools are surprisingly—and some might say frighteningly—complex. However, the following guidelines will help make certain you are always making the most effective use of your tools.

> Paper and pencil are often best.
> Make tool dependencies explicit.
> Use simple tools and simple configurations of complex tools.
> Avoid tools failing to meet your needs.
> Develop tool-specific knowledge.
> Share tool-specific knowledge.
> Tell your manager what tools you need.
> Change tool generated source code *carefully.*

Paper and pencil are often best.   Many developers avoid using paper and pencil for problem solving and instead try to always do their work using some computer-based tool. This approach does have its merits: The process of change is made easier once you've created the initial outcome, and you can save and restore your work.

Yet, this approach has its drawbacks, and these drawbacks are significant. Even the best tool is no match for paper and pencil (or a whiteboard when working with a team) when you are in the initial stages of solving a complex problem, for any more sophisticated of a tool will constrain your thoughts to the structure provided by the tool. Paper and pencil, on the other hand, provide minimal constraints (by providing minimal structure). This, in turn, gives you the mental freedom necessary for the exploration of alternative solutions. Once you are *reasonably* certain of your outcomes, transfer them as appropriate to a more sophisticated tool.

Make tool dependencies explicit.   Are you relying on specific features of the implementation technology (language/machine)? For example, are you using a nonportable extension of your compiler? If you are, make certain you make these dependencies explicit.

Use simple tools and simple configurations of complex tools. Choose the simplest tool available that enables you to accomplish your task, and use simple configurations of complex tools [Wirth 1971]. Why? Good tools can be seductive. Instead of focusing on the problem, you focus on the tool. You begin to explore the capabilities of the tool, becoming more concerned with the tool than the task you are trying to accomplish. The moment this occurs, you are focused on the wrong thing.

I don't mean to imply that you should completely avoid all advanced features of a tool. It is often appropriate to pick an advanced tool *because* the structure it provides enables (or forces) you to examine your problem from a different perspective. The key point here is that you should not use the tool for the sake of the tool. Instead, use the tool to focus on the problem from the structural perspective provided by the tool.

The tools I used in writing this book illustrate this concept quite well. Although I had been thinking about this book for quite some time, I didn't take the first step until I purchased a project notebook (described later in this chapter). As I reviewed the books and articles I have saved over the years, I started to make notes in my notebook using paper and pencil. These notes included several alternative outlines for the book.

When I started writing, I didn't begin by using a powerful word processing package. Instead, I used Microsoft Write for about two months, generating potential outlines and about 50 pages of text. Write was an excellent choice. I didn't care about spelling, it was simple and easy to use, and I could easily transport all my text on one disk. I switched to Microsoft Word when I wanted to incorporate graphical examples, use a thesaurus, spell check, and standardize formatting.

The first investment I made in the conversion was to read the sections of the Word manual explaining how to manage long documents and how to format text under different styles. I also learned that by creating a standard document template, all my documents could share the same visual appearance. In a similar manner, most of the figures in this document were generated using the relatively simple line graphics program included in Word. When a figure became too complex for Word, I drew it in Visio. By choosing the simplest tool possible at every step of the way, I was able to maintain my focus on the outcome.

Avoid tools failing to meet your needs.   Beware of tools promising, but failing, to meet your needs. The only way to get past marketing hype is to try the tool in *your* environment, making certain it meets your needs. If it doesn't, *don't use it.*

There is a need for balance in selecting your tool. For example, I've been disappointed with the modeling tools I've used in the past. Quite often they are overstructured and impose too many restrictions on processes (e.g., the tool requires a diagram to be drawn in a specific order). Too much structure kills mental processes. Moreover, most modeling tools fail to support local customizations to method notation. These customizations are not necessarily personal preference. At times, they are absolutely required to address method-defined inconsistencies. Thus, for most of my modeling work, I stick with Visio, a simple but powerful diagramming tool adequate for most of my needs.

By using Visio, I gain flexibility. But what do I *lose?* First, I lose the automated support for a data dictionary provided by dedicated modeling tools. Second, modeling tools provide support for automatically generating source code, database tables, and so forth directly from the model. Third, such tools provide consistency in the models, facilitating the sharing of models between developers. In general, the larger the team, the greater the need for an automated tool.

Develop tool-specific knowledge.   Learning to use your tool effectively is a wise investment. You will avoid unnecessary rework and wasted process. It is especially important to briefly explore significant new features accompanying a new product release, for they may quickly and easily solve sticky problems for you.

Share tool-specific knowledge.   In general, teams of developers share the same set of tools. As you increase your knowledge of a tool, share this knowledge with others. You may have uncovered some feature providing direct benefit to a problem they face.

Tell your manager what tools you need.   Your manager cannot possibly keep current on the plethora of available tools. You must keep him/her informed of your needs. However, just asking for a tool does not mean you will get it. To really get the attention of your manager, show them how acquiring the tool will benefit the bottom line. In other words, justify the acquisition in economic terms.

A developer called me on the phone not too long ago to tell me how he had convinced his management to purchase a faster computer by clearly stating his request and justi-

fying it in economic terms. He did this by comparing compilation times on his current machine with his requested machine, calculating the "cost" of each compile in terms of his salary, and establishing the break-even point based on the capitalization of the desired machine. It was one of the most gratifying phone calls I have ever received, because he said: "I didn't see the value of your insistence of clear writing and economic justifications when I was working for you, but I'm sure glad I gave it a try."

Change tool generated source code *carefully*.   Many tools generate some portion of source code for you automatically. Avoid directly changing this source directly, as most tools are not effective at detecting your changes. Thus, you will lose them if someone else regenerates the source.

ADVICE TO MANAGERS

You have two responsibilities with respect to tools for your staff. First, you must provide them with a good suite of essential and supplemental tools. Second, you must monitor their use to ensure they are used effectively.

> Provide good tools.
> Upgrade tools.
> Avoid the tool pit.

Provide good tools.   How many of the tools described in Table 5–2 are readily available for your staff? Providing good tools is especially important if your team is inexperienced, because they need more structure to support their problem-solving processes. If you are uncertain what tools are appropriate for the team or the project, consider asking more experienced developers and/or managers from other teams for their opinion. Alteratively, you could hire a consultant to help you make good tool selections.

If you need any more motivation on the use of tools, here is the most important: Good tools can significantly improve the quality of the software shipped to your customers. One group I managed developing PC programs in C didn't have any static or dynamic analysis tools. When I learned of this, I immediately authorized the purchase of a static code analyzer and a dynamic memory profiler. Combined, these tools found more than a dozen previously unknown defects the first time they were used!

Upgrade tools.   Developer tools are continually increasing in capabilities. Unfortunately, many managers delay the purchase of new versions of such tools far too long. Quite often this is a budgetary oversight: You simply forget to plan for upgrades. Don't let this happen to you. Always budget some money for upgrading tools.

An uncontrolled upgrade process can negatively impact performance. Maintain control of the process by first purchasing the new version of the tool and then assigning one or two developers to explore its use. Have them prepare a concise impact analysis addressing three areas:

1. problems with the current tool corrected by the new tool
2. problems in the new tool and known workarounds
3. the recommended process to use when converting existing work to the new tool

You may want to enlist the aid of the tool vendor in preparing this report.

Avoid the tool pit.   The right tool can result in substantial productivity increases. For example, consider two developers building a set of relational databases. One is using a CASE tool that converts entity-relationship diagrams directly to an appropriate relational database schema. The other is drawing and translating diagrams by hand. Which developer will be more productive in generating the desired schemas quickly, consistently, and with a minimum of rework? The answer is obvious: the developer with the better tool!

But what happens if the right tool doesn't exist? What if the first developer is trying to translate the entity-relationship diagrams into a relational database not supported by the tool? Should they skip use of the tool entirely? Or, should they use the tool for diagramming and then convert the resultant models to hand?

All tools provide a structure for engaging in work. When the tool provides the right structure our productivity is high. When the tool provides an inappropriate structure our productivity is low, and in the case of a really terrible tool, our productivity can actually decrease when compared with not using the tool at all. I think of this situation as *the tool pit* (see Figure 5–1).

The tool pit contributes to an unfortunate approach in selecting tools: *Either* I have the high-productivity tool providing the structure exactly meeting my needs *or* I am forced to abandon a tool entirely or (at best) choose the lowest common denominator.

The tool pit is a dreadful thing. It forces us to look for perfection when perfection doesn't exist. No matter how rapidly tools increase in their ability to solve problems in your domain, they will always be imperfect. To manage the tool pit, throw away the *either-or* approach and instead use an *integrative* approach. Instead of looking for the perfect tool with the perfect structure solving all your needs, look for many tools that can help you solve part of your needs as shown in Figure 5–2. These combinations of tools help form a bridge from the low- to the high-productivity side of the tool pit.

Low Productivity
(i.e., Poor Structure)

High Productivity
(i.e., Optimal Structure)

Figure 5–1   The Tool Pit

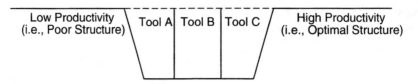

Figure 5–2   Bridging from Low to High Productivity

Consider the developer using the CASE tool described above. Instead of avoiding the use of the CASE tool entirely, the second developer should use the CASE tool to draw the diagrams even if they must subsequently translate these diagrams by hand.

5.2 USE A PROJECT NOTEBOOK

Most of us take some notes when solving a problem, and for good reason. First, the act of writing what you know about a problem helps clarify your understanding. Second, notes help provide a structure that help you explore the problem space. By writing our thoughts down, we can selectively concentrate on different aspects of the problem, secure in our knowledge we won't forget something important. Finally, notes provide a structure that makes it easier to compare two or more alternatives.

There is empirical evidence supporting the use of notes. Adelson and Soloway [1985] found that expert designers write down aspects of their mental processes *and* refer to these notes at appropriate times during problem solving. Especially important were notes taken to "remind" the expert of potential problems with a proposed solution (e.g., constraints and invariants of the problem domain). The same study found that designers working in unfamiliar problem domains took fewer notes, presumably because they didn't know where the potential trouble spots existed.

Unfortunately, like the novice designers in the study described above, we don't always make effective use of notes. We misplace them, forget to review them, or even worse, throw them away when we think we are finished. This tendency to throw out notes is especially damaging when you consider that notes are one of the easiest mechanisms we have to grow our cognitive libraries. By reviewing our notes, we can remember what worked and avoid what didn't. Our notes also contain our false starts and potential solutions rejected for one reason or another. Unless we save our notes, others are likely to waste time retracing our steps during maintenance or other system enhancement activities. The remainder of this section shows how to improve performance by taking notes in a structured manner.

5.2.1 What Is a Project Notebook? What Should It Contain?

A *project notebook* (or *journal*) is your repository of notes, thoughts, ideas, and sketches regarding one or more projects. It is a tool to help you in the messy process of solving a problem by providing a place to record all of the things you think about during the life of the project. It supports the exploration of alternative designs and can help you when you have to backtrack to a prior solution. It is like a portable, historical whiteboard. It can be shared (via photocopying) or given away (by ripping out pages).

Of course, a project notebook doesn't have to be paper. It could instead be a portable computer or a Personal Digital Assistant (PDA). On one assignment, I used a portable computer, carrying it with me everywhere. It was extremely effective for taking notes, and I loved being able to instantly search the notes of prior meetings. It was not nearly as effective for drawing. In the long run, going digital was a good choice.

5.2.2 How to Use a Project Notebook

My description of a project notebook thus far does not yet constitute an effective structure for managing notes. Why? Recall from Chapter 1 a structure also prescribes a preferred process. This section details the processes you should follow to make most effective use of your notebook.

♦ *Keep it with you at all times.*

The structure for taking notes provided by your notebook isn't very helpful if you are in one room and your notebook is in another.

♦ *Use it.*

The most fundamental process associated with a project notebook is putting as much information into it as you possibly can. The more information it contains, the more effective it becomes. Anything goes: an outline for a technical report; a list of tasks that will form a project schedule; sketches of preliminary object models or user interfaces; internet sites containing useful source code, and so forth.

♦ *Review it.*

Periodically review your notebook to make certain questions have been answered, issues have been addressed, and good ideas capitalized upon. You may have to work on this until reviewing your notebook becomes a habit. You should also consider having a colleague review it for breakthroughs or patentable ideas, for your notebook is a legal document that can be witnessed.

♦ *Keep accurate dates.*

The only precise piece of information required in a notebook is the date information was added. This is important for two reasons. First, it meets legal requirements should the notebook be used as evidence. Second, it facilitates learning by helping you reflect on where you have been and *how long* it has taken to get to where you are now.

♦ *Save it.*

Save your notebook in a safe place when finished with the project or when it becomes full, for it represents a long-term, valuable resource. How can saved notebooks be used? When asked about design decisions, you can refer to your notebook for the answer. When a new project is started to enhance the current system, you can refer to your notebook for all of the wonderful ideas you explicitly deferred "until the next time."

Using a notebook effectively requires a certain amount of discipline, but you will find you quickly develop your own "notebook style." For example, when I was in school I took notes on unlined paper to help me draw diagrams; a colleague prefers the use of graph paper for exactly the same reason. At the present time I use a spiral bound notebook. I also keep a small stapler and scotch tape dispenser in my briefcase. This way, if I jot something down on a piece of paper (such as the notepad on my car dashboard), I can easily transfer it to my notebook.

I write notes to myself in the margins to help me keep track of what needs to reviewed, tasks assigned to me and tasks assigned to others, and tasks remaining to be finished before I can move on to a different problem. As issues are addressed and tasks completed, I cross them off, making any additional notes as needed. I like to review my notebook every few weeks, which helps ensure I am spending my time on the right problem and allows me to track progress against long-term objectives.

Since many of us work on more than one project at the same time, the question naturally arises as to how many notebooks should be kept: one for each project, or one for all projects? I've tried both and prefer the following arrangement. If I'm working on several projects at the same time, each of which has a slightly smaller duration, then I use one notebook. If I am working on one large project, then I use one notebook for that project and one for everything else. While working on this book, for example, I kept two notebooks: one for the book and one for work-related projects. And yes, this means I do sometimes carry two notebooks to a meeting.

ADVICE TO DEVELOPERS

If you don't already use a project notebook, the advice is simple: Get one. Use it. It may feel a bit uncomfortable at first, but stick with it. Once you have become comfortable with the basics, consider the following.

> Reflect on your use of the notebook.
> Try multiple folders instead of a notebook.
> Use an on-line mini-notebook during implementation.

Reflect on your use of the notebook.   First, consider structure. Would a different style or kind of notebook work better for your current project (see next item)? Would a loose-leaf notebook, where pages can be inserted in random order, be more effective? Second, consider process. Are you reviewing your notebook on a regular basis? Is it always available?

Try multiple folders instead of a notebook.   Robert Glass, in an early review of this book, noted there are other approaches to the use of a project notebook and provided this alternative: "I choose to use multiple folders, one per topic, as repositories. This has the advantage that clippings, etc., can be inserted unchanged, and means there is never a need to 'rip out pages.' Of course, you can't take such folders to meetings, but you can take notes [in the meeting] for later insertion into one (or more) folders."

Use an on-line mininotebook during implementation.   During the implementation phase of a project, I keep a special on-line mini-notebook for all of the little details arising during programming in a simple text file. As issues are addressed, I either delete them (if truly minor) or add the decision to the notebook. This approach has two distinct advantages. First, it doesn't slow you down. The moment you think of something not directly related to the source code you have a place where it can be easily recorded. You can address it later. Second, such notes are easily distributed to other developers via e-mail.

ADVICE TO MANAGERS

If your team doesn't already use project notebooks,

> Make notebooks available to your team.
> Use a project notebook, or its equivalent, yourself.
> Establish ownership of the notebook.

Make notebooks available to your team.   Purchase several notebooks and store them in your supply cabinet. Schedule a special meeting and review the information provided in the beginning of this section. Specifically, describe the advantages of a project notebook and let your staff know there is a readily available supply of notebooks in the supply cabinet. *Don't hand them out.* This will make a project notebook seem like a management fad. Each developer must make his own decision on the use of the notebook. Your goal is to motivate, not dictate.

Use a project notebook, or its equivalent, yourself.   Leading by example is the best way to convince others of your thoughts regarding project notebooks.

Establish ownership of the notebook.   Notebooks are absolutely essential if you expect to obtain intellectual property value from the work performed by your staff. It is therefore critical that your staff understand the company owns the contents of the notebook. There are numerous advantages to company ownership of the material. Having project notebooks can help protect copyright and patent rights, can assist other developers in understanding how a system was implemented, and can establish an "idea warehouse" that can be mined for future applications. Be certain you consult with your legal department on the exact policy that should be adopted.

5.3 MANAGING TIME

Software development requires a significant amount of time spent *concentrating intently* on the desired outcome. Ideally, you concentrate so intently the rest of the world seems to fade away. You even lose your sense of time. This mental state is referred to as *flow*. When you are "in" a state of flow, you are completely focused on the problem.

Unfortunately, achieving flow is not necessarily easy: It can't simply be "turned on." Instead, we must "ramp up" our concentration on a given problem. This takes about 15 minutes of uninterrupted time. In addition, an individual in a state of flow is in a rather fragile state for even the smallest interruption can break his concentration. They must then begin the process of attaining flow all over, another 15 minute process [DeMarco 1987].

There are two main objectives in effective time management for software development. The first is to create large blocks of time, roughly two hours in length, where you have the opportunity to create a state of "flow." The second is to learn how we really spend our time when creating software, so that we can learn how to improve our personal process. As Boehm so aptly stated, "The main [opportunity for improving individual productivity] comes when each of us as individual programmers becomes aware of where his time is really going . . ." [Boehm 1973].

The remainder of this section details the structures, processes, and outcomes associated with effective time management.

5.3.1 Structures, Processes, and Outcomes for Time Management

The basic structures, processes, and outcomes of an effective time management system are surprisingly simple and readily available. If you are already using a time management system (e.g., the Franklin Day Planner™, Day-Timer™, or equivalent), you may want to skip this next section and proceed immediately to the practical advice.

♦ *Structures*
   The basic structures are a calendar for recording appointments and a notebook for organizing and prioritizing tasks. Many developers use their project notebooks in combination with a small calendar. Others purchase a more formal time management system such as the Franklin Day Planner. Keep your calendar with you at all times so you can always be certain of your availability for

an appointment. Most importantly, use a *single* calendar. When everything is in one place, you know where to find it, you will avoid scheduling conflicts, and it is less likely something will slip through the cracks.

♦ *Processes*

There are two main processes involved with effective time management. The first is task review and prioritization. This involves listing all tasks that need to be accomplished in a given day and reviewing these tasks in the morning (or at night before you sleep). Next, order the tasks so the most important tasks are completed first. This should take only about 10 to 15 minutes each day. Any longer than that means you are spending too much time on planning! The second is ongoing task management. As you complete tasks, place a check mark next to each task, recording additional information as appropriate in your notebook. Be certain your process includes reviewing the tasks of previous days to ensure important tasks have been completed.

♦ *Outcomes*

The most easily identified outcome is a series of completed task lists and notes concerning these tasks. A less easily identified, but no less important, outcome is the enhanced feeling of satisfaction from improved performance in your personal and professional life.

ADVICE TO DEVELOPERS

Developers are typically given a large amount of personal discretion concerning time management. Learning to use this flexibility wisely is the primary focus of this section.

> Waste less time playing games and save Internet surfing 'til after work.
>
> Be consistent.
>
> Create blocks of time for "flow."
>
> Beware of fading.
>
> Dismiss unnecessary interruptions as quickly as possible.
>
> Post a sign.

Waste less time playing games and save Internet surfing 'til after work.   The single most important question you can ask yourself before engaging in *any* activity is this: How will this activity help me achieve the goals of the project? If you can't answer this question don't engage in the activity.

Be consistent.   Establishing a consistent daily review is the most important *process* of time management. Without this consistency it is impossible to achieve effective time management.

Create blocks of time for "flow."   While you can't "force" yourself to achieve a state of flow, you can increase your opportunities for achieving it by scheduling uninterrupted blocks of time throughout the day. In general, a person can handle a state of flow for approximately two to three hours, so aim for this in your scheduling. One extremely effective way of doing this is to schedule yourself for an appointment—with yourself!

> *I find I have three or four blocks of time throughout the day when I am maximally productive. Early in my skating career I started training at 6:30 A.M., which required getting out of bed at 5:30 A.M. After several years of training I became accustomed to getting up early and now, I usually get up around 5:00 A.M. Thus, my first block of "flow" time is in the early morning, between 5:30 and 8:00 A.M. Between 8:00 A.M. and 9:30 A.M., I like to read mail, catch up on important conversations, and otherwise prepare for the day. I've tried working intensely in this time frame, but it is difficult and potentially antisocial. The next big block of time begins around 9:30 A.M. and lasts until lunch, when the office settles down and everyone seems to be a bit more intense. After lunch, I like to handle phone calls, e-mail, and other administrivia. Depending on my afternoon schedule, I can usually find one or two more additional blocks of time.*

Beware of fading.   You may find your use of a time management system "fades" a bit after you have become comfortable with its structures and processes. Unfortunately, fading means following a less effective process. Grab your calendar and make an appointment with yourself one year from now and reread the advice presented in this section.

Dismiss unnecessary interruptions as quickly as possible.   A time management system is an effective tool for planning, but your calendar won't prevent unnecessary interruptions. How can you quickly dismiss them? When someone disrupts you, don't engage in idle chatter. This will only encourage more interruptions in the future. Instead, ask them a pointed question such as "How can I help you?" or "What can I do for you?" This question transfers "ownership" of the conversation to the interrupting party, in effect asking him/her to justify the intrusion—and preventing him/her from wasting your valuable time. Similarly, be considerate of other developers, and find ways to minimize your distractions on their time. For example, ask questions via e-mail rather than barging into their office or cubicle.

Post a sign.   If you are really busy or working on an especially difficult project, post a sign announcing this to your fellow teammates. Here is a sample.

Please Do Not Disturb

I am working on the final product release for XYZ. I will be available to handle interruptions, meetings, etc., at 11:30 A.M.

ADVICE TO MANAGERS

Working to instill proper time management is not difficult. It is something you can easily encourage in your staff through a few simple actions.

Provide time management structures.

Go on-line.

Use structure to facilitate the creation of "chunks" of time.

Minimize morning meetings.

Watch for chronic overtime.

Provide time management structures.   Provide your staff with time management structures (e.g., calendars, a Franklin Day Planner, etc.) and associated training. These tools are not expensive and will more than pay for themselves.

Go on-line.   If developers use different time management systems, scheduling meetings easily and consistently can be problematic. Fix this problem by going on-line with one of the many readily available calendar/appointment scheduling systems. Doing so will provide a consistent mechanism for scheduling meetings, as well as a repository for recording when a developer will be in or out of the office. It will help minimize interruptions between team members asking for meeting availability.

Use structure to facilitate the creation of "chunks" of time.   Limit meetings among developers to no more than two hours. For example, you could require code inspections to begin at 10:00 A.M. or 3:30 A.M.

Minimize morning meetings.   The morning is often the most productive development time. People are fresh and ready to start their day. Minimizing morning meetings should help the team find opportunities for flow when they are most prepared for development activities requiring intense concentration.

Watch for chronic overtime.   There are several reasons why a developer may be working overtime, most of them bad. You may have simply assigned too much work. Or, a well-intentioned developer may simply have agreed to take too many tasks. Even worse, a developer may be hiding a serious deficiency. They may *seem* able to get the job done, but only because they are putting in an extraordinary amount of effort. Compared to a normal developer, they could be quite unproductive. No matter what, watch for chronic overtime on your staff. In the long run, it is terribly unproductive, sapping energy, excitement, and concentration from the project.

5.4 WORKING WITH SUPPORT STAFF

Even the smallest organizations employ support staff, people whose jobs are to help you to be more effective in your job. Learning to use them effectively can provide a noticeable improvement in your productivity. What can they do for you? It depends on who they are and the help you need. Network administrators can install software, configure printers, connect you to the Internet, and so forth. Secretaries can help schedule meetings, review documents, navigate the corporate bureaucracy, shield you from unwanted phone calls, and so forth. How do you make the most effective use of their services? By creating (and following) appropriate structures.

♦ *Identify your support staff.*

Just because they exist doesn't mean they are easy to find. The first step to using their services is identification. Create a small list of the groups and/or individuals who can help you. Try to think inside as well as outside the company. Creating this list before you start a major project can help, as it will provide a structure helping you find help. Of course, this approach is slightly paradoxical: How can you know what help you will need in the future? One technique is to apply future perfect thinking by imagining all the help you will have needed to complete the project. Because the contents of this list is likely to grow over time, you should consider keeping it on-line.

♦ *Make your request specific and put it in writing.*

A frantic plea for "help" is not likely to be successful. Like you, your support staff are busy people, and they don't have the time to interview you extensively in an effort to determine your requirements. Make your request specific. Be clear and concise and let them know the date when the task must be completed. Putting it in writing doesn't necessarily mean creating a lengthy, formal, internal memo! Attaching a simple and legible handwritten note is sufficient.

♦ *Watch lead times.*

Many support organizations define *lead times,* the amount of time they need to complete a task. I once worked for a company whose audiovisual department specified a lead time of three days. If your request was made three days or more before the completion date, they *never* failed to deliver. If your request was made with less than three days, they tried hard but there were no guarantees. Keep track of lead times associated with specific support staff.

♦ *Say "thank you."*

When they have completed your assignment, saying "thanks" will go quite a long way. If they have completed an especially difficult assignment, you may want to consider giving them a small token of your appreciation. I have found gift certificates to the movies or the local ice cream parlor are simple, but much appreciated, tokens of gratitude.

♦ *Treat them with respect.*

You may have more education than your support staff. You are likely to be paid more. And, they may appear to jump at your every request. None of this gives you the right to treat them in a rude or disrespectful manner, or to make their job difficult.

ADVICE TO DEVELOPERS

Working smarter doesn't mean doing all the work yourself. Use your support staff to magnify your productivity.

> Be aware of your background.
> Don't think you can *always* do a better job.
> Coordinate the use of your time.
> Use external organizations.

Be aware of your background.   Learning to use support staff effectively can be especially difficult if you have an extensive engineering background. Engineers have a tendency to micromanage tasks. Don't do it! Ask for help, and then let others do their job. Recent graduates also experience difficulty in learning to use support staff. When in school, we usually have to perform all aspects of a task—few students I know had support staff available for research, photocopying, and the like!

Don't think you can *always* do a better job.   One of the most consistent complaints I hear from managers is that their development staff wastes time doing tasks—such as replacing a hard drive or "fine-tuning" the network server—that are really the responsibility of another organization.

Coordinate the use of your time.   Do you need to upgrade your PC? If possible, time the installation request with the next time you won't need your PC for a long period of time. For example, you could wait for your next vacation or a business trip.

Use external organizations.   Be on the lookout for ways in which external organizations can provide support. Governmental organizations, such as libraries, the post office, and so forth, can be quite helpful *if you ask.*

On one project I helped a client design a direct marketing application linking a Geographic Information System (GIS) with address information. The U.S. Postal Service and the U.S. Census Bureau were invaluable resources. I was literally amazed at the number of helpful articles, brochures, and informative booklets that were available free for the asking. For example, the Census Bureau sent me "Maps & More: Your Guide to Census Bureau Geography," [Hatchl 1992] which explains the wide variety of geographic tools—maps, reports, computer tapes, and so forth—provided by the Census Bureau. This information not only helped me understand the problem domain more completely, it also helped my client make better decisions about how to position his product in the marketplace. More recently, I had to place a conference call from my home. The AT&T teleconference operator was cheerful, friendly, and made the overall task easy. The point is that there are a large number of organizations that can help you get your job done—provided you ask.

ADVICE TO MANAGERS

You want your staff creating applications, not photocopying requirements documents.

> Continually educate your developers on the use of support staff.
>
> Share your assistant with a developer.
>
> Set a good example.

Continually educate your developers on the use of support staff. When you witness a developer engaging in a task that should be performed by someone else, remind him/her of the appropriate support staff.

Share your assistant with a developer.   One novel approach to promoting the use of support staff is to "share" your administrative assistant with one developer each week. Encourage your assistant to "pester" the developer, continually asking the developer how they can help the developer be more effective. Over time they'll get the point. Of course you run the risk of never seeing your assistant again once they learn just how effective a good assistant is at magnifying your talents.

Set a good example.   Unfortunately, many managers are just as guilty as their developers when it comes to proper use of support staff. Do you follow your own advice? Do you continually tinker with your own machine, or do you let the network (and other) support organizations do their job?

6

TRAINING

The brief history of software development has been characterized by massive and enormous change. New technologies—software, programming languages, design techniques, and so forth—are introduced at an ever-increasing rate. But how can you learn of the existence of such things, let alone how to apply them accurately and effectively? One way is through training, the focus of this chapter.

Chapter Overview

Section 6.1 begins by providing a definition of training. Section 6.2 follows by showing how training impacts the SPO framework. But who is really responsible for *your* training? The short answer is you. The detailed answer is found in Section 6.3. Sections 6.4 through 6.6 work together to provide the structures necessary for taking control of your training. Section 6.4 and Section 6.5 discuss depth and breadth of knowledge. Section 6.6 focuses on individual learning style and delivery mechanisms.

6.1 WHAT IS TRAINING?

Mintzberg, a researcher in organizational behavior, defines training as "formal instruction to establish and standardize in people the requisite skills and knowledge to do a particular job in the organization" [Mintzberg 1992:161]. The Capability Maturity Model developed by the Software Engineering Institute provides essentially the same definition: "The purpose of the Training Program is to develop the skills and knowledge of individuals so they can perform their roles effectively and efficiently. Training is an organizational responsibility, but the software projects should identify their needed skills and provide the necessary training when the project's needs are unique." Some authors (e.g., [Pressman 1993]) go even further and provide precise estimates of the amount of time developers should spend in training programs. The two salient features of these definitions are as follows. First, training should be designed to provide the skills necessary to accomplish well-defined job-related tasks. Second, training is an organizational responsibility.

6.2 TRAINING IN THE SPO FRAMEWORK

Imagine that someone has just invented a powerful new object-oriented programming language (I'll call it *Vivid*) that you wish to learn. In terms of the SPO framework, you must learn three things. Structurally, you must learn the language and the tools used in the creation of Vivid programs. Procedurally, you must learn how to create a Vivid program—when and how these tools are used. The outcome associated with this training are the skills (e.g., plans) you have acquired for designing, developing, and maintaining Vivid programs. More specifically, can you create a well-constructed Vivid program? Can you distinguish between a "good" Vivid program and a poor one? Do you know when Vivid is a suitable choice of language given the constraints and context of your current problem?

Thinking of problem solving in terms of structures, processes, and outcomes motivates a different approach to training. Training in structure helps us learn the right processes to follow in creating outcomes as well as the specific outcomes themselves. This kind of training helps build the syntactic-semantic plans described in Chapter 1. It can happen quite rapidly, as when a developer learning Vivid has prior knowledge of a different object-oriented language. Knowledge associated with structure tends to be static in nature.

Training in the process of creating Vivid programs is experiential knowledge, best learned through the act of actually building Vivid-based systems. In other words, training in structure is like telling someone "Here are the things you do," while training in process is having the person *do* those things.

The most important outcome of training is the knowledge (e.g., plans) created during the course of the training. Specifically, the learner should have added appropriate plans to his/her cognitive library regarding the structures and processes associated with the creation of specific outcomes. After attending a Vivid class, the developer should understand the basic structure of Vivid programs and the process by which they are created. They should have also acquired the ability to create Vivid programs of varying complexity.

Does this imply structure should be taught first? Not necessarily. The best training begins with an overview of the kinds of problems that can be solved by what is being taught. Without an understanding of the limitations of past solutions, we can't really be certain the proposed new solution is better. This overview also helps prepare us for learning by creating a contextual structure for the new plans. The best way to learn Vivid is to first learn the kinds of problems Vivid has been designed to solve. This enables us to better place Vivid-plans within our cognitive libraries.

There is another way of thinking about the structures and processes associated with training. This perspective focuses not on the material to be learned (and the structures and processes associated with this material) but with the mechanism by which training is delivered. One kind of training structure is lecture-style instruction, which supports the process of delivering course material from an expert. An alternative training structure is a self-based tutorial, which supports a considerably different learning process. Choosing the right kind of training structure is based on many factors and is covered in greater detail later in this chapter.

6.3 SELF-LEARNING

The definitions of training provided earlier are consistent in their view that training is primarily (or solely) the responsibility of the organization. I disagree. Training is *at least* a shared responsibility. Yes, your company has a responsibility to provide *certain* kinds of training. But you must also take responsibility for your training. Why? Rather than answer this question directly, I'll answer it indirectly by posing (and answering) three different questions.

First, what if your organization has not completely defined the skills you need to accomplish your task? According to the training definitions provided above, you will become increasingly unproductive.

Second, what if you disagree with what the company thinks are "required skills"? You're out of luck, because they are only responsible for providing training in the skills *they* think are necessary. Convincing your manager to provide you with training in other skill areas you consider important can be next to impossible because of budgeting, scheduling, other training needs, and a host of other factors.

Third, what if the training provided by your organization does not match your personal goals? In other words, do *you* only want to learn advanced features of your current programming language? If you think about it, I'll bet there are probably a plethora of subjects you would like to know more about—from new programming languages to managing your investments to scuba diving. Learning can be especially fun when you control the content, and learning about new areas almost always has unexpected dividends.

> Some time ago I became friends with a wonderful gentleman who is a professional salesperson. This man's skill, dedication, motivation, and ethics impressed me so much I asked him to recommend a book on sales. He said one of the best was How to Master the Art of Selling by Tom Hopkins [1982]. I purchased the book to try to learn more about my friend and his job. Having read it, I now know a little about the art of being a salesman and I've gained a greater appreciation of what my friend does for a living. The best part of this learning has been the unexpected benefits it has produced in my

*career, such as the time I had to "sell" my manager on the need to make some modifica-
tions to a class I had created. Or when the sales department asked me to provide them
with a demonstration of a product I had helped develop. Rather than wondering what
they could possibly need from such a demonstration, or why they were bothering me, I
was able to use my knowledge of selling to show them ways in which they could demonstrate the value of the product to a prospective client more effectively.*

Do you plan to work with your current organization for the remainder of your career? If not, then you better take charge of your training. What are considered to be
necessary skills change between companies and even between groups within the
same company.

Perhaps the most critical motivation for taking charge of your learning is this:
Best practices in software development change rapidly. New algorithms and development techniques are constantly invented, even in languages that are well established. Failing to stay abreast of these techniques means failing to improve yourself
as a developer. Athletes are constantly on the prowl for improved training techniques. As a developer, you should remain similarly vigilant for improved development techniques.

*I value self-learning so highly that I interview for it. During the interviewing process, I
try to assess how the candidate handles his/her own learning. How you approach self-
learning is an expression of your values. Do you value your craft? Are you willing to
take charge? Sadly, the interview often goes something like this.*

Hohmann: What was the last book you read about software development?

Candidate: I can't remember. I think in college.

*Normally, this response does not bother me too much, because I know reading an entire
book is a fairly substantial investment in time. Cost is not a factor—most books on software development cost less than a nice dinner with your significant other.*

Hohmann: What computer-related magazines do you read?

Candidate: None.

*This is a very bad sign. If this person is not reading any computer-related magazines,
how is he/she staying current in his/her field?*

*Hohmann: When was the last time you made a conscious decision to improve your pro-
gramming habits? If within the last six months, describe this change in detail.*

Candidate: Let me think. I started to use const *instead of* #define *because of the
new coding standards.*[1]

---

[1] const is a C++ variable declaration marking a variable as read-only. A C++ compiler will generate an error if a developer attempts to modify the value of a const variable. In contrast, the #define
statement is a preprocessor directive often used to declare constants. Because const retains variable
type information, its use is preferred over #define.

This is close, but doesn't count, because their change was not motivated by any form of learning. Instead it was motivated by adherence to a standard. Adhering to a standard is good, but failing to understand the deeper issues motivating the standard is not.

Given this final answer, what would you do with this candidate? I hope you say "Dismiss him/her." They have demonstrated no motivation for self-learning in his/her chosen profession. Without a desire to increase his/her ability, how will he/she improve? Of course, I wish I could say I have always followed my own advice, but I haven't. Sometimes I have made exceptions for candidates who appeared to have the skills I needed. It has always been a mistake. While they may have been able to address an immediate need, they failed to continue to grow in their skills and remain a contributor over the long haul.

Finally, does it annoy you when an author begins to praise your intelligence for purchasing his/her book and "improving" your skill set? This practice used to really annoy me, because I thought it was not too subtle a ploy to encourage me to purchase more books, or to tell others to buy the author's book, or whatever. Now I think those other authors were correct. I am continually shocked at the number of programmers I meet who don't read any books or magazines on software development. So . . . congratulations on purchasing this book and improving your skills as a software professional! And sure, if you find it useful, recommend it to a friend.

6.4 A COMPETENCY FRAMEWORK FOR SELF-LEARNING

There is more to being a software professional than simply knowing the latest programming language. Expert developers are well-rounded individuals, possessing many diverse skills. They can communicate clearly and effectively. They can manage themselves (and others, when needed). They typically know one domain deeply, often through work, but remain interested in other aspects of life. They are strong, but balanced. Is there a way you can organize your self-learning so you can gain the needed technical competence while remaining balanced? There is.

A *competency framework* provides a structure to organize the variety of knowledge and skills we wish to acquire. Figure 6–1 presents a three-layered competency framework for organizing self-learning in a balanced manner. The innermost layer identifies a broad subject area. The middle layer identifies a specific topic of importance within the subject area. The outermost layer lists specific skill-based competencies within a topic. A *skill-based competency* is a specific identifiable behavior that can be assessed in terms of performance (i.e., there is a way to measure proficiency in exhibiting the skill).

The competency framework presented in Figure 6–1 is designed to be both minimal and extensible. It is a mistake to think you must have six sides with exactly three layers. Your personal framework may have five sides (or seven) with four layers (or two). For example, C++ could be further broken down into specific skills associated with C++, such as the correct use of exception handling or templates.

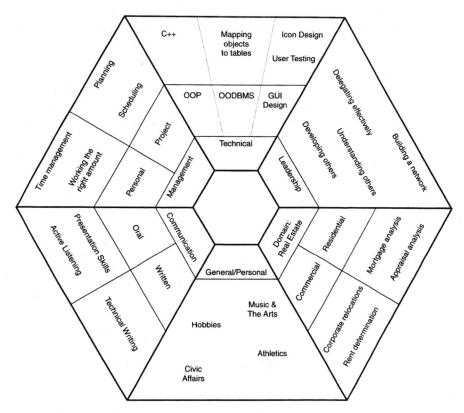

Figure 6–1   A Competency Framework

Initially, the skills layer is likely to be blank, as it is quite difficult to identify specific skills for a topic you know little about. As you begin to learn about a specific topic area, desired skills can be added to this layer. Figure 6–1 lists some skill-based competencies for selected topic areas. Examine the Domain sextant carefully: It will change based on your current problem domain. Figure 6–1 uses real estate as a representative domain.

The use of a competency framework as a structure provides several benefits. First, it helps keep us under "control." If you are like me, you want to learn everything about everything. Fortunately, my competency framework helps keep me focused on those skills most appropriate for my current job, company, and personal interests.

Second, it allows for the specification of multiple kinds of competency. For example, the *Technical* sextant is likely to contain more topics and skills than any other sextant. You are, after all, a software developer, and creating software-based systems is what we do.

Finally, and perhaps most importantly, it reminds us of the importance of symmetry. While the technical sextant is the most important, a successful developer possesses more than just technical skills. Management, leadership, and even our hobbies are all worthwhile interests.

Have you ever been to a bodybuilding competition? If you haven't, you should go. Rock and roll music pounds from speakers high overhead as powerful and quite serious athletes engage in a series of poses. It is pure energy. What allows one competitor to win? It isn't huge arms and skinny legs, or a broad back and slim forearms. It is symmetry, carefully forged to reach the maximum potential of the competitor. Because symmetry is so important to competitive bodybuilders, it is easy to spot them at the gym: They are obsessed with it. Yes, of course, they work to improve their "best part" (an important aspect of the competition), but they know simply having a single best part won't enable them to win. They need one best part and many very good ones. Competitive bodybuilders stand in stark contrast to individuals who lift weights without regard to symmetry. These people tend to avoid symmetry, because achieving symmetry is hard. They fall into the trap of working on the same muscle groups during each visit to the gym. The result? Big guns and chicken legs—strength in a particular area (usually the upper body) but a distinct overall lack of symmetry.

Unfortunately, many developers forget about symmetry when thinking about improving their skills. Instead, they work to improve only those areas of software development they are already good at. For example, let's assume you have a talent for testing systems. A common way to improve your skills would be to attend a software development conference and spend all your time on the presentations and workshops devoted to testing. Unfortunately, this is similar to making a strong muscle stronger.

A wiser investment would be to attend the conference but spend some time learning about other topics or subject areas. For example, attending a presentation on project management might give you ideas on how to best organize system testing to benefit other developers. Attending a workshop on data modeling might provide clues on how to create more effective test plans.

Learning in other areas of the framework can provide unexpected benefits. A class in accounting may introduce you to double-entry bookkeeping, a technique for automatically detecting and preventing common accounting mistakes. Could this idea be incorporated into your current project so errors could be more easily identified? How about a class providing further background on the problem domain? Such a class will help to ensure you are generating test plans mimicking the behavior of the system in a production environment. A class in technical writing may teach you how to organize test plans so other developers can understand them quickly. Of course, I'm not advocating stopping all learning associated with testing the system. As with a bodybuilder, it is desirable to have both one best part and overall symmetry.

6.5 BREADTH VERSUS DEPTH IN THE COMPETENCY FRAMEWORK

While the competency framework provides a structure for organizing an overall approach to training, it provides little guidance as to *how much* training is needed. It deals with breadth, not depth. To describe the depth of training (i.e., how much) requires a different structure. Rather than invent my own, I'll use the seven levels of competence defined by Meiler Page-Jones [1990]. I've taken the liberty of slightly modifying the descriptions associated with these terms. Their essential meaning, however, remains unchanged. (Quinn [1988] provides a competency framework for managers with a different characterization of depth.)

1. *Innocent.* You have not been exposed to a given area of knowledge and are unaware of its existence. In other words, you have absolutely no plans associated with the topic in your cognitive library.

2. *Aware.* You have been exposed to an area of knowledge (such as a new programming language), perhaps by reading an article, and can see its relevance but have not yet applied or used it. Your cognitive library may have one or two plans regarding the body of knowledge. These plans are at best rudimentary. You are still unable to use them for any useful purpose.

3. *Apprentice.* You have had some formal training in the structures, processes, and outcomes associated with an area of knowledge, perhaps through a five-day workshop. You have begun the task of creating and storing plans in your cognitive library. At this stage of learning, structures tend to be viewed as absolute, not to be violated. You can produce simple outcomes for well-defined problems but require the assistance of more expert individuals to solve ill-defined or new problems.

4. *Practioner.* You are able to accomplish moderately difficult tasks without assistance. Your cognitive library is fairly well developed, but you must still rely on experts to accomplish very complex tasks.

5. *Journeyman.* You regularly use the body of knowledge in your work and begin to question and/or modify structures to suit your needs. At this stage your cognitive library is reasonably large. You begin to apply existing plans in novel ways. Individuals at levels 2 through 4 seek your guidance.

6. *Master.* You have mastered the body of knowledge and can effectively apply it in many different situations. Your cognitive library is both large and sophisticated. It contains plans enabling you to solve well-known problems quickly and easily. You are adept at applying plans in novel ways. You can easily adapt or invent appropriate structures to aide in problem solving.

7. *Expert.* With substantial expertise, you move beyond the master stage by extending the collective body of knowledge through lectures, writing articles and/or books, or applying the knowledge in new problem domains. The difference between a master and an expert is subtle, but important. Both possess extensive cognitive libraries, but the expert works at externalizing their library in a form suitable for use by others.

There are two additional points concerning this list. First, a certain amount of time must pass before an individual is recognized as an expert or master. You can't "skip" a phase of development, and depending on your ability, experience, and environment, it may take a surprisingly short (or, more likely, a frustratingly long) amount of time to

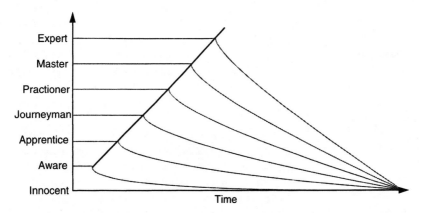

Figure 6–2   Learning and Forgetting

attain progressively higher levels of excellence. Second, a given level of proficiency can change if you pursue a different competency. In other words, we forget!

Both of these ideas are illustrated in Figure 6–2, which represents the attainment of increasing expertise linearly as a solid line and forgetting as a dashed line. In terms of the cognitive library presented in Chapter 1, it can take quite a while to create our library, and sometimes even longer to forget!

Please note Figure 6-2 is a *gross* simplification. Gaining higher levels of expertise is *not* linear. It is a step function. Learning happens in "chunks" as new plans are internalized. Second, it takes many *years* of hard work to gain increasing levels of expertise. Reaching the level of expert in any field takes at least eight to twelve years. Finally, as expertise increases, it takes longer to "forget" what we have learned. In fact, I'm not certain a master or expert can ever forget *everything* about a given body of knowledge. There are just too many plans in their cognitive library to forget them all.

6.6 LEARNING STYLE AND DELIVERY MECHANISMS

Learning style describes individual differences in how people learn a body of knowledge. Understanding your learning style can help you choose effective delivery mechanisms.

One kind of learning style is motivated from research in Human-Computer Interaction, which among other topics explores how people learn to use computer systems. In a classic study, Carroll and Carrithers [1984] identified two distinct modes of learning. The first, which they refer to as the *reckless explorer*, is an individual who "immediately begins to play with the system, frequently with only a superficial reading of the manual. This type of learner commits many errors and spends much of the time in error recovery, but sometimes stumbles on the correct solution."

In stark contrast to the reckless explorer stands the plodder. The *plodder* "will not try anything until certain of the results. This learner will sit and read the manual and stare at the screen trying to think things through." The plodder and reckless explorer do not represent different kinds of learning. Instead, they represent different extremes on the same continuum of learning style, much as the KAI measures the continuum of cognitive style. The good news is the study found both styles to be equally successful when learning a given system.

Most of us will find our own learning style to be somewhere in the middle, affected by the kind of task we are trying to accomplish. Given a task perceived to be simple or inexpensive, we probably find ourselves operating more like the reckless explorer. We may just jump right in and try to accomplish our task as best we can until we *need* to refer to some other body of knowledge. I know I often take this approach when trying to do things at my home, such as repairing chipped paint. I'm *far* from an expert "handyman," but I will try to compete simple tasks without much help.

Conversely, if the task is perceived to be expensive, we take the approach of the plodder. We read the manual until certain of how to accomplish the task, hoping to save time as well as completing the task more effectively. For example, if I am doing electrical work at home, I will take the approach of the plodder—risking electrical shock is far too "expensive" for my tastes!

All delivery mechanisms associated with training must ultimately stimulate one or more of our basic senses—our basic "input" ports, if you will. The applied psychology field of Neuro-Linguistic Programming (NLP) studies how stimulation of our senses affects our internal representation of reality, how we model reality, and how we communicate our models to others. While a full discussion of NLP is beyond the scope of this book, one specific aspect of NLP is relevant to this section. According to NLP, each of us is predisposed to learn most effectively through one of three distinct "input mechanisms": auditory, visual, and kinesthetic. Auditory people learn best by listening; visual through reading, and kinesthetic through "doing" (e.g., trying the method or technique).

As with the reckless explorer and plodder, it is a mistake to think of these classifications in an extreme manner. None of us learns in only a single way, and the most effective delivery mechanisms will provide a mixture of auditory, visual, and kinesthetic stimuli. For example, the core of a class on a given topic should consist of the hands-on exercises and assignments designed to impart the necessary knowledge to students in the given topic area. This represents kinesthetic learning, or learning by doing. To be most effective, exercises and the material supporting them need to be introduced by a lively and engaging instructor (auditory) who is supported by excellent overheads and other visual stimuli. Alternatively, a well-designed computer-based tutorial could provide appropriate stimuli. Ideally, the class would provide additional supporting material, such as a reference manual, to support the needs of both the reckless explorer and the plodder long after the class has finished.

I spend a great deal of my time in two classrooms. The first is the training rooms of ObjectSpace, where I teach a variety of classes in object technology. The second are the training rooms at numerous fitness clubs in the Dallas metroplex, where I teach a variety of aerobics classes. Differences in NLP are easily identified in an aerobics class. Some students appear disinterested in the class. These students aren't really looking at me or other students, but, amazingly enough, they follow the choreography flawlessly. Such students are auditory. They are able to follow the class simply by listening to my verbal cues. Visual students are just as easily identified. They tend to stand near the front of the room, prefer the use of hand cues, like eye contact, and find the class easier if they can see themselves in the mirror. Finally, there is the group of students who just don't seem to "get" the movement until I walk over and place their body into proper form. This often requires direct manipulation of their body. As you can guess, these students are primarily kinesthetic. Like a good aerobics class, a good technical class will support all three styles.

ADVICE TO DEVELOPERS

If you have read this far I hope I have convinced you to take control of your training. If I have, great! The advice in this section is designed to help you follow through on this conviction.

> Develop your own training plan.
>
> Balance reckless explorer and plodder approaches.
>
> Choose a delivery mechanism that supports your NLP preference.
>
> Participate.
>
> Consider negotiating for training.
>
> Apply new skills to old problems.

Develop your own training plan.   Establish your plan for self-learning by customizing Figure 6–1 (Figure 6–3 is provided for this purpose). In the first layer of the hexagon, fill in the domain sextant with your current domain (e.g., "banking," "life insurance," "telecommunications," and so forth). I have found the other five subject areas are broad enough to cover the needs of most developers. Of course, you should add or remove subject areas as you deem appropriate, creating a five-sided shape or even an eight-sided shape. The important point is to *use* some structure to organize your training plan.

In the second layer, put specific topics. In the third layer place the skills you wish to develop. You may also want to add a fourth layer listing how you can acquire the skill. These would include training classes offered by your company, books, magazines, courses at a community college, and so forth. Consider recording the information in pencil so it easily can be updated.

At the same time you are identifying skills, think also about depth. How much knowledge is required to accomplish your goals? For example, let's say you have started to work on a project with your accounting department. This is not just another

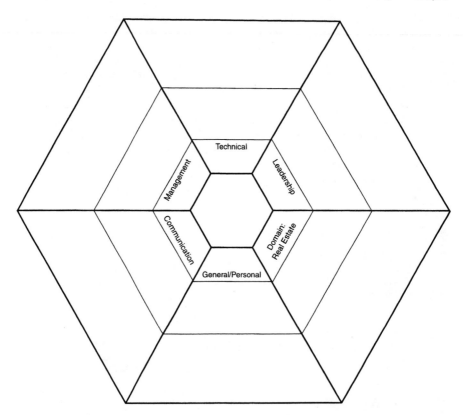

Figure 6–3   A Personal Development Framework

job, but a way to expand your knowledge in a new problem domain. To be most successful, you will have to learn enough accounting to meet their needs effectively, the depth of which is determined by the specific requirements of the project. Assuming the project is fairly simple, it is unlikely you will have to obtain more than a novice level of knowledge. Developing this depth of knowledge could easily be accomplished by reading a short accounting primer.

In contrast, let's say you have identified yourself as a journeyman Visual Basic developer, and you'd like to move to the level of master or expert. To accomplish this goal, you must find ways to extend your skills beyond their current capabilities. A friend of mine did this by moving beyond Visual Basic and into the world of MS-Windows Dynamic Link Libraries (DLLs). By creating DLLs for Visual Basic, he was able to expand his already considerable knowledge and is now what I would consider a master of Visual Basic. He is presently considering writing a book on the subject which would enable him to attain his ultimate goal—a recognized expert in Visual Basic.

Balance reckless explorer and plodder approaches.   Reflect for a moment on the definitions of the reckless explorer and plodder provided in Section

6.6. Which one describes your general approach to learning? How can you use descriptions from the other style to improve your performance?

Suppose you think of yourself as a reckless explorer. Be aware there are times when reading the manual or consulting another developer will make learning a new concept considerably easier. It simply doesn't make sense to try and hack through every aspect of learning a new system or programming language. Among other things, you risk creating dangerously bad programming habits if *all* your learning is on your own.

Conversely, if you consider yourself more of a plodder, remember there are times when the manual may not provide the exact answer you need. You will simply have to "jump in" and try something to determine the answer.

Choose a delivery mechanism that supports your NLP preference.
Refer to the definitions of NLP provided in Section 6.6. Are you more auditory, visual, or kinesthetic? If you are stuck, ask a friend—mine told me I was kinesthetic. I'd suspected this, but until she told me, I wasn't certain. Use Table 6–1 to help you choose delivery mechanisms matching your dominant NLP learning style.

Participate.   Learning theory is overwhelmingly clear on one point: Students who actively participate in a class by asking questions and doing assignments learn more. Even if you are a more reserved or shy person, find ways to participate in the class. Always do the assignments!

Consider negotiating for training.   Your manager may not be able to control vacations or cash bonuses, but they may be able to get you additional training. Thus, you may consider negotiating for training in lieu of a more traditional bonus.

Apply new skills to old problems.   The most common complaint I hear from students is this: "They sent me to training, but it will be at least two or three months before I can use this on the job. I don't know why they sent me here at all. I'm just going to forget everything! What a waste!" While this complaint has some

TABLE 6–1   Training Delivery Mechanisms

Learning Style	Effective Delivery Mechanisms
auditory	lecture-style classes with a strong lecture component
	theory-centric classes providing the opportunity for discussion with the instructor and/or other class members
	panel discussions at conferences; speakers at trade shows
visual	books, magazines, and other printed material
	videos
	computer-based tutorials with an emphasis on graphics or videos
kinesthetic	hands-on classes where the majority of the class is spent using a system
	interactive demonstrations at conferences and trade shows

merit—it is good to utilize new information as quickly as possible—it is counter-productive.

You *can* find ways to retain and extend what you have learned. Instead of fo-cusing on "how much you are going to forget," concentrate applying your new skills in your present job. For example, if you have just taken an introductory Smalltalk class, you probably learned about the importance of information hiding and how it is realized in Smalltalk. While the support for information hiding is often not as strong in other languages, you can always do a better job through disciplined use of these languages. Doing so will serve to reinforce and refine object-oriented and Smalltalk concepts until you can use them in your day-to-day work.

> *I have found learning a new programming language to be easier if I concentrate my ef-forts on solving a well-known problem using the new language. For example, to learn C++ I redesigned a system I had originally written in C. I tried to take special care in learning where the two languages differed and concentrated on applying principles of object-oriented design. The benefit of using an "old" problem is that it frees you to con-centrate on the differences in the languages. In effect, I was able to learn C++ more quickly because I was learning only one thing: the language, not the problem.*

ADVICE TO MANAGERS

The primary purpose of this chapter has been to motivate developers to take charge of their training. If your staff does this, do you still have a role? Of course! You can provide assistance and guidance to your developers as they create their personal training plans. More importantly, knowledge of these plans will help you create training opportunities meeting these goals.

> Provide guidance.
> Don't use training as a motivator.
> Embrace differences in learning style.

Provide guidance.   With all the managerial advice given in this book, it may seem your busy job just keeps getting busier! Fortunately, creating personal training plans is the responsibility of your staff. You are only responsible for providing guid-ance as they create this plan, which should not take an extraordinary amount of time.

Don't use training as a motivator.   If a member of your staff possesses the requisite skills to perform the job but is not using them properly, you have a mo-tivation problem, not a training problem. Sending the individual to training will at best defer the problem, not solve it.

Embrace differences in learning style.   Don't make the assumption your staff learns in the same manner as you. Remain open to alternative forms of de-livery mechanisms.

Part Three

There is a straightforward reason for programming in teams: Most commercial software is too complex for an individual developer to create working alone. But, how do teams work? The primary goal of Part Three is to show how the basic ideas associated with structures, processes, and outcomes presented in Part One can be extended to teams. To do this, it moves from cognitive models (which describe the individual) to organizational models (which describe groups of individuals). By integrating organizational models with software methods, it shows how the SPO framework is useful as a single, cohesive framework helping us to understand, predict, and guide both individual and collective behavior.

Section 7.1 begins by taking a closer look at the problem-solving behavior of teams. Elaborating and expanding on the definitions provided in Chapter 1, Chapter 7 provides a deeper understanding of structure, process, and outcome. In Chapter 1, special importance was given to process, for the mental processes of a developer *are* the primary means by which we solve problems. In Chapter 7, the emphasis shifts to outcome, for developers can only communicate their knowledge and solutions to problems by sharing outcomes.

As discussed in Chapter 2, individual problem-solving behavior is strongly influenced by values, personalities, and goals. Teams, as collections of individuals, have natural counterparts: Values, culture, and goals all serve to guide collective behavior. In addition to these parallels between individuals and teams, teams are also guided by strategy and corporate knowledge. Chapter 8 examines all of these factors in the development of an integrated framework for teams.

7

DEVELOPMENT TEAMS AND THE SPO FRAMEWORK

Recall from Chapter 1 that problem solving can be described using three simple concepts: structure, process, and outcome. Structure defines the form and content of outcomes and prescribes and supports the processes we use to create them. Process refers to the mental and physical activities we use to produce outcomes. Outcomes are the things produced.

How do these concepts apply to teams? More specifically, how do teams solve problems? How do they use structure? Are the processes of a team guided by a method? Does a team exhibit process leveling? And what about outcomes? What purpose do they serve? Why are they generated? How are they generated? This Chapter, and the next, answer these questions by showing how the SPO framework can be used to both understand and guide teams of developers.

Chapter Overview

Section 7.1 begins by clearly defining the size of a "team." Section 7.2 follows by introducing problem solving in teams and showing how a method makes working together that much easier. Of course, methods alone do not specify every activity associated with software development. Additional activities and their motivations are described in Section 7.3

Before discussing structures, processes, and outcomes within teams, we need a basic definition of a team. Developing this understanding motivates the brief review of organizational theories presented in Section 7.4.

Chapter 7 takes the same general approach to discussing structures, processes, and outcomes as was taken in Chapter 1. Specifically, processes are discussed first in Section 7.5. The critically important role of outcomes in the team is discussed in

Section 7.6. Structures influencing, supporting, and guiding the team are discussed in Section 7.7. The essential structures of system architecture and organizational topology are discussed in detail.

The SPO framework for teams is discussed in Section 7.8. Section 7.9 addresses feedback loops and cross talk between frameworks, and Section 7.10 reviews and summarizes the chapter.

7.1 A BRIEF WORD ON SIZE

This book defines a *team* as a group of between two and twelve developers. As a lower bound, two is the minimum for social interaction. As an upper bound, twelve is more than sufficient if you accept the notion of bounded rationality as proposed by Simon [1957;1981] and the idea individuals can only manage a limited number of social interactions in a meaningful way [Weick 1979]. (*Bounded rationality* states that humans have information and perceptual processing limits preventing them from solving complex problems in a completely rational manner. The "rationality" of our decision making will be discussed later in this chapter in further detail.)

Does this prevent the ideas presented here from being applicable to very large teams? No, for three reasons. First, if you do accept the premises presented above, then size really isn't the critically important variable associated with teams. Most of our day-to-day working is based on interactions with a limited number of people.

Second, very large teams will form smaller teams to handle specific problems. This process continues until it bottoms out in teams of the size defined above. Thus, while large teams must be assembled to complete large projects, small teams are where all the action lies. Concentrating on understanding and improving their performance is an appropriate investment.

Third, the problems faced by large teams—communication, coordination, working together—are also faced by small teams. Thus, understanding and managing these issues in small teams provides insight into understanding and managing them in large teams. Of course, these issues become more complex and difficult to manage as size increases.

Size *is* important. It substantially changes many aspects of working together. Coordination mechanisms that work well for three developers are likely to be woefully inadequate for thirty, communication among three people is radically different than communication among thirty, and so forth. Although my focus is on smaller teams, I will show how the topics covered in this and the remaining chapters in Parts Three and Four of this book change with respect to size.

7.2 METHODS AND TEAMS

Imagine you are a member of a small development team—say, five or so members—given the task of moving an existing COBOL mainframe system to a Smalltalk client-server application with a graphical user interface. At the present time you are relatively unfamiliar with the other members of the team, although you have briefly met some of them through lunch with mutual acquaintances. The project is quite appealing. You will have the opportunity to learn many new things: a new programming technology, graphical user interfaces, a new way to do analysis and design, and so forth. And, although you are not the senior technical lead, you will be given the opportunity to analyze and design some of the major subsystems.

The project just described is fairly typical. I've encountered similar projects dozens of times in consulting and teaching. It is important: Companies are continually making large investments in the rewriting of existing applications, moving them from monolithic mainframe systems to object-based client-server applications. It is exciting: Developers have the opportunity to learn new skills, and in the process hope to deliver more effective applications. It is complex: How can the staff learn all the required skills *and* build the system in the specified time frame?

As described in Chapter 1, methods are the way we systematically control our approach to problem solving. The basic activities of requirements determination, analysis, design, implementation, and verification are universal. It does not matter if we are a single developer or a team of 12. Methods can help us solve the problem. Thus, one specific recommendation for the team described above is simple: Adopt the use of a method and follow the processes it prescribes to produce the outcomes it defines.

This advice is just a bit too simple. *How* a team engages in the use of a method is substantially different from how an individual uses a method. Even though both may follow the processes prescribed by the method, they do so in substantially different ways. If I'm working alone on a problem, I will likely engage in the processes prescribed by a method *in my mind* as much as possible. If I am working with just *one* other developer, I must communicate to ensure we share the same understanding. If I am working with seven other developers, the very nature of this communication changes.

To illustrate, consider what it really means to develop an understanding of the problem within a team. First, each member of the team must develop his or her own understanding (i.e., each developer must create his or her own mental mode). Once this idiosyncratic understanding is created, it must be shared with others. These two activities are intertwined: My understanding of the problem is influenced by yours, and yours by mine. It is a communication process, facilitated through and mediated by the outcomes defined by the method. Without this shared understanding, my part of the solution is not likely to mesh well with yours.

As this description illustrates, software development is far more than individuals working alone developing programs. As much as 40 to 50 percent of an eight-hour day can be spent on legitimate activities associated with teamwork, such as preparing for and participating in outcome reviews, attending project meetings, and the like [Fairley 1985]. In the end, problems are solved by individuals, but focusing solely on individual problem solving (or the technology) just misses the boat. Although technology *is* important, Jim McCarthy [1995: 87] got it right when he said: "I see software development as primarily a sociological or cultural phenomenon."

To "work together" means the team has established or adopted acceptable forms of interaction among themselves and the larger organization. Initially, these interactions will follow those of the organization and society from which the team was formed. The adoption of a method facilitates this social interaction, for the outcomes defined in the method enable efficient communication.

The familiarity of the team with the method breaks down into the familiarity of each team member with the method. Higher initial knowledge facilitates group interaction and supports more complex approaches to problem solving. This phenomenon has been studied in improvisational jazz quartets, in which members who are experienced in the rules of jazz (i.e., the structures), and the preferred mechanisms for interaction during a concert (i.e., the processes) can create new compositions (i.e., outcomes) in a fairly short time frame [Bastien 1992]. A "jam" session is ineffective without such prior knowledge, much as software development is difficult, at best, without prior knowledge of the structures and processes associated with chosen development strategy.

> *An aerobics studio is another place where you can witness the effect of prior knowledge of method facilitating group processes. The International Dance Exercise Association (IDEA) has published guidelines as to the format, content, and structure of an aerobics class. These guidelines include patterns of class organization, tempo of music, and appropriate movements for participants of different fitness levels [IDEA 1987]. By following these guidelines, a "method" for teaching an aerobics class, aerobics instructors ensure students taught by one instructor can participate in a class led by another in a safe, fun, and healthful manner.*

> *Although aerobic students are rarely taught this "method" in a formal way, they nonetheless learn this "method" fairly quickly. After just a few classes, they know the prescribed processes and can work primarily individually (and at times, collectively) to obtain desired outcomes. When the entire class knows this method, interaction happens quickly and students can expend all their energy on achieving the desired outcomes (physical fitness). When students don't know this method—as when teaching a class to beginning students—the instructor must spend far more of their time teaching how an aerobics class is taught. The net result is students obtain a less-intense physical workout because more time was spent in teaching the method.*

> *In a similar manner, a design session by a group of developers who share a common knowledge of the design outcomes defined by the method will be more efficient than a design session where the developers are unfamiliar with the preferred outcomes. In the former, developers will be free to concentrate all their efforts on solving the problem. In the latter, developers must expend valuable energy in additional communication designed to make certain their outcomes meet the notations defined by the method.*

Use of a method by the team can take many forms, as each member of the team brings his or her personal cognitive library of plans regarding the method to the project. At one extreme, no one will be familiar with the method. In this case, considerable effort will be spent learning how to solve the problem as opposed to solving the problem. While somewhat undesirable, this extreme is acceptable and at times necessary, such as when an organization is making a strategic change from one method to another.

At the other extreme, each member of the team will have experience in the method. Such knowledge enables the team to focus their efforts on solving the problem, for they already know *how* it should be solved. They may even engage in a "meta analysis" of the method, reviewing their past experiences and customizing method-defined structures to match the needs of the project more effectively. Of course, customization can lead to other problems, for without discipline an experienced team can spend an inordinate amount of time customizing.

My discussion of methods presupposes a method was selected by (or, as is usually the case, for) the team before the project was initiated. This is not always the case. Teams are regularly asked to begin working on a system without the benefit of a method. This is unfortunate because a method provides one of the most important structures for guiding the processes of a team. In the absence of a method, a smaller coalition of the team (or a single member) may try to establish some other mechanism for control, in the hopes this will form the foundation for the coordination of activities. Barring this, each member of the team must follow his or her own idiosyncratic approach to problem solving. The net effect is severely reduced performance.

To briefly summarize, the purpose of a method is to structure the processes of software developers so they can create the necessary outcomes to build a software system. Because of this, methods are relatively impervious to size. In other words, I have never read about a method prescribing substantially different processes and outcomes for an individual versus a team of developers.

Although a method provides a structure that facilitates group processes, a method is not a panacea. Methods do not address important issues of teamwork such as the partitioning of work, the coordination of activities, or the integration of individually produced outcomes. Understanding and resolving these issues require the integration of methods with organizational models. What will emerge is the use of a method as a central component of group activity, supported by a deep understanding of how groups engage in problem solving.

7.3 BEYOND METHODS: GROUP ACTIVITIES

Strict adherence to a method alone is insufficient to ensure a team of developers can work together in a coordinated and controlled manner and build a software system. There are simply too many additional activities that must be done! To illustrate, consider User Acceptance Testing (UAT), an activity whose purpose is to determine if the system is fit for delivery to the customer. While UAT is essential to the success of any system, it is often only partially specified in a method. Moreover, UAT requires at least two kinds of coordination. The first is external. The interactions between the development team producing the software and the organization running the tests or supplying the users must be properly coordinated. The second is internal. As problems are identified they must be assigned to specific team members for review and correction. All of this activity must take place in the context of some structure—ideally, the *right* structure.

Several of the more common coordination and control mechanisms used by software development teams are presented in the following list.[1] Many of these are not specific to software development but instead represent coordination and control mechanisms required by any team.

- ◆ *Configuration Management.* An integrated sequence of process that enables developers to identify appropriate outcomes (e.g., data models, source code, requirements documents, and so forth) so they can review, compare, extend, or otherwise modify these outcomes in a coordinated manner.

- ◆ *Outcome Reviews.* Outcome reviews (e.g., code reviews, formal inspections, design reviews) are controlled examinations of outcomes. Reviews are usually conducted by a subset of the development team and/or other teams from the larger organization. In general, reviews produce additional outcomes recording the appropriateness of the outcome reviewed, including the detailing of any necessary changes. Outcome reviews represent critical feedback loop in the development process.

- ◆ *Status Monitoring.* The development team and its management must determine progress toward milestones established for the project. If progress is inadequate, appropriate action must be taken to ensure the team reaches appropriate objectives.

- ◆ *Customer Interaction.* A development team must communicate with a customer, either directly or indirectly. Unfortunately, development teams are often far removed from the actual customer they serve and are forced to rely on indirect communication. Filtering customer feedback in this manner delays dilutes its impact.

- ◆ *Management of the Use of the Method.* Methods are rarely used "as is." Instead, teams, through experience, implicitly and explicitly modify their use of the method to deal with new problems.

- ◆ *Managing Development Costs.* Software development can be a costly process. While assessing and managing these costs is generally thought to be a management discipline, all members of the team can contribute expertise and assistance in this critical activity.

- ◆ *Release Packaging.* It is rarely sufficient to ship an executable file and say "we're done." Instead, a controlled sequence of activities must take place to bring the product to the customer. The activities usually require the coordinated efforts of multiples teams (e.g., marketing, sales, service support, and so forth).

---

[1] Additional lists of activities can be found in the base and generic practices defined in the Software Engineering Institute Systems Engineering Capability Maturity Model [SEICMM-94-04] or the key operations defined by Holdsworth [1994].

The combination of activities in this list and a method does not necessarily define all the activities necessary for success on a given project. The specific activities required vary from project to project. However, there is a much higher chance for success when a project adopts a method and the appropriate activities supporting its use.

If the activities of the preceding list are so important for success, why are they not defined by more methods? There are three primary reasons. First, many of these activities exist only to support the development team in the application of the method. In a way, these activities represent metastructures, metaprocesses, and metaoutcomes supporting the team in the application of the structures, processes, and outcomes prescribed by the method.

Second, the specific application of these activities is more properly detailed by a specific organization. No method could adequately and completely specify how *every* software company should engage in *every* activity listed above. It is simply not feasible. These activities must instead be defined by the organization in support of its needs.

Third, and most importantly, specifying all these activities in a method would create a method so large and unwieldy it could not be used effectively by a development team. Such a method would overstructure the development process, effectively stifling it.

Finally, you may have noted some of these activities are as much the province of the individual developer as the team. Experienced developers, for example, will self-monitor their status and proactively take corrective actions when milestones are likely to be missed. Similarly, they will create and adhere to configuration management structures, processes, and outcomes even when working on their own source code. They are listed here because each of them is a *social* activity, usually taking place through interactions with other members of the team and the larger organization.

7.4 ORGANIZATIONAL THEORIES

Recall from Chapter 1 that a software development method is a prescriptive guide for behavior, while a cognitive model is a description of actual problem-solving behavior. The SPO framework links methods and cognitive models through process, forming a simple yet comprehensive tool for understanding and improving problem-solving behavior. A similar approach is useful in understanding and guiding the working of teams. More precisely, organizational theories provide the foundation needed to understand group behavior, while methods provide a means to guide it. This section provides a brief overview of some of the most important descriptive aspects of organizational theories.

7.4.1 What Is an "Organization"?

Describing an "organization" is tough! Organizations are complex, multifaceted entities. Which facet do we pick? Why was *that* facet chosen? Rather than try to describe all aspects of a organization in a single definition, it is more helpful to review several definitions. Each highlights a different facet, providing slightly different ways to answer the question, "What is an 'organization'?"

> *Organizing is "a consensually validated grammar for reducing equivocality by means of sensible interlocked behaviors. To organize is to assemble ongoing interdependent actions into sensible sequences that generate sensible outcomes." In Weick's view, the ongoing process of organizing produces an organization, "a shared sense of appropriate procedures and appropriate interpretations, an assemblage of behaviors distributed among two or more people, and a puzzle to be worked on." [Weick 1979: 3–4]*

> *An organization is "an identifiable social entity pursuing multiple objectives through the coordinated activities and relations among members and objects. Such a social system is open-ended and dependent for survival on other individuals and sub-systems in the larger entity—society." [Hunt 1972]*

> *A group [organization] is defined as the largest set of two or more individuals who are jointly characterized by a network of relevant communications, a shared sense of collective identity, and one or more shared goal dispositions of associated normative strength. [Smith 1967]*

The basis of Weick's definition is the interactions among group members as they seek to make sense of their environment. *How* individuals make sense of their environment is essential and will be covered in greater detail later. Ideally, the result of these interactions is a set of structures supporting the processes of organizational members engaged in generating outcomes.

Much of Weick's work deals with how structure is created. Specifically, much of what we think of as organization's "structure" is created *through* the processes (interactions) between people. However, this does not mean Weick believes process can take place without structure. Like myself, Weick believes all activity, including the activity of organizing, takes place in the context of structure. However, Weick places a much greater emphasis on process, for central to his characterization of organizations is the idea that they are continuously constructed, sustained, and changed through the processes of their members. This idea has considerable merit in understanding how change within an individual (e.g., the growth of personal cognitive libraries) changes the organization.

Hunt's view more explicitly recognizes the need for coordination. The creation of an organization as the result of interactions between people requires coordination mechanisms to sustain these interactions in an effective manner. Without coordination—which works best when explicitly structured—interactions will be inefficient and may potentially break down. This view is neatly captured by Mintzberg, who asserts: "Every organized human activity—from the making of pottery to the placing of a man on the moon—gives rise to two fundamental and opposing requirements: the *division of labor* into various tasks to be performed and the *coordination* of those tasks to accomplish the activity. The structure of the organization can be defined simply as the total of the ways in which its labor is divided into distinct tasks and then its coordination achieved among those tasks." [Mintzberg 1992: 158; italics in the original]. The trick, of course, is creating the right structure.

Finally, Smith's view moves away from process and coordination to softer aspects of organizational theories by stressing the importance of collective identity, shared goals, and normative behavior. In Smith's view, it is these things that enable two or more people to work together in a coordinated manner. While these softer issues (as compared to the "hard" issues associated with structure or outcome) will be covered in greater detail in the next chapter, it is worthwhile to further clarify the concept of a "shared goal."

Smith claims that without a shared goal the activities of the group lack cohesion and become meaningless. But, is a "shared goal" really needed? It depends on how you define the term "shared goal." When I think of a shared goal as guiding my interactions with another person, I think of something we both agree upon to the degree it supports a harmonious working relationship. We "share" the desire to create the same outcome, attribute nearly identical meaning to the outcome, and agree on the structures and processes to be used in its creation.

While shared goals enhance working relationships, are they a necessary prerequisite for working together? In other words, can we work together without shared goals? Certainly. You and I may be working on the same system but seek to accomplish different goals. If this is the case, then what allows us to work together in the absence of shared goals? In other words, the intuitive meaning of a shared goal seems to have substantial merit. We must agree to *something* in order to work together, right?

Yes, of course. We need to agree on the eventual outcome we are trying to create even if we don't agree on the process. Donnellon, Gray, and Bougon [1986] refer to such an outcome as an *equifinal meaning*, a collective understanding of what is to be achieved. An equifinal meaning does not mean we have the same goals. It does not mean we share the same structures. It does not even mean we work well together or even like one another. All it means is we agree on the outcome we are to achieve.

To illustrate, suppose you and I are given the assignment to write an Application Programming Interface (API) to some legacy code. Once we agree to the API (the equifinal meaning), each of us can generate our respective source code using whatever process we wish. You might use a method, while I might simply hack-and-slash something together. You might despise my process, and I yours. In the end, if we work together hard enough and long enough, we will eventually create something that works.

Is the difference between a shared goal and an equifinal meaning important, or is it just sociological mumbo jumbo? Although the difference between the two *is* subtle, it is nonetheless important. Research by Thamhain [1987] has shown that teams who focus their efforts too heavily on softer aspects of teamwork (e.g., the development of shared goals or group harmony) are less effective than teams who concentrate on the outcomes needed to solve the problem.

Equifinal meanings provide two additional advantages over shared goals. First, it is usually easier to obtain agreement on an equifinal meaning than a shared goal. This does *not* mean shared goals are unimportant and we should avoid working to create them. Shared goals *are* powerful motivators, for when they exist, work is far more enjoyable. It simply means a shared goal is not a prerequisite for coordinated work.

Second, equifinal meanings say nothing about process. Once the outcome is agreed upon, we are free to create outcomes using different processes. An equifinal meaning even supports the concept of radically different structures, as long as the agreed upon outcome can be created. This enables an organization to experiment on the best way to achieve outcomes by trying different structures and/or processes. A shared goal, on the other hand, implies the sharing of both structures and processes.

> *I've witnessed this effect firsthand when consulting with clients in the process of adopting object technology. Some clients spend a lot of time and energy trying to create harmonious "shared goals" regarding the use of object technology. They want every project to agree on the "right" way to use object technology before they begin using it. They discourage innovation and force conformity. Other clients approach the adoption of object technology by concentrating on the specific outcomes they expect to achieve (e.g., increased reuse, easier maintainability, and so forth). These clients are often willing to accept differences in how specific projects adopt object technology as long as the previously identified and agreed upon outcomes are realized. Invariably, clients who focus on outcomes are far more successful. They are more effective at dealing with the inevitable differences that come with the adoption of the new technology.*

Finally, both Smith and Hunt allow for the pursuit of multiple goals or objectives. A development team can seek to simultaneously reduce error rates while at the same time adopt a new method. In addition, individuals are equally free to pursue personal goals in the context of organizational goals. I can choose to work on a project (which accomplishes an organizational goal) *because* it is allowing me to learn a new programming language (a personal goal). Ideally, personal goals are consistent with organizational goals, a topic discussed at length in the next chapter.

To summarize, we organize as a means to create one or more outcomes through stable processes. These outcomes can be ill-defined or abstract, in which case a valid objective of organizing is to define the outcome. Processes can be more or less stable. Of course, more stable processes are preferred. How we organize is based on our prior experience and the context of our environment. Once organized, ongoing coordination is required to ensure desired outcomes are created in an efficient manner.

7.4.2 Organizational Interdependence

What is the degree of interdependence within the team and between the team and the larger organization from which they are drawn? Clearly, the idea of a "team" implies each member of the "team" is in some way dependent on another member for overall success. If you and I are creating a system, I'm *dependent* on *your* adhering to the specifications of the module I've just created. If you don't, *we* can't work together.

The same can be said for your module. I must adhere to your specifications. In this manner we are interdependent. Of course, if you *never* use any of the source code I've created, we are independent of each other—although I would question why we would be considered members of the same team! An explicit recognition of this interdependence contributes to higher performance—the realization "we are all in this together!"

The issue of interdependence between the team and the larger organization is more complex. Independence from the larger organization shields a team from any changes in the organization that could detrimentally affect the team. This is similar to loose coupling among modules within a software system. In a loosely coupled system, changes to one module don't affect others.

However, even the most autonomous team is interdependent (and most often dependent) on the larger organization which produced it. Why? Two reasons provide the answer. First, most teams are formed from members of the existing organization. Because of this, they naturally gravitate towards structures, processes, and outcomes familiar to their constituent members. The form of dependency is quite subtle. It can be difficult for newly formed teams to do things differently, even when asked!

The second form of dependency concerns the services provided to the team. In addition to human resources, the larger organization usually provides other resources (e.g., hardware, office space, capital, and the like). Such dependence can be critically important to the success of the team, as when a large software development organization provides financial support for a smaller team learning a new implementation technology.

The preceding two paragraphs have presented the larger organization in a very positive light. They provide well-known structures, processes, outcomes, and resources necessary to accomplish the task. But, the larger organization can just as likely *impose* inappropriate structures or withhold important resources.

A team is the result of a complex set of interactions among a group of people, their environment (which includes the larger organization), and the task to be accomplished. Ideally, the degree of interdependence between the team and the larger organization from which it is formed is such that the team derives a clear benefit from the larger entity.

7.4.3 Rationality

Have you ever had the experience of trying to make sense of someone else's decision, and no matter how hard you try, you just can't do it? You *know* if *you* were making the decision, it would be *the right one*. In other words, you wouldn't be so irrational!

An organization is thought to act *rationally* when outcomes are the result of the planned, calculated, or intended actions of its members. What makes rationality so interesting is that what is considered rational (good or sound decision making) may not be shared. In other words, we often have to live by the decisions made by others, and this can be especially difficult when we think these decisions are irrational! Perhaps even more interesting is the fact that what may appear rational may later prove irrational. Alternatively, apparently irrational behavior may be viewed as perfectly rational when the final outcomes are known.

Why might this be so? One reason is that organizations are comprised of people, and people act both rationally and irrationally at the same time. Sometimes we make decisions in a rational manner. We are deliberate, thoughtful, and apply reason. At other times, we are irrational. We speculate, gamble. We try something new, just for the heck of it.

Think back to the descriptions of stepwise refinement provided in Chapter 1. Although we are *supposed* to solve problems in a top-down rational manner by thoughtfully, carefully, and methodically applying specific criteria, we don't often do this. Instead, we pursue promising solutions in an opportunistic manner based on the plans within our cognitive library.

However, even if we (the organization) try to act rationally, we may still make irrational decisions. Why might this be so? The idea of bounded rationality presented earlier provides one explanation. *Bounded rationality* states that humans have information and perceptual processing limits preventing them from always acting in a completely rational manner. Moreover, the uncertain state of the future, and the unknowable actions of others, means that even when a decision appears to be rational, it may ultimately prove to be irrational through no fault of the decision maker.

An analogy to bounded rationality appears in the artificial intelligence-based searching technique known as hill climbing. In hill climbing, a set of possible solution states are organized into a search tree. The algorithm searches the tree by examining the possible steps from one node to another, taking the best possible step each time. The process is metaphorically based on the following algorithm for climbing a hill whose top you cannot see.

1. At each step, pick the direction which seems to lead uphill most steeply.

2. Take a new step in that direction.

3. Repeat steps 1 and 2 until you cannot find a direction leading uphill.

The problem with this algorithm is that it may not lead to the actual top of the hill but instead may settle on what is known as a local maximum (see Figure 7–1). According to bounded rationality, human decision making operates in a similar manner. We pursue what we believe to be the best course of action, but, unfortunately, we may not obtain the best possible final outcome.

Don't confuse *rational* decision making with logic. A rational decision is a sensible decision based on explicit reasoning using the best available information. A logical decision, on the other hand, is one based on the correct application of rules regarding the transformation of logical expressions. Logical expressions, in turn, are comprised of symbols, predicates associating properties with objects, and relation-

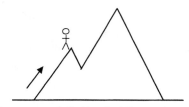

In the process of climbing the hill, we may settle on a local
maximum instead of reaching the top of the hill.

Figure 7–1 Hill Climbing

ships between objects. Logic and logical reasoning is an abstract exercise *unless* an
accurate and valid interpretation can be given to the symbols, predicates, and relationships within the expression.

To illustrate different kinds of reasoning, assume you are asked to select the
programming language for a new project and you have three choices: C, C++, and
Smalltalk. An irrational and illogical process is to flip a coin twice, once to pick between C and C++, and again to pick between Smalltalk and the winner of the first
toss.

A logical process would consist of establishing appropriate logical expressions
representing the languages, the project, and the host of other factors associated with
the project. The heart of this process would consist of establishing axioms for each
of these factors, absolutely true statements regarding the properties associated with
each factor. Even assuming this could be done in a valid manner (an almost impossible task), the sheer effort of doing it would preclude the regular and systematic use
of formal and rigorous logical reasoning.

Since random guessing and logic are out, all we have left is rationality. A rational process might be to first obtain data regarding the needs of the project, existing
skills of the development staff, relative costs associated with each language, and
other factors deemed important. Once these are known, simply select the language
appearing to "score" highest on each identified factor. Of course, some languages
will score higher in some areas than others, complicating the process and forcing
you to view certain factors as more important. Moreover, there is always the very
real possibility you will score the languages incorrectly. My point is that you are
making a concerted effort to make the best decision given the available data.

Suppose the data indicate the right choice is Smalltalk. This means selecting
Smalltalk is the "rational" decision. What if you pick C++ instead? Perhaps you are
a manager and you feel selecting C++ will enhance your prestige. Or, maybe you are
a developer and you want to enhance your *personal* knowledge of the language.
Such a decision is likely to appear *irrational* to anyone having access to the data.
Anyone but you, as you were *rationally* influenced by other factors *not known* to
them.

This observation illustrates the original point of this section. What you or I
think of as *rational* is ultimately a personal decision, based on our own experiences.
Of course, if the project is a success, you can later claim your apparently irrational

decision was perfectly rational—you "knew C++ was the best choice all along!" In summary, while we might *want* organizations to behave rationally, organizations are still collections of individuals who *do not* always act in a rational manner. If individuals do not always act in a rational manner, how can an organization?

7.4.4 Topologies

Organizational topologies[2] are used to describe formal relationships within the organization. While there are numerous topologies, all are derived from the most universal topology of all, the hierarchy. Figure 7–2 shows two such topologies in an idealized way, the pure hierarchy and the pure matrix. Of course, any topology is an *idealized* representation. Few, if any, organizations approach these idealized structures [Mintzberg 1992; Tropman 1989].

Formal and informal lines of communication are only partially portrayed in Figure 7–2. By formal communication, I mean communication explicitly supported or mandated by the processes used in the creation of outcomes. Informal communication, on the other hand, may not be explicitly supported and is certainly not mandated. For the pure hierarchy, I assume formal communication exists between the members of a single functional area and between selected members of differing functional areas. To verify that the second assumption holds, simply move up the hierarchy. For the pure matrix, I assume some formal communication exists both hori-

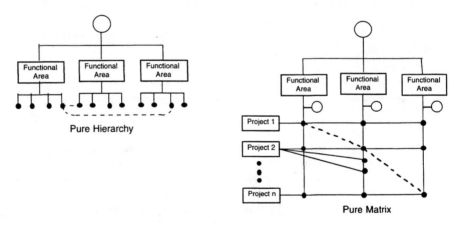

Pure Hierarchy

Pure Matrix

___ Managerial authority and/or specific teams

● Individual team members

- - Informal lines of communication

■ ▪ Formal lines of communication

Figure 7–2   Common Organizational Topologies

[2] An organizational topology is usually called an organizational structure chart, or more simply, an "org chart." I use the term *topology* to avoid any confusion with my use of the term *structure*.

zontally and vertically and between selected members diagonally. Informal communication within a pure matrix is not shown but is nonetheless present.

Why do we spend so much time, money, and energy in creating typologies? The answer lies in the critically important descriptive and analytic properties of a topology. For example, by examining the topology, we gain an understanding of the flow of information. Each level within an organization is a kind of barrier, potentially impeding or otherwise distorting important messages. Usually, fewer levels means communication is more effective. However, even this is not universally true: An organization with many levels can exhibit more effective communication if the manager at each level *works* at disseminating information in a timely manner.

Topologies also represent authority relationships in a practical, straightforward manner. For example, I can use the topology to identify the managers of key groups and contact them about an important event. These managers can then decide which members of their teams need to participate. What is even more interesting about the topology is what it tells us about corporate culture. Consider an organization using a hierarchy to represent authority relationships. Examining the topology provides some clues on which managers are more likely to closely supervise the work of their subordinates, under the assumption managers with many subordinates can exert only a limited amount of control over each one. The topology can also represent the explicit accumulation of power; managers with large numbers of subordinates are more powerful than managers with few.

Alternatively, by choosing a topology other than the hierarchy, an organization can choose to emphasize different aspects of the organization other than reporting relationships. For example, topologies can be drawn to emphasize unity or pockets of expertise rather than subordination. And, no matter what the "formal" reporting relationship, there are *always* an infinite number of informal topologies within and among members of the organization. While the formal topology may be intended to model the preferred form of communication between subordinates and their superiors, the actual flow of information can be substantially different. Put more bluntly, I may not receive any useful or important information from my manager but instead may rely more on my close friend in a different department for the *real* news regarding the company. The point is not that formal topologies are unimportant. They are. The point is that when the formal topology does not provide an optimal structure, we can craft informal topologies to effectively meet our needs.

7.4.5 Summary

By examining how humans organize and operate in groups, organizational theories address issues methods cannot. Like cognitive models, they provide the necessary descriptive component for understanding how a software development team works together in problem-solving activities. The remainder of this chapter will show how the SPO framework unites organizational theories and organizational models into a consistent framework, helping to create the link from individual to collective problem-solving behavior.

7.5 GROUP PROCESSES

Group processes consist of four distinct subprocesses: Identifiable *subtasks* must be *distributed* among members of the team who *coordinate* and *integrate* their work to complete the larger group task. This section discusses each of these subprocesses in greater detail using the foundation of individual problem solving presented in Chapter 1. Following this, I'll address the issues of process leveling in teams during group processes, the role of experience, and the impact of individual and collective ability.

7.5.1 Identification and Distribution

The first subprocess of the team is identification. Because identification is closely tied with distribution they are covered together in this section. Thinking of identification and distribution immediately raise two questions: W*ho* identifies tasks? W*ho* distributes them?

A trivial answer might be "the team leader," "the senior architect," or "the manager," but each of these answers is as unsatisfying as it is overly simplistic, naive, and just plain wrong. Examine each of these choices carefully: They centralize control and problem solving in the minds of one or two people. Such an approach is ineffective for the complexities associated with professional developers engaged in problem solving [Page-Jones 1985; Mintzberg 1992]. Sadly, it is very easy for software developers to adopt such a model for two reasons. First, there *are* times when a senior architect can accurately identify and distribute subtasks. Second, each of us has a fair amount of experience in top-down decomposition, and we inappropriately extend a *technical* approach to a *social* problem [Weinberg 1982].

A more accurate answer is "the individuals comprising the team." Specific members of the team identify and self-distribute tasks through a combination of volunteering ("I know how to do that"), election ("Jane can do that. She did something very similar on the last project"), elimination ("Everyone has an assignment except you, Phil, so I guess this one is yours"), and, in rarer cases, direct assignment ("Stephanie, you must be the keeper of the project plan").

But *how* does a group of individuals engage in volunteering, election, elimination, and direct assignment? Recall from Chapter 1 that the process of identification is ultimately based on the plans each of us has within our cognitive library. We identify problems based on our experience. In turn, we tend to offer ourselves for tasks we "know" how to do—precisely those tasks we have done successfully in the past! Alternatively, we offer ourselves for tasks we perceive will allow us to achieve our own goals (e.g., taking a more complex, but presumably more prestigious, task, in the hopes of career advancement).

What is the role of a method in the identification process? The processes prescribed by a method are designed to increase understanding of the problem. "Understanding" the problem to be solved *means* identifying the right subproblems. Thus, a method facilitates the proper identification of tasks within the team, just as it does for the individual. In the absence of a method, prior experience is the only means by which the discovery process is enacted. Ultimately, this results in erratic performance, as teams miss potential problems simply because none of the members has the necessary experience to ask the right questions.

The processes prescribed by a method also help in the distribution of tasks in the following way. A method-prescribed process *is* a task that must be accomplished. By using the method as a high-level guide, a manager can assign the responsibility of making certain a task is completed to specific developers. To illustrate, consider a three-member team using Structured Analysis/Structured Design. At a minimum, this method prescribes the creation of three models: the data model, the data flow model, and the state transition model. All other things being equal, a gross distribution of tasks would be to assign the responsibility of creating one model to each developer. Of course, *how* each developer realizes this responsibility (by creating its associated outcome) is a different matter entirely.

In addition to experience and method, other factors strongly influence the identification and distribution of tasks. Certain members of the team can partially dominate the process if they are perceived to be more powerful than other members of the team, either by formal organizational structure, experience, political acumen, and/or actual ability. Seniority is also a factor, and members with greater seniority tend to have greater influence over the distribution of tasks (e.g., "I've paid my dues. I don't have do that. You do it." or "I have been here longer, and know the best way to distribute tasks.").

Both identification and distribution processes can be guided. For example, a senior architect may be asked to guide the identification process not because they know more about the problem domain, but because they have more experience in asking the right questions to identify appropriate subtasks. A manager may guide the distribution process to achieve objectives not known to every member of the team (e.g., they may know vacation schedules and may wish to assign critical tasks to developers who have not planned to take a vacation for the next few months).

To summarize thus far, the beginning of problem solving in a group is the process of identifying work assignments and distributing them to specific individuals or coalitions, both of which represent outcomes. Coalitions recursively repeat this process until specific assignments are given to individuals. Individuals create the required outcomes using the problem-solving principles described in Chapter 1.

7.5.2 Coordination and Integration

Once tasks have been identified and distributed, group processes turn to coordination and integration. These processes are special, as both involve interactions based on individually and collectively created outcomes.

The first subprocess deals with coordination. *Who* should coordinate the tasks? The team leader? Each team member? Both? Neither? (I.e., the team leader's manager coordinates the task, or perhaps a secretary.) Determining exactly who should be responsible for coordination can be a problem as complex as the identification and distribution of the original tasks! Although I risk stating the obvious, coordination is essential for successful development. What may not be obvious, however, is that coordination is an *ongoing* process in which the team engages to manage the creation of desired outcomes. The kind and degree of coordination are based on many variables, among them the size of the team, the nature of the current activity, and the degree of formality required in the coordination.

Many people confuse coordination—which is a process—with the structures supporting it. Establishing a configuration management system and a system administrator who maintains the system creates a *structure* in which the coordination *process* can take place. Coordination will suffer unless each member of the team uses the processes defined by the structure thus created. Thus, the answer to the earlier question—*who* should coordinate tasks—is *each member of the team.*

The last subprocess is integration, where individually produced outcomes are put together to form the larger solution. Integration sounds simple enough, but it is often during integration where the most problems are found! Because integration is inextricably bound to individually produced outcomes, detailed discussion of this topic will be deferred to later in this chapter.

7.5.3 Process Leveling in Teams

Suppose our team has been given the assignment of developing an analysis class model. An analysis of our process would show each of us exhibiting process leveling (i.e., shifting among different levels of abstraction based on the plans within our cognitive library) as we contribute to the creation of the model. Indeed, leveling *must* exist in the team, because the problem-solving process of the team is based on the problem-solving process of its members.

Suppose our team consisted of four developers. Process leveling in a team means you and I may be working on analysis while our two colleagues are working on completely different activities (e.g., one may be working on the system architecture while the other is designing a preliminary user interface to help clarify an ambiguous requirement). Process leveling can cause problems in our collective process. How can you and I communicate effectively with our colleagues when we are engaged in completely separate activities?

We can't simply tell everyone to work at the same level (e.g., "Everyone must now do analysis and only analysis."). This is not how problem solving works. But, we can make certain everyone agrees upfront that the objective of our shared efforts is the creation of an analysis object model. This equifinal meaning facilitates effective communication. How so? Effective communication relies not only on actual behavior, but on the *expectations* of behavior created when the team agrees on an activity. Thus, even though we cannot be certain of the specific mental processes of a colleague, we can communicate with them effectively through the expectation that *the other person* is working on analysis.

Can the idea of your colleagues engaging in process leveling while you collectively work on a problem have any positive benefits? Certainly! One is *anchoring*. If I am having trouble completing an assigned task, an understanding of the task I'm *supposed* to be doing helps me return to it (i.e., "I know I'm supposed to be doing analysis, but I really need to write some code to understand this problem. But everyone else on the team is expecting an analysis model. I'd better find a way to turn the result into analysis.").

The inverse of anchoring is *cutting the tether*. If I know *you* are doing analysis, I am free to explore the impact of your analysis decisions on the proposed design. Of course, if you ask me, I'll cast an anchor and say I'm not *really* doing design. But of course I am "doing analysis," for good analysis can never be done without a partial understanding of how analysis level will impact design.

The point is that the explicit expectations of one activity allows the safe exploration of another. When the benefits of anchoring and cutting the tether are applied to the entire team, the most important motivation for creating a shared expectation of activity (an equifinal meaning) quickly emerges. A shared expectation of activity simultaneously encourages and controls the process leveling of the team.

Two ways to take advantage of process leveling are immediately obvious. First, use a method, for a method facilitates communication by creating consistent expectations of group processes. This need for shared expectations is so strong developers often find it difficult to communicate without them. Quite literally, "If I don't know what activity we are supposed to be doing, how can I communicate with you effectively?" Second, structure work so developers are working in teams of two as much as possible, as both anchoring and cutting the tether are both based on social interactions (which require *at least* one other person) [Coplien 1995].

One way to visualize the process leveling of a team is to imagine a loosely woven string created from a set of elastic fibers. Each fiber represents one member of the team and is colored with five different colors, one for each stage of the development process. Take the string and tie the verification end to a post and hold the requirements determination end in your hand. Snapping the string sends a high-energy wave of development effort down the string. The amplitude of the bulge represents effort.

As an analogy for software development, the movement of the string has several uses. First, it is rare for a team to immediately stop one activity and begin another because of the dampening effects of communication among team members. The string as a whole moves in a sine wave, not as a step function. This stands in stark contrast to the process leveling of a single developer, who can exhibit process leveling approaching a step function. Coupling between developers—how tightly the fibers are woven—determines how much freedom each is given to pursue process leveling in the context of the team.

Second, feedback is nicely illustrated: When the string hits the wall, a smaller wave of lower amplitude is returned. Third, as the initial wave of energy moves down the string, it consumes energy. The team gets tired. Effort levels near the end of a project are often not as high as in the beginning.

Finally, the string illustrates the dangers associated with long development processes. The longer the string, the harder you must snap it to make certain you have enough energy to reach the end. Better be careful in how you snap the string.

Snap it too hard and it will break. A shorter string requires less initial energy to make certain the wave can reach the wall. What is desired is a smooth and continuous harmonic series of sine waves moving through the string to produce a software system. Each "wave" representing a single stage of controlled growth.

I remember organizing a meeting for a project that had been started—and stopped—many times. Requirements, data models, and even a prototype existed. As you might guess, the project was being started again. The primary mission of my team was to get a handle on the mess and get something implemented. I thought a good way to restart the project would be holding a "kickoff" meeting. My goals included revisiting the strategic importance of the system, obtaining the necessary financial support, and introducing myself and my team. Most of all, I wanted to generate a renewed enthusiasm for the project.

The attendees included managers from around the world, many of whom had been associated with the project for quite some time. Very early in the meeting the participants—many former developers—demanded to know what "phase" the project was "in." I vividly remember the uproar I caused when I stated the project could be in any "phase" we wanted. All they had to do was pick a phase, and I would justify why the team was "in" that phase. Based on the collective body of prior work the project could be in any phase: requirements, analysis, design, prototype review . . . whatever.

When things calmed down, it was decided (not easily!) the best "stage" to be "in" was "requirements." More plainly, the best stage was trying to determine the true business requirements of the system and to examine the most effective mechanism for meeting these requirements. By agreeing to this conclusion, the team gained an immediate cohesiveness that had not previously existed. Everyone knew, in both a general and specific way, what needed to be done. And, they had a clear dictate for managing the previously created outcomes. Each could be examined in the context of the question, "Is this what we want this system to do?" Thus, each previous outcome could be used to provide value to the project. Although my team felt good, the managers in attendance didn't, and the "kickoff" meeting generated much less enthusiasm than we had hoped for.

As I've thought about this meeting over the years, I've come to realize the source of the frustration between the managers and the new development team was their prior experience with previous incarnations of the project. The members of the newly formed team, including myself, had to be "in" requirements because we were new to the project. We didn't know what needed to be created, and the best course of action was to learn! The managers, on the other hand, had learned through the failures of the other teams exactly what the system needed to do. All they wanted was for my team to get on with the job of doing it. Quite simply, each group was operating at a different level. It was the differences between levels that caused so much frustration.

If we apply the idea of process leveling to very large software development projects, it becomes easy to see it is impossible to characterize such projects as being in a single "stage" in the overall development process. Consider a large system, say, two million lines of source code. It will almost certainly be the case that different teams within the organization will be working on different aspects of the system. One group may be working on additional functionality required for the next release and could be characterized as being "in" analysis. Another could be in the process of fixing a known defect—"implementation/verification." Understanding process leveling means understanding that the actual phase of the development process is precisely the phase the team agrees upon. Because of this, it is worthwhile to make certain each member of the team understands the expected activity of the team. As described above, a method can help create these expectations in a consistent way.

7.5.4 Collective Mind and Groupthink

Suppose you are comparing two teams, Team A and Team B. Team A is obviously more effective than Team B. The question is, "Why?" Lots of potential variables come to mind. Team A might have better tools, a better working environment, more experienced developers, and so forth. But what if you could make all these variables equal? What could now cause Team A to be more effective than Team B?

The answer lies in how the members of Team A have molded their collective experience into a sum greater than the parts. Somehow, Team A is more effective when working together than when working apart. But how can this happen?

Think about some of your earliest interactions with your colleagues. What did you know about them when you first met? What do you know about them now? As we work together, we learn about each other. We learn Jill is an excellent analyst, Raji is a great designer, and Ruth is a powerful motivator. The team forms a *collective mind*, in which the interdependent actions of the team create a "a separate transactional memory system, complete with differentiated responsibility for remembering different portions of common experience" [Weick 1993a]. More plainly, we not only know Jill is an excellent analyst; we also *rely on our knowledge* of Jill's being an excellent analyst and begin to assign her tasks capitalizing on her skills. We remember the tasks she has been given and rely on *her* memory when we need information about those tasks. A collective mind enables the team to become more effective in problem solving precisely because each member of the team can *rely* on other members to provide experience and skills we do not possess as individuals.

Conversely, just because the raw potential of the team exceeds the individual does not mean it will be realized. There are times when a team can perform much worse than any single individual. One way this happens is when teams fail to account for their own poor performance. Instead of working to identify what is wrong and fix it, effort is spent identifying other groups that can "take the blame" [Kahn 1994]. Another way this can happen is through *groupthink*. Groupthink occurs when each member of the team stops critically examining decisions in order to make them better. Instead, effort is spent finding ways to justify a poor decision [Janis 1971]. Collective mind and groupthink represent two extremes: one optimal and the other to be avoided at all costs.

What are the implications of collective mind? First, the potential of each team is unique, initially based on the individual ability of each team member.

When harnessed, this can produce incredible performance, as when the Macintosh team created the first Macintosh or when the Chicago Bulls won three NBA championships in a row. Second, individual talents alone do not imply success. A collective mind is based on the *collective* skills and experience of the team. No matter how good the star, he or she needs a supporting cast. Third, a collective mind can only be formed as the result of interactions among team members. This takes time. How long did it take the Bulls to win their first NBA championship, even with Michael Jordan leading the team? Fourth, a collective mind is a fragile thing, easily lost and not easily recreated. Did the Bulls immediately win the title when Michael Jordan returned to the team in 1995? Finally, because team members rely on each other for information, skills, experience, and ability, changing the composition of the team can have substantial repercussions.

7.5.5 The Impact of Individual Ability

Although the collective potential of a development team is based on its constituent members, it would be ludicrous to assume each member of the team contributes equally. The impact of individual ability is far too strong. Recall in Section 3.4 the research from Curtis [1988] demonstrating that the success of even very large software projects often depends on *one* or *two* key individuals. As described in Section 4.6, Sackman et al. [1968] found a 28:1 variation in the abilities among different developers. Other researchers have found similar results. For example, Curtis [1981] found a 23:1 variation in ability. Boehm [1981] reports that differences in personnel, managerial practices, and team capability are the single most significant factors affecting productivity. The data are clear, but not wholly surprising. Even though most software is created by teams, the stars are critically important.

The practical results of these realizations are so obvious they are almost not worth stating. First, hire the best developers possible. Second, assign the most difficult tasks to the most capable developers. Third, find ways to maximize the skills of the stars through specific policies and organizational structures (this topic is discussed more extensively below). Fourth, invest time in grooming possible stars through assignments designed to increase their abilities.

7.5.6 Other Aspects of Process

While the most basic processes of a team are identification, distribution, coordination, and integration, these are certainly not the only processes. I have chosen to concentrate on these processes because they are intimately involved with understanding, predicting, and guiding problem-solving behavior within a team, and providing techniques to understand such behavior is a primary focus of this book. However, there are other many processes influencing the team (refer to Section 7.3). I'd like to talk about each of these processes, but this is beyond the scope of this book. However, you should be aware other processes do exist, and they do have an influence in problem solving.

Of course, all is not lost. One of the greatest benefits of the SPO framework is how you can apply it to more completely understand processes not directly covered in this book as discussed in Section 2.1. Consider release packaging, a specific process involving the creation of a final "shrink-wrapped" product suitable for shipment to a customer. To understand this process better, ask the following questions. What structure(s) prescribe, support, and otherwise define the processes associated with release packaging? What are all the forms of outcomes associated with each of these processes? Are these processes appropriate? What modifications, if any, are needed to the structure(s) associated with release packaging?

7.5.7 Summary

The problem-solving process of the team, while similar to that of the individual, is more rich, more varied, and more complex. It involves the active engagement of team members in multiple, interrelated, complex processes as they work both individually and collectively to solve problems. It is guided, not bound, by individual experience. As the team works together, collective experiences and the development of a shared history can increase the effectiveness of the team. Contrary to the popular slogan, there is an *I* in TEAM. It is precisely this *I* that is *essential* for success.

7.6 OUTCOMES

An individual creates an outcome as the result of mental and physical processes associated with problem solving. Extending this simple description to a team seems to work: The result of team processes are the outcomes created through these processes. Consider a "team" outcome created as the result of engaging in an integration process. Integration involves taking individually created outcomes, merging, blending, consolidating, and unifying these outcomes into a new outcome which is then measured against previously established criteria. When this new outcome does not meet the criteria, we engage in the process of identifying deficiencies, create new tasks to correct these deficiencies, distribute the tasks as appropriate, and return once again to the integration phase of individually created outcomes. There is a definite cyclical nature to the overall process.

During integration, individual outcomes tend to lose their association with their creators. Because of this, outcomes produced by a team are best described as *shared* outcomes.

Thinking of an outcome as "shared" changes the way we think about how they are created. It also helps us understand how the result of the team (an outcome) is viewed by others. Consider the bricklayers who worked on my home. While I know each brick was placed by a human hand and that certain of the bricklayers were more skilled in their work, I can't escape my perception of the final outcome: a house covered with bricks. Moreover, my memory of the individuals has faded. I no longer think about individual

artistry or sacrifice but instead judge the team based on the final result. As I judge my
house, so too do customers judge the final system we create as a software professionals.
Does it meet their needs? Was it constructed on time, and within budget? Even though
we know individual accomplishments must be wrapped up inside the final system, these
thoughts become lost over time. In all but the rarest of cases, we remember the outcome
of the team, not the individual.

The most important shared outcomes are those that control, guide, or are used as
input to subsequent processes. Understanding how these outcomes are created, and
what they mean, is critical to understanding and controlling team processes based on
these outcomes. The remainder of this section explores the creation and meaning of
shared outcomes.

7.6.1 The Creation of Shared Outcomes

A shared outcome is created through a complex sequence of interactions
among team members. Each specific interaction is based on individually created outcomes. The "sharing" takes place as we try to create a consistent meaning to these
outcomes.[3] This process is illustrated in Figure 7–3, which takes as a starting point a
specific, individually created outcome submitted to the team for review, refinement,
and/or acceptance. In response, the "team" decides on the appropriateness of the outcome, providing feedback to the individual.

This feedback often consists of additional tasks designed to further transform
the outcome into something suitable for sharing. A shared outcome is created when
each member of the team has attributed a consistent meaning to the outcome. The
overall process can be amazingly fast, as when an individually produced outcome is
deemed immediately acceptable ("You hit the nail on the head! That is exactly what
we've been looking for all along!"), or can appear glacially slow ("Do we have to
have *another* review meeting!" Yes, you might—and for good reason).

In order to fully understand the model, several words and phrases in the preceding paragraphs must be expanded. First, an *individually produced outcome* is any

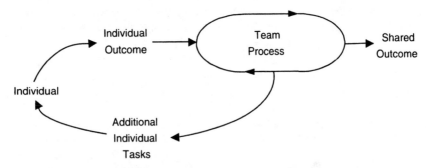

Figure 7–3   Individual Outcomes, Team Process, and Team Outcomes

[3] Outcomes have no inherent meaning. Humans *give* meaning to outcomes.

outcome generated by an individual. Examples include body language, utterances, sketches of a user interface, a detailed design specification, or a fully tested software component submitted for review. This is why Figure 7–3 specifies outcomes in an abstract way.

Second, by *submitted to the team for review* I do not mean to imply there is a formal submission or review process. Most of the time, neither of these exist, nor are they necessary

Third, although Figure 7–3 depicts a "team" process, in reality *there is no "team" process.* To illustrate, suppose you and I are creating an analysis class model for a bookstore retail management system with two other developers. When you propose `Customer` as a candidate class you have just created an identifiable outcome. When the other two developers and I indicate our agreement by nodding, saying "yes," or otherwise communicating agreement (each of which are identifiable outcomes), a shared outcome has been created.

Fourth, it is not necessary for each member of the team to attribute the same meaning to an outcome or even agree to the shared outcome created. I may propose modeling a trinary relationship as multiple binary relationships. You can easily understand this proposal but may disagree with it. We have achieved a shared outcome in the process. This idea is so important it is explored in greater detail in the next section.

Of course, all sorts of team dynamics greatly increase the complexity of this process. For example, I may disagree with the addition of `Customer` but be "outvoted" by the other two developers. Again, my disagreement is an identifiable outcome as are the overrides of the other two developers. And the process of resolving the issue can be understood by applying the model depicted in Figure 7–3 once again. Trying to show all of this graphically is too complex, which is why these multiple independent processes are simplified and abstracted into a single "team" process.

Finally, the additional tasks generated by the team do not have to be assigned to the person who first created the outcome. In many cases it is appropriate to reassign ownership from the creator to another member of the team (e.g., to provide an opportunity for education or to utilize the skills of an especially experienced person).

The most important part of the model is its emphasis on outcomes as the *sole* means of linking members of the team. We are not telepathic. We cannot share thoughts and mental processes. As humans, our *only* choice for communication is through outcomes.

This model does not allow for the generation of team outcomes before individual outcomes. *All team outcomes must be created from individual outcomes.* Do you find this surprising? Are you thinking: "*Individuals* don't *always* produce outcomes which are further processed by the team. Why, I was just in a data modeling meeting last week, and none of us went into the meeting with any so-called previously generated models. We started with nothing but the requirements and by the end of the meeting we had generated a pretty good data model. We did it as a team, not as a group of individuals."

While appealing, this point of view is incorrect for two reasons. First, even though the team may not have started with any previous outcome, in the sense there was no previously created data model, each team member *did* start with something: their cognitive library of previously stored plans. These internal plans were shared through the outcomes (e.g., sketches, speech, body language, and so forth) each member of the team created throughout the meeting.

Second, Donnellon [1986] has shown that the creation of *every* shared outcome can be traced through a series of specific transformational processes to the source originally creating it. It may be hard, but it can be done.

In practice we prefer to achieve a shared outcome as quickly as possible. One powerful technique for doing this is ensuring that individually produced outcomes adhere to structures known by all members of the team. For example, suppose I have been given the assignment of creating a preliminary data model for a new system and I understand two different notations. To facilitate the creation of a shared outcome (i.e., a data model everyone on the team can understand, verify, and use as guidance in future development efforts), I should choose the notation understood by a majority of the team. If I use a different notation, even one I personally favor, the overall process will be slower. I will have to teach others the new notation, explain its meaning, and show how my outcome accurately models the problem domain. Of course, individually produced outcomes are not always prepared with such noble intentions. Suppose instead I want to control the team, influencing them to use the data model I prefer. I would then choose the notation *least* understood by others, thereby making the team more easily influenced by my outcomes. Choosing a notation only I understand gives me the upper hand!

7.6.2 The Meaning of Shared Outcomes

Just because a shared outcome exists *does not* mean each member of the team attributes identical meaning to the outcome. Return to the example of the bookstore described above. In addition to Customer, assume the team also agrees on the class labeled Book. If I am responsible for the mailing list and you are responsible for the management of special orders, do you think each of us attributes exactly *identical* meaning to Customer and Book? The answer, of course, is no. Each of us will view these entities slightly differently as influenced by our development assignments, cognitive libraries, and other factors related to project.

When these differences are great it can cause severe problems in software development. This is *precisely* why so much effort is put into creating shared outcomes having a minimum of ambiguity and equivocality. *Ambiguity* means something can be understood in two or more ways. *Equivocality* refers to our degree of certainty over the meaning of a shared outcome. To say an outcome is unambiguous means each individual shares the same meaning associated with the outcome. To say it is unequivocal means we have a high degree of certainty as to the meaning we share. When ambiguity or equivocality are high the degree of sharing is correspondingly low.

The dangers of ambiguous and/or equivocal outcomes are especially important in software development because so many outcomes are used to guide, control, or provide input to further processes. When an outcome is such that it is either ambiguous, equivocal, or both, mistakes are bound to occur in these subsequent outcomes when decisions are made based on the outcome. And these mistakes are costly. Boehm [1981] estimates that fixing an error caused by an ambiguous or equivocal requirements document is ten times more costly when the error is found during implementation instead of during requirements determination. The ratio increases dramatically from there, and it can be up to 1000 times more costly to fix an error found during system operation. It is therefore paramount to find ways to increase the likelihood of creating outcomes with a minimum of ambiguity and equivocality.

7.6.3 Reducing Ambiguity and Equivocality in Shared Outcomes

One way to reduce ambiguity and equivocality is through training [Mintzberg 1992]. Consider two teams, the first having taken a formal class on creating analysis models using a specific notation. Which team will be able to achieve a minimum of ambiguity and equivocality in the analysis models created by team members? Which team is likely to experience rework because of miscommunication occurring through incorrect use of the notation? Which team is more likely to create a "shared" outcome in a rapid manner?

Another way to reduce ambiguity is to prepare outcomes in a formal manner (equivocality is another matter). By formal, I mean that outcomes are created with an absolute minimum of deviation from the structures which define them. Formal outcomes are communicated with less ambiguity than informal outcomes, and communication is the heart of the process of creating shared outcomes.

Formality can be difficult to achieve in practice because it appears to be at odds with equivocality. What good does it do to be formal (i.e., unambiguous) when I am not certain of my understanding (i.e., the outcome I propose is equivocal). Actually, it does quite a lot of good. First, preparing outcomes with a minimum of ambiguity encourages precise thought about what is being created. Precise thought, in turn, helps reduce equivocality. Second, there can be very little that is "shared" about an ambiguous outcome. When there are multiple ways to interpret an outcome, it is a certainty different developers will choose different interpretations.

A third way to reduce ambiguity and equivocality is by increasing review processes *and* creating structures to guide review processes. One such structure is a specific checklist created for each reviewable outcome and rigorously followed during the review process. Suppose we are reviewing the bookstore class model searching for sources of ambiguity and equivocality. Our checklist might include some of the following questions:

1. Is each class and relationship drawn from a specific, identifiable requirement?
2. Do all identifiers in the model have corresponding entries in the data dictionary?
3. Is each conceptual entity represented once and only once?
4. Are there any contradictory relationships?

5. Is there more than one way to interpret a class or relationship? If so, which specific way will we choose?

The single most important shared outcome of all in the software project is the requirements specification, for it guides, controls, and provides input for all subsequent outcomes. When requirements specifications are ambiguous or equivocal, costly errors will occur. When they are extremely low in quality or nonexistent, the project may fail completely. Techniques for reducing ambiguity and equivocality in requirements specifications are so important they deserve their own book. I've used *Exploring Requirements Quality Before Design* by Don Gause and Gerald Weinberg [1990] for years and recommend it highly.

7.6.4 Managing Shared Outcomes

It is not enough to simply create a shared outcome and then leave the team to work from it. Even if I agree an outcome is both unambiguous and unequivocal when first created, any number of factors may shake this belief (e.g., an increased appreciation of the complexity of the problem, increasing understanding of the problem domain, new requirements, and so forth). It is only through periodic review of previously created outcomes (perhaps through reference to the data dictionary or talking with another developer) that I can maintain my confidence.

The management problem is worse in rapidly changing environments. Consider a process model painstakingly prepared by a team over a four-week period in support of an automation project for a manufacturing environment. The purchase of a new piece of equipment automating several discrete production operations will invalidate the model, and a new one must be created.

Two problems can occur. First, unless the new model is deliberately and carefully shared with *all* members of the team, decisions will be made under the old, and incorrect, mode. Communication plays a special role in the process, which is why rapidly changing problems are often best addressed by small teams until they stablize. It is simply easier to achieve shared outcomes when the number of minds involved in the sharing is low.

Second, even though an individual may acknowledge the new model, he or she may *still* make a decision based on the old model if a great deal of effort was expended in creating it. There are simply more plans associated with the old model in their cognitive library and these plans are more firmly entrenched.

7.7 STRUCTURE

In Chapter 1, structure was defined as defining the form and content of outcomes and prescribing and supporting the processes we use to create them. Ideally, the *right* structure is chosen. Such a structure defines outcomes appropriate for the problem along with the best possible processes for generating these outcomes. The axiom of Chapter 1 still holds: All human activity takes place in the context of structure. Give the team good structure and problem solving is that much easier. Give them a poor structure, and problem solving becomes more difficult. The team must deal with *two* problems instead of one: the problem they are trying to solve, and the bad structure they are working within.

Like process and outcome, structure takes on a different meaning for the team. In Chapter 1, the primary structural influences in problem solving were characterized by the use of a method, our cognitive style, and discipline. A method provides a systematic structure for solving a problem. Our cognitive style represents our individual preferences for structure during problem solving. The application of structure—following processes and preparing outcomes—occurs through discipline.

Structure for the team, on the other hand, has a considerably broader connotation. It is not enough to say the structure of the team defines the form and content of outcomes and then prescribes and supports the processes generating these outcomes. Nor is it enough to say some teams prefer more or less structure, although both of these things are true. An expanded definition of structure is required to accurately describe the concept of structure for a team. A good starting point of what to add is provided by Donabedian, who characterized structure in the following way:

> By "structure" I mean the relatively stable characteristics of [the individual developers], the tools and resources they have at their disposal, and of the physical and organizational settings in which they work. The concept of structure includes the human, physical, and financial resources that are needed to [develop software systems]. The term embraces the number, distribution, and qualifications of professional personnel. The basic characteristics of structure are that it is relatively stable, that it functions to produce [software] or is a feature of the "environment" of [software development] and that it influences the kind of [software that is created]. [Donabedian 1981: 81, with modifications]

These additions increase the breadth and complexity of the conceptual definition of structure. It addresses the ways different groups of people are organized to work together on a project; the manner in which the organization responds to inputs from the environment; the classification of jobs and the distribution of responsibilities; the interactions between teams focused on different aspects of the system; and the mechanisms established for coordinating and controlling work processes.

This does not mean every aspect of structure should be considered at the same time. Such an approach would be both overwhelming and confusing! Instead, it is best to think about the different aspects of structure separately and then examine their effect on the other interrelated aspects of structure. Thus, we can think about topology (the physical structure of the team) separately from the method, even though the different topologies are likely to motivate different uses of a method.

While the first two parts of this book focused primarily on those aspects of structure most influencing the cognitive processes of problem solving, it is impossible to separate our cognitive processes from the aspects of structure described by Donabedian. I cannot work effectively, alone or in a team, if I am not given the proper tools, training, an appropriate working environment, or relevant feedback.

7.7.1 Essential Structures: System Architecture and Topology

Two aspects of structure have a particularly strong impact on the creation of a software system. These are the overall system architecture and the topology. This section briefly introduces how these aspects of structure influence the team. These issues are discussed in much greater detail in Chapter 12.

A system architecture defines the basic "structure" of the system (e.g., the high-level modules comprising the major functions of the system, the management and distribution of data, the kind and style of its user interface, what platform(s) it will run on, and so forth). Topology, as described above, specifies formal communication patterns and reporting relationships. Conway's law [1968] states: "Organizations which design systems are constrained to produce systems which are copies of the communication structures of these organizations." Instead of simply using any topology, Conway's law motivates us to ask, "Which topology best supports the creation of a system with the desired architecture?"

Consider a team building a system based on a three-tiered architecture. One "tier" is responsible for managing the details of data storage, the second for the internal representation and manipulation of data, and the third for the user interface. Conway's law cautions us to create a topology in explicit support of these layers.

More generally, the best approach is to establish a high-level system architecture and then craft topologies supporting the growth of the team in the context of the architecture. Why? Most architectures live far longer than the teams who created them. Estimates of system longevity range from 12–30 years, while developer longevity ranges from 2–4 years. A good architecture is designed with an eye toward long-term growth, modularity, and a host of other factors. Because of this, it is far more preferable to support the long-term goals of the architecture than the more transient topology involved in its construction.

This does not mean topology is subservient to architecture, or that topologies which have worked well in the past should be discarded in the development of new systems. Such an approach is far too simplistic! An architecture and a topology provide essential *starting points* for creating the overall structure that enables the team to engage in productive, satisfying, and enjoyable work. These starting points will be modified as needed during the actual construction process.

Do you think I am putting too much emphasis on the interplay between topology and architecture? Would a better approach be to simply define the architecture, group some developers together, and then let them self-organize as necessary to build the system? Surprisingly, this is a viable solution *if* the group has the right experience base. When given a challenging task and little explicit structure, teams will attempt to self-organize to produce a structure supporting their collective processes as they solve the task. Thus, while the initial engagement of process will *appear* to be devoid of structure, structure will rapidly emerge as the team finds it cannot coordinate its activities without structure [Weick 1993].

But does this mean the emergent structure is good? By good, I mean: Does the structure appropriately, effectively, and efficiently support the processes of the team in the production of the system? In general the answer is no. Structures created in an ad hoc manner through process are usually based on social interactions. The likelihood that these social interactions will effectively support the desired architecture is slim. Conway's law, in turn, predicts the preferred architecture will be compromised or even abandoned.

Unfortunately, I have witnessed this approach ("throw-em together and let them learn on their own") in many organizations adopting the Total Quality Management (TQM) technique of a "self-managed" team. In my view, a self-managed team has the skills, expertise, and authority necessary to refine their structures and processes to meet the needs of their current project. For example, a self-managed team may decide a particular outcome is not needed and simply omit it. Or, they may choose a different topology to support an agreed-upon change in the system architecture.

Sadly, I know of at least two large software development organizations who regularly bring a group of developers together and say: "Here is a problem. Solve it. And don't forget, you're a self-managed team. Figure out the best structure on your own." To make matters worse, this often happens at the same time the organization is in the middle of adopting a new technology!

Structure does emerge in these teams, but its creation is fraught with tension, misunderstanding, and frustration as people struggle to see their individual view of structure govern the team. Moreover, self-managed teams tend to increase the number of pairwise communication links established among team members, often resulting in unnecessary and redundant communication. Why? When there is no leader, there is no one you can turn to for information, guidance, or decision making. No one is given responsibility for breaking deadlocks, and creating shared outcomes can only be achieved through extraordinarily complex communication patterns. Ultimately, this results in a topology that poorly supports, if at all, the system architecture (if one even exists!).

Like any other team, a "self-managed" team requires some minimal set of structure in order to work effectively. This is best achieved by giving the team an initial topology in support of the desired architecture. Being "self-managed" means the team is free to modify this and other structures to effectively support their processes. If the objective is to foster individual empowerment in problem solving and to reduce managerial bureaucracy, the solution is not to remove all structure. Instead, teams should be given successively more freedom in structuring their own approach to problem solving.

7.8 THE SPO FRAMEWORK IN TEAMS

The SPO framework was created to help explain the mystery of how individuals and teams create software. By linking cognitive and organizational models with software methods, it provides the tools we need to understand, predict, and guide how software is created. Although the way an individual solves a problem *is* different from the way a team solves a problem, the SPO framework provides a means to understand both behaviors.

The many different processes and outcomes associated with software development (refer to Section 7.3) cannot be supported through a single structure. Instead, multiple SPO frameworks are needed. The remainder of this section discusses some of these frameworks, paying special attention to the role of the method.

7.8.1 Methods, Teams, and Topologies

Mintzberg [1992] identifies four key aspects of coordination of work within a team requiring standardization:

1. the work processes that must be followed in the creation of outcomes,
2. the outcomes themselves,
3. the skills required to engage in the work processes, and
4. the shared set of beliefs about how the work should be done.

A method addresses all four of these coordination mechanisms. By defining outcomes and prescribing the processes creating them, a method makes coordination through standardization easier. A method, for all intents and purposes, *is* the standard! Once selected, it explicitly and implicitly defines the skills needed to engage the processes producing the outcomes. Of course, a method does not define every required skill. The multitude of other structures used within the team, from the configuration management system to the underlying implementation technology, define additional skills required in the team. Finally, the selection of the method creates an *expectation*—a shared belief—of how work will be done.

The importance of a method is not only that its use facilitates coordination. A method, like a familiar system architecture or topology, provides a starting point for high-performance teams. Normally, we think about groups forming and then developing rules for how they wish to organize their processes to achieve desired outcomes. Yet, for even the most basic forms of interaction to occur, some kind of rules must first exist [Weick 1979]. By providing a consistent starting point of what *cognitive* processes are desirable in producing outcomes, methods provide the starting point for the *social* processes necessary to achieve shared outcomes.

A method concentrates on structuring the processes of the developers and the outcomes most directly related to the production of the software system. The structural components of a method deal with how developers move between stages and the completion criteria associated with outcomes. This, of course, is different than the topology (see Figure 7–4).

Throughout this book, methods are assumed to be rather dimensionless with respect to the size of the team. It is not the method that changes when size changes. It is the other structures and processes associated with the production of outcomes that change to support a larger or smaller team.

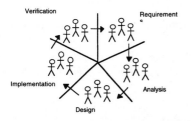

Verification   Requirement

Implementation   Analysis

Design

A method governs the movement between activties by structuring each activity and defining exit criteria for the processes associated with each activity.

An organizational topology shows formal relationships, facilitates communication, and defines the place of the team within the larger organization.

Figure 7–4   Method and Organizational Topology

The advantage of a dimensionless view of methods is that our approach to their use becomes more consistent and the importance of organizational issues become prominent. Rather than focusing on how we can change the method, the focus becomes "how can we create appropriate structures and processes to produce the best possible outcomes as defined by the method?"

Suppose a team of 11 developers has decided to adopt the Coad method for developing object-oriented software systems (as described in [Coad 1995]). One of the most important outcomes in the Coad method is the object model. Once everyone on the team knows the structure of the object model and the process by which it is generated, they can focus on creating the best possible organizational structures to support the creation of object models. Examples of these structures include ready access to domain experts, meeting rooms with whiteboards and flip-charts, CASE tools making it easy to generate and modify object models, and so forth.

Finally, by adhering to the structural relationships among processes as specified by the method, our abilities, both as individuals and as teams, in producing consistently correct and appropriate outcomes are greatly enhanced. In other words, when you haven't been there before (and, much of software development *is* going where we haven't been!) following the processes of the method in a systematic manner helps you get there. These ideas are congruent with the main focus of the Software Engineering Institute's Capability Maturity Model (SEI-CMM), that of defining consistent practices for the development of software systems. As stated by the SEI-CMM:

> *One of the advantages of systems engineering based on a defined process is the precept of fully investigating the nature of the environment around the system and the effects that the environment will have on the system under all circumstances. Systems engineers using processes based on SEI-CMM practices are not any more likely to know the parameters of a particular problem, but are likely to follow disciplined investigative methods that draw out the risk areas of a system. [SEI-CMM-94-04: vi–vii].*

While the SEI-CMM does not do an adequate job of differentiating structure, process, and outcome, it has the same basic intent. When you haven't been before, systematically following the processes defined by a good structure helps you identify the most important aspects of the problem domain. By following the process, we are less likely to "forget" an activity, or an outcome, in the development of the system. This is where the SEI-CMM and the SPO framework resonate: By consistently following processes, the quality of the systems created by developers will increase (sometimes dramatically) over time.

7.8.2 Multiple Integrated Frameworks

The development of a software system is a complex task comprised of multiple processes producing numerous outcomes (refer again to Section 7.3). Ideally, there is an appropriate structure prescribing each process and defining each outcome. These observations lead to a view of software development as a series of multiple, integrated SPO frameworks, as shown in Figure 7–5. Any single framework supports a single aspect of the development process. Multiple frameworks are needed to support all the activities inherent in the creation of the system.

Ultimately, each framework should be selected based on the manner in which it directly contributes to the creation of the software system. Thus, each of the outcomes displayed in Figure 7–5 should somehow be traceable to the creation of the system. Is there some higher-level structure we can use to classify or categorize the effect of various frameworks so we can pick those that are most appropriate?

The answer is yes. Two very well-established measurement and certification mechanisms rely on the use of multiple frameworks and provide substantial guidance in selecting ones most appropriate for software development. The first is the SEI-CMM, and the second is the International Standards Organization's 9000 series

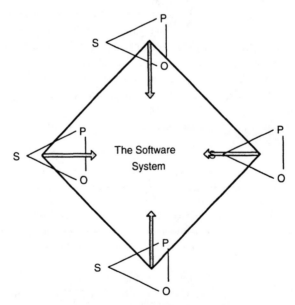

Figure 7–5   Multiple Integrated Frameworks

of management system standards (usually referred to as ISO 9001). The SEI-CMM describes several *process areas* associated with systems development. An example of a process area is configuration management and change control. Process areas are grouped by the SEI into *maturity levels*. Each level constitutes a measurable difference between organizations; organizations at higher levels are (according to the SEI-CMM) capable of developing software in a well-defined, organized manner and are more likely to complete a project than an organization at a lower level. As stated above, the SEI-CMM is process- and outcome-centric. The trick in adopting the SEI-CMM is creating the right *structures* for these processes and outcomes for your organization.

ISO 9001 is "the standard to which an organization can be certified for the design, development, installation, and maintenance of products and services such as software development operation, and support" [Jenner 1995]. The standard addresses many different areas such as training, document and data control, change control, and so forth. All of these are tied together through the quality manual, and all are designed to ensure that customers of the organization obtain a quality product or service.

There is a strong relationship between the SPO framework and the ISO 9001 standard. For example, the ISO 9001 definition of *process* is the "application of methods, procedures, work instructions, and standards to achieve a result" [Jenner 1995]. Similarly, the ISO 9001 definitions of policy and product equate to my definitions of structure and outcome. The SPO framework differs from ISO 9001 in that it is a tool that can be used in a theoretical way to understand organizations, and in a practical way to improve them. The focus of ISO 9001 is almost exclusively practical in nature. Finally, the SPO framework places a greater emphasis on structure and is equally useful for understanding both individual and collective problem-solving behavior.

The scope of SEI-CMM and ISO 9001 are much, much greater than the few paragraphs listed here. Why are they important to you? First, both forms of assessment and certification represent the maturation of our industry. Second, customers are using SEI-CMM and ISO 9000 certifications to help them select software organizations. Given two organizations, one with a high SEI-CMM maturity rating and one completely unrated, it is easy to see the motivation to award business to the more highly rated firm. The same can be said for ISO 9000. As one student in a recent project management class stated, "We've just tried to introduce our software in France and found a lot of resistance because we are not ISO 9001 certified. We are now committed to achieving this certification."

Another way of characterizing the multiple frameworks associated with software development is through categories of related issues (motivated by Donabedian [1981:95–7]), rather than by addressing specific aspects of software development, or defining specific structures, processes, or outcomes. Especially important categories are presented in Table 7–1. Note the components of structure, process, and outcome are purposefully intermixed in Table 7–1. My motivation is not to prescribe specific frameworks, but to provide a means of thinking about which frameworks have spe-

TABLE 7–1   Categories of Issues

Category	Issues
Accessibility	The geographic location and distribution of developers with respect to each other and the customer.
	Well-known entry points for requesting services related to software development (e.g., change requests to existing systems).
	Scope and nature of software services provided.
	Management of the customer interaction.
Technical Management	Physical structures, facilities, and equipment and the manner in which these are obtained, upgraded, and serviced.
	Numbers, types, and qualifications of staff.
	Fiscal organization.
	The presence and organization of quality monitoring and assurance mechanisms (e.g., outcome reviews, metrics, testing).
	System architecture, method, and formal topology.
	Adherence to the method.
	The manner in which staff is selected, trained, and evaluated.
Interpersonal Management	The nature, degree, and quality of communication.
	The presence of mechanisms to capture feedback.
	Courtesy, respect, and trust among developers and between customers and developers.
	The quality of interactions and other "soft" issues associated with work.
Continuity	The overall development process, from initial conception to final delivery and ongoing maintenance.
	Stability of the team (membership) and environment (tools and procedures).
	The manner in which change is identified and enacted.
	Degree of follow-up and control.

cial importance. The different aspects of structure, process, and outcome can be broken out to address specific circumstances related to a development effort.

In reviewing this table, it is striking to note how much of the software engineering literature is dominated by books focusing on only a few aspects of technical management or continuity. This book, on the other hand, contains material relevant to each category, concentrating its efforts on technical and interpersonal management. Even more importantly, it provides the theoretical tools whereby you can address aspects of software development not directly covered in this book.

A final benefit of thinking of software development in terms of multiple frameworks is the decoupling of one framework from another. Thus, we can vary our testing procedures with a minimum of impact to our metrics procedures. Decoupling is an essential aspect of introducing improvements (change) to a component of any single framework: Instead of changing *every* aspect of the system at the same time, we can identify specific aspects and work to optimize them.

7.8.3 Timing

In Chapter 1, the issue of timing between components in the framework was posed as "Which comes first?—structure, process, or outcome?" The answer to this question is the same for the team as the individual: Structure must come first. Ideally, it is the structure most effectively supporting the needed processes and desired outcomes.

Unfortunately, the simplicity of this answer is unappealing. In the presence of multiple, integrated frameworks, *which* structure of *which* framework should come first? Should one specific framework come before all others? Or, should the team try to define, as much as possible, all of the frameworks thought to be needed and then immediately put them in place?

While there is no right answer to this question, I believe the best approach is to define or select a minimal set of mutually supportive structures guiding the development process. Consider a development team starting work on a new project. The first such structure to select is the method, which prescribes the overall processes of the team and defines the form and content of outcomes. The second structure to define is the *preliminary* topology in support of the initial activities of the method, usually requirements determination.

Once requirements have been gathered (and sometimes during), the team should define their third important structure, a preliminary system architecture. This architecture can change over time, but defining it as early as possible provides a critically important equifinal meaning guiding the interactions in the team. Using the system architecture as a guide, the team should make any necessary modifications to the topology to directly support this architecture. Over time, as the project grows in complexity and as needs are better understood, additional structures can be added to support the team.

Of course, many structures are not selected or defined by the team but simply accepted as given. For example, an implementation language and hardware platform are often given to the team in the beginning of the project. Similarly, teams are often given other structures, such as configuration management systems.

This general approach is consistent with the one proposed by Bailey, Basili, and Youseffi [1984]. They propose the organizing process begin with "a set of requirements . . . derived from user's goals and expectations." This approach has considerable merit, for a major part of the organizing process is determining exactly what *outcome* is to be produced. In other words, the first outcome of the group (the requirements) is the specification of the final outcome they are to produce (the system). By making certain a method and topology exist, the approach outlined above makes certain an appropriate structure and topology exist to capture the requirements and use them in a productive manner.

You may find fault with my selection of the method, topology, and system architecture as the specific set of minimal structures needed on a new project. Additional structures considered "minimal" could easily include a change control system, inspections, or meeting structures. In reality *any* given structure can be essential depending on the needs of your project. We must never forget all human activity takes place in the context of structure. The goal of any single structure is to prescribe an *optimal* set of processes producing appropriate outcomes.

7.9 FEEDBACK LOOPS AND CROSS TALK

As discussed in Chapter 1, feedback loops exist between the components of any single SPO framework. However, the complexities associated with multiple frameworks mean feedback is different, in kind and degree, within the team.

First, in order for feedback to be useful, structures must be put into place to detect and analyze it. This is often much harder than it sounds! Organizations are often structured to prevent themselves from detecting feedback, especially feedback motivating change to the status quo [Schon 1986]. Even when structural impediments are absent, feedback often goes unnoticed simply because we haven't taken the time to observe and think about the manner in which outcomes were created [Weinberg 1992]. This is why the group activity Management of the Use of the Method (described in Section 7.3) is so important. Without some form of mechanism to capture feedback, we have little hope of deriving benefit from it.

Second, the existence of multiple frameworks introduces the notion of cross talk between components of different frameworks (see Figure 7–6). Cross talk occurs when the structures, processes, or outcomes of one framework impact another. For example, the establishment of a metrics program, in which specific metrics are gathered at well-defined intervals, usually has an impact on the development team's processes (e.g., I may spend a few hours on Friday morning cleaning up my code because I know the metrics sample will be taken on Friday afternoon). Sometimes, cross talk is intentional, as is often the case in the establishment of a metrics program. Othertimes it is not, as when a change in the method invalidates an established (and successful) review program.

Another interesting difference between individuals and teams with respect to feedback is the rate of change feedback motivates. In general, larger numbers of people take longer to incorporate, process, and analyze feedback. In other words, it is far easier for a single person to modify their use of method based on feedback from the last project by adding a new outcome than a team of developers.

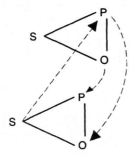

Figure 7–6   Cross Talk between SPO Frameworks

7.10 REVIEW

The operation of a software development team can be described in terms of group processes, shared outcomes, and structure. Group processes, which include identification, distribution, coordination, and integration, result in the creation of shared outcomes, a collective understanding of what is (or has been) accomplished. Group processes take place in the context of structure. The SPO framework provides a means of characterizing any single set or related group of activities associated with software development.

One critical SPO framework is the selection of the method. A method defines one or more outcomes and the processes by which these outcomes should be created. As such, a method provides an essential aspect of structure to the development process. Other essential aspects of structure include the topology, which defines the formal communication structures of the team, and the system architecture, which defines high-level structure of the system.

All human activity, whether for the individual or the team, takes place in the context of structure. How much structure is needed? Enough to support the process. Enough to define the final outcome. Enough so individuals can distribute, coordinate, and integrate their work. Enough, and no more, to solve the problem.

8

AN INTEGRATED FRAMEWORK FOR TEAMS

Developing software in a team *is not* a technological activity! It is a *social* process, founded on interactions, beliefs, expectations, and shared meanings. Some of this process is supported and guided by the structures selected or defined by the team: the method, topology, the system architecture, and the like. Some of this process is guided by other aspects of structure.

As discussed in Chapter 2, individual problem-solving behavior is strongly influenced by values, personalities, and goals. Teams, as collections of individuals, have natural counterparts: Values, culture, and goals all serve to guide collective behavior. In addition to these parallels between individual and collective behavior, there are two other important aspects of the social and organizational behavior: strategy and corporate knowledge. This Chapter examines these factors in the development of an integrated framework for teams.

Chapter Overview

Sections 8.1 through 8.3 discuss values, culture, and goals. Strategy is addressed in Section 8.4 while corporate knowledge is addressed in Section 8.5. The integrated SPO framework for teams is presented in Section 8.6. One benefit of using the same basic concepts to describe individual and collective behavior is the way it can be used to link individuals and groups. This linking is discussed in Section 8.7. Power and politics are not separate components of the framework but can instead be understood in terms of it. These are discussed in Section 8.7. Finally, Section 8.9 reviews and summarizes the material.

8.1 VALUES

In the development of the integrated framework for individuals, values were described as one way to understand decisions not dictated by method. When we ask "What do I consider to be important?" we are making explicit aspects of our internal structure guiding decision-making processes. Answering similar questions for the team (i.e., "What do *we* consider to be important?") has the same impact. Shared values help focus our attention on a common theme, promotes consistency in decision making, and assists in the socialization of new members [Phillips 1980].

Values expressed in a visible manner can have a remarkably strong operational effect. Structures are chosen to match these values, processes adhere to them, and outcomes shown to support them are given the most importance and long-lived meaning. Consider the well-known value of Caterpillar regarding superior customer service as expressed in the following goal: "24-hour parts service anywhere in the world." The software team responsible for the inventory management system could select a fault-tolerant database in support of this value.

This does not imply values are important solely because of their "operational" impact. Many individuals try to work in a company (or team) whose corporate values can reaffirm and give further meaning to their own personal values, even when they find it difficult to articulate these values. Unfortunately, the spiritual component of values is often overlooked or ignored. The idea that an employee seeks meaning from work consistent with their inner meaning may not be culturally acceptable[1] but continues to be a growing motivational force in the workplace [Pascale 1981].

Consider the team who created the first Macintosh. As eloquently described by Guy Kawasaki in *The Macintosh Way*, "The Macintosh Division shared a dream, the Macintosh Dream, of changing the world by bringing computers to people so they could improve their personal creativity and enrich their lives" [Kawasaki 1990:18]. The values reflected in this statement are not the "financial improvement of the corporation." Instead, they tap into deeper, more humane beliefs about doing what is right and helping others. In addition to these utilitarian values, there are highly personal values of making a lasting impact by "changing the world." All these values provided substantial meaning, motivation, and commitment among members of the Macintosh team as they pursued this dream.

When values are expressed in written form, they tend to be rather broad statements of intent that allow for considerable flexibility in their interpretation and implementation. This is for several reasons. First, values must often support multiple aspects of the business, from marketing and sales to product development and customer service. Broad values provide for multiple interpretations, and by tapping into common themes, they can stand the test of time. Too narrow a focus may unintentionally restrict one or more of these areas from pursuing necessary objectives.

---

[1] The cultural reference is to the United States, the country of the author. Other cultures from around the world embrace the notion that workers find a great deal of meaning in their work, and tend to more explicitly support the reification of values in the workplace [Hofstede 1980].

Second, organizationally held values are more difficult to change over time than individual values because of the expectations individuals make concerning these values and ongoing behaviors reifying these values. It is difficult to put much faith in a corporation whose values constantly change in response to market demands. It is far better to have a stable, but broad, set of values whose *expression* changes over time.

Finally, organizational values must appeal to a wide variety of individuals. The importance of a value lies not in what it states, but in the beliefs and the meanings we attribute to the value.

In addition to the externally stated values of the corporation as found in such things as mission statements, value statements, and policy statements, there are also implicit values associated with any team. For example, a team *valuing* design processes based on known and repeatable solutions may find themselves *realizing* this value through the use of design patterns [Gamma 1995]. Ideally, this means *each* member of the team values the use of repeatable solutions, for when our internal values match those of the team, there is a greater likelihood for increased job satisfaction, reduced stress, and clear decisions about ethical dilemmas [Boyatziz 1991].

There is a difference between espoused values and actual values. *Espoused values* are the values of the corporation as found in company mission statements, pamphlets, brochures, and the like. *Actual values* are the values expressed through the tangible actions of the corporation (i.e., its workers). When actual values are inconsistent with espoused values (e.g., a corporation publicly announces a concern for the environment but uses environmentally damaging manufacturing processes; a corporation promotes products scientifically validated as carcinogenic; a computer software firm ships software known to have bugs potentially causing loss of human life; and so forth), employees are likely to experience decreased job satisfaction, increased stress, and be unsure of what decisions are expected of them when faced with a complex ethical problem.

8.2 CULTURE

An organization's culture is the realization of its values through the interactions of its constituent members. It is "how we do things around here" [Quinn 1988:66], and "encompasses the traditions and beliefs of an organization that distinguish it from other organizations and infuse a certain life in the skeleton of its structure" [Mintzberg 1992:157]. More formally:

> *Organizational culture is the* pattern of basic assumptions *that a* given group *has* invented, discovered, or developed in learning to cope *with its* problems of external adaptation and internal integration, *and that have* worked well enough to be considered valid, *and, therefore, to be* taught to new members *as the correct way to* perceive, think, and feel *in relation to these problems. [Schein 1981:370, italics in original.]*

Culture serves many purposes within the organization. It is a powerful—perhaps *the* most powerful—integrating force [Tropman 1989]. It helps provide an identity to members of the team; by adopting the culture, a new team member can find acceptance in the group. It is the personality of the team.

A positive and healthy culture both reflects and reinforces values. Consider two software teams, the first of which has a clearly stated disdain for "hidden agendas." Which team will have a culture emphasizing clear and direct communication? What could be the ramifications of this culture in such common group activities as requirements gathering or architectural design?

To illustrate, I value a development process that builds systems in an iterative-incremental manner. Iterative means the system is constructed through multiple applications of the processes prescribed by a method. Incremental means the total functionality of the system is grown through well-defined product plans. This value is shared by my colleagues at ObjectSpace. It is realized through our culture. At ObjectSpace, nearly *everything* is built using an iterative-incremental process. In other words, using an iterative-incremental process is part of the ObjectSpace culture.

There is no single culture that works best for software development. Microsoft, for example, has a culture that has been characterized as an "armed truce." Individuals are not necessarily expected to reach consensus on a particular topic but instead agree to approach a problem a certain way until their personal point of view has a greater chance for success. Then, when an opportunity presents itself, the truce is called off, and the alternative point of view is vigorously pursued.

ObjectSpace, on the other hand, has a slightly different culture. At ObjectSpace, individuals (especially leaders) are expected to make decisions by talking with as many people as possible in order to gain their insight and experience. One benefit of this approach is that consensus is generally reached on the best course of action. Where consensus cannot be reached, it is expected the leader will put into place a plan that makes the best sense given current knowledge and abilities—a culture that could be called "benevolent dictator."

This is not to say any given culture is devoid of any drawbacks. Individuals engaged in "armed truce" expend energy in looking for weaknesses in their opponents. Such energy could be better spent in furthering the goals of the team. Some of the problems with "benevolent dictator" is that decision making takes a long time—sometimes far too long. Even worse, team members may feel frustrated if their carefully given input is subsequently ignored (i.e., "Why did they ask for my opinion when they just made a different decision anyway?").

Cultures cannot be selected off the shelf and simply applied to the team. The culture of the team is grown in the context of larger organizational and societal cultures. This growth can be guided but rarely can it be dictated.

The influence of culture as a mechanism for governing behavior may appear stifling and even confusing to the outsider. Culture *is not* a rigid conformance to some predetermined, static set of "rules" or "parliamentary procedures." As an expression of values, culture can, and does, change over time. Such a change can be seen right now at IBM, which for years mandated a conservative dress policy. Now, many divisions within IBM are relaxing the dress code, and "business casual" is becoming the new standard. One analysis might conclude the motivation for the relaxed dress code was the desire to obtain top-notch developers, who often prefer to work in more casual clothing. Another might conclude the dress code was relaxed to allow greater expression of individuality. And a third might determine the motivation was external: Customers have relaxed their dress code and IBM was merely responding to their implicit and explicit requests.

No matter what the analysis, it is important to realize the core values of IBM (among them treating employees with dignity and respect while returning a fair profit to stockholders) have not changed. Their cultural expression has.

8.3 GOALS

Successful organizations have clearly stated goals guiding the short-term and long-term behavior of their members. Conceptually similar to values (which govern behavior and are expressed through culture), goals are differentiated from values by their explicit operational effects. The Macintosh team shared the value of "changing the world by bringing computers to people." This value, in turn, helped create the goal of creating the Macintosh. Of course, this value could have been realized by different goals. The Macintosh team could have worked on creating new applications and hardware devices to allow mainframe computers to improve "personal creativity" (although I suspect they would have invented a different name).

Three development teams from different companies may share common values on the importance of writing defect-free code but may have substantially different operational goals due to their environment. One may be developing a system running in diverse operating environments, another may face strict performance requirements, and the third may have the goal of complete compatibility with a diversity of file formats.

Values are realized through the attainment of goals. Consider the following pairings, all of which have been adapted from conversations I've held with other managers.

Value: Take care of the employee.	Goal: Remain profitable, so a fair wage can be paid and job security will be enhanced.
Value: Staying current with new technology is important.	Goal: Provide at least two weeks of training per year in an aspect of technology considered "new."
Value: Provide superior customer service.	Goal: Control growth within the company so each client is given appropriate attention.

As discussed in the previous chapter, explicitly shared goals are not a necessary prerequisite for organized action. Teams should focus first and foremost on creating appropriate equifinal meanings.

But wait! Don't take this line of reasoning too far! There is also a substantial amount of research demonstrating that clearly defined, challenging goals have a substantial impact on motivation. Well-chosen goals assist in creating a shared meaning of effort for the team. Goals also have great power in effecting change. By identifying where the team is now, and defining what is desired, goals give the team something to strive for [Phillips 1980; Waterman 1980]. In the long run, goals are not required for teamwork—but they *do* enhance it.

Much can be accomplished when the operational goals of the team (cross-platform portability) are consistent with the personal goals of team members (learning how to create cross-platform systems in the belief this will enhance future career opportunities). Alternatively, I may be willing to temporarily subordinate personal goals if I think other benefits can be obtained through the pursuit of team goals (such as the enjoyment of working with people I respect and admire).

There are some very specific benefits related to team goals. First, they can be used during conflict resolution by providing the means to objectively assess differing courses of action. Second, they are another mechanism preventing divergence in the creation of individually defined outcomes. In the absence of goals, team members often have no choice but to pursue their own goals, which may or may not be appropriate. For example, if performance goals are not well known, then only individual goals and preferences can help the team make tough decisions regarding the selection of algorithms having different time and space requirements. When such goals are clearly defined, the team can evaluate the different proposals with respect to the specified operational goals.

8.4 STRATEGY

With the replacement of culture, the integrated framework for teams is identical to the integrated framework for individuals. This should not be surprising. Organizations are comprised of individuals! However, when a team exists, two additional components must be added to the theory before it can be considered complete. The first is strategy, discussed in this section. The second is corporate knowledge, discussed in the next.

Strategy is a set of mutually supportive SPO frameworks designed to accomplish the major objectives of the organization. The best strategies are consistent and cohesive. Each framework within the strategy makes sense with respect to the whole. For example, an "object-oriented, GUI-based, client-server strategy" would entail the selection of

- ♦ a method supporting object-oriented development;
- ♦ an object-oriented implementation language;

- tools supporting object-oriented development;
- training in all of the above *and* in the design of both graphical user interfaces and client-server systems;
- a migration plan defining how and when existing systems will be converted;
- and so on!

Crafting a strategy is not easy, and usually occurs in two phases [Mintzberg 1992]. The first is formulation—deciding what to do. The second is implementation—doing it. During formulation, the organization strives to clarify values, identify goals, assess current abilities, and gain an understanding of the competitive environment. During formulation, the organization asks: Why do we want to adopt an object-oriented, client-server strategy? Is such a strategy consistent with our values? What goals will it accomplish? What capabilities do we gain? What do we lose?

Strategy implementation concerns the establishment of structures and processes necessary to produce the outcomes achieving the strategy. The real effects of strategy are felt during implementation, especially if the strategy represents a substantial change over the status quo. While underlying corporate values remain stable, new structures, processes, and outcomes are put into place. Even culture must undergo change, for a new strategy often requires a modified culture. Ideally, the chosen strategy is viewed as an equifinal meaning so that different teams are given some flexibility and autonomy in its implementation. This enables teams to customize the strategy as needed in response to the specific demands of the problem and their internal and external environments.

Thinking of strategy in terms of mutually supportive SPO frameworks can seem daunting. After all, selecting "mutually supportive SPO frameworks" sounds pretty hard. There is, however, a simpler way to think about strategy. Strategy is a perspective, a way of thinking about the future that transcends a focus on the immediate. Creating a personal strategy involves answering the questions: Where am I now? Where am I going next? How might I get there? Answering these questions for the team provides a team strategy, and for the corporation, a corporate strategy.

One final aspect of strategy must be discussed. Like individuals, organizations are not free to pursue *any* possible strategy. The environment in which we operate serves to govern, constrain, influence, and control us. For example, telecommunications and tax-preparation companies are often required to make substantial changes to their software in response to regulatory requirements. Other examples include organizations operating in highly competitive environments, those at the mercy of their suppliers, or those lacking the skills necessary to immediately pursue an otherwise desirable strategy.

Perhaps more importantly, our prior actions constrain our strategy. Thus, a Macintosh software firm wishing to develop software for Microsoft Windows is constrained by their existing customer base (unless they want to drop them entirely, which *is* a strategy, but certainly not a good one!). In addition, because organizations are not rational systems, strategies may make sense only when subjected to a retrospective analysis. An example of the latter is when a senior manager pursues a "skunkworks" project based on a "hunch." When the hunch turns out to be successful, it can easily be analyzed in hindsight as a "brilliant new strategy."

8.5 CORPORATE KNOWLEDGE

Corporate knowledge represents the skills and abilities members of the larger organization have accumulated and made available to the team. Corporate knowledge enables us to capture the essence of what a corporation is known for doing best [Waterman 1980]. It impacts software development teams in two crucial ways.

First, corporations tend to develop experience in certain kinds of programming skills, styles, and algorithms. In the long run, these represent crucial aspects of competitive advantage. For example, Broderbund is known for its skill in creating ground-breaking edutainment software. EDS, on the other hand, is known for its skill in developing traditional, business-oriented, mainframe-based, high-reliability data processing systems. Members of these organizations can rely on the body of knowledge produced internally to support ongoing efforts in these areas. Thus, a developer who works for EDS can gain access to COBOL programming techniques not generally available to employees outside of EDS. Developers at Broderbund can share similar information on video compression algorithms for CD-ROMs.

Second, corporate knowledge is often reflected in enhanced general domain knowledge. Thus, a developer who works for the Principal Financial Group (an insurance conglomerate) will develop a significantly different set of domain knowledge than an individual who works at Sprint (a telecommunications company). Such knowledge, in turn, enables team members to communicate effectively with one another and with other teams in the larger organization.

8.6 THE INTEGRATED FRAMEWORK

The integrated framework for teams is largely identical to the integrated framework for individuals. With the replacement of culture for personality, teams, as well as individuals, can be characterized through structures, processes, outcomes, values, and goals. The inclusion of strategy and corporate knowledge leads to an even richer understanding of teams.

In Figure 8–1, the integrated framework for teams is shown resting on the support provided by corporate knowledge. Strategy is shown as giving the team direction as they pursue corporate objectives. Values are not shown directly but are instead embedded in the corporate knowledge supporting the other components. Culture is also not shown directly but is realized among the members of the team through their interactions.

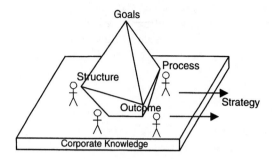

Figure 8–1   The Integrated Framework for Teams

8.7 LINKING INDIVIDUALS AND TEAMS

One advantage of the similarity between the integrated frameworks for individuals and teams deals with how individuals become linked with teams. By using the same framework, we have a consistent means of dealing with the individual in the context of the team. This section explores how this occurs in greater detail, at times summarizing and extending the results of previous sections.

There are two primary means by which individuals can be linked to teams. The first has an operational emphasis: Are the structures, processes, and outcomes used by an individual consistent with those of the team? The more individuals who can answer this question in the affirmative, the greater the likelihood the team will operate with a minimum of wasted effort. Individually produced outcomes will be more easily understood, and the creation of shared outcomes will occur more quickly. The core of this form of linking is the method, which is why this book places such an emphasis on methods.

As described in Chapter 7, outcomes are the only means by which humans can communicate. Thus, focusing on outcomes as the primary means of enhancing teamwork is a sound technique. This does not mean we should ignore process or structure! Because processes are the means by which outcomes are created, working to achieve common processes among team members is similarly a sound strategy for improvement. And, because structure prescribes and supports process and defines outcomes, a team will be more effective if each individual adheres to the structures established by the team *even* when solving a problem on their own.

The second form of linking, and one I feel is significantly more powerful, occurs when individual values, personality, and goals mesh well with team and corporate values, culture, and goals. In the ideal world, the things *I* consider important *we* consider important; *my* personality fits well into *our* culture; achieving *my* goals is synonymous with achieving *our* goals. This kind of linking results in increased motivation, reduced interpersonal conflict, and a greater appreciation for how other team members approach the same task (to name only a few) [Schein 1981].

8.8 POWER AND POLITICS

Power and politics represent two undeniable aspects of organizational life [Salancik 1977]. They do not, however, represent separate components of an integrated framework. Instead, they can be understood in terms already described.

Power is the ability to directly influence or control others into doing what you want. One model of power is called the strategic-contingency theory, which states that power accrues to those individuals and teams dealing most directly and effectively with organizational problems. In other words, power accrues to those individuals who have influence over the creation of outcomes deemed valuable to the organization. Sometimes, this allows for individual, team, and organizational success, as when a manager in charge of a critical department is able to exercise his or her power in obtaining a larger budget for the purchase of new equipment, thereby enhancing productivity (and ultimately benefiting the organization).

On the other hand, power can be misused, especially when the external environment in which the organization operates shifts. An example of this is when resources are allocated to a currently powerful manager whose team provides increasingly less benefit. These resources would be better utilized by a currently rising star. Ideally, power "flows" through the organization, from those more powerful to those less powerful when those who are less powerful can provide more appropriate outcomes. In reality, this is not often the case, as those in power will actively work to keep it.

Politics is the means by which we indirectly influence others. Unlike power, politics are engaged through persuasion, favors promised and exercised, and the like. Like power, politics can be used for positive or negative ends. Politics are often required to resolve issues associated with individuals of relatively equal power, status, or when organizational objectives are incomplete or difficult to understand.

To illustrate one beneficial use of politics, suppose you and I are managers at XYZ corporation. I have nearly finished with my project, but a few additional testers would really help ensure a high quality product (this way the development team can concentrate on *fixing* bugs, not *finding* them). Unfortunately, I'm already over budget, and my boss has flat out refused any additional funding. What do I do? Unpaid overtime is an option, but I've already been working my staff pretty hard. I could accept lower product quality and ship a product with more bugs than I'd like. Or, I can call you on the phone, discuss the situation, and try to convince you to loan me one of your developers for further testing.

Why should you consider loaning me a person? There are several reasons. You may have some idle resources, and the company would be better served by putting them to work. You may want to provide cross-training for a member of the team. You may owe me a favor, or, conversely, you may want to try to extract something from me in the future. If the political process is successful, I will obtain the extra resource. Of course, I run the risk that your motives may not be this noble. You may give me your worst performer!

Part of learning to operate effectively in an organization is knowing when one can, and should, use power and/or politics to accomplish your goals. Very early in my career I worked on an object-oriented expert system designed to assist MVS operators in dealing with a complex, internally developed bulk-data transfer application. The project, which had started in the research and development department, received strong resistance from operations managers. Common complaints were based on the newness of the technology, a concern for the damage the expert system could wreak if it were to make a bad decision, and the lack of experience among operators in supporting the unfamiliar hardware.

As my manager and I worked to develop organizational support, I consistently advocated a forceful "ram the new system down their throat" approach. In this case, the "power" approach was ill-advised, and I learned much by watching my manager engage in "political" maneuvering. He worked to create buyin from managers through controlled product demonstrations, called old favors, and promised new ones. He played on egos by implying other managers were going to adopt the new technology— did this manager want to be perceived as being any less innovative? (Innovative managers who successfully introduce new technology are more powerful, aren't they?) Over time, I realized our group, which was primarily engaged in technology transfer, simply did not have the power necessary to force changes in other areas. Our best chance for change was through political approach.

Of course, this is not to say the "power" approach is not effective. It was equally instructive to watch my manager introduce a similar technology within his own organization. In this case, no "politics" were used. He simply told subordinates adoption of the new technology was mandatory and gave specific deadlines for phasing out the current system in favor of the new. How his subordinates were to achieve the goal was their responsibility, but all departments under his direction had to meet the deadline. While substantially different than his usual approach of using politics to develop consensus for organizational change and the adoption of new technology, his exercise of power was both appropriate and effective.

8.9 SUMMARY

If you have managed to read this far into the book (bravo!), you may now realize why I took the time to develop a new model for describing and managing organizations, even though numerous excellent models already exist. Recall from the preface the primary goal of this book is to help unravel the mystery of how software is created by providing a simple yet comprehensive theory of individual and collective problem-solving behavior. As shown in Parts One and Two, the integrated SPO framework meets this requirement.

The ideas contained within the framework transcend any specific method or implementation technology. It is my sincere hope that by applying the concepts of structure, process, and outcome, you can better understand, predict, and guide behavior.

Part Four

Part Four provides practical advice for improving the effectiveness of teams. It begins with Chapter 9 which discusses the foundations of teamwork: interpersonal relationships.

The popular stereotype of a software developer is that of a more-or-less introverted person who prefers to work alone. The reality, of course, is much different. Developers spend an extraordinary amount of time communicating with their colleagues, customers, and managers. Chapter 10 explores communication in detail, along with several strategies on communicating more effectively.

Name the last book or article that you read that discusses the "culture" of a team. Examine this discussion carefully. Did it include explicit advice on how to shape, control, or guide it? Probably not. The integrated framework for teams describes the importance of values, culture, and goals, but, without advice on how to shape, control, and guide these components they are of little value. Chapter 11 is devoted to providing the tools and techniques needed to manage these aspects of the team.

Chapter 12 examines how engineering techniques learned in the creation of successful software systems can be applied to organizations. Beginning with coupling and cohesion and ending with structure *as* process, Chapter 12 will help you build on your engineering knowledge to create effective and dynamic organizations.

Chapter 13 concentrates on managing change within the SPO framework. It deals with two kinds of change: *innovations,* which are tools, techniques, and/or outcomes that are perceived as new, and *reorganizations,* which are changes in and among members of the team over time.

Chapter 6 was devoted to a single theme: Software developers should take responsibility for their training. However, training is also the responsibility of the organization. Managers must not only define the training that is required but also provide for it. Chapter 14 shows how the SPO framework and the tools developed in Chapter 6 can be used to create a training plan for the entire team.

9

INTERPERSONAL RELATIONS

Developing software in a team is a social process taking place through interactions with other people. (Interactions, in turn, can themselves be thought of as outcomes.) The quality of these interactions determines, to a great extent, the enjoyability, sustainability, and efficiency of the overall development process. The purpose of this chapter is to explore structures and processes that serve to increase the quality of these interactions.

Chapter Overview

Section 9.1 begins by exploring the structure of our assumptions and expectations of interactions with others. Section 9.2 follows this by exploring the use of a specific style of interaction based on this structure and human physiology. Trust plays a critical role in creating high quality interactions. Section 9.3 examines the impact of trust in detail and presents a structure and a process for increasing it.

9.1 REASONABLE PERSONS

A large portion of human interaction is based on the assumptions and expectations we have of others. An *assumption* is something taken for granted. An *expectation* is an outcome considered probable or certain. Both form mental structures guiding our interactions. Consider the team doing analysis described in Chapter 7. The assumption was "Everyone is doing analysis." The expectation was "Outcomes will be analysis outcomes."

Of course, we have more assumptions and expectations than those provided by a method. When I meet you for the very first time and extend my right hand, you have the reasonable expectation it is in friendship, and not a precursor to a sharp jab from my left! (Indeed, the handshake was "invented" to help ensure others knew your intentions were friendly.) Similarly, when you attend a code review, I hold the assumption you have prepared for the review. During the code review, I expect you to raise issues, not redesign my solution. If I assume or expect otherwise, the quality of interactions will plummet, regardless of your actual behavior before or during the review.

The integrated SPO framework for individuals presented in Chapter 2 provides a tool helping us understand the behavior of others. Can we also use the framework to create expectations and assumptions about behavior? The answer is yes, and the result is the Reasonable Person Theory (RPT). Motivated partly from the rationality principle proposed by Card, Moran, and Newell [1983], the RPT states:

> *People act in a reasonable manner for any given situation according to the structures of their environment, their cognitive library of plans, cognitive style and personality, values and goals.*

The integrated SPO framework helps us understand how others behave. It reminds us that others, like ourselves, are guided by past experience, have bounded rationality, and solve current problems within the constraints of their environment. It puts a positive spin on this behavior, creating a mental structure promoting beneficial interactions with others. By *assuming* and *expecting* another person's behavior is reasonable, we can achieve shared outcomes more quickly.

ADVICE TO MANAGERS

The most obvious managerial implications of the reasonable person theory manifest themselves in how you view the behavior of your subordinates. Your staff will try to create outcomes using the best possible process within the constraints of the structures you provide. Because of this, your primary responsibility is to choose outcomes appropriate for the problem and create the structures supporting the processes leading to these outcomes.

Change structures, processes, or outcomes, not developers.

Change structures, processes and outcomes when changing deadlines.

Cultural biases influence what is thought of as reasonable.

You get what you manage for, not what you ask for.

Change structures, processes, or outcomes, not developers.   Reasonable behavior is based on the structures and processes given to developers as they create required outcomes. When outcomes are deemed undesirable or unacceptable, your first approach to improving them should consist of carefully examining the structures and processes leading to their creation, modifying them as necessary to correct the problem(s).

All structures are not good, and all processes are not optimal. A poor structure can actually prevent a good process. A poor process, in turn, will result in poor outcomes. A developer cannot accurately diagnose a bug if configuration management tools are not available to recreate the source code shipped to the customer. Developers cannot be held responsible for a lack of testing if appropriate test machines are not available. Developers who design poor solutions in unfamiliar environments because they have been given inadequate training cannot be held responsible for all of their design decisions.

Even apparently similar problems or application environments often have surprisingly different design approaches. One example of this is the difference in the design of COBOL batch programs for IBM mainframe systems versus COBOL programs for Tandem high-speed transaction processing systems. Even though both systems run on mainframe computers and the basic language is the same, the appropriate design principles to apply in each environment are substantially different. Another example concerns applications designed using C++ versus those designed using Smalltalk. While both languages are object oriented, the differences between the two are sufficiently large to motivate substantial design, implementation, and testing strategies.

This advice draws heavily from the writings of Edward Deming [1986]. As Deming studied workers engaged in (primarily) manufacturing environments, he concluded management is the source of most problems workers experience as they attempt to complete their tasks. Exhortations to "work smarter" or "implement the system right the first time" are unlikely to change, in any substantial manner, the quality of the outcomes produced by developers. The real avenue to improved quality is to systematically improve the structures and processes associated with the creation of specific outcomes.

Change structures, processes, and outcomes when changing deadlines. Although I plead guilty to advocating the extension of project deadlines in other areas of the book, it is an unavoidable fact that at times you *will* have to cut the deadline. There are many appropriate reasons this may happen. Your largest and most important customer may *demand* that the system be delivered more quickly, the government may require the change, or you may risk losing market share to a competitor. All of these, and many more, represent quite legitimate reasons for cutting deadlines. What might be the best way to do this?

First, let me explain what I mean by changing a deadline. A *deadline* is a time constraint governing the creation of one or more specific outcomes. Cutting the deadline means preparing these outcomes more quickly than originally specified. Preparing an outcome more quickly *means* changing the structures or processes associated with an outcome *or* changing the outcome itself. Usually, it means changing all of them, because you can't engage a different process (i.e., doing things faster) without changing the outcome.

Consider a development team whose deadline has been cut. One way to modify their process in an effort to save time is to reduce the amount of time devoted to code inspections. Therein lies the problem. Reducing code inspections increases the likelihood of errors in the final product. Changing the process of what is built *changes what is built.*

The right way to change a deadline is to consider first what changes can be made to the outcome. From there, the structures and processes devoted to creating this outcome can be appropriately modified. The classic, and best, approach is to see if completeness criteria associated with the outcome can be relaxed. For a requirements document, this might mean detailing only the most important aspects of the desired system. For an actual system, it might mean delivering only a portion of the originally requested functionality. This allows the new outcome to be prepared using originally planned for processes. For example, reducing the functionality of the system enables the process of code inspections to take place, contributing to originally planned quality targets.

A second approach is to remove the creation of specific outcomes not deemed essential to the overall system. This approach should only be attempted under the guidance of an individual who has built a system *with* these outcomes so the decision on *what is not produced* is made from experience. An alternative approach would be to "skip" process steps associated with the creation of an outcome with full knowledge of the risks associated with skipping each step.

Avoid, at all costs, simply setting a new deadline and leaving it to your staff to determine how to change development structures or processes. This will not solve the problem, because each developer will make the changes *reasonable* to them. Unfortunately, idiosyncratic changes are not likely to translate into an effective approach for the entire team.

Cultural biases influence what is thought of as responsible.   There *are* important cultural differences in behavior (here, the use of the term culture refers to a societal culture, not an organizational or team culture). Hofstede [1980] has measured culturally motivated differences in behaviors in the following four dimensions (adapted from Hofstede [1980], with permission).

Power Distance. The extent to which a society accepts the fact that power in institutions is distributed unequally.

Uncertainty Avoidance. The extent to which a society feels threatened by uncertain and ambiguous situations and tries to avoid these situations by providing greater career stability, establishing more formal rules, not tolerating deviant ideas and behaviors, and believing in absolute truths and the attainment of expertise.

Individualism-Collectivism. Individualism implies a loosely knit social framework in which people are supposed to take care of only themselves and their immediate families. Collectivism is characterized by a tight social framework in which people distinguish between in-groups and out-groups; they expect their in-group (relatives, clan, organization) to look after them, and in exchange for that they feel they owe absolute loyalty to it.

Masculinity-Femininity. This dimension expresses the extent to which the dominant values of the society are "masculine"—assertiveness, the acquisition of money and things, and not caring for others, the quality of life, or people. According to Hofstede, these values are considered "masculine" because "*within* nearly all societies, men scored higher in terms of the values positive sense than of their negative sense (in terms of assertiveness, for example, rather than its lack)–even though the society as a whole might veer toward the "feminine" pole. [p. 351]

Before prejudging on individual's behavior, ask yourself if the behavior may be culturally motivated. Consider a developer from India versus one from the United States. According to Hoftstede's data, both counties score about the same in terms of uncertainty avoidance (weak). Thus, these two developers are culturally conditioned to such behaviors as risk tasking, changing of structures when they are not perceived to work, and willingness to accept deviation.

However, the countries are not identical and score quite differently in terms of power distance, with the United States having a "small" power distance and India having a "large" power distance. Because of this, substantial differences in behavior could be expected in, for example, interactions with superiors. The American developers are likely to think of their superior as someone like themselves, while the Indian developer is more likely to think of their superior as someone substantially different. Americans are more accepting of the concept of interdependence and trust between superiors and subordinates; Indians are far less accepting.

Of course, these represent broad generalizations. Specific individual behavior is likely to be different. The important point is that reasonable behavior does have cultural biases, and it is worthwhile ascertaining what these biases might be in understanding behavior.

You get what you manage for, not what you ask for.   No matter what you *say*, what you *do* will create the environment in which people operate. Unfortunately, what you *do* may not create the environment you *want*.

Consider Linda, a manager who wants to adopt an iterative process to create her current system. After creating an initial plan, she presents it to her team. As she tells her team, the iterative process means the system is constructed in iterations. Each iteration consists of a complete pass through all of the steps in the method (e.g., requirements, analysis, design, implementation, and verification). As Linda explains, the core philosophy behind iterative development is to create an initial system that is subsequently developed to meet all the requirements.

The response is overwhelmingly enthusiastic, and the team becomes energized at creating the first iteration. None of them, including Linda, has ever done iterative development. The thought of having a complete system (albeit with extremely limited functionality) up and running within six short weeks is truly exciting. And, through hard work, many tough decisions, and a few long nights, the team achieves their goal: A prototype of the system *does* exist and can be used as the foundation for future iterations.

How did the developers achieve this goal? One technique involved making certain the core features of the system were present (in a simplified form) and complex aspects of the system (such as error processing) were deferred. This is a reasonable assumption. Isn't the point of iterative development to increase the functionality of the system and its sophistication (with respect to such things as error processing) over time?

Which brings us to the crux of the story: *How* Linda evaluates this first approach will determine, to a large extent, the subsequent behavior of the team.

Suppose Linda reviews the initial set of outcomes associated with the project as follows: "I was looking over the requirements document and couldn't help but notice the following problems. Don't you realize if a customer orders more than $10,000 in merchandise in a year and has not been late on a single payment in the last six months, he or she is entitled to a 5 percent discount on every subsequent purchase over $500? Even worse, the prototype lets me enter all kinds of invalid data! Didn't you add all the necessary validations to a customer order? And what about distributed databases? I thought this system was going to seamlessly connect the laptops used by our sales force with the data on the mainframe. There was nothing in the prototype demonstrating this capability!"

While Linda may have been well intentioned (and even correct) in her criticisms, the likely result of such a harsh review is that the development team will engage in self-protective behavior. More specifically, the *reasonable* response to this evaluation is to spend *more* time in each step of the method in order to "get the system right." Instead of decreasing the amount of time to obtain feedback from the customer, the team will increase it! Thus, instead of taking six weeks for the next iteration, the team may take 10 (or 20).

If Linda evaluates the next iteration in the same manner, the developers will unconsciously return to a completely waterfall model. Why? The *promise* of the waterfall is that by taking the time to perform a complete analysis, you will get your system "right the first time." This leads us to the moral of this story: The quickest and surest way to kill the movement to iterative development models (which are far better than their waterfall equivalents) is to be highly critical of early versions of the system. (Recall that one of the best techniques to combat this is the use of burned pancakes described in Section 3.8). This story really also illustrates that the actual behavior of developers will always be reasonable in the context of what you manage for, not what you ask for.

ADVICE TO DEVELOPERS

The reasonable person theory provides a structure for creating positive assumptions and expectations of behavior. Here are some additional pieces of advice for using this structure most effectively.

We judge ourselves based on intention, but others based on outcomes.

Good expectations produce good results.

The RPT applies to your manager.

We judge ourselves based on intention, but others based on out-comes.   Our actions are generally grounded in good intentions. No matter what the final outcome, we can rationalize or justify our behavior because we were trying to do the right thing. Unfortunately, we tend to judge others based solely on their outcomes, not their intentions. What makes matters worse is that in the highly stressful environments often accompanying software development (e.g., tight deadlines, unproven technology, and so forth) it is far too easy to associate malicious intent to an action.

When you are trying understand the actions of another, there are two good approaches. The first, and easiest, is to try and imagine what might have motivated their behavior according to the reasonable person theory. What is their personality? What plans might exist in their cognitive library motivating the behavior? What do they value? Are they operating under different goals?

Avoid simply comparing what you might have done in the same situation with what they did—there are simply too many potential differences in the variables motivating behavior. Taken to extremes, comparing their actual behavior with your imagined behavior leads to negative thoughts (e.g., "Why in the world did they act *that* way? I would have done it much differently. They *must* be incompetent."). Remember, your colleague wants the project to succeed as much as you do.

A second, and usually far more effective approach, is to *ask*. Specifically, ask your colleague their intention in a nonthreatening manner (e.g., "John, I don't understand why you feel my selection of algorithm is inappropriate. Can you elaborate?").

Good expectations produce good results.   Our expectation of how people will interact with us determines, to a large extent, their actual behavior, *because we shape their behavior to meet our expectations!* If we walk into a code review expecting to be attacked, we are likely to respond negatively to criticism intended to improve the code. This response, of course, will motivate a similar response from the reviewer, and a negative spiral will ensue. If, however, we approach a code review as a learning experience, in which we can increase our knowledge and skill based on the reviewers, we stand a much better chance at interpreting a fellow developer's criticism as it is intended: a sincere attempt to improve the success of the project by promoting the highest quality code possible.

The RPT applies to your manager.   It can be pretty hard to think of your manager as a reasonable person, but you should try. Managers often have far less control of the overall environment than you might realize. Before you become too frustrated with the overall decisions, remember that like yourself, your manager really is working for the good of the team given the constraints of their environment.

There are many good reasons why your manager may appear to make unreasonable (or irrational) decisions deals with information. Managers usually possess information you don't (or can't). This information impacts decision making in ways you can only guess. Sometimes this information is related to the business, as when a company is engaged in a legal action (e.g., due diligence). Other times this information is personal (e.g., someone may announce they are moving out of state but would rather not tell the entire team until they have found an offer for their home, or when they are experiencing extreme stress, such as finding a nursing home for a parent who just had a stroke).

Before I became a manager I was under the impression—mostly through the effects of corporate culture—that managers had complete control over the compensation of their subordinates. When I became a manager, I learned otherwise. In reviewing the salaries of my subordinates, I was immediately concerned: One of my very best programmers was being substantially underpaid given the volume and quality of his work and depth and breadth of his experience. I was also haunted by the suspicion that this man had experienced a slower salary growth than most other individuals of similar (and even lower) abilities because of his minority status.

Unfortunately, I learned the hard way that I could do nothing to redress this situation. He did not meet the corporate established and salary administration structures. My manager refused to allow any deviation from this structure. When he had finally reached the structurally defined "acceptable" time limit for a raise, I was practically ashamed to give him a raise of only 4 percent. He had earned considerably more and could find it in the open market if he cared to look. Although I had acted in the most reasonable manner I could given the structural constraints, I know my behavior appeared unreasonable. The proof came six months later, when he walked into my office and announced he had found another job with a much better salary. This example illustrates two things. First, management can make seemingly unreasonable decisions based on poor structures. Second, dogmatically following the processes of poor structures has severe consequences. When my manager refused to allow an exception to the salary administration process, the result was the loss of a valuable employee.

9.2 PULLING, NOT PUSHING

Muscles in the human body are physiologically designed to do only one thing: *contract*. In other words, a muscle can only pull. Though we may refer to a complex movement as a push, muscles can only contract. Even the popular "push"-up does not consist of any "push"-ing. In reality, a push-up is a complex sequence of muscle contractions involving muscles of the shoulder, chest, and arm. When we "push" ourselves away from our desk, a similar sequence of coordinated contractions enable us to extend our forearms with enough force to move us away from the desk.

I believe humans respond emotionally much as they do physiologically. Using muscle contraction as a metaphor for guiding the process of interactions with others, I believe *pulling is better than pushing*, especially when trying to motivate or influence behavior. To illustrate, let's listen as Sarah, the manager of a development team at SuperSoftware, explains the SuperSoftware coding standards to Ramesh, an applicant.

> *Ramesh, there is one final aspect of the development environment I must discuss with you before you make your decision to join SuperSoftware. We have a firmly established coding standard. If you join our team, you must follow it. I allow no exceptions. Although I understand you may have developed your own coding style over time, I'm here to tell you it cannot be used. You must follow our standard. There is a biannual review of the standards, but we haven't changed them in over a year, so you'll be expected to follow them as is.*

Before reading further, answer the following questions:

Is Sarah pulling or pushing Ramesh to follow the standard?

Would you do it differently? If so, how?

Sarah has just exhibited a classic push: She *told* Ramesh what must be done. If I were Ramesh, I would have some serious doubts about joining this organization. What if the coding standard is terrible? What if Sarah has no real clue about what is going on, and everyone ignores the standard? What if my personal coding style is much better than the standard? At a minimum, if I were Ramesh I would want to review the standard to make certain it was something I could support. After all, if I am expected to follow something, I should probably know what it is. And if the standard was poorly designed, I probably wouldn't join SuperSoftware!

The real heart of the problem described above is not the standard. It's how Sarah motivated its use. By pushing the standard on Ramesh, she is not likely to obtain the behavior she wants. This is not to say Sarah's *intentions* in wanting Ramesh to follow a standard are unsound. In reality, her intentions are quite good. A good coding standard facilitates communication, promotes reuse, and helps make source code easier to debug and maintain. Regardless of her actual intention, I agree with Sarah: Ramesh *should* follow the coding standard, for failing to do so will negatively impact the team.

I'm equally certain Ramesh has similarly good intentions with respect to how he thinks of the standard. Quite simply, the team may fail to capitalize on Ramesh's skill and experience if he simply follows the standard blindly—and he probably knows it. Before reading onward, see if you can think of a way to convert Sarah's push into a pull. The goal is to try and motivate Ramesh to follow the standard while still gaining the benefit of his experience. Perhaps Sarah should try this approach. (As you read on, note how Sarah showed how use of the standard supports the values of the team.)

Ramesh, there is one more aspect of our team I must discuss with you before you make your decision to join SuperSoftware. About one year ago we did an extensive review of our development process. One key structure found missing was a coding standard. The objective of the standard is to improve readability, maintainability, and understandability of source code. The standard isn't very long—about 12 pages—but it is consistently followed.

I guess you could say writing code in adherence to the standard is a matter of pride: Everyone wants to write easily understood source code. I'd like you to think about your feelings toward standards, and the idea of promoting teamwork by following them. I'll give you a copy of the standard to review. You may find it acceptable as-is, or you may find your own style differs from our standard. I must caution you to read the standard carefully, for even if you dislike it, you will be expected to follow it. This doesn't mean your input is unimportant. In order to improve our standards we hold a biannual review meeting. All suggestions for change are carefully considered at the meeting. Although the standard doesn't change often, you can be assured your concerns will be listened to by a receptive audience. Do you have any questions?

Quite a change, isn't it? By converting a push into a pull, Sarah presented the importance of the standard in a nonthreatening manner. Of course, it may be the case Ramesh is not interested in following any standard other than his own. Ideally, Sarah would detect this during the interview process and use it to safely exclude Ramesh as a candidate. Ultimately, by converting a push to a pull Sarah is more likely to achieve her goal: adherence to the standard.

ADVICE TO MANAGERS

Achieving a pull style of management is tough as many traditional approaches to management lend themselves to pushing, not pulling. Even though pulling is often harder than pushing, make the commitment to pull whenever possible. In the long run, the results will be worth your efforts.

> Beware of a push disguised as a pull.
> Don't forget to stretch.
> Know when—and how—to push.

Beware of a push disguised as a pull.   The following techniques can help you distinguish between a push and a pull.

♦ Pushes are usually commands or direct orders given with no explanation. Pulls are more often directives whose intentions are clear. The motivation comes from the realization the directive represents the best alternative course of action.

♦ A push offers little or no opportunity for variation. A push has little or no structural support change and virtually no mechanism for capturing feedback. A pull has one or both.

To convert a push into a pull, review the above list. Is a direct command really necessary? Usually, only a moment is needed to give you the time to convert a push to a pull.

Don't forget to stretch.   *Flexibility* is the capacity to move a joint throughout its entire range of motion [Howley 1992]. If you always exercise the same way without stretching, you will lose flexibility. Your developers will respond in a similar manner. Pull them too long or too often in the same direction (e.g., keeping them on the same project or working in the same language) and they will begin to lose some flexibility. Increase their flexibility by helping them *stretch*: Try new things, new projects, new languages. Of course, stretch with care: Muscles (and people) stretched too hard, or too fast, can sustain significant damage!

Know when—and how—to push.   Achieving a "pull" style of management does not mean relinquishing authority. As a manager, you have a responsibility to act in the best interests of your team, and you may find yourself faced with certain situations seemingly unsolvable in a pull manner. For example, assume in the story above that Ramesh joins SuperSoftware but consistently violates the coding standard. If, after discussing the matter with him and stressing the importance of standards as they relate to the overall team, Ramesh still does not follow the standard, it is time for a push.

Push using the following four-step process:

1. State the problem in a simple and direct manner. This problem statement must refer to the problem in terms of job requirements.
2. State what must be done to correct the problem.
3. State the consequences for failing to correct the problem.
4. (optional) Record the incident in the personnel file of the employee.

Using three steps, the conversation with Ramesh would go something like this:

Ramesh, you are not following the coding standard. It is a requirement that all developers follow the standard. Accordingly, from this day forward you must follow the standard. Failure to do so may result in reassignment to a different job. It may also result in termination of your employment.

Termination of employment is recommended in only truly *extreme* cases. Does failure to follow a coding standard constitute grounds for termination of employment? Probably not. But, if Ramesh continues to violate the standards, it is your responsibility to exercise your legitimate authority as a "push."

ADVICE TO DEVELOPERS

The primary use of pushing versus pulling deals with motivating or influencing the behavior of others. In other words, when we want someone else to do something for us, a pull is usually more effective than a push. While you may not have as much cause for changing behavior as your manager, pulling is also effective for you.

> Demo or die.
> Stabilize.

Demo or die.   You are absolutely *certain* you have a great idea, but you just can't seem to convince anyone else it should be pursued. You've told them incessantly about how wonderful the idea is, but you can't seem to convince them to give it a try. And you are pulling, aren't you?

Actually, you're not. Incessantly whining about your "better idea" is not a pull. It is a push. What you *should* do is demonstrate the effectiveness of your idea. This advice is drawn from the MIT Media Lab, which has a tradition of encouraging its members to demonstrate good ideas rather than talking about them. Stop talking. Start doing. Over time, if your idea really is better, others will be *drawn* (i.e., pulled) to adopt it.

Stabilize.   Two kinds of contractions are needed to perform any complex movement. The first involves the muscles moving the limbs involved with the movement. The second involves muscles contracting work to stabilize the body. Consider, again, the push-up. In order to keep our body in proper alignment, our abdominal muscles must contract to stabilize the spinal column. Without this support a push-up is done poorly, if at all. How can this metaphor help teamwork? You don't always have to be the "muscle" moving the team. Sometimes the best way to help the team is to stabilize and let others pull.

9.3 DEVELOPING TRUST

When you first meet someone, it is beneficial to assume they are reasonable. Over time, continued interactions form repeated patterns. When these patterns are stable, you develop something even more powerful than a reasonable expectation: You develop trust. *Trust* is an assured reliance on the character, ability, strength, and truthfulness of another person and the feeling we are free to say or do things without fear or misgiving. This section explores trust in greater detail and presents a structure and process for increased trust in the team.

9.3.1 Impact of Trust

The concept of trust and the feelings and expectations it produces has a large and pervasive impact. Driscoll [1973] found our feelings of trust in our colleagues and managers was the single most important variable in measuring job satisfaction. Not surprisingly, we enjoy jobs where we can trust people!

Trust has an equally strong impact on the degree to which we will support structures, engage processes, and utilize outcomes. Simply put, when we trust our structures, we follow the processes they prescribe. In turn, we trust the outcomes produced by these processes to be of high quality.

The concept of trust has important implications for managers who wish to change structures. We are more likely to support changes in our working environment if we *trust* our leaders, *even* if the motivations, goals, and ramifications of the change are not completely understood.

> *I often find many of my students resist the rigorous use of a method when I'm teaching object-oriented analysis and design. Perhaps they have been successful in the past without using a method and cannot think of why they need one now. More commonly, perhaps they've tried to use a method in the past and found the method to be overly constraining or just plain cumbersome. For whatever reason, it is quite common for me to spend a major portion of the class helping students develop trust in the method. In the end, I want students to trust that using a method will help enable them to produce higher quality systems.*

To measure the impact of trust, Zand [1972] and Boss [1978] conducted studies examining how conditions of high and low trust affect the quality of problem solving. Each study gave a management team a problem to solve and a set of simple instructions establishing expectations of trust or mistrust. For example, the instructions given to the high-trust teams contained phrases such as, "You have learned from your experience during the past two years that you can trust your colleagues." While the instructions given to the low-trust team did not explicitly state the existence of low trust, low trust expectations were created by statements of extreme competitiveness among the members of the team.

Several differences emerged in the communication patterns and subsequent performance of the teams. Members of the high-trust team were characterized by frequent differences of opinion, explicit statements of encouragement and disappointment, a high degree of information sharing, and mutual support. The low-trust teams, however, exhibited opposite communication patterns: Information was not readily shared, differences of opinions and alternative points of view were rarely explored in detail, and there was little or no support shared between members of the team.

The bottom-line results? In terms of performance, the high-trust teams were significantly more effective. The studies concluded the key determinant of problem-solving effectiveness among these teams was the degree of trust among team members. Given the importance of trust in team effectiveness and problem solving, it is somewhat surprising that few books on software engineering discuss issues of trust.[1]

---

[1] Some books on project management do discuss trust; see O'Connell [1994] for a discussion of the different managerial approaches that are appropriate for individuals the project trusts to complete assigned tasks versus those that have not proven themselves trustworthy.

Compare the quality of interactions of a high-trust team to a low-trust team during a code review. In the high-trust environment, developers are more likely to assume feedback is directed toward improving the quality of the system. Conversely, in a low-trust environment, the same feedback may instead be viewed as a personal attack (especially if the reviewers, because of prior interactions, use the code review to "get back" at the reviewee). This goes beyond the egoless programming approach described by Weinberg [1971]—sometimes my "ego" is just a protection mechanism erected to protect myself in a low-trust environment!

A similar effect can be evidenced in communication patterns between developers during analysis or design sessions. Effective analysis relies on a great deal of general domain knowledge from our cognitive library. Other members of the team can only gain the benefits of your cognitive library if you share it. The likelihood of sharing such information is substantially higher in a high-trust environment.

Feelings of trust impact the quality of communication. Development teams often complain of communication problems between themselves, or between their team and other teams within the organization. Many times there is no problem with communication. There is instead a problem with trust. The communication problems are merely symptoms of the deeper problem.

Consider the impact of low versus high-trust environments in debugging. As I wrote this book I asked numerous students what their thoughts were in this matter, and the answers are almost universally the same. In a low-trust environment, individuals are more likely to think *some other developer* is the source of the problem and spend their time trying to *prove* that person is at fault. Conversely, in a high-trust environment, where one feels safe and secure, individuals are more likely to think *they* are the source problem and first spend time verifying *their* code is correct. Moreover, in a high-trust environment we are more likely to seek help from other developers in resolving the problem. Conversely, in a low-trust environment we will spend more time working on our own, *even when we know others might help us solve the problem more quickly!*

Perhaps even more astonishingly, the level of trust among members of the team is directly reflected in the structure and style of their source code. I have seen more than one system spend far too much time on the error checking of module parameters because, as one frustrated developer told me, "You can't trust anyone around here to call your function with arguments in the ranges we agreed upon! I've just decided to validate *every* parameter in *every* function call, *even though I know we are losing money because of the increase in transaction times*, because I just can't trust people around here to call my functions with the correct arguments." This result is a natural extension of Conway's law. The structure of the system reflects not only the structure (and communication patterns) of the team that created it, but also the *degree of trust* within that team. *How* effectively we communicate and the manner in which we communicate are reflected in the system.

> *Once trust is lost, even simple gestures designed to promote it are misunderstood and taken as further evidence of mistrust. I once assumed leadership of a team engaged in*

client-server development who were in the process of developing a communication protocol needed to support programs running on a mainframe with their counterparts running on PCs. Unfortunately, by the time I came on board, the working environment was one that could easily be characterized as low trust.

During design, the two teams would specify aspects of the protocol apparently meeting everyone's needs. Not surprisingly, during implementation the designs would require modification. Unfortunately, changes were often made by one group without consulting with the other. Of course, the difference between specification and implementation would be uncovered during testing, which then caused a round of finger pointing. Each team would take turns showing how they were correct. The environment rather quickly degenerated into one of mutual distrust. To illustrate just how bad things were, I remember one episode in which a developer from one team specifically made a change to help make it easier for the other team to use the protocol. Unfortunately, this act of good will was received as the final straw in the ongoing conflict.

Thinking of the problem in terms of structures, processes, and outcomes, I felt the teams did not have enough "structure." I tried to add more structure by suggesting each team sign a "contract" stating the format of the protocol. By explicitly signing a binding document as to the structure of the protocol, my goal was twofold. First, I suspected part of the problem was too little time spent exploring the ramifications of design decisions. I hoped the perceived importance of the contract would motivate everyone to spend a little more time in design. Second, I hoped the larger cultural influence of adhering to a contract would help the teams work together. A contract represents an important structure describing the processes and outcomes between two or more parties. Signing a contract means we will try to follow its terms.

Of course, there are many times contracts don't work, and neither did the contract between the developers: Problems due to changes in the communication protocol kept occurring, except this time my suggestion had made the situation worse. Now developers could point to specific breaches of contract and would come to me demanding punitive (and sometimes even compensatory) damages from the offending parties. As a manager, I had still not addressed the root cause of the problem: A lack of trust within the environment.

9.3.2 The Johari Window

The Johari Window, developed by Joseph Luft and Harry Ingham [Hall 1973; Quinn 1990], provides a structure for thinking about our interactions with others. We can use this structure to support a process for increasing the amount of trust. The remainder of this section is devoted to explaining this structure and how the process it supports leads to high trust.

The Johari Window is an information processing model representing two kinds of communication processes: solicitation and exposure. *Solicitation* is the process by which we actively obtain information from others. *Exposure* is our willingness to apprise others of relevant information we possess and others may not. Organized as a grid, these processes produce four regions of communication space between ourselves and others with respect to the information needed to make a sound decision. The grid provides the necessary structure for understanding the effects of the solicitation and exposure processes as shown in Figure 9–1 (when reviewing the model, it is important to think of *self* as *yourself*).

The most important region is the *arena*, which is the information known to both self and others. The Johari window predicts, and empirical evidence confirms, this is the region in which teams operate most productively and interpersonal relationships are most rewarding. Teams operating in this region are operating under a maximum of trust, because there is a high degree of mutual sharing.

The *blind spot* is that information which is known by others and unknown by self. When operating in this region, we can become confused by the actions of others, primarily because we don't have access to their information. Because we are confused, overall trust (and effectiveness) decrease. This, in turn, motivates us to act in a distrustful manner.

The *facade* is the inverse of the blind spot. It represents information we possess that is unknown by others. In a sense, the tables are turned, and others are forced to guess our motivations. Many individuals prefer to operate in this region, under the assumption they gain some advantage in decision making. While hoarding information may indeed provide a temporary advantage, it increases distrust, especially when someone finds out you withheld critically needed information.

The facade increases distrust because others will remember your actions. In response, they will be more likely to withhold information from you in future interactions. Thus, although the facade rarely has an immediate causal effect, you cannot

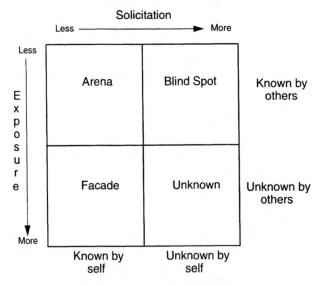

Figure 9–1   The Johari Window

escape its long-term consequences. At best, the facade can only provide a *temporary* advantage. Unfortunately, individuals who change jobs frequently can operate using the facade in an apparently effective manner for years without experiencing its negative effects, as the realization of the facade's ill effects require sustained interactions.

Finally, the *unknown region* represents information not known by anyone. Bounded rationality predicts the existence of this region, although we prefer it to be as small as possible. This is not to say the unknown should be ignored or is unimportant. Many times learning what is unknown (and then sharing it with others) leads to the best decisions.

9.3.3 Interaction Styles

There are four basic interaction styles exemplified by the Johari window: reclusive, questioning, opinionated, and balanced (see Figure 9–2). Each of these increases or decreases the size of the arena. Ideally, we seek interaction styles increasing the arena.

The *reclusive* style avoids both exposure and solicitation. Talking with a reclusive person feels cold, mechanical, and impersonal. They neither communicate their feelings and/or opinions nor do they ask for or acknowledge our own when given. Over time, these feelings translate to a lack of trust: If no information is shared, then how can there be trust? Eventually, the reclusive style decreases the arena: You don't know what I know, and I don't care about what you know.

While the next two styles are not reclusive, they each exhibit dysfunctional communication patterns reducing trust in the long run. The *questioning* style is based almost entirely on solicitation. Quite simply, we ask too many questions. Taken to extremes, individuals try to "get" as much information from others while trying to "hide" their own motives and knowledge.

When I think of the questioning style, I image a lunch meeting between Ralph and Christine, two CEOs. Christine is highly competitive, while Ralph is a bit more genteel. As lunch begins, we find Christine asking a lot of questions. Over time, Ralph will slowly realize Christine is just seeking information and begin to withdraw. At the end of the lunch, Christine is still asking questions, but Ralph is no longer answering them in a way providing any real data. Political enemies are also people who base their interactions on questioning.

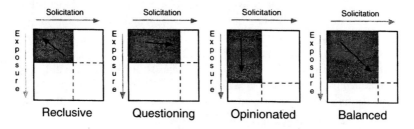

Figure 9–2   Interaction Styles of the Johari Window

Alternatively, individuals who use the *opinionated* style base their interactions on exposure. Not too long ago I needed a new pair of sneakers. No matter what I told the salesman, he kept trying to sell the same brand. It took only a few minutes to realize I could not trust him to help me select the best sneaker. He was too opinionated. Software developers are often quite opinionated and can easily lapse into this style. Pushing your solution (or even pulling too hard) is another example of the opinionated style.

The ideal style is a *balance* between solicitation and exposure. Sometimes we are asking questions to clarify, understand, and increase our knowledge. Other times we are answering them, sharing our knowledge and helping others to increase theirs. A balanced style is characterized by a sense of candor, openness, and sharing. Everyone obtains the benefits of trust, and problem solving is most effective because it takes place in the largest possible arena.

> *Using the Johari window and associated communication styles as an analytical tool, it is easy to see that the mainframe and PC development groups described earlier suffered from a very small arena as a result of an opinionated style. Suppose a member of the PC team needed a change in the protocol. A balanced style would involve discussing the proposed change with one or more mainframe developers. An opinionated style (which was dominant) would simply make the change and implement it ("I know what I'm doing. Your opinion is unimportant."). Instead of promoting a balanced style, the introduction of the contract motivated a confrontational questioning style (e.g., "Are you adhering to the contract? Why not?"). Some developers did try to increase the arena of trust using the contract (e.g., by proposing amendments), but the adversarial patterns established in the past were just too strong.*

9.3.4 Increasing the Arena of Trust

Patterns of trust or mistrust are developed and perpetuated through reciprocal behavior. If I perceive you to be acting in a trustworthy manner, then I am more likely to act the same way. If, however, I think you are being distrustful, then I am likely to respond the same way. The previous section showed the best way to increase the arena of trust was to use a balanced interaction style. Specifically, to increase the arena we must use a balance of solicitation and exposure (i.e., we must ask others for their opinion as well as give our own).

The question is: What is the best sequence for using a balanced interaction style? Here is where things get a little tricky. If we try to use solicitation first, others may perceive us as too questioning, and incorrectly assume we cannot be trusted. Thus, to increase the arena, we must first use exposure. By sharing information (facts, feelings, wild guesses, articles in magazines, and so forth) in a candid, timely, and thorough manner, we begin to increase the arena. Once this has begun, we can then use solicitation to obtain information from others. Of course, their willingness to provide information is directly based on the amount of information we may have first shared with them. The best avenue to a balanced style is summarized in Figure 9–3.

To increase the   we must first   before solicitation.
arena of trust,   use exposure

Figure 9–3   Increasing the Arena of Trust

Increasing the arena by starting with exposure can be extremely difficult, especially when there is little trust to begin with. How can we make the first step when exposure puts us at risk with people who may use this information against us? The work of Louis Barnes [1981] is extremely helpful in providing guidance on how to start this process. He suggests the most effective way to change a low-trust environment is by consciously acting in ways that are different from established patterns. In other words, *act trustful in a low-trust environment.*

This is not necessarily easy. Sustaining paradoxical behavior requires patience and a thick skin. As others experience increased exposure, they may indeed use it to their advantage, releasing pent-up feelings and frustrations. However, if the paradoxical behavior is practiced long enough these feelings of frustration will be drained, and the arena will begin to increase in size. Once the arena increases in size, problem-solving effectiveness will flourish as previously wasted energy can be focused on the problem at hand. As the environment moves from low to high trust, the initially paradoxical high-trust behavior will become standard operating procedure, and you will be able use both solicitation and exposure in a balanced style.

In summary, the optimal use of information is to increase the arena of *shared* information guiding decision making. We can increase the size of the arena through two specific behaviors, exposure and solicitation. If necessary, we can engage in paradoxical behavior to start the process of increasing the arena. Most importantly, you have control over this process, and thus the quality and levels of trust found in your interpersonal relationships.

> *Returning to the dueling development teams, I had another opportunity to solve the problem when the mainframe team broke the contract. As the PC developers sat in my office demanding something be done, the conversation went something like this.*
>
> *PC Team: They violated the contract: They changed the fourth field from numeric to mixed alpha-numeric and broke our code in the process!*
>
> *Luke: Yes, I know. And you're frustrated. But, why are you so upset? The change looked reasonable to me.*
>
> *At this point one of the developers immediately butted in.*

Developer: Yes, but they didn't adhere to the contract! They don't know what they are doing! If they did, they would have thought of this in design. You're lucky I'm on the PC team, because I'm good enough to make the necessary changes fast.

Luke: I didn't say I agreed to the manner in which they made the change. I simply said the change made sense. I am not condoning their behavior. But, let me see if I understand your comment. Do you mean they can't respond to changes in the communication protocol as quickly as you can because you are more highly skilled?

Developer: Yes.

Luke: Well, if you are so much better, why not stop fighting and simply accept every change they propose or make? Just let them be the driving force in the creation of communication protocol. When they make the change, don't complain, but do what you need to do to make the system work.

Developer: But, they'll have all the fun of designing the protocol. And, they'll get all the credit.

Luke: No, they won't. First, I will know you and your team are working overtime to make the project a success because you are willing to respond to their changes. Second, keeping up with any changes will be a real test of your ability. Didn't you say earlier you are more highly skilled? Are you suggesting those unskilled mainframe developers are going to design a communications protocol you and your team can't implement quickly?

The developer thought about this for a second, nodded agreement, obtained buy in from the other members of his team, and agreed not to sign any more contracts and just respond to changes in the system proposed by the mainframe developers.

At first, the mainframe developers couldn't believe the PC team decided not to sign a contract regarding the next set of communication protocols. Moreover, they practically fainted when they made a change to the protocol and heard nothing more than "OK." In the next few weeks, the mainframe team continued to make changes, being surprised every time at the willingness of the PC team in accommodating these changes. Most of the time these changes were legitimate, but every now and then I did have to intervene to make certain the change made sense. Usually all I had to do was ask the mainframe team to justify the technical merits of the proposed change. This simple question was more than enough to stop any inappropriate behavior.

The entire interaction and communication style between the two teams quickly changed as the level of trust increased within the environment. What surprised me was just how quickly. It took less than two months to go from an environment of low trust and warring factions to one of moderate to high trust and more effective teamwork. In retrospect, the speed of the change should come as no real surprise: Most people would rather work in a high-trust environment.

In the low-trust environment, both teams had learned to avoid consulting the other team on changes because discussing the change was unpleasant (at best). Instead of debating the technical merits of the change, other developers would take the opportunity to deride your ability. Quite simply, it wasn't worth exposing yourself to such abuse, so both teams had simply learned to make the change and deal with it later. This is not to say anyone liked the situation. They didn't. They just didn't know how to change it.

By "exposing" themselves to the mainframe team, the PC team made the crucial first step to increasing the arena of trust. Over time, a high-trust environment was created as both teams learned that sharing information was the best way to manage the inevitable changes in the communication protocol. In other words, even though the mainframe team knew they could make a change to the protocol without consulting the PC team, they quickly learned the best change was made when the two teams co-designed the new specification. Such an approach allowed each side to capitalize on their experience and learn more about the other platform in the process. Ultimately, these teams didn't need a contract. They needed trust, and the ideas behind the Johari window helped create it.

ADVICE TO MANAGERS

A manager has many jobs, one of the most important being the creation of a high-trust environment. Use the information in this section to increase trust not only within your team, but also between yourself and your peers.

> Increase your use of solicitation with subordinates.
> Increase your use of exposure with peers and superiors.
> Be reliable.
> Be honest.
> Be prepared for the demands of leadership.

Increase your use of solicitation with subordinates.   In general, managers tend to use too little solicitation with subordinates. This results in feelings of frustration and resentment: Who wants to work for a manager who does not seek your input? Even worse, who wants to work for a manager who *ignores* your input?

Consider the case of John, a harried manager whose boss just told him he must get the next release of the system out the door two months ahead of schedule because a competitor just announced an enhanced version of a competing product. John's team must get the system to market first, otherwise the entire company could lose a significant amount of market share. During the next team meeting, John informs the team of the competitive threat and announces the new development schedule. The good news is that by exposing the team to the competitive threat, they are likely to be more understanding of the need for the shortened schedule. The bad news is that John created the revised schedule without any input from the team.

John would be more effective if he were to inform the team of the competitive threat and present them with a preliminary revised schedule for review. By soliciting ideas on how to complete the system two months ahead of schedule—and acting on it—John's team is more likely to meet the new deadline. For example, someone may come up with a creative idea John never considered, such as delaying the introduction of certain performance optimizations to a subsequent release, or creating split schedules in order to provide developers with better access to the testing machines.

Increase your use of exposure with peers and superiors.   While managers often use too little solicitation with subordinates, they make the opposite mistake with peers and superiors. They tend to use too little exposure.

One reason for this deals with the overall corporate environment. A strongly hierarchical, political, or militaristic organization is not conducive to exposure. There is simply too much at risk. Of course, avoiding exposure contributes to such an environment!

I'll assume, for the moment, you work in a more-or-less normal environment. What are some of the advantages of increasing your use of exposure? First, you gain the experience of peers and superiors in solving problems. Second, you help to establish long-term, mutually beneficial working relationships (e.g., sharing resources with another manager, another kind of exposure, increases the chance they will reciprocate in the future, a clear sign of mutual trust).

Similarly, increasing your exposure with your superior (where the gap between solicitation and feedback is often the greatest) enables you to gain their expertise while increasing their image of you as a competent manager who is willing to explore options and then pick the best alternative. But, this is easier said than done. How can you engage in exposure with your superior, especially when referring to a difficult problem, without appearing ineffective? One way is to prepare a potential solution to your problem before discussing it with your manager. Share your problem (exposure) with your manager *and* your solution, and then ask them for their opinion (solicitation).

Be reliable.   Warren Bennis [1989] has written extensively about leadership and has concluded that one of the four essential qualities of the effective leader is reliability. *Reliability* is behaving in a predictable manner consistent with your stated values. If you let your developers know where you stand and then act in a manner consistent with these values, you will increase their trust in your leadership abilities, *even when they disagree with specific policies!*

Be honest.   It is impossible to establish a high-trust environment if subordinates perceive you as deceitful or misleading. For example, assume your manager has told you some confidential information. One of your staff comes into your office and asks you to confirm or deny a rumor. You guessed it. The rumor they want you to confirm or deny just happens to be related to the confidential information your manager expressed earlier.

At this stage it is irrelevant *how* this developer came to hear of this information. The real question is this: What is your response? You could tell a "white lie," but doing so will hurt you in the long run should the confidential information ever become public. It is far better to state simply and directly that you cannot discuss the situation at this time rather than offering misleading information. Furthermore, you should encourage the developer to refrain from engaging in rumor mongering, for rumors are damaging to the moral of the team and to the company in general.

Be prepared for the demands of leadership. Developers are constantly evaluating their managers to determine if these people are "worth" trusting. Developers ask: "Do I agree with that decision? Would I have done the same thing?" At times you may feel as if you are under a microscope, and in a way, you are. Yet, it is the sum total of these evaluations that establish your trustworthiness in the eyes of your subordinates. Scrutiny comes with the territory when you are the manager of a high-trust environment.

> *The perception of trust in many people is based on their individual morals, and like it or not, followers often judge a leader based on them. I remember how one friend continually complained about his manager. As he put it, "I just can't trust his decisions. I don't think they are in the best interests of the team." Despite what my friend said, I couldn't really think of anything that was so terrible about the decisions made by his manager as to create feelings of low trust. Indeed, every decision made by his manager seemed reasonable enough to me.*

> *The real source of the problem surfaced during lunch one afternoon when my friend revealed he knew his manager was involved in an extramarital affair. This behavior was in strong opposition to the deeply held religious beliefs of my friend, who summarized his feelings by asking: "If he can't be trustworthy to his spouse, with whom he is supposed to share a lifelong commitment, how can he be trustworthy to me? His nickname is even 'Screwy Huey.' Am I the one who is going to be screwed next?"*

> *My goal is not to moralize! I merely wish to point out that feelings of trust are often based on individual perceptions of morality, and how subordinates feel about their working environment can be influenced by how we behave outside of work.*

ADVICE TO DEVELOPERS

The feelings of trust between you, your colleagues, and your management will determine, to a large extent, the quality of your working environment. The first step in moving toward high trust is to act in a trustworthy manner.

> Trust your co-workers' code.
>
> Be reliable.
>
> Managers can't tell you everything.

Trust your co-workers' code.   In his 1983 ACM Turing award lecture, Ken Thompson [1984] describes in detail how a developer can create a simple Trojan horse in a C compiler. He then concludes: "The moral is obvious. You can't trust code that you did not totally create yourself." In many respects Mr. Thompson is correct. In one sense it is impossible to entirely trust another developer's code. A malicious developer can easily hide a difficult to find bug in a system of any reasonable size.

Yet, we *must* "trust" another person's code if we are to develop systems, because we can't build them alone. One can surmise Mr. Thompson feels the same way, for he begins his address with, "To what extent should one trust a statement that a program is free of Trojan horses? Perhaps it is more important to trust the people who wrote the software." To the extent that teamwork is founded on trust, we must learn to trust the code developed by others.

This means that when we are debugging, we should examine *our* source code first on the assumption *other* developers are doing their job competently and effectively. This is often referred to as the *contractual* model of programming: If you adhere to the terms of my calling conventions, I will faithfully compute an accurate output result [Meyer 1988].

Be reliable.   Being reliable is an important component of trust. When you are reliable, other developers learn they can "count" on you to do your job competently, effectively, correctly, and with a certain predictable quality.

Managers can't tell you everything.   The Johari window motivates us to increase the arena of trust by exposing information relevant to the problem at hand. This does not equate to a complete and full disclosure of all information related to a specific matter of importance. Many times managers have information they simply cannot share (e.g., salary information, potential alliances with other companies, proposed changes to company policies, possible changes to the project schedule, and so forth). Base your expectations of information from your manager on reasonable expectations.

10

COMMUNICATION

Take a moment to think about how you spend your time throughout the day. Do you spend a lot of time in meetings and on e-mail? Do you spend *more* time talking, meeting, and conferring with other developers than writing code? Creating a software system requires an enormous amount of communication among a wide variety of people. We have meetings with customers to generate and clarify requirements. We have meetings among the development staff to create and agree upon architectures, models, standards, and the like. We tell vendors about problems and work with them in resolving them.

Communication is the ongoing process whereby developers work to create shared outcomes. It links the team, internally and externally. It is governed by the structures (e.g., organizational topology, e-mail, sufficiently large and readily available meeting rooms, and so forth) supporting or inhibiting the team. Because communication is what leads to the creation of shared outcomes, communicating effectively is perhaps the single most important factor influencing success or failure. It easily overshadows method, topology, and implementation technology.

As a subject area, communication is given far too little focus in traditional books on software engineering. If included at all, it is often talked about in reference to Brooks' [1995] discussion on the difficulty of achieving effective communication in a large team because of the large number of potential pairwise relationships. The focus of this chapter is on developing a deeper understanding of communication: the structures supporting it, the processes defining it, and the outcomes derived from it.

Chapter Overview

Section 10.1 begins by returning to the idea of a shared outcome. It shows how communication is the foundation for creating shared outcomes and discusses what it means to communicate meaningfully.

The remainder of the chapter discusses various aspects of communication especially important to development teams. Section 10.2 explores the special role of notation. Section 10.3 discuss the beneficial role of standards and provides an easy to follow structure for creating them if none exist. Status reports are essential for keeping a project under control. Section 10.4 will show you how to write effective, informative, and useful status reports.

Running a meeting requires a separate set of structures, processes, and outcomes. These are discussed in Section 10.5. Finally, Section 10.6 concludes with a discussion of the project repository, the project notebook of the team.

10.1 THE CREATION OF SHARED OUTCOMES

As described in Chapter 7, shared outcomes are created through transformational processes operating on the outcomes created by individuals. The heart of these transformational processes is communication. But, what *is* communication? What does it consist of? How can these elements be shaped to make certain we are using them effectively?

10.1.1 Modeling Communication as Messages

A *message* is an exchange of information between two entities. In communication networks, a message is a data packet sent between two computer systems. In object-oriented programming, objects communicate via messages. If you think about it, there is a surprisingly large number of message-related terms we use quite regularly. We speak of broadcast messages, synchronous versus asynchronous messages, appropriate bandwidth, transmission rates, error rates, and so forth.

Software developers have an advantage in understanding human communication because we can use most computer-related message terms to describe human communication. In fact, Webster's dictionary *defines* message as "a communication sent between persons." We broadcast an e-mail or an announcement at a soccer game; we share conversations on the phone (i.e., exchange verbal messages using a synchronous protocol) and listen to voice mail (i.e., receive an asynchronous verbal message).

Of course, computer-based analogies fail to describe accurately all the subtle complexities of human communication. A human transmits multiple kinds of information in a message: facts, feelings, attitudes, and the like. In a computer message, the data are largely *in* the message. In human communication, the "data" may be in the *context* as well as the data. In some cases, the context can even be the message.

A human receiver is rarely passive, especially in conversation. Conversation is a nearly *constant* stream of messages. You say something and I reply with a nod, a frown, or a quizzical look—all of these represent messages. Humans also have a much richer means of sending and receiving messages than most computer systems. We can send messages directly (e.g., verbal communication in a meeting) and indirectly (e.g., body language). We can send them formally (e.g., status reports) and informally (e.g., "heads-up" e-mail). We can even exchange them physically (e.g., a handshake).

Perhaps the most important difference between computers and humans regarding communication deals with understandability. The ability for a computer system to receive a message correctly, barring any gross errors in transmission, is based solely on the skill of the developers who created the system. If my program creates a message formed according to the rules of communication, then the system should process it correctly. Human communication is far different. Even if a message is formed properly and transmitted effectively, processing it (i.e., *understanding* and *acting* on it) is based on a multitude of factors, among them the skill of the sender, the knowledge shared between sender and receiver, the skill of the receiver, and the predisposition of the receiver to the contents of the message. In addition to these factors, specific transmission mechanisms require specialized skills. For example, oral communication skills include the ability to speak at an appropriate volume and speed, while written skills include the ability to organize material in a format accessible to the reader.

10.1.2 What Is Meaningful Communication?

In order to better understand communication, linguists have devised a three-layer approach to describing messages [Martin 1989].

♦ The *lexical* content of a message is comprised of the individual tokens or symbols structured inside the message. A well-formed message is constructed from the defined set of tokens understood by both sender and receiver. In written communication this would include words formed by letters of a commonly shared alphabet. In the creation of a class diagram using the Unified Modeling Language, this would consist of using the symbols defined by the Unified Modeling Language.

♦ The *syntactical* content refers to the structure of the tokens and the message itself. A syntactically correct message is formed according to the rules of the language used by the sender and the receiver. Adhering to syntax is importance because properly formed messages are easier to understand. This means spelling and punctuation *are* important, even in e-mail! It also means a class diagram prepared using the Unified Modeling Language should organize its tokens in a proper manner.

♦ The *semantic* content of the message refers to the meaning of the message. Fortunately, we usually attribute greater importance to the semantic content of the message and are usually forgiving of slight lexical or syntactical mistakes. Thus, in a book such as the one you are reading right now, the occasional (and pretty much inevitable) lexical (e.g., a misspelled word) or syntactical (e.g., an unbalanced parentheses mistake is usually forgiven when the semantic content can be inferred.

If the sender and the receiver do not
share a minimum understanding of the
lexical, syntactical, and semantic
contents of a message, the message
will be meaningless.

When shared knowledge exists,
messages can be successfully
exchanged.

Figure 10–1   Shared Knowledge in Communication

Meaningful communication requires two things. First, both sender and receiver must possess a shared understanding of the lexical and syntactical contents of the message. Second, there must be a minimum shared semantic content serving as the starting foundation upon which further understanding can be constructed. By using this shared knowledge, we can communicate effectively (see Figure 10–1).

How can these ideas be applied in software development? What kinds of shared knowledge are important for effective communication? One is the semantic-syntactic knowledge of the outcome used as the vehicle for communication as discussed in Chapter 1. A class written in C++ or a function written in C are as much a message from one developer to the computer ("Do this") as they are to another developer ("This is what this does"). If either receiver does not understand the message, it will be meaningless. For the computer, it means the message must conform to the rigidly specified lexical and syntactical aspects of the language. For the human, it means they must understand the language so they can infer the semantic intent of the source.

Viewing source code as a message from one developer to another puts an entirely new spin on the meaning of good formatting, consistent naming conventions, and the like. The idea isn't new: Bentley and Knuth [1986] presented a similar idea called *literate programming*, in which a developer could sit down with a glass of wine and well-written program and enjoy it much like a good novel. While programs are an important form of communication between one developer and another, literate programming may take the idea a bit too far. Nonetheless, the idea has some merit in motivating well-written source code.

Especially important, and often overlooked, is the metacommunication often needed in teams to establish the ground rules for subsequent communication. By "metacommunication" I mean "communication about communication." Examples include the structure of meeting agendas, coding standards, the "ground rules" for how the meeting will be conducted, and how minutes of the meeting will be distributed. Metacommunication is important because it can help make subsequent communication efficient.

Shared knowledge and well-formed messages are not enough for effective communication. The receiver must truly receive the message in order for it to be effective. A manager who writes several memos to a subordinate may believe s/he is communicating effectively, but effective communication can take place only if the subordinate reads the memos. Effective communication requires the active participation of the receiver, and not merely the efforts of the sender.

10.1.3 Communication Structures

Communication structures include not only the lexical and syntactical aspects of messages, but also the senders, receivers, and communication channels used for the transmission of messages. Focusing on communication structures enables us to make certain the right messages are transmitted to the right people in the best possible manner.

The most common senders are receivers of messages within the team are . . . members of the team! While this result is intuitively obvious, what is not necessarily obvious is that most messages sent between team members are not sent to all members of the team. Messages are instead sent to the smaller coalitions in which the sender participates. Coalitions form in response to job and task requirements—when two people share responsibility for a subsystem they form a natural coalition. Coalitions also form by mutual selection among team members who share similar attributes such as education, beliefs, social status, and the like. Finally, coalitions can form across team boundaries for both task and socially motivated reasons. One way to identify coalitions is to examine the flow of messages within the team as shown in Figure 10–2.

Managing the number of people with whom you communicate (or are expected to communicate) is of special importance. Brooks [1995] showed that the number of *pairwise* communication paths for a team of size n is $n(n - 1)/2$. This means for a small team of 5 developers there are 10 possible pairwise communication paths. However, the *potential* number of communication paths is far greater! Quinn [1975] shows this number is $n[2(n - 1) - 1]$, or 75 for a team of five developers (see Table 10–1).

If it is difficult to communicate effectively with a large number of people (and it is), what is the best thing to do? The simplest, best, and most obvious solution is to keep project teams as small as possible (but no smaller), ideally between three and ten developers. Another approach is to establish topologies encouraging the formation of coalitions around subsystems, which naturally reduces communication. Each coalition, in turn, would be as small as possible. This technique is discussed later in this section and again in Chapter 12.

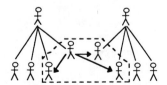

Organizational topology structures much communication among members of the team, such as when a manager sends a message to all members of the team.

The dominant form of communication, however, occurs among the coalitions that form between team members and across topological boundaries.

Figure 10–2   Method and Organizational Topology

TABLE 10–1   Team Size, Communication Paths, and Communication Channels

Team size	1	2	3	4	5	6	7	8	9	10	11
Pairwise paths		1	3	6	10	15	21	28	36	45	55
Potential paths	1	2	9	28	75	186	441	1016	2295	5110	11,253

A third approach is to use advanced technology to facilitate communication, but this should be done with some caution. Research by Perry [1994] shows even the most feature-laden e-mail system is still no match for a whiteboard and face-to-face communication. Why? Ultimately, e-mail is a relatively low bandwidth means of communication. Body language, intonation, gestures, and much emotion are lost in e-mail. And, its asynchronous nature means feedback is delayed. A real-time video-based collaborative tool can compensate for some of these losses, but it too has drawbacks. Fidelity is still an issue, not every sense is captured, and the cost is prohibitive.

A related aspect of communication structure concerns how different coalitions and teams are linked. Teams need such people, for without them "islands of understanding" form around isolated aspects of the problem. Consider a complex system comprised of multiple subsystems, each created by a different team. If a large number of problems are found during subsystem integration you can be absolutely certain the different teams did not communicate effectively. No one linked the teams.

A linking individual also smooths relations between development and nondevelopment groups. Angela is a developer with an interest in marketing and has formed a friendship with Don, a member of the marketing department. Together, Angela and Don represent a critically important coalition serving to transmit information between their respective teams. Angela's explanations of marketing department decisions (as told to her by Don) serve to generate understanding, and perhaps even support, for such decisions in the development team. Don can give similar explanations to his team, such as explaining why a compiler bug causing an error in the last product release really isn't the fault of the development team. Both Angela and Don represent conduits of information that would not otherwise exist.

Integrating disparate coalitions can be a tricky thing. I doubt that Angela's manager told her, "Go hang out with the marketing department so we can get information." Yet, by doing so, everyone benefits. Linking coalitions can be especially difficult in the ethnically diverse environments characterizing many development organizations, for coalitions naturally form along shared language and cultural boundaries. Linking individuals are essential in such environments. I first realized this in graduate school, when many class discussions did not include all students unless the professor explicitly integrated ethnically based coalitions. The instructors who could do this most effectively spoke multiple languages fluently and could help bridge communication gaps due to differences in language.

More recently, as ObjectSpace has continued to grow, we have hired several individuals from around the world, including India. Quite naturally, coalitions have formed

along shared cultural and language boundaries. We are also fortunate in that another employee, who hails from Canada, lived a few years in India and can speak Hindi. Many times I have watched him play a linking role among those whose native language is English and those whose native language is Hindi. His presence substantially improves the effectiveness of the team.

Communication channels are the structures by which messages are transmitted. These include everything from face-to-face conversation to e-mail, voice mail, and so forth. Even the physical environment can provide a communication channel, as when we are informed it is time to return to our seats after intermission by the dimming of the house lights at the symphony.

Communication channels are part of structure because they determine communication processes. Certain channels facilitate the transmission of a message to a large audience, while others permit higher sensory bandwidth. For example, e-mail can be used to transmit a message quickly and efficiently to all members of the team. An effective conversation can only be held with a limited number of people but gives the speaker more flexibility in adjusting messages to transmit subtle shades of meaning often difficult to convey in a written form. Without the structure provided by an internal Web site, a company could not think to communicate operating procedures using Java. By providing multiple channels, managers can enhance communication within the team. By choosing the right channel, developers can increase the likelihood the messages will be received.

The most important aspect of communication structure is the common knowledge between sender and receiver regarding the lexical and syntactic contents of a message, for this understanding is a necessary prerequisite to sharing semantics. Receiving a message *means* the sender and receiver increase their shared understanding of the semantic contents of the message in some meaningful way.

Suppose you and I are working on a project using the Fusion method [Coleman 1994] and I want to obtain feedback on a preliminary object model. The lexical aspects of the model (a message) are the symbols used within the model. The syntax is defined by Fusion and includes the legal ways in which the symbols can be linked. The semantics of each symbol are the meaning we attribute to the different symbols. The semantic content of the entire model is the aggregate semantic content of each symbol. Thus, you could understand parts of the model but not others. We say the model is correct if the semantic meaning of the model accurately reflects the problem domain and requirements.

Our communication is enhanced if I adhere to the symbols defined by Fusion. If I use a new symbol, one not defined within Fusion, our communication is made unnecessarily more difficult. Why? Unless I establish the syntactical and semantic properties of the new symbol, you will not understand what it means. If you don't understand what the symbol means, you will be forced to "guess" its meaning or ask me what it means. In either case, effective communication is reduced: What are the chances you will guess correctly? How long will it take you and me to reach a shared understanding of what the symbol means?

10.1.4 Communication Processes

Communication processes are the means by which a sender creates messages and transmits them to a receiver(s). A simplified view of this process is as follows. A sender decides some information is to be transmitted to a receiver. A message format is selected, based on the sender's perception of the shared knowledge between the sender and the receiver and the type of information to be transferred. The message is created according to the lexical and syntactic rules associated with the chosen communication structure. Finally, the message is transmitted over an appropriate communication channel, also dictated by structure.

It sounds like a lot of work, doesn't it? Fortunately, most of the time this process happens so naturally we don't realize it is composed of discrete steps. When you have a question regarding some aspect of the system, it is simply natural to walk down the hall and ask a colleague or simply send an e-mail. Of course, the very fact the process is "natural" can cause us problems: We sometimes do not take care in creating messages effectively! Because we are careless, we do not choose effective message formats, prepare messages properly, or transmit them effectively. The result is ineffective communication—a failure to create a shared understanding.

By thinking of the process of how we create messages, we can substantially improve our effectiveness in communication. The first step is selecting the right kind of message structure. If you are dealing with most technical aspects of the system, such as analysis or design, the best first choice is the message structure defined by your method. If you are dealing with a nontechnical aspect of your system, or some technical aspect not covered by your method, the best choice is based on what you think the receiver will understand. Avoid picking message structures you know well *just because* you know them well! It is far better to pick a message structure understood by *both* you and the receiver.

The next step in a good communication process is preparing the message appropriately. The *formality* of a message is the degree to which the message adheres to the lexical and syntactic rules describing the message. *Clarity* is the degree to which the receiver can understand the semantic meaning of the message in an unambiguous and unequivocal manner. Formal messages tend to enhance clarity, as they are subject to less interpretation by the receiver.

A preliminary sketch of a data model on a whiteboard is likely to be prepared with less formality than the same model prepared in a CASE tool. Both models (which *are* messages) can communicate effectively in the right context. I'd prefer the informal version in an early planning meeting, because formal messages take time to create, and I don't want to be slowed down by details. On the other hand, I'd much prefer the formal version if I had to distribute the model to a large number of developers.

Careful communication refers to the effort the sender puts into the creation of a message that conveys information accurately, correctly, and unambiguously. Like formality, carefully created messages enhance clarity. However, carefully created messages do not have to be formal; formality and carefulness are two different dimensions. Being careful means being conscientious, purposeful, attentive, and consistent. Being careful doesn't necessarily mean being unequivocal. I can be unsure about something but communicate about it in a very careful way, as when I am asking you to review two different ways of expressing a difficult requirement.

Time is always a factor in software development. Among other things it impacts our communication processes. Because highly formal, carefully prepared messages take longer to create, we tend to expend such efforts only when we think it necessary. Unfortunately, creating messages quickly tends to reduce their clarity, resulting in miscommunication. In the long run this can actually increase the overall amount of time it takes to achieve a shared understanding—eventually the miscommunication will be discovered, and we will have to go back and "fix" what is wrong! Taking more time to carefully prepare a message would have saved time in the long run.

Time also impacts our selection of a message structure because certain kinds of messages take longer to create. A graphical picture of the system architecture may convey it most effectively, but it may take so long to create given a very simple drawing tool we instead choose to describe it textually. The trick, of course, is to find the right balance between message structure, formality, and carefulness.

10.1.5 Communication Outcomes

According to communication theory, "communication" has not taken place unless one or more identifiable changes have occurred in the receiver as a result of the message [Whitman 1983]. Quite often these changes are not externally visible. A change in knowledge level is a successful communication outcome, as is a change in attitude. Many times they are visible, as when we change the way we write source code as a result of reading a book on improving coding practices. The most important specific kind of outcome in the creation of a software system is the creation of a shared understanding among the members of the team. Most communication related to systems development is geared toward achieving this goal.

Outcomes build on outcomes creating a communication context. A context, in turn, guides further communication. Consider the following conversation among two members of the team [after Whitman 1983].

Developer 1: Have you decided?

Developer 2: Not yet.

Developer 1: We need your decision by Friday.

Developer 2: I know. I'm thinking about it.

Are these developers talking about the project plan, the calling specifications between two modules, or the company soccer team? If we don't know the previously established communication context, we cannot understand the conversation.

A communication context is similar to the "shared understanding" required for communication but differs in that it is a result of the ongoing communication process.

It may help to think of communication like a program. The shared understanding is the static representation of the source code. The communication context is the dynamic execution state of the program as it is run (as we communicate). The shared understanding we seek in software development is often defined by the context, which enables developers to communicate using highly encoded words and knowledge structures.

Recall that simply sending or receiving a message *is not* communication. An identifiable change must occur in the receiver as a result of a message. Suppose I send you a message but it becomes lost or garbled in transmission? Or, suppose you don't quite understand the message and would like to discuss it with me in greater detail? One way to address these kinds of problems is to save messages for future use. Doing so enables us to search, compare, and review messages as we attempt to increase our understanding of the problem or the communication context. Like saving the stack trace of a program, saving messages enables us to review past messages and aids in "debugging" the decisions made regarding the system during the development process.

10.1.6 Changes over Time

Because communication forms the foundation for interactions among members of the team, the nature, form, and content of communication will change over time as the team develops. For example, in the early stages of team development, body language may not have a great impact during a meeting because team members do not understand the body language of other team members. Over time, body language will assume greater importance as members of the team learn the significance of how other members of the team react to situations and communicate their reaction through body language.

Other changes occur regarding the formality of communication. When someone is new, we are quite likely to engage in more formal communication, either by social convention or in the hopes of communicating with greater clarity. Over time, we relax. Communication becomes less formal, and we begin to rely more and more heavily on our collective mind, the communication context, and the shared understanding the context has created. Needless to say, even though the formality associated with communication can safely change over time from formal to informal, effective teams should never send careless messages. The sender should always assume the responsibility of choosing an appropriate level of formality, and, when needed, use highly formal communication processes.

ADVICE TO MANAGERS

The creation of structures and processes supporting effective communication is one of the basic functions of management, for how the team operates is inseparable from how the team communicates. In addition to managerial advice contained in this section, the developer advice also discusses several strategies for improving communication. Because it is not possible to be an effective manager without possessing good communication skills, you should also read the developer recommendations.

Periodically review the basics.

Know the implications of Brooks' law.

Choose the communication topology based on the organization topology.

Change organizational members to produces changes in communication.

Provide numerous communication structures.

Integrate frequently.

Establish "ground rules" early.

Hire a mercenary analyst.

Give your undivided attention.

Periodically review the basics.   The basic ideas presented in this section are these: Communication structure is whom I communicate with; communication process is how I communicate, and communication outcome is the degree to which I achieve a shared understanding with the receiver regarding the semantic content of the message. All are important for effective communication. By periodically reviewing these basics, you can make adjustments to ensure your communication and the communication within your team are maximally effective.

Know the implications of Brooks' law.   In *The Mythical Man-Month* Brooks [1995] traces the impact of adding developers to a late project in terms of coordination, management, communication, and training. As described earlier, the number of communication channels and the number of pairwise communication paths increase nonlinearly. This means adding even *one* person can substantially increase the burden of communication! Brooks simplifies his result with a simple management dictate that has stood the test of time. Known as Brooks' law, it states: "Adding programmers to a late project makes it later." Among other things, Brooks' law motivates us to consider the communication impact of adding developers to the team (even if the project is *not* late!).

Choose the communication topology based on the organization topology.   Examining the flow of communication—who communicates with whom, and why—results in a communication topology. Effective organizational topologies support optimal communication topologies. In other words, a good organizational topology encourages communication among the right people in the project by providing natural structures for this communication.

Take advantage of this idea when designing organizational topologies. Beginning with a proposed organizational topology, draw a communication topology minimizing unnecessary communication. Then, work to create this communication topology by assigning tasks to people who communicate according to the communication topology. Try to assign tasks to the smallest coalition possible, as smaller coalitions communicate more effectively. Expect to iterate through this process once or twice. The primary objective is to ensure the right people are communicating about the right problems.

I have used this technique often and have found it especially helpful when the team is working under a tight deadline. Why? One of the biggest time wasters on any project is unnecessary communication. By structurally minimizing unnecessary communication, the team is more likely to meet the deadline. To illustrate, on one project I was asked to prepare the next version of a system on an extremely tight deadline given five people. As project lead, I was responsible for organizing the team.

At first, I considered a democratic team, structuring each developer as "equals" but rejected it because four out of five team members were unfamiliar with the implementation language. Their inexperience would create unnecessary and redundant communication. I decided a traditional hierarchy was best, because it offered the best chance to allocate independent tasks and minimize pairwise communication. However, two of the team members were best friends (indeed, one had convinced the other to join the project). These two friends were going to communicate intensely regardless of the project, so I leveraged their friendship and created a single larger task suitable for two people (see Figure 10–3).

To structure communication further, I created a formal system of scheduled communication. Each subteam submitted weekly status reports into a shared a project repository (both of these are described in greater detail in subsequent sections). Two meetings were scheduled each week: One with each subteam and myself, and one with the entire group (thus, I had five meetings each week, but any one team member had at most two). By carefully structuring the communication of the team, everyone was able to focus on their assignment. The result? The project was completed on time, with 11 out of 12 major system enhancements.

Changing organizational members produces changes in communication. Drawing the communication topology makes it easy to see that when

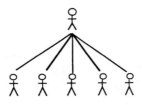 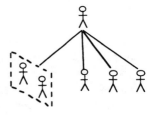

Organizational topology provides the starting point for effective communication...

...but explicitly designing the communication topology and encouraging the formation of coalitions can significantly boost productivity.

Figure 10–3 Organizational and Communication Topology

there is a change in the membership of the team, communication changes both qualitatively and quantitatively. Because the membership of any team changes over time, always consider the effects of changing membership on communication.

Consider the effects of adding a developer. Should you assign them a mentor to guide them in their work? (Microsoft has great success with this approach.) Do they bring a special set of skills to the team you hope to propagate? Assign them a task encouraging communication with others.

Provide numerous communication structures.   How we communicate (process) is based on the available communication structures. I cannot communicate with you over the Internet if I don't have an Internet accessible mail system! Your team cannot have effective meetings if there isn't a free meeting room! By providing as many structures as possible, communication is enhanced. Voice mail and Internet accessible e-mail are bare minimums.

Integrate frequently.   How can you be certain the teams or developers associated with the development of disparate subsystems (or modules or objects) communicate frequently enough to ensure the system is built on time? In one way you can't, because you can't "mandate" communication. You can't "force" people to send e-mail, verify calling conventions, or ensure performance requirements. You can, however, schedule frequent integrations (at a minimum, once or twice a week).

By integrating subsystems frequently, you create communication demands on all parties. Integration requires the resolution of all sorts of nasty little issues that *only* surface during integration. Resolving these issues, of course, requires communication—communication about the problem, the domain constraints, the proposed solution, and the actual implementation—communication which leads to a better system.

Of course, improved communication is not the only benefit of a frequent integration schedule. Frequent integrations provide valuable feedback to the team: It lets them know where they stand and how they are doing. Frequent integration helps people feel good about themselves and their work: There is always a working system, and watching this system grow in functionality is just plain fun. Finally, frequent integration identifies problems early, when they can be fixed before they cause a lot of damage.

Jim McCarthy [1995] reports how many projects at Microsoft integrate *every day*. A complete build of the system is conducted every day by a developer given special responsibility for making certain the build happens. McCarthy readily admits performing a daily build is a *very* demanding discipline but notes many projects at Microsoft have used the approach with great success.

Establish "ground rules" early.   *Ground rules* provide explicit structures establishing acceptable and unacceptable behaviors with respect to specific communication contexts. Usually, ground rules focus on meetings [Scholtes 1988], but using them only for meetings discounts their importance. Although they can sometimes sound corny, they provide an important structure. Adhering to this structure *does* improve communication.

An effective exercise is to establish ground rules with your team. Here are some sample ground rules to help you get started:

♦ *Respect*. Everyone's opinion is valuable. Everyone is entitled to it.

♦ *Courtesy*. Avoid interrupting others. Listen attentively. Go to a private place if the communication is about a sensitive issue.

♦ *Honesty*. Say what is on your mind.

♦ *Facts*. Opinions are OK, but opinions disguised as facts are not.

♦ *Participation*. Everyone needed to make a decision should have input. Being domineering is not tolerated. Include as many as people as are needed to obtain a good decision.

Once ground rules have been established, post them in a conspicuous place. When communication processes fail to adhere to the structures prescribed in the ground rules, note the difference and modify the communication process as necessary.

Hire a mercenary analyst.   Jim Coplien [1995] notes that supporting all the analysis and design notation required by a method is too complex a job for a single developer, especially when this developer has other project responsibilities. When a developer is asked to do both, either the documentation quality suffers (or, as is more likely the case, is not done at all) or their "real" work suffers. In either case, the team suffers.

To correct this situation Jim suggests hiring a "mercenary analyst," a technical writer (or articulate developer) who is proficient at creating the necessary documentation for the project. By elevating the role of documentation, you give it respect. By dedicating a person to the job, you ensure it is done in a timely manner. Jim also suggests the documentation be maintained on-line (I fully agree with this) and that this be a full-time position. I'm not certain I agree with this second point. A full-time position is only required on the largest projects, and even then it is most important during the initial analysis and design of the system. Once the major architectural decisions have been established, you may then have less of a need for a full-time position.

Give your undivided attention.   I know you are busy. I know you have many things to do. Yet, failing to give your undivided attention to a subordinate discounts their value. If you can't give undivided attention when they want to talk, delay the conversation until you can.

ADVICE TO DEVELOPERS

Effective communication is based not only on the messages you send, but also on the manner in which you receive them from others. Preparing messages with clarity, and receiving them effectively, will help you achieve the communication you desire.

> Take greater care when communicating with new team members.
>
> Use communication to control process leveling.
>
> Communicate with appropriate formality.

Take greater care when communicating with new team members.

Sometimes it can be quite frustrating to talk with new members of the team—you have to explain everything in excruciating detail! They just don't seem to know anything, and when you tell them something, they always seem to return in a few hours, asking more questions about the obvious.

Obvious to whom? Do they have your knowledge of the problem domain? Do they have knowledge of the communication context created in the team? Do they share the same understanding about previously created outcomes? Do they even know the basic operating processes of the company (most new employees don't)? Do they know when and how your team acts differently with respect to these processes? Are they integrated into the collective mind?

Taking special care when communicating with new team members has at least four dividends. First, it saves you time and frustration. By making certain what you communicated was understood *the first time*, you prevent repeat questions. Second, you help the new team member feel as if they are a valuable member of the team, helping to ease their transition to their new assignment. Third, you establish your reliability and increase the arena of trust. Finally, you bolster their self-esteem. No one, especially when they are new to an organization, wants to asks too many questions for fear of being labeled as incompetent. By making certain you are well understood, you eliminate these fears by removing the need for the question.

Use communication to control process leveling.

One of the differences in process leveling between individuals and teams is that communication within teams tends to slow the speed at which process leveling occurs. Use this to your advantage. When you sense another developer is working at a different level, determine if you think it is appropriate. If the answer is yes, be quiet. Let them continue, and only "return" them to a different level if they don't return on their own. If the answer is no, ask them: "What are you thinking? Why?" The question will engage communication, slowing process leveling.

Form coalitions with other groups.

Try to find other groups within the company with whom you share interests. By increasing the size and richness of your communication topology, you will obtain more information more effectively.

Communicate with appropriate formality.

Taking one of my analysis and design classes can be tough. During class, I require students to be highly formal in the preparation of outcomes. As you can guess, I often get a lot of complaints. Preparing formal outcomes is hard, especially when you are learning a new method! Every now and then a student asks me: "Luke, do you always prepare outcomes with such formality?" When I answer I *don't always* prepare outcomes with such formality, my students often think they've got me. If I don't always prepare formal outcomes, why should they?

One reason is since I *know* the notation, my *need* to prepare formal outcomes is less than theirs. In other words, preparing formal outcomes is a highly effective educational tool for learning the notation. Another reason is that because I know the notation well, I can convert informal outcomes (such as a sketch) into a formal outcomes (a well-drawn object model with all the adornments) easily. Without this ability the long-term effectiveness of communication is severely hampered.

However, my students are correct: Being formal is not always appropriate. Here are some rules of thumb to help guide your decision on formality.

◆ Formality increases as the number of receivers increase.

◆ As discussed, be formal when communicating using a new notation or when learning new lexical and syntactical message structures. Doing so will facilitate learning and minimize misunderstanding.

◆ Formality increases when communicating with superiors, especially as you communicate with people who have greater positions of power or who are not in your direct line of command.

◆ Formality increases when there is greater chance for ambiguity on the part of the receiver.

◆ In general, it is better to err on the side of formality.

Since much of our general communication involves verbal communication, you can substantially improve the effectiveness of our communication by improving your speaking—and listening—skills.

> Speak in an appropriate tone of voice.
> Respect personal space.
> Silence implies a failure to communicate.

Speak in an appropriate tone of voice.   Speak loudly enough for others to hear you clearly, but as quietly as possible so as not to disturb others. Achieving the right volume, especially if you work in a room full of cubicles, is especially important.

Respect personal space.   I once worked with a gentleman I will refer to as "John" who could not communicate effectively. At first, I thought only I felt this way, because John was articulate. So, to double-check my feelings, I asked some other people on the team what they felt. They all replied they felt talking with John was very difficult, but no one could quite figure why. Unfortunately, John was asked to leave the team before we understood the problem. Although John spoke clearly, he did not

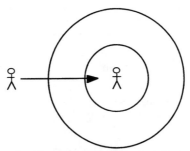

Figure 10–4   Personal Space

Avoid moving into the personal space of another person during conversation.

communicate effectively. Only later did someone remark during a conversation how John would stand very close to you when speaking. Too close. *Uncomfortably* close. He violated personal space.

Our *personal space* is the distance separating us when talking (or otherwise interacting) with others. Think of two concentric circles, the inner circle with a diameter of about 5"–7" and the outer circle with a diameter between 14"–30" (see Figure 10–4). The boundary of the inner circle is my intimate space; the boundary of my outer circle is my personal space. The actual diameter of the circles varies— each of us prefers different sized boundaries, and our preferences are influenced by societal norms.

When you are outside the larger circle, we are engaged in what is generally considered "normal," or "public" conversation. Being between the two circles makes our conversation more intimate, more private. The closer you become, the more private our conversation. However, moving closer than 5"–7" puts you into my intimate space. Unless you are my wife, one of my closest friends, or are telling me a secret no one else should hear, I'm likely to feel uncomfortable. John usually stood about 8"–12" from another person, far too close for normal conversation. Because we felt uncomfortable when he was nearby, we could not communicate effectively.

Be especially careful of touching another person during conversation. Touch is perhaps the most intimate form of communication and is generally not appropriate for the work environment. Note also what is considered acceptable "social touching" is highly culturally dependent. Someone from a different culture can even find the American custom of shaking hands to be offensive. Learning to communicate effectively, especially in conversation, means respecting the personal space of others.

Listen aggressively.   The first step to becoming a more effective listener is making the decision to do so. You have to want to improve your listening skills, because while hearing is easy, listening is hard work. One way to improve is to listen "aggressively." Why? The average listener can process speech at least twice as fast as the average speaker can generate it. As a result, it is easy to let your mind wander off the topic. The result? You hear, but don't listen. To listen more effectively, try the following.

♦ Attempt to identify the main points and central ideas the speaker is trying to convey. Think of how subsequent topics fit these ideas.

♦ Continuously review previous points made by the speaker. Periodically ask questions to ensure you have summarized this information accurately.

♦ Avoid jumping to conclusions, but do try and anticipate what the speaker will say next and then compare what is actually said with what you thought. The discrepancies will provide important feedback on your understanding of the material.

♦ Remain aware of the stylistic and/or emotional aspects of the communication. Concentrate on both *content* and *presentation*, for how a message is transmitted (itself a form of communication) may provide great insight into how an individual really feels about a problem. If a colleague prepares a highly formal document when you were expecting just a simple sketch, you can safely infer they have prepared something they feel is important.

♦ Do not finish sentences. Even if you finish them correctly, the practice is at best discourteous.

Silence implies a failure to communicate.   If other members of your team are unusually or uncharacteristically silent, they are not likely to be giving you "consent." In general, silence implies a failure to communicate, and you should be especially careful about silence. Don't try to "force" someone to communicate—they may really want to be silent. Instead, give them the opportunity to communicate [Scholtes 1988]. For example, suppose you are in a meeting with four other developers. Anne is dominating the conversation and Ajay has been unusually quiet. To include Ajay, you might say: "Thanks for your input Anne. Let's hear what others have to say. Ajay, what do you think?" This will give Ajay the opportunity to provide his thoughts in a nonthreatening manner.

Because e-mail is such a pervasive tool in our industry, it is worthwhile to examine special techniques on using it effectively, including what could be considered "e-mail etiquette."

E-mail is a *corporate* resource.
Use descriptive subject headings.
Save e-mail because it can be searched.
Anything digital can easily be distributed to the entire organization.
Distribute humorous e-mail with care.
Use humor and sarcasm with care.
Turn on spell checking.
Be brief.
Explicitly state the response you expect.
Close threads.

E-mail is a *corporate* resource.   Unless you are paying for your e-mail connection and using it on your own computer, e-mail is a corporate resource. This means your employer has the right to search your mail, monitor how you use it, and even terminate employment in cases of a misconduct [Weisband 1995]. Use your e-mail system in a responsible manner, just as you would any other corporate resource.

Use descriptive subject headings.   The purpose of the subject is to provide a concise description of the contents of the message. Ideally, it should enable the reader to safely and effectively decide if the message must be read.

Save e-mail because it can be searched.   Most systems provide facilities for searching the subject and contents of mail messages. This can save a considerable amount of time when trying to recall relevant communication on a specific topic. Of course, if you do save your mail, make certain you have an appropriate backup plan.

Anything digital can easily be distributed to the entire organization.   Things digital have a surprising tendency to be replicated and distributed. Your e-mail is digital. Once created and sent, it can be forwarded without too much work to the entire world! The implication is this: You cannot be entirely certain who will read the mail you create. More than one career has been damaged by an ill-conceived e-mail. If you are at all uncertain about the consequences of a message, it is better not to send it. Instead, choose a different communication channel, one more appropriate to the transmission of secure information.

Distribute humorous e-mail with care.   Your employer may not share your sense of humor, especially when your humorous e-mail is forwarded to the entire organization, overloads the mail system and causes it to crash. Certainly, a little humor can brighten our day. But, can you justify your mail on *business* terms?

Use humor and sarcasm with care.   Humor is extraordinarily difficult to convey in writing. Attempts at humor within e-mail can be easily perceived as flippant, technically incompetent, immature, or just plain offensive. Writing with clarity is hard enough—really funny writing is considered by many to be the hardest writing of all!

One way to use humor effectively is to refer to only what *your team* thinks is funny. Most teams develop "inside jokes" that have meaning to members of the team, but not to people outside the team. By referring to these jokes in your mail, you will most likely find a safe mechanism for expressing humor.

Turn on spell checking.   The on-line community has a distressing tolerance for poor grammar and spelling. Most mail systems allow you configure some form of spell checker. Use it.

Be brief. E-mail is not the best mechanism for communicating large amounts of complex information. First, complex information is communicated most effectively when given an appropriate structure (e.g., tables, diagrams, graphs, multiple fonts, and so forth). Most mail systems do not provide nearly enough control over the formatting of messages. Second, long documents can take a long time to transmit, and remote users may become annoyed. Third, long documents consume valuable resources on the server—I know of at least one mail system that *replicates* messages to every receiver. Your well-intentioned 3-Mb attachment could consume 30 Mb of disk space if sent to ten other people! If you do have a large document to share with others, put the document in a shared file server (or similar medium) and send the name of the file to others. Being succinct in your e-mail messages will help you use the medium to its greatest potential.

Explicitly state the response you expect. Much of the e-mail I send is designed to inform my peers, subordinates, and superiors of some pertinent or relevant information. Sometimes I don't want a response. Other times, I expect a response. And, sometimes I need one, usually by a specific date. To make certain my intentions are clear, I often put the following tag lines in my e-mail:

```
— No reply necessary —
— Reply requested by mm/dd/yy —
— Reply required by mm/dd/yy —
```

Your mail system may provide automated support for any of these requests. If so, use it.

Close threads. A *thread* is a sequence of messages about a particular topic. In the on-line community it can be difficult to determine when the "end" of the thread is reached—there is no on-line equivalent of simply nodding agreement and walking away. On-line threads just seem to fade away . . . they lack closure. To help rectify this situation and to let others know when I am finished, I try to close threads by ending my messages with "End of thread?" If others have finished, they won't respond. If they do respond, they usually tell me why they are continuing the thread (which further enhances effective communication).

10.2 KNOW YOUR NOTATION

When solving a problem you must deal with two issues. The first is understanding the problem well enough to create an appropriate solution. The second is documenting your solution in a manner allowing you and others to use, extend, and maintain it. As discussed in Chapter 3, many of the solutions associated with software development are models of the system. Because they are models, we need ways to communicate about them in an unambiguous and concise manner. This goal is achieved through notation. A *notation* is a specific *language* created to communicate specific kinds of information. It is defined through specific lexical and syntactical rules defining how semantic information is transmitted using this language.

ADVICE TO MANAGERS

Making notations work for your team consists of two primary activities. First, you must make certain everyone who is using the notation, including yourself, understands it. Second, you must make certain you are using the right notation, one meeting the needs of your team.

> Make certain everyone knows the notation.
> Modify when necessary.
> Control modifications.

Make certain everyone knows the notation.   The most important aspect of a notation is understandability: Does *each* member your development staff understand the notation? If not, schedule some form of training to instruct the developer in using the notation.

Modify when necessary.   A notation is a language, and all languages evolve through use for quite legitimate reasons. One reason concerns ambiguity. The designers of a method are human, and although most do an excellent job in defining notations with a minimum of ambiguity, the possibility exists. Addressing ambiguities in method-defined notations is a perfectly legitimate reason to modify a notation.

A more common motivation is to increase communication efficiency. To illustrate, the Fusion notation for modeling classes of objects during analysis is shown in Figure 10–5. Each class is represented as a box, with the name of the class at the top. The class name is separated from the rest of the class by a line. The attributes of the objects belonging to the class are named below the line.

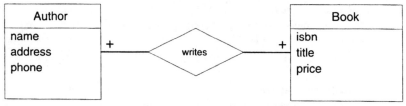

Fusion notation, as defined by [Coleman 1994]

Figure 10–5   Fusion Object Model Notation

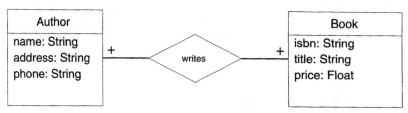

Fusion notation, extended to show attribute type information

Figure 10–6   Extending the Fusion Object Model Notation

In Fusion, analysis attributes cannot be objects. They can only be simple values of well-defined "atomic" types such as integers, strings, numbers, dates, and boolean flags. A common extension to Fusion is to annotate each attribute with its associated type. This is shown in Figure 10–6.

You may find some developers resist extending notations out of concern of using something "nonstandard." Is this a problem? Not really. The inventors of methods are not dogmatic people who refuse to allow any changes or extensions. They are, by and large, engineers who have created their method as a means to engage in more effective problem solving. They *want* us to use their methods as *tools*, not restrictions. As far as I know, they universally encourage us to modify, extend, or otherwise change their notations as needed in problem solving.

Analyzing an extension in terms of structures, processes, and outcomes, we find the following. The goal is to structure the process of notation modification to achieve two related outcomes. The first is modification truly enhancing the existing notation. The second is a shared understanding of the meaning of the new notation among all members of the team.

First, a developer identifies a problem with the current notation. Perhaps this is through prior experience, or perhaps it is through current use. To begin the modification process, have the developer describe the problem and the proposed solution in a form easily distributed for review. Initiate a formal inspection to ensure the proposed modification meets these needs. Once the change has been approved as accurate, make certain it is appropriately communicated to all members of the team.

Of course, the formality of the actual process should be based on the size of the team and the complexity of the modification. Consider the simple modification to Fusion proposed above. A small team could probably get by with an e-mail from the senior architect describing the change. A large team should follow a far more formal process and record the modification in an appropriate standards manual.

Control modifications.   Having opened the gate to notation modification, I must caution you to resist extending notations unless absolutely needed. Many proposed extensions are often unnecessary and are motivated more by a lack of knowledge of how to correctly use the current notation than a problem with the notation itself.

ADVICE TO DEVELOPERS

The notations defined by a method are one of your most powerful tools for developing software systems. They enable you to condense and communicate a surprisingly large amount of information in a precise manner. Taking the time to use your notation effectively is worth the effort!

> Learn your notation.
> Don't get hung up on presentation.

Learn your notation.   Knowing your notation well allows you to express yourself clearly and precisely. Because you know *how* to document your solution, you can focus your energy on *solving* the problem. Conversely, a poor understanding of your notation will make problem solving more difficult. Instead of focusing on the solution, you focus on documenting your solution—an entirely different problem!

Recall that all human activity—even thought—takes place in the context of a structure. Knowing your notation well provides the means by which you can *think* clearly and precisely about the solution to the problem. Extensive knowledge of a notation is like a large vocabulary; it provides us the means to express ourselves with clarity.

Knowledge of the lexical structure of the notation is especially important because each token (e.g., each $\prec$, $\rightarrow\bullet$, $\square$, $\rightarrow\blacksquare$ or $\boxminus$) defined within a method is precisely defined. If your understanding of the token is incorrect, you cannot do anything *but* miscommunicate! Suppose you create a data flow diagram but reverse the meaning of two elements: source and process. Instead of showing a process as a circle and source as a square, you instead show a *source* as a circle and a *process* as a square. Please, don't give this diagram to me! I probably won't understand it. If I do manage to make some sense of it, I am sure to be wrong!

Resist the temptation to learn multiple notations at the same time. It is best to first learn one notation in a thorough manner. Why? First, most notations are much more expressive than people realize. Only by learning the notation thoroughly can you express yourself completely. Second, there tends to be a high degree of similarity among notations documenting similar kinds of models. For example, there is a high degree of similarity between the various notations for entity-relationship diagrams. Knowing one notation well facilitates learning another, much like knowing C++ makes learning Java easier. Third, it is rare your current project will have a need for a specific conceptual model communicated through two or more specific notations. As such, there is virtually no chance you will have the opportunity to learn more than one notation on the job.

My high school French teacher once told my class we would really know French once we had our first dream where everyone spoke French. I never learned French very well and consequently never experienced such a dream. In a similar manner, you know a notation well when you naturally express your solutions in that notation. Following DeMarco and Lister's [1987] advice about interviewing, I always give applicants a small problem to solve. This allows me to assess their problem-solving skills and their knowledge of a method.

Sometimes the applicant will ask what notation they should use to solve the problem. I always respond: "Pick any notation you feel comfortable with. If I don't understand it, I'm confident in your ability to explain how it is used." What happens next is most unfortunate. Most applicants proceed to solve the problem without using any notation! Because they abandoned their notation, they have no mechanism for expressing their solution. Even worse, such people often have great difficulty explaining their solution. Both of these are strong indicators they have not learned their chosen notation well enough to enable them to express their solution or they don't have the skills necessary to solve the problem.

Don't get hung up on presentation.   Let's say you are preparing a class diagram using the Unified Modeling Language. (A class diagram shows the objects with the system and the relationships between them.) In the Unified Modeling Language, objects are drawn with a solid rectangle with three compartments. The class name is placed in the top compartment, attributes in the middle, and behaviors in the bottom. You spend 20 minutes drawing the classes in your system. After spending another 10 minutes drawing relationships, you spend another 30 minutes making certain each box is *exactly* the same size. Sadly, you've just wasted 30 minutes that would have been better spent thinking about the problem. The purpose of notation is to communicate. Invest your time wisely. Does spending half your time making certain shapes are the same size increase communication effectiveness by a similar amount?

10.3 STANDARDS AND GUIDELINES

An analysis model prepared according to the guidelines of your favorite method is unlikely to be easily shared among the team if everyone follows different naming conventions when preparing the model. Filenames are not easily understood unless naming conventions are established and followed. Source code written by many different people is easier to understand when it follows the same formatting (e.g., indenting, capitalization, and so forth) conventions.

Recall that a message has three specific aspects: lexical, syntactic, and semantic. A *standard* is a formal specification of *required* lexical, syntactic, and semantic features of the outcomes routinely shared among developers. Outcomes prepared in violation of a standard should be rejected. A *guideline* is formal specification of *desired* lexical, syntactic, and semantic features of the outcomes routinely shared among developers. Outcomes prepared in violation of guidelines are less desirable than outcomes prepared according to the standard but are nonetheless acceptable.

Think of standards and guidelines in the following way. A good standard could be used as the specification for a computer program taking as input an outcome prepared according to the standard and producing as output a single binary answer: Yes or No. Yes, the outcome faithfully adheres to the standard. No, the outcome deviated from the standard in these ways. If the answer is No, the outcome is rejected.

A guideline could also be used as the specification for a program. The difference is what we do with the result. If the outcome violates the guideline, we may still find the outcome acceptable.

Standards and guidelines often receive a negative reaction among developers. They shouldn't. Instead of deriding them, developers should embrace them. Standards and guidelines provide much needed structure to the communication process. Knowing this structure, in turn, creates expectations of how outcomes will be communicated. When you follow the coding standard, I find your code easier to understand. When you don't, I have to waste time trying to understand what you have written.

ADVICE TO MANAGERS

Standards can be an especially volatile topic, especially naming and code formatting standards. Leading your team to agree to a simple, consistent, and concise set of standards *and* having the team follow them is well worth the effort.

Use someone else's standard rather than create your own.

Use the following structure and process to create a standard.

Keep standards small.

Monitor conformance to standards.

Establish a change process.

Establish a process to handle standard violations.

Use someone else's standard rather than create your own.   The best approach to establishing a standard is to reuse someone else's tried and true standard rather than invent your own. I consider it nearly absurd to establish a formatting standard for a programming language when the environment comes with a built-in formatter. The time your team spends debating about the format of the source code would be better spent solving the problem. Another example of standard reuse concerns naming conventions. Why invent your own when plenty of good ones exist? (See McConnell [1993] for an especially good discussion of naming conventions, including the popular Hungarian naming convention.)

Use the following structure and process to create a standard. While it is preferable to adopt previously accepted standards, there are times when you must create your own. Perhaps the programming environment does come with a source code formatter, but everyone on the team universally hates it. Perhaps your team is using a new language and part of your assignment is to create a corporate standard for this language. Creating a standard has additional benefits as well. Done correctly, it is a powerful exercise in team building. And, because everyone has a role in building the standard, they should follow it more closely.

Creating a standard is not necessarily a simple or straightforward process. Everyone has an opinion and they want it to be heard. Everyone has prior baggage they are bringing to the standards creation process, and this baggage can slow (or wear) you down. Using the right structure will help to ensure everyone supports the standard. Begin by identifying two members of your team who have the experience and maturity necessary to lead the effort. These people form the standards management team, the primary structure for creating and managing the standard. They are given complete responsibility for the process outlined below (this process can also be used to amend an existing standard—see the next section).

1. The standards management team creates a draft standard. Allocate appropriate time for this process; it is a legitimate task. Make certain each item in the standard is uniquely identified and the standard is appropriately time and date stamped.

2. The draft is submitted to the team for review. Feedback is given directly to the standards management team who tracks each response. Establish and enforce a *hard* deadline for the review. If someone wants to provide feedback, they can do so in the allotted time frame (one to two weeks is about right). Accepting no feedback on the draft once the deadline has expired lets everyone know you are serious about the standard. You may wish to warn the standards management team to expect a wide range of feedback on each item, from complete acceptance to considerable resistance.

3. The standards management team reviews the feedback and prepares a final version of the draft. Items with unanimous acceptance are left as is; simple corrections and noncontroversial modifications are made; controversial items are identified, and each alternative is contained in the document in preparation for the final review meeting. Make certain each alternative is clearly identified.

4. Schedule a final review meeting to achieve a binding resolution on each contested item. Encourage everyone to attend. The structure of the meeting is as follows. Each contested item will be reviewed for no more than ten minutes. If, after the end of ten minutes the team has not reached a consensus, the standards management team will make the final decision. They may decide to include the item as is, or may decide the item is too controversial for the standard and instead make it a guideline. It is helpful to review each contested item with the standards management team before the meeting so they are certain of your position.

5. The results of the final meeting are collected. The standards management team prepares the final version of the standard, versions it with an appropriate tracking number, and distributes it to the team.

The end result of this process is the newly created or properly amended standard.

Establish a change process.   Even the best standards show their age over time and require periodic enhancement to incorporate new working habits, new technologies, and enhanced understanding of the problem domain or method. Establish a structure supporting the change process. First, include in the standard a sample change request (see Figure 10–7). Users of the standard use the change request form to request changes in a controlled manner.

The standards management team tracks change requests by giving them appropriate identification numbers and filing them for further review. Every six months the standards management team reviews the change requests and submits modifications to the standard for review by the team following the process outlined above.

Keep standards small.   The most common mistake made when creating standards and guidelines is blurring the distinction between the two. A hallmark of a good standards document is that it is *small,* easily followed, and clear. Examples are numerous and serve to illustrate *exactly* how the outcome(s) addressed by the standard should appear. Each example is meticulously prepared and completely unambiguous. Counterexamples are provided as needed to illustrate violations of the standard. Ask yourself: "Can this standard be used as a complete specification for a

Standard Change Request Form	
Submit to: _____ **or e-mail to:** _____	**Tracking No.:** _____ **Date Recvd:** _____ **Status:** _____
Contact Information Name: _____ Phone: _____ e-mail: _____	
Reference *List the specific reference number associated with this change request.*	
Problem *Describe the problem, not the solution.*	
Proposed Change *Describe a proposed solution. This solution may or may not be accepted upon further review.*	
Impact Assessment *Evaluate the impact of the problem on your work on a scale from 1 to 5, with one being low impact and five being high impact.*	
Comments *Provide any additional comments necessary.*	

Figure 10–7   Change Request Form

program?" If the answer is no, the standards are probably too long or contain guidelines. Guidelines, on the other hand are typically longer than standards—although this is by no means permission to create a lengthy set of guidelines! Both standards and guidelines are harder to follow (and easier to ignore) when they are long.

Monitor conformance to standards.   Routinely ignored standards are useless wastes of time and energy. Consider a coding standard. Once the standard has been created, enforce it: Any *new* or old code modified during maintenance failing to meet the standard is rejected. The distinction between new and old code is important. I'm not advocating you rework all of your old sources just to meet the new standard. This is simply not feasible. Previous outcomes should only be recreated to conform to the standard if absolutely necessary. However, it is imperative that all new code adheres to the standard.

Establish a process to handle standard violations.   Because standards are created by humans, we can't expect them to be perfect or address every possible situation. By establishing a mechanism to handle standard violations, you achieve two goals. First, you enable your staff to work efficiently. They don't have to slow down when they uncover a problem with the standard. Second, you provide a feedback loop for the standard management process. By identifying shortcomings in the standard, you can ensure the standard is grown to address them.

What is the best process? When a developer must deviate from the standard, s/he should document the deviation by referring to the relevant section of the standard and stating their motivation for the deviation. This enables reviewers to understand the deviation and correct it as necessary.

ADVICE TO DEVELOPERS

Your primary responsibility with respect to standards is quite simple: Follow them!

> Participate in the standards creation process.
> Avoid standard deviations.

Participate in the standards creation process.   If you have the opportunity to participate in the creation of a standard, by all means do so! You will have to live with the result—it is in your best interest to participate. Failing to participate forfeits your right to complain about the final result.

Avoid standard deviations.   Even if your team has not established a process of handling standard violations, you should act as if such a process exists. Doing so provides three benefits. First, it makes your motivations clear. Second, it alerts those who are in position to change the standard that a change is necessary, provides evidence of the need for the change, and a possible way to address the change. Finally, it helps others perceive you as a responsible, self-disciplined developer who acts in a rational manner.

10.4 STATUS REPORTS

Status reports serve an essential role in the management of any project. They provide formal feedback from developers to their managers on the state of specific tasks. Without such feedback, keeping the project on schedule and addressing problems are nearly impossible. Status reports act as early warning systems, identifying problems when corrective action can be taken in the most effective manner. They can also serve as a motivational tool. Generating a team-related status allows everyone to share in the progress of the team. Finally, status reports can aid developers in planning their activities by providing them with a specific opportunity to reflect what needs to be done.

What follows next is a simple structure for a one-page status report that I have used successfully for several years. Each section has been designed to provide useful information to both managers and developers. I will describe this format from a

---

date

developer

Accomplishments
Tell me what you have accomplished in concise, single-sentence statements, focusing on significant items.

Current Work
List the work expected to be done this week.

Future Work
List the work expected to be done over the next several weeks.

Comments/Concerns/Problems
Outline any comments, concerns, and/or other problems you may have with the development organization. Concentrate on bringing to my attention issues you are having difficulty resolving through your own efforts (e.g., "Don't forget my PC is scheduled for repairs in two weeks, and I will need a temporary machine to continue development work." or "The LAN group has not completed the installation of the fourth floor server. If installation is not completed by 10/23, testing will be delayed."). I will act on this information. If you indicate this information is confidential, I will not redistribute it to any other party, including any other member of the team.

Status Relative to Plan
What is your status relative to your schedule? Refer to explicit time frames wherever possible. If you are behind schedule, outline how you intend to address the problem.

managerial perspective, elaborating further on both its contents and the process used to generate the report in the advice given to managers and developers.

The contents and purpose of each section, in greater detail, are as follows.

- *Accomplishments* provides a means for the developer to explicitly state and record their accomplishments and gives managers a means for tracking the workings of the team.
- *Current Work* assists developers in reflecting on their activities for the coming week and helps promote sound time management principles. Managers should briefly review this section looking for activities unnecessarily detracting from the project (e.g., "What benefits will accrue to the project if you attend the sales meeting on Thursday?").
- *Future Work* helps managers and developers alike prepare for upcoming activities and events by highlighting the work just around the corner. The time frame for this section is roughly two to four weeks in the future. A healthy project will show a natural progression of items from this section to the current work section, and from there to accomplishments. For example, if unit testing is scheduled in two weeks, listing the event here enables everyone to prepare for the test as necessary (perhaps by scheduling activities with other departments involved in the testing). By focusing on a slightly longer time frame, this section also provides developers with a means for rising above thinking only about day-to-day development activities. Such a perspective is invaluable to projects of long duration.
- The *Comments/Concerns/Problems* section is the means by which organizational problems are identified for further action. It is discussed in greater detail for both managers and developers below.
- Finally, the *Status Relative to Plan* gives developers the opportunity to describe the progress made on their current assignment with respect to the overall project plan. If progress is slipping, they are expected to detail how they are going to respond to the problem. In turn, the manager can review each status report with respect to the overall project plan, adjusting resources as necessary.

Two additional rules must be followed. The first deals with structure. The report must fit on one page, be neatly typed or submitted on-line, and dated. Keeping the status report to a single page helps developers focus on what is essential and assists managers in preparing the integrated report for the team. The formality of typing reinforces the importance of the report, and dating it allows it to be appropriately filed for future reference.

The second deals with content. Each developer is given complete responsibility for determining the exact content of each section of the report. If a manager needs specific information on a topic not selected for inclusion in the report, s/he can easily request it through other means. Alternatively, and in rarer cases, special sections can be added to the report.

ADVICE TO MANAGERS

Requiring written status reports is a simple and effective manner to inject structure into the development process. If you already employ status reports, examine your communication goals. Does your format address all the topics presented above? If not, consider amending your report as described above. If you think your reports are sound, consider how they are prepared with respect to the following.

Allocate 15–20 minutes for the preparation of the report.

Prepare and distribute a similar status report to the team.

Prefer the use of on-line status reports.

Establish a consistent time—preferably Monday morning—for receiving status reports.

Explicitly respond to all Comment/Concern/Problems.

Make certain all developers have a plan.

"More of the same" is not an acceptable accomplishment.

Allocate 15–20 minutes for the preparation of the report.   While preparing a good status report only requires 15–20 minutes, your developers will only take the time to generate a good report if they believe you value the report by reading and acting on its contents.

Prepare and distribute a similar status report to the team.   Accentuate accomplishments and show how the team is moving forward to complete project goals. Be careful of distributing information contained in the Comments/Concerns/Problems section. If information is given to you as confidential, it *must* be treated as such. If you feel that one member of the team can help another solve a problem you can engineer this outcome through any number of private mechanisms. The promise of confidentiality cannot be broken.

You can and should list Comments/Concerns/Problems if they are well known to the entire group or if the manner you will address a specific Comment/Concern/Problem will affect the entire group. In the example given earlier, a developer wrote "The LAN group has not completed the installation on the fourth floor server. If installation not completed by 10/23, testing will be delayed." Because addressing this concern will likely impact the entire team, you should include the resolution of this problem in the team status report (e.g., "The LAN group will be installing the fourth floor server on 10/15 in preparation for testing.").

Prefer the use of on-line status reports.   On-line reports are more easily searched and incorporated into larger documents. If necessary, you can print out a copy of each status report for paper-based storage.

Establish a consistent time—preferably Monday morning—for receiving status reports.   A consistent time frame enables developers to proactively schedule the time needed to prepare a status report and enables you to collect all reports in a consistent manner. Why Monday morning? Consider the alternatives. Writing a status report on Friday afternoon is too difficult—developers are tired from the work week, and the distractions of the coming weekend make it too easy to prepare the report in a haphazard manner. Preparing the report at any other time during the week feels unnatural because there is no closure to activities. Monday morning gives each developer time to reflect on the activities of the coming week, reaffirming the importance of time management skills. A colleague of mine, David Nunn, notes that waiting until Monday also provides an opportunity to "forget the details" of the previous week and instead "remember the essentials." Finally, preparing the report on Monday morning can provide an initial burst of motivational energy, as each developer reflects on the accomplishments of the prior week and thinks about the accomplishments they will realize by the end of the current week.

Explicitly respond to all Comment/Concern/Problem listed in the report.   By definition, this section of the status report lists organizational problems your developers cannot handle without your intervention. As such, it is the single most important section of the status report. You must respond to each listed item. A simple acknowledgment of the item is often sufficient. It is not required that they know *how* you are going to address an item, only that you *will*. Of course, if you know how you plan to address the problem, you may wish to inform the developer directly, but this is not required.

Make certain all developers have a plan.   There are two key assumptions in the status report structure described above. First, the developers know their assigned tasks. Second, they have a plan for accomplishing these tasks. You also know these things. Together, you measure progress. This does not mean every developer has a complex sequence of activities micromanaged through your favorite project management tool. An overstructured approach stifles process. A simple list of tasks along with estimated completion dates often provides the necessary structure.

"More of the same" is not an acceptable accomplishment.   In a long or complex development effort, your staff may spend multiple weeks performing the same activity. As such, they may be tempted to list an imprecise accomplishment (e.g., "Completed more analysis for the XYZ project."). A clear warning sign is the same item appearing in the Future Work section for more than six weeks (too long a time frame) or the Current Work section for more than two weeks (too large a task was listed).

Discourage this for several reasons. First, lumping together discrete activities into a general activity is a common way of masking serious problems in the project. Without an accurate listing of accomplishments, you cannot determine exactly where the project is with respect to the overall project plan. Second, even within large projects, every task can be decomposed to the point where you can track progress toward identifiable subgoals. If this cannot be done, the quality of the entire project plan is suspect. Finally, the same item listed from week to week is an indication your staff is not taking the time to reflect on their progress in the preparation of the status report.

ADVICE TO DEVELOPERS

Status reports are as much a tool for you as they are for your manager. Using them effectively will help you improve your own productivity and will help you keep track of your accomplishments.

> Prepare a status report every week.
> Always include an explicit Accomplishments section.
> Document all Comments/Concerns/Problems.
> Protect yourself.

Prepare a status report every week.   A status report provides a concise record of your activities from week to week. By recording each accomplishment, you make certain your managers are aware of your excellent work. A well-documented record of accomplishments is a valuable asset. When preparing for your annual review, quickly peruse your status reports. When negotiating for a raise, refer to your accomplishments. When updating your resume, you can select specific accomplishments depending on your desired emphasis in searching for a new job, and so forth.

Always include an explicit Accomplishments section.   Whatever the format of status report requested by your organization, make certain you clearly list your accomplishments of the prior week. If one is not included, send them to your manager as a separate message.

Document all Comments/Concerns/Problems.   Failing to document Comments/Concerns/Problems prevents your manager from obtaining the information he or she needs to perform the job. The real question is determining exactly what information should be included in this section. *Any* information you feel should be added is appropriate for this section of the report, *especially* information directly or indirectly impacting your ability to perform your job.

For example, let's say a customer calls you on the phone and asks for a small modification to the system. Because you perceive the change to be small and you are already working on the specific module in question, you bypass the formal change mechanisms of your organization and agree to make the change. Unless the change is truly trivial (e.g., less than one hour of work), make certain you inform your manager. Why? Your manager is the person responsible for coordinating your schedule with respect to other members of the team and the larger organization. Undertaking this modification on your own could seriously impact the schedule. Moreover, your manager has information about the overall team you do not have and may have already assigned this modification to someone else. You have created double work! It would be better to suggest to the customer they utilize the existing change process and inform your manager customers are asking for changes directly from developers—something s/he *needs* to know.

Your comments don't have to be completely "work" related. One of the best comments I've ever received was "I think the energy of the team is really low. We're kinda tired. Can we do something fun?" I didn't realize it, but this person was right! My team had been working incredibly hard, and *needed* some time off, only I didn't realize it. So, I found a way to give them a day off!

> *You may have to document your concerns repeatedly. One project leader, a capable young man, was leading the implementation of a new financial management system. It was well known in the development organization that this project was considered crucial for the future success of the company. It was also painfully obvious this project was considerably understaffed. Each week he would state in his "comments" section he felt his project was understaffed and asked when he would get some relief. Unfortunately, this was an area where I was unable to give immediate help. All existing resources were allocated to other projects, and my requests for additional personnel were denied by my manager. To his credit, the project leader continued to state this comment, even though he fully understood the situation. Eventually, I was able to get him more help. He removed the item.*

Protect yourself.   The Comments/Concerns/Problems section is not only designed to provide information to your manager on what he or she can do to improve your job, it is also designed to provide you with a protection mechanism. Suppose during implementation you run into a brick wall. You cannot build the system as specified because of a serious but previously undetected analysis flaw. While I know you will immediately bring this matter to the attention of your manager or team leader, don't stop there. Formally document the situation in your status report, in both the Comments/Concerns/Problems and Status Relative to Plan sections. This will ensure there is a formal record of the problem.

10.5 EFFECTIVE MEETINGS

Does the idea of having an *effective* meeting surprise you? It shouldn't. Meetings are one of the most important tools available for promoting effective communication, for a well-run meeting can accomplish several objectives. It can distribute important information obtaining feedback in the process. It can bring together people with disparate skills to solve a tough problem. It can be the single fastest way to create a shared outcome. Finally, meetings fulfill a very deep social need within members of the team and serve as a good starting point for creating and nurturing culture [Ware 1977].

Unfortunately, many meetings fail to accomplish their communication goals for a variety of reasons. They fail because they start late. They fail because all the necessary individuals are not present, or, alternatively, because too many individuals are present. They fail because individuals are not prepared. Mostly, they fail because structures, processes, and outcomes associated with effective meetings are not known or not followed. By identifying the structures, processes, and outcomes associated with effective meetings, we can repeat and improve on the entire process.

10.5.1 A Model for Effective Meetings

A successful code review provides an excellent model for effective meetings. (What is a code review other than a special meeting?) What makes a code review successful?

- *Well-known objective.* Recall from Chapter 3 that the singular purpose of a review is to assess the appropriateness of an outcome for its intended purpose. Thus, the purpose of the code review is to assess the appropriateness of the source code. All outcomes produced during the review are structured to ensure this objective is met.
- *Appropriate structure.* Material necessary for the review is prepared and distributed well in advance to allow participants ample preparation time. The review is not conducted if participants are not prepared. The review is held in a sufficiently large room. Participants have well-defined roles.
- *Well-known process.* During the review, specific aspects of the outcome are assessed. Issues are raised.
- *Well-known outcome.* The final outcome of the review is a report signed by each participant assessing the quality of the outcome reviewed. Additional outcomes that may be produced detail required changes to the outcome. This report is signed by the reviewers, distributed to all relevant parties, and placed in the project repository.

We can generalize our experiences with successful code reviews into a model for effective meetings.

Structure.   A meeting room adequate for the purposes of the review was secured *before* the review. An agenda outlined the general flow of the review, highlighting as needed any aspects of the code needing special attention. The structure also defined the expected content and form of the outcome of the meeting, in this case a report detailing the appropriateness of the code. The right number of participants were asked to attend the meeting—enough to make certain the review was successful, but not so many the review process was painfully slow (a symptom of overstructuring).

Effective meeting structures include:

♦ A convenient meeting place, large enough to hold all participants and appropriate supporting material (e.g., flip-charts and tape, overhead projectors, and so forth).

♦ A well-known date and time.

♦ The right number of participants. Ideally, include as participants only those individuals who can materially contribute to the objective of the meeting.

♦ An agenda prepared in advance and distributed to all participants. The agenda states the time, place, and objective of the meeting. Each agenda item has an associated time limit, as does the entire meeting. Breaks are inserted, as appropriate, for long meetings.

♦ Specific roles participants assume during the meeting. At a minimum, a meeting should have the following roles. The *recorder* records the relevant conversations and agreements in the meeting. The *organizer* reviews the agenda, making certain participants understand the purpose of the meeting and each item. A *facilitator* may be present. Facilitators have special training in keeping the meeting focused, making certain important items are not overlooked, and bringing discussions to a close.

Processes.   The overall process of conducting a successful code review consists of preparing for the review, conducting the review, preparing outcomes during the review, and finally distributing these outcomes to relevant parties after the review. Of course, the same process applies to any effective meeting. Before the meeting, appropriate information should be distributed to meeting participants, who are then responsible for taking the time to review it. During the meeting, the group should maintain a focus on the overall purpose of the meeting, as well as sticking to the agenda. After the meeting, appropriate outcomes are distributed as needed.

Effective meeting processes include:

♦ Reviewing the agenda to ensure it is appropriate, noting discrepancies, and addressing them during the meeting as needed.

♦ Sticking to the agenda and adhering to preestablished time limits.

♦ Taking breaks when scheduled.

♦ Recording action items.

♦ Minimizing interruptions. The most popular rule for minimizing interruptions is known as the "100-mile rule" which states "no one should be called from the meeting unless it is so important the disruption would occur even if the meeting was [held] 100 miles from the workplace" [Scholtes 1988].

♦ **Ending on time.**

Outcomes.   The primary outcome of a code review is a report assessing the quality of the code. This outcome is very well defined. Likewise, every meeting should have *at least* one outcome: the minutes. Most meetings should have additional outcomes: action items, an evaluation of the meeting itself, and a list of items that should be addressed in the *next* meeting.

Outcomes produced in effective meetings include:

◆ A list of the participants present at the meeting.

◆ A list of action items with each individual responsible for the item explicitly listed along with the expected completion date.

◆ A list of items not covered in the allotted time or deferred to another meeting. This list should be used to ensure each item is appropriately addressed in the future.

◆ An evaluation of the meeting: Were all objectives accomplished?

◆ A draft of the next meeting. This is especially useful during a long running project.

ADVICE TO MANAGERS

While you may participate or organize a large number of meetings, your primary job is to make certain your staff know the processes, structures, and outcomes associated with effective meetings. Improving their meeting performance will have a far greater net effect in the organization than simply focusing on your own. Of course, you should work to improve your meeting performance, especially with respect to the meetings you organize with your staff. Knowing when and how often to have such meetings is a sign of your managerial competence.

Schedule regular meetings.

Provide the necessary structures.

Organize meetings around specific themes.

Publish meeting outcomes in the repository.

Avoid monster meetings.

Schedule regular meetings.   A regularly scheduled meeting is a consistent and effective way to impact relevant information to the entire team. Such meetings, which are most appropriate for small teams (e.g., between two to twelve developers) do not have to be long, just regularly scheduled. I have found a weekly or bi-weekly schedule works best. There are at least four advantages to establishing and keeping a regular meeting schedule. First, you establish a *structure* helping to ensure important information is communicated to the team. Second, such meetings help build cohesiveness within the team. During an intense project this meeting might be the only time the entire team comes together at the same time! Third, preparing an agenda helps you make certain important aspects of the project are discussed. Fourth, your staff will learn how to run their meetings more effectively by following the positive example established by your meetings.

> *My preference is to hold such a meeting every Friday morning with the agenda distributed via e-mail on Thursday night or very early Friday morning. To help create the agenda, I keep a file for each week and periodically add items as needed. I usually have multiple files, adding agenda items to the most appropriate week.*

Provide the necessary structures.   Strangely enough, many development organizations preach the benefits of establishing good meeting processes yet fail to provide the structures necessary to engage in a good process. It is impossible to hold an effective meeting without the appropriate organizational structures, the most basic of which are meeting rooms with appropriate supporting material. Think about it. Is the cafeteria the preferred meeting room? Are napkins the "next best thing" to a flip-chart?

Publish meeting outcomes in the project repository.   If everyone on your staff feels they must attend every meeting associated with the project, you've got a problem! Most of us despise attending unnecessary meetings— at best, they are a needless waste of time, distracting us from our work. Yet, in certain organizations, you *must* attend every meeting, because if you don't, you'll be in trouble. How? Someone might assign you an action item. Or, important decisions might be reached directly affecting your part of the system. One way to prevent bloated meetings is to publish all meeting outcomes in the project repository (see below). This removes any perceived "penalties" for not attending a meeting.

Organize agendas around specific themes.   It is helpful to organize agenda items (or entire meetings) around one of the following themes:

- ♦ Planning: Creating a plan for achieving a stated objective.
- ♦ Communication: Disseminating relevant information to team members.
- ♦ Problem Solving: Developing one or more solutions to a pressing problem.
- ♦ Deciding: Selecting a specific option from a list of alternatives.

Sequence agenda items effectively.   Good techniques for organizing and sequencing agenda items [Ware 1977] include:

- ♦ Build agenda items on each other.
- ♦ Put the easiest and least controversial items first.
- ♦ Avoid more than seven items.
- ♦ Avoid items representing problems more effectively handled through delegation to specific individuals or subteams.

Avoid monster meetings.   A *monster meeting* is an extremely large meeting, often including more than 20 participants. Their sheer size means they are not effective vehicles for dialog or interaction. Such meetings are usually only effective for making announcements.

ADVICE TO DEVELOPERS

Why should you waste your time in ineffective meetings? You shouldn't! Follow the advice in this section and use meetings as tools in the creation of shared outcomes.

> Avoid attending unnecessary meetings.
> Avoid assigning tasks to individuals who are not present.
> Offer to record action items and minutes.
> Beware of "agenda-itis."

Avoid attending unnecessary meetings.   When asked to attend a meeting, simply ask yourself and, if possible, the organizer: "Is this a meeting I need to attend?" If the answer is no, *skip the meeting!*

Avoid assigning tasks to individuals who are not present.   Many of us have had the experience of missing a meeting only to realize later we were "volunteered" for an assignment. Avoid doing this, as it can create a cycle of mistrust in the team and motivate people to needlessly attend meetings as a way of protecting themselves from unnecessary work. If you must assign a task to an individual not present in the meeting, do so in a tentative manner. Give them or their management the opportunity to review the assignment.

Offer to record action items and minutes.   Controlling the minutes means you control the "spin" put on all items discussed in the meeting.

Beware of "agenda-itis."   While having an agenda *is* a proven tool for more effective meetings, don't go too far! As a form of structure, agendas should exist only to facilitate the meeting *process*. When you start concentrating more on the agenda than the meeting, you are missing the point. Distributing the agenda before the meeting is nice, but this is not always possible. Suppose you have a meeting but fail to publish the agenda first. What should you do? Simply spend the first five or ten minutes writing one on a flip-chart.

10.6 PROJECT REPOSITORIES

Software development teams generate a surprising number of outcomes, each serving one or more purposes. Some are the physical trace of communication between the development team, customers, users, and other entities associated with the development effort. Status reports, project plans, questions from developers to customers and the response of the customer, marketing plans, and formal evaluations of the system all fall into this category.

Others are generated in the context of good software engineering. Examples include the outcomes prescribed by the method, results of code reviews, handbooks for using configuration management and/or other tools, standards manuals, and the project plans of individual developers. Many documents (such as project plans or high-level requirements) serve to communicate externally and internally at the same time.

Each outcome should be directly related to creating a quality system. As such, outcomes represent the formal and informal knowledge and experience of the team. Collecting, organizing, and sharing this information have a substantial impact in overall quality and productivity. The question is how?

Earlier, I advocated the use of a project notebook as a tool for recording "important stuff" about the project. A *project repository* organizes all outcomes generated by the team for future use. The term project repository is known by other names. Brooks [1995] refers to it as a "project workbook." Constantine [1993] refers to it as "a structured, externalized group memory." In effect, it is the project notebook of the team, as shown in Figure 10–8.

ADVICE TO MANAGERS

A project repository, like a project notebook, is an inexpensive mechanism for significantly improving the quality of communication and sharing of information.

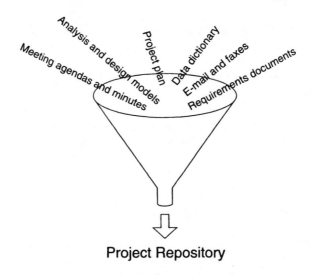

Project Repository

Figure 10–8   The Project Repository

> Make the repository visible and accessible.
>
> Structure it.
>
> Index it.
>
> Organize and index *on entry.*
>
> Store contents digitally whenever possible.
>
> Establish the role of a caretaker to manage the repository.
>
> Provide for expansion.
>
> Explicitly show the repository to new team members.

Make the repository visible and accessible.   How can the repository provide value to the team if it is kept under lock and key? Ideally, the project repository is located in a special, well-known, easily accessible location.

By making the project repository visible and accessible, you also help to promote a culture valuing openness, honesty, and shared communication. As discussed in the previous chapter, one way individuals try to gain a temporary advantage over others is by hoarding information. The project repository states in a very real and public manner information regarding the project is to be shared equally and that all members of the team have the right to this information.

Structure it.   Needless to say, some form of structure is needed before the team can make effective use of the repository. Constantine [1990, 1993] recommends the following organization (recast in terms of the SPO framework):

Outcome Record. Contains a copy of all outcomes produced by the team. The outcome record is further organized into specific kinds of outcomes. The *reject* "bin" contains outcomes formally rejected along with the motivation for the rejection. The *deferred decisions* bin contains outcomes needing further attention by the team. Such outcomes usually represent problematic outcomes. Finally, the *bright ideas* bin records potentially useful outcomes so they are not lost. Outcomes should be further organized as to their "type": project plans, meeting agendas, minutes, review outcomes, change requests and their resolution, and so forth.

Process Record. Describes the processes used in preparation of these outcomes.

Structure Record. Contains descriptions of the structures in place as the outcomes were created. The structure record is important because as structure changes so do processes and outcomes.

Each item placed in the repository contains a date and time stamp indicating when it was added and a brief abstract describing the item. This information should be maintained in an on-line format so it can be easily accessed and searched, as described below.

Index it.   The decisions and information related to specific topics on a project are often threaded through many different outcomes. A specific requirement (e.g., response time) might be addressed in a host of outcomes. Finding all of them is impossible without the structure provided by a good index.

Consider using at least two kinds of indices. The first is a *keyword* index driven by the glossary of terms. As each outcome is added to the repository, appropriate keywords describing the outcome derived from the glossary of terms are used to describe it. These are automatically added to the keyword index.

The second index is a *tracking* index. This index is derived from the specific identifiers associated with well-written requirements documents. Johnson and associates [1995] refer to these as "trace anchors" because they allow a specific requirement to be traced through the entire development process. Consistent use of these anchors allows *all* aspects of the project impacting requirements to be identified quickly and easily.

Organize and index *on entry*.   It would be a nearly impossible task to try to organize and index even a small repository all at once. Make it easy on yourself and your staff. As each item is added to the repository (time and date stamped with the name of the contributor) *immediately* file it under the correct category and index it appropriately.

Store contents digitally whenever possible.   The basic repository described thus far consists of two distinct parts. The first is the electronic abstract and index, and the second is the physical contents (e.g., drawings, faxes, and the like). Of course, the contents don't have to be physical. They can be digital.

Creating and maintaining a digital repository is a bit more work than a simple physical repository, but going digital has clear benefits. First, free-form searching can be performed on *any* textual item in the repository, not just the abstract. Try finding all the meetings Sandra attended regarding the invoice subsystem in a purely-paper-based repository. You get the idea. Ideally, the tool helping you manage your digital repository will provide extensive, customizable cross-referencing, cataloging, and other capabilities to make finding information in the repository easy and fast.

Establish the role of a caretaker to manage the repository.   Like a garden, the project repository will not flourish unless someone is given the responsibility of maintaining it. The caretaker makes certain outcomes are added to the repository in an appropriate manner, creates abstracts, and keeps the keyword index up to date.

Provide for expansion.   By definition, the repository will grow over the life of the project. You should choose a storage mechanism supporting growth.

Explicitly show the repository to new team members.   One of the earliest steps in bringing a new member to the team should be showing them the project repository and explaining its content and purpose. Encourage them to explore the repository as necessary as they learn their role in the project.

ADVICE TO DEVELOPERS

The project repository is one of the many tools at your disposal to ensure the right system is being constructed. Use it.

> Record design decisions in the repository.
> If in doubt, add it.

Record design decisions in the repository.   As described in Section 3.6, recording *every* design alternative in great detail is a waste of time. The other extreme is just as bad. Failing to record *any* design decisions means others are doomed to duplicate your work.

Where's the balance? What decisions should be put into the repository? Decisions regarding the system or technical architectures affecting more than one subsystem should be put into the repository. Why did you choose C++ over Smalltalk? Was it because *at that time* the majority of the team knew C, and you felt learning C++ would be relatively easier?

Decisions regarding the selection of vendors and/or tools should be placed in the repository. Vendors come and go, and the motivations for using one vendor should be clearly stated.

Mandates from the customer, either from the requirements or from some other source, must be placed in the repository. Certainly other categories of decisions are important—these two represent the bare minimum. How much detail should be added? Enough so others will not have to duplicate substantial portions of your work to understand your conclusion. Typically, all that is needed is a simplification (or abstraction) of the actual work.

If in doubt, add it.   If you think something should be added to the repository but are not certain, add it. It is far better to err by putting too much information into the repository than too little.

11

FORTIFYING THE TEAM

Values, culture, and goals integrate and coordinate the team. When faced with a difficult decision, a shared set of values helps ensure the decision I make is one you are likely to support. When you don't, our culture—an outgrowth of our values—helps you find constructive ways to express your disagreement. Together, we work to achieve a common goal—a long-term objective outcome guiding our mutual efforts. This chapter is devoted to showing how managers and developers can shape these components of the integrated SPO framework in order to achieve more effective work teams.

Chapter Overview

This chapter parallels the structure of Chapter 8. Section 11.1 discusses values. It concentrates on functional values and includes a structure for generating a concise set of functional values. Culture consists of five distinct components: norms, symbols, stories, rituals, and shared language. Section 11.2 shows how to use these components to shape culture for the benefit the team. Section 11.3 concludes with a discussion on managing goals.

11.1 VALUES

Values are the "things" considered important in the team. Often expressed as broad statements, values serve many purposes. First, they guide behavior, especially decision making. Second, they provide meaning to work. As discussed in Chapter 8, there are two kinds of values: those associated with the larger organization and those associated with the team.

Values usually associated with the larger organization can be summarized under the following categories [Pascale 1981]:

1. Relationship with employees: as a place to work, identify with, and serve.
2. Relationship with external entities: what product or service your provide, and how you go about providing it; your competitors, and the rules by which you compete.
3. Internal operations: what things are important (speed, lowest cost, highest quality, and so forth).
4. Relationship to "higher orders": the social welfare of employees, the corporation, and the state; adhering to the law and/or existing sociological values.

While organizational values do serve all of the purposes described above, they are often not directly useful to the team. First, organizational values are often so broad they can be used to justify multiple kinds of behavior, even apparently inconsistent or conflicting behavior. Second, because organizational values are established when the firm is very young, they tend to reflect the beliefs of the founder(s). This is not necessarily a problem, as we tend to select firms whose existing values match our own. However, it is undeniably more exciting to state and follow *your* values rather than "the organization's."

Third, because organizational values are set when the firm is young, older firms may experience a generation gap (or two) in the values considered important. Customizing values for a specific team can mitigate this gap. Finally, we developers are an interesting lot. Many of us have deeply held values on how software should be created. There can be tension between personal and organizational values unless personal values can be consistent with organizational values.

The best way to address this situation is to customize organizational values to meet the needs of the team. This customization process produces a hierarchy of values ranging from broad (the entire corporation) to slightly more specific (a single department) to rather specific (the development team), each appropriate for guiding the activities of a particular group of people.

What kinds of values are most appropriate for the development team? The heavy use of communication and the importance of sound interpersonal relationships motivate two distinct kinds of values: interpersonal and functional. *Interpersonal* values are associated with how team members interact. Positive interpersonal values include honesty, integrity, respect, a disdain for hidden agendas, a preference for simple and direct communication (e.g., "It doesn't matter who is right, it matters what is right" [Spangenberg 1995]), a desire for direct interaction with the customer, and the realization that at times compromise *is* necessary in the development of a large system.

Functional values guide us in our daily actions with respect to how we perform our job duties. I've already introduced functional values in Chapter 4: By valuing code clarity over efficiency, you've identified (or established) a functional value that helps guide decision making. Other desirable functional values include a belief in the usefulness of a method, underpromising and overdelivering, and a general orientation toward writing code others can understand, test, and maintain. Many developers share similar functional values but differ significantly in how they are prioritized.

If you were to record each statement made by a group of developers in a design review (or similar meeting), you would find many of the statements shaping the flow of communication are value statements. I recently attended a meeting of fellow consultants. The purpose of the meeting was to create a consistent means of addressing several inconsistencies in the method used by one of our clients. As each proposal was presented, its various advantages and disadvantages were discussed. During one especially heated exchange, the group began to take sides, with each group lining up with the proposal they supported the most. Eventually, objective evaluations of the proposals were dropped altogether, and the focus merely become "winning."

Finally, one frustrated developer said rather loudly to another: "I would agree with you, but you are just wrong, and so is the way we are conducting the meeting . . ." and then proceeded to refocus the meeting back to objective evaluations of the differing solutions. The strength of the comment—hearing "you are wrong" at roughly 80 decibels will always get your attention—forced everyone present to reconsider our process. But, what was more important than the loudness of the statement was the dramatic realization of how blatantly our process conflicted with our values. Having a meeting to resolve a customer's problem should never be about "winning." It should be about serving the customer.

ADVICE TO MANAGERS

A broad statement on a piece of paper has little meaning. Values do. Your role is to make them explicit through action and to nurture them to effectiveness. Before addressing any specific interpersonal or functional values, it is best to consider general principles.

Approach values with care.
Support values through structure.
Change structures to change values.
Engineer reward systems consistent with stated values.
Counsel when they fall short.
Label values with care.

Approach values with care.   Recall from Chapter 8 that *espoused values* are the values of the corporation as found in company mission statements, pamphlets, brochures, and the like. *Actual values* are the values expressed through the tangible actions of the corporation. Approaching values with care means realizing most people (developers included) are amazingly good at spotting inconsistencies in behavior.

Support values through structure.   The specific structures you create, the processes you expect, and the outcomes you require support or erode the values held by you, your team, and the larger organization. Consider the project repository. Keeping its contents under tight lock and key erodes values of honesty and open communication. Making certain the repository is easily accessible structurally supports these values.

Explicitly linking structures, processes, and outcomes to values has the greatest effect (e.g., "The reason I want you to prepare a project plan is that our customer needs to have the software by 11/23. Without this plan we cannot communicate effectively with them on changes."). Without such linking your staff is forced to guess the relationship.

One value often shared by managers is a desire for increased productivity. One value often shared among developers is working in an environment of their choosing (e.g., absolute silence, continuous rock 'n' roll, and so forth). One structure I find extremely effective in meeting both goals is to allow developers to work at home. Developers enjoy the arrangement because it is out of the ordinary and gives them a much needed change of pace. By removing common distractions, I expect developers who work at home to be more productive (and make certain they are aware of this expectation). In some cases developers have faster machines at home than at work, so the chances of increased productivity are usually pretty high! While there is potential for abuse, I've not found it difficult to administer such a structure.

Change structures to change values.   Well-established values are extraordinarily resistant to change, because we actively support them through ongoing processes, existing structures, and known outcomes [Phillips 1980]. Thus, the first step to changing values is to establish new structures that support different processes and outcomes. The second step is allow for enough time for these new values to take hold in the context of these new structures.

Engineer reward systems consistent with stated values.   A reward system is a special organizational structure: Engaging in the process prescribed by the structure results in a *very* desirable outcome (e.g., "Get the project finished by the deadline and you get a bonus."). The problem occurs when reward systems motivate processes or outcomes at odds with organizational values. When this happens, developers are likely to experience stress, disillusionment, and frustration. Critically examine every reward system to ensure it is consistent with stated values.

Counsel when they fall short.   The greatest developers not only have a passion for creating great software, but their personal values are also so deeply held we call them idealists. Three aspects of such individuals are important. First, they can be incredibly difficult to manage or work with. They never let you or anyone else take shortcuts or get away with anything less than perfection. Second, even though they are difficult to manage, you want at least one on every project, and sometimes two or three.

Third, and most importantly, an idealist tends to judge their own behavior with greater intensity and scrutiny than anyone else. Invariably, they will feel they fall short of their ideals. This is *not* failure, but humanity. Be prepared to counsel them when this happens. Yes, they may have failed to follow their own process. Yes, they may have produced an outcome of lower quality than originally planned or desired. Yes, they are human. Don't let their ideals become a burden.

Label values with care.   Many developers are suspicious of "values" because they perceive them to be hollow words created by corporate bureaucrats needing to justify their existence. Even worse, they may have worked for a manager whose actual values consistently violated espoused values and have thus learned values don't really mean anything in their work environment. One way around this problem, especially if you are trying to turn around a dysfunctional team, is not to refer to them as "values." Instead, use phrases like "ground rules," or more even more simply "this is the way I (we) like things done." Doing so will help defuse any negative experiences associated with values and will give you the time to instill them in the daily working habits of the team.

Managing interpersonal values among the development team is an especially demanding task for at least two reasons. First, our profession does have a disproportionally higher percentage of introverts when compared with the normal population (see Chapter 4). The very idea of "interpersonal" values may strike an introvert as a bit odd. Second, developers spend an extraordinary amount of time interacting with machines, not humans. After a long stretch of programming, it can be difficult to think about "interpersonal values." Doing so, however, helps the team.

> Your interpersonal style sets the interpersonal style for the team.
> Clearly defined values help potential team members select an
>   appropriate team.

Your interpersonal style sets the interpersonal style for the team.
The best mechanism you have in establishing beneficial interpersonal values is your own interaction style. By continually focusing on the needs of the customer, avoiding hidden agendas, and squashing rumors, you will find your interpersonal values, as realized by your visible behavior, will set the tone for the team. Of course, the converse is also true. If your team learns that to communicate effectively with you they must engage in innuendo, insinuation, and allusion, they will utilize similar communication patterns with each other.

Clearly defined values help potential team members select an appropriate team.   Values are, by definition, the things we feel are important. By clearly defining the values of your team, both you and a candidate are better able to ensure there is a good "fit" between them and the team. This advice also works in the

reverse direction. Clearly defined values enable a team to properly evaluate a potential candidate during the selection process, rejecting those whose values are obviously inconsistent.

As the project moves through its normal progression of phases, from requirements determination to implementation, developers will spend an increasing amount of
time working and making decisions on their own. A well-known set of functional values increases consistency in decision making. Ideally, such values are established near
the beginning of the project but can be created at any time during the life of the team.

> Place emphasis on functional values.
> Clarify coding values.

Place emphasis on functional values.   There are many values enhancing the effectiveness of the team, among them a concentration on the task at hand,
clear and direct communication, a desire for group cooperation and cohesiveness,
and so forth. Research by Thamhain [1987] has shown that teams who concentrate
too heavily on interpersonal values (e.g., group harmony, team building, and the
like) are less effective than teams who concentrate on functional values and how
these relate to the problem. Yes, group harmony is important. However, it is not built
through multiple retreats or forced outings held every Saturday. Harmony is created
when everyone knows their role and their task in relation to the whole, with each
person working as hard as they can to create the best system possible.

Clarify coding values.   Peter and Tim are two developers who have just
joined the project from quite different backgrounds. Peter is a 15-year veteran who
specializes in building embedded systems for military purposes. Tim just obtained
his master's degree. His thesis discussed the use of expert systems in learning how to
perform object identification from digitized stereoscopic images. It's not much fun
to think of how they will interact when Peter reviews Tim's proposed design.

Peter: Your design is unacceptable. It uses way too much memory.

*Tim: Why do you always bring up size? Things get too complicated when you are al-
ways trying to create fancy data structures. Buy more memory!*

The sad part of this story is that both Peter and Tim are making entirely reasonable decisions based on their experience. Both styles of design (e.g., minimize space
or maximize clarity without regard to space) are entirely appropriate given the right
context. However, unless they take steps to clarify and understand their *collective*, as
opposed to their individual, values, they will continue to clash. As a manager, the potential for similar disagreements over functional values in your own team is just as
high. By establishing a shared set of well-known functional values, you will prevent
such deeper problems before they can start. I think of these functional values as *coding* values, because they ultimately influence how we code the system.

Because of the highly personal and potentially controversial nature of coding values, a structured form of group interaction should be used to guide the team in selecting such values. A good candidate is a mix between multivoting and the nominal group technique, both of which are slightly modified here for the purposes of this exercise [Scholtes 1988]. Make certain you read this entire process completely before you begin, as you have special responsibilities in making certain it is successful.

Begin by making a copy of the table in Section 4.1, adding any items you feel are especially appropriate for your environment. Organize a meeting whose purpose is to develop a shared set of coding values for the team. (Instead of selecting the items, you may want to brainstorm the potential values as the first step in the meeting.) The first item on the agenda is a review of the structure and process you will use to create these coding values. It is as follows.

1. Distribute a copy of the potential coding values to each team member along with three to four 3" × 5" index cards. Each card represents a vote and a weight factor for a specific value (such as "Portability" or "Efficiency"). Increasing the number of cards increases the number of "values" supported by the team and makes the process of identifying them more difficult. Fewer cards help to focus developers on selecting truly important values but may miss values supporting important aspects of your development environment. It is better to start small, with three or four cards, and only increase the number of cards as necessary.

2. Members select values from the list by writing down one item per card. Once a value is selected it cannot be used again. Encourage everyone to concentrate on their personal preferences, whatever they may be, and not the perceived preferences of you or the group.

3. Numeric scores representing the strength of preference for each value are written next. The scores are distributed in the following way. If there are four cards, there are four scores: 1, 2, 3, and 4. Team members assign the highest score to their most important value, the next highest score to the next most important value, and so on.

4. Collect the results and divide a whiteboard in four columns. The whiteboard structures decision making as follows. The first column contains the raw scores associated with each item. The second column contains the number of votes each item has received and is a measure of the breadth of support. The third column contains the point totals and is a measure of the depth of support. The fourth column will contain the actual values of the team—the outcome of this exercise.

   The process is as follows. Write the raw results in column 1. Write the number of votes each value has received in column 2 sorted from most to least. Write the point totals of each value in column 3 sorted from highest to lowest.

5. This is the hardest step, the one which will produce the values of the team. Review the second and third columns. In general, items receiving the most votes

will have the highest point totals. These will become your values. However, because of the way the exercise is conducted, some items may not receive many votes but will still have high point values. This means a small coalition values something strongly. Ignoring this coalition is dangerous—if you do you may lose essential knowledge. Instead, you must thoroughly discuss each potentially controversial item. Unless everyone can truthfully and openly support these values, you can expect trouble down the road.

If the team cannot agree on one or two items, the following two options are effective at reaching a final resolution. First, before the meeting, inform the team you will make the final decision on any contested item if they become deadlocked. This is a structural device with the advantage of making certain the values of the team are consistent with your own values. The danger of this approach is your staff will reject these values if they perceive them to have been forcibly dictated. Second, you can repeat the process, focusing efforts on those items receiving the highest scores. You could, for example, quickly repeat the process, but this time only use two or three index cards instead of six. Do not close the meeting until an agreed-upon set of values has been created.

6. Record the values and have every member of the team sign the tally. Obtaining their signature reinforces the importance of values and further solidifies their commitment. Place the original in the project repository and distribute a copy to every member of the team. Post a copy in a conspicuous place. Refer to these values as often as possible and share them with other teams.

Here is an example.

Sarah is beginning a project to integrate the sales database used by salespeople on their laptop computers with multiple-mainframe databases. The objective is to make certain customer information is maintained and shared in a consistent and correct manner and to facilitate the tracking of sales information. Her team consists of six developers with extremely diverse backgrounds. Because everyone has experience in C and four of the six have experience in C++ (one is considered an expert), she has selected C++ as the implementation language. She has chosen three values as her goal. The results of her exercise through step 5 are as follows:

Raw Scores		Votes		Point Totals	
Highly portable:	2,1,1,2,3,3	Highly portable:	6	Highly portable:	12
Very efficient:	2,1,1	Follows standards:	3	Follows standards:	6
Easy to test:	2	Very efficient:	3	No "tricky" language features:	6
Follows standards:	1,3,2	Easy to maintain:	2	Easy to maintain:	5
No "tricky" language features:	3,3	No "tricky" language features:	2	Very efficient:	4
Small size:	1	Small size:	1	Easy to test:	2
Easy to maintain:	2,3	Easy to test:	1	Small size:	1

Thus, "Highly portable" has received the most votes (6), but "No tricky language fea-tures" has a small but vocal coalition as evidenced by its high point total (6). What should Sarah do now? She could choose the first three values listed in column 2 and ig-nore the small, but vocal coalition. Or, she could simply assume that because "No tricky language features" has a more vocal coalition, this value is more widely held and ignore the more broadly held value of efficiency.

Neither of these approaches is satisfactory. The problem is that Sarah, and the rest of the team, don't know which language features are considered "tricky." It turns out Ned, the C++ expert, has convinced Sal multiple inheritance is so tricky it must be avoided at all costs. Because the current coding standard does not explicitly disallow the use of multiple inheritance, both Ned and Sal decided it needed to be stated as a value of the team. After further discussion, in which the team agreed to amend the standard, it was agreed the final values of the team would be (in order of importance):

1. Follow standards
2. Highly portable
3. Very efficient

Identifying coding values is a simple and rewarding exercise and should take no more than one hour from start to finish (especially if you quickly model the process for the team). In addition, once this has been done, you will find the team can successfully cre-ate values to guide them in other aspects of system development. On one consulting as-signment a team designing a GUI interface couldn't decide which of two alternatives was more effective.

As you might guess, I was hired to "tell" them which design was better. Rather than doing this, I used the technique described above to create a set of GUI design values based on the stated preferences of the customer and the personal experiences of the team. Once these values were stated, it was easy for everyone to agree on the alterna-tive best supporting them.

ADVICE TO DEVELOPERS

Organizations are collections of people. Ultimately, our personal values impact our work environment. Use your knowledge of values to do so in a positive way.

> Reinforce values.
>
> Learn the values of your organization.
>
> Be courageous in pursuing values but avoid sacrificing yourself for them.

Reinforce values.   There are countless opportunities to reinforce your val-ues and your team's values during the course of a working day. Take advantage of these opportunities. Suppose you value standards highly, even if other members of the team do not. I'm not suggesting you pontificate endlessly about the importance of following standards. What good is that? I am suggesting that whenever you submit your code for review, you make certain it follows the standard meticulously. If someone comments on how well your code follows the standard, simply state, "Standards are important to me. I'm going to follow them." Positively referring to your own behavior is more effective than pointing out the perceived shortcomings of others.

Learn the values of your organization.   Many organizations publicly state their values. Quite often, these values reflect those of the founder and are distributed to new hires in the form of speech reprints or pamphlets. For example, when I first started to work for EDS I was given a small booklet entitled "Success in Business," a reprint of a speech delivered by Ross Perot, founder and (then) chairman of the board of EDS.

Much of the speech stated the implicit and explicit values of EDS, among them support for pursuing multiple career paths, promotion from within, and a long-term view of personal and career development. While such publications may seem trivial or appear to have little impact on your daily working habits, it is worth the 10- or 15-minute investment to read these statements carefully. These values are guiding the decisions of your top management team. It is in your best interests to understand where they might be headed, and why.

Be courageous in pursuing values but avoid sacrificing yourself for them.   While it may be romantic to view yourself as a heroic figure fighting villains in the name of truth and justice, it is generally unwise to sacrifice your career for a value. Losing your job over a difference in values is only appropriate in *extreme* cases, such as when you are convinced your manager or fellow team member is acting illegally and have evidence to prove your claim. Otherwise, work to instill and support your values but know when to back off.

11.2 CULTURE

Culture is a human artifact, created by and sustained through our interactions. As an expression of values, culture nurtures and sustains the team. But, what *is* culture? How *can* it be changed? The definitions of culture provided in Chapter 8 are too vague and abstract to be of practical value to managers and developers who wish to influence it. To fully understand culture and how it can be molded, it is necessary to identify its components: norms, rituals, symbols and stories, and shared language.

11.2.1 Norms

Culture finds expression through *norms*, which are the social conventions established by a team serving to guide, control, and regulate behavior. They are known by a majority of the team, and members of the team can identify behavior consistent with the norms. Following the norms of the group contributes to team effectiveness and a feeling of shared identity. An individual deviating from established norms can cause conflict and strife and risks censure [McCaskey 1990].

Normative behaviors are rarely formally planned. Instead, they develop over time in the context of established patterns of interaction from the larger societal and organizational culture. For example, in Japan, where the efforts of groups are highly valued, work groups organized around specific tasks are common.

In contrast, the cultural emphasis on the individual in the United States can be seen in the tendency to assign an individual to a task, who may then organize a team (and be subsequently recognized as the "leader" of the team). In this sense, norms represent a customization by the team of preestablished acceptable mechanisms for interaction. What come first are general rules and expectations of how individuals should interact. These rules enable the team to form and work together in a reasonable manner. Team-specific norms are then created by the team in the context of these interactions, refining and extending behavior.

These observations can pose some especially difficult challenges when trying to change culture. Consider a development team moving from traditional development technology to development based on object technology. One of the most important values associated with object technology deals with reuse. The object technology culture supports these values through specific norms promoting reuse. What if the team suffers from "NIH"—Not Invented Here—the distressing tendency of developers to reject solutions they or their teams did not directly invent? Do you think the normative behaviors of such a team support the use of objects?

> *Not all norms serve as a positive force within the group. In one assignment, I was surprised to see fellow managers privately discuss the actions and behaviors of other managers in a highly critical manner, yet publicly praise these same people. Because I believed such a norm was dysfunctional and inhibiting the effectiveness of the team, I tried to confront it during a staff meeting. Unfortunately, as a new member of the group I was unable to change a firmly entrenched norm apparently sanctioned by our common superior who often engaged in such behavior. Eventually, he was replaced and a new manager began the task of changing the norms of the group. As it turns out, bad norms were made even worse. Instead of instilling positive norms through leadership, he simply promoted, demoted, or transferred subordinates who did not do exactly as he wished. In effect, he changed one dysfunctional norm—cloak and dagger communication—for another—"my way or the highway."*

11.2.2 Rituals

Rituals are semiformal or formal *repeated* patterns of behavior among members of the team often associated with specific actions and behaviors or providing stable frameworks for such actions and behaviors. They serve to promote kinds or modes of interaction considered beneficial and help define what behaviors are important enough to be given special attention. Where norms are primarily "internal" and not always easily identified, rituals are "external" and are thereby far more easily recognized.

They are "the things you can count on," and can be informal (e.g., sharing lunch on Tuesdays), or formal (e.g., the annual holiday party).

Rituals often provide an avenue for the expression of certain kinds of behavior that may not otherwise exist. For example, the norms of a conservative company might make it difficult to express enthusiasm about a job well done, but at the celebration party held for each release of the product, enthusiastic displays may not only be condoned, they may be expected, even from the most reserved members of the team. A formal company may discourage subordinates from talking with senior executives unless the dialog takes place at a specific ritual. Thus, a senior executive may virtually ignore a junior employee in the cafeteria but will hold a deep and meaningful conversation with that same employee *if* it is shared in the monthly "get to know the boss" luncheon.

Rituals often develop in surprising ways, often outliving their originators even as the membership of the team changes. To illustrate, imagine you are a member of a five-person development team. The team has decided to begin every week with a one-hour planning/review meeting. One morning Shrikant decides to bring donuts. This kind deed is repeated once or twice more by other people. Over time, the kind deed becomes "ritualized" as everyone takes turns in a friendly, fun, and low-cost competition of seeing who can bring the most creative breakfast for under $10. The ritual is likely to be maintained even if Shrikant transfers to another team. Although new members may fail to appreciate the significance of the ritual, it will likely persist until the team is disbanded or the planning meeting stopped.

11.2.3 Stories and Symbols

Establishing and maintaining a culture is often accomplished through common symbols and stories ("folklore") told about the organization. Stories are often created when the organization (or team) is young and often serve to specifically reinforce specific company values. Ideally, a story is positive, appropriate, and supportive of the culture. This is not always the case, and it is quite common to hear stories promoting (or warning of) *negative* aspects of culture. The important point is that as stories are told and shared, they establish, strengthen, and broaden the common bonds shared by the team. Bad deeds or actions become worse; good deeds or jobs well done become heroic feats.

One can learn a substantial amount of information about a culture, including which values are considered especially important, by listening to corporate stories. In one well-known example, IBM employees learn Thomas J. Watson, Jr., once fired a salesperson for selling the customer a larger and more expensive system than the customer needed [Phillips 1980]. This story reinforces corporate values on providing superior customer service (i.e., selling a larger and more expensive system can hardly be considered "superior customer service"). Consider the story of how Steve Jobs led the team who created the first Macintosh. By making certain every employee knows this story, Apple strengthens core values of individuality, creativity, and entrepreneurship.

In a similar manner, symbols identified by the team serve to communicate important values both within and outside the team. When a symbol is shared, it can become a powerful motivating and integrating force. Obvious symbols include the corporate logo, but many development teams find it effective to create their own symbols directly reflecting their own culture (e.g., the dark mustaches of the testing team described in *Peopleware* [DeMarco 1987]).

Culture is often reflected through the symbols chosen by the corporation and the meaning given to these symbols by individuals within the corporation. For a number of the years I worked at EDS. An important symbol in the corporation was a bald eagle, a proud image of strength, courage, and individuality. At the completion of one project I received a beautiful ceramic sculpture of an eagle in flight, a highly recognizable and valued representation of EDS culture.

However, symbols can be confusing, both to those within organization and those external to it. When I called my wife to tell her about my award, she commented: "Are you telling me the corporate symbol is an eagle?" I replied, "Informally, yes." She responded: "Isn't that a poor symbol for a group of developers? Think about it. Eagles are primarily solitary birds. They don't flock. If everyone is an 'eagle,' how do you get anything done?"

As I reflected on her comments, I began to see she was correct. A culture emphasizing individualism too heavily makes it difficult to achieve teamwork. Such a realization must have occurred at the highest levels of leadership within EDS, because there has been a slow movement away from using the eagle as a symbol. Indeed, two years later a team I was working on received another award from the same manager who had given me the eagle. The award? A pewter mobius strip, symbolizing the unity of the team. It was also a symbol of a different kind. It was a symbol of a manager supporting a cultural change from a single symbol of individuality to a diversity of symbols, each chosen by the manager for their team and reflecting the team and project to which it was given.

11.2.4 Shared Language

Perhaps the easiest component of culture to identify is the shared language of the team. Special acronyms, cryptic shorthand, and other language idioms serve to reinforce culture. Language special to the team reinforces identity with the team's culture and enables team members to communicate in an especially efficient manner.

Larry Constantine [1995] reports how one team he worked on developed a special language to handle office interruptions. When interrupted, developers responded with "NAK" (negative acknowledgment—"I'm busy, please don't bother me now") or "ACK" ("I can see you now"). At ObjectSpace, we speak of "qwacking" (quality hacking), "ObjectShirts" (a company symbol), and other "Object" things. To an outsider, especially one not familiar with interrupt handling or object-oriented programming, such a language is confusing, at best.

A shared language not only serves to differentiate the group, but it also serves to link disparate groups. Consider a large, geographically dispersed development project. It is desirable to encourage each subteam to develop their own culture, including language. This must be balanced by the need for cohesiveness across geographic boundaries. A shared language is one mechanism to achieve this: No matter where the team is located, members can identify a means of communication that is theirs and theirs alone.

11.2.5 How To Influence Culture

How can we use the components of culture defined above effectively? To illustrate, suppose you wanted to adopt the use of design patterns as a part of your culture? (Recall from Chapter 1 that a pattern is a stereotypical solution to a problem that has been documented in such a way that it can be shared.) What should you do? The answer is surprisingly simple! Define appropriate pattern-related cultural artifacts and introduce them into the team. For example, a *symbol* of pattern development could be a plaid shirt (or a piece of plaid cloth). Any member of the team who documents a pattern is encouraged to wear something plaid (e.g., a shirt) each day of the week. Does this strike you as corny? Remember, it is not the external view of culture that guides the team. Rather, the internal view of culture—how each member of the team *feels* about the culture—is what is most important.

Table 11–1 provides a starting point. You can use it in three ways. First, use it to plan the artifacts you feel support patterns most effectively. Brainstorming is essential at this stage! Second, use it to gauge your progress toward creating a "pattern" culture. Of course, you will have to extend the examples into a form suitable given your existing culture. While suggesting everyone in the office wear plaid shorts on "pattern" day (a symbol and a ritual), you may find an unreceptive audience in most companies! Third, use the structure provided by the table and the processes of changing culture to create a culture supporting other beneficial software engineering practices. For example, the quality assurance group can use these techniques to create a culture of quality assurance.

Finally, remember that identifying specific cultural components for change is only one step of the overall process. Cultural change cannot be achieved by simply introducing new cultural artifacts or speaking in a different language. The more established the culture, the more resistant it is to change. Moreover, a change in culture usually occurs in conjunction with a change in other aspects of the work environment. For example, the creation of a "pattern" culture usually occurs in the context of the more general adoption of object technology. In other words, there is usually a *lot* of change going on when there is a cultural change. The most universal advice is "go slowly." Do not expect an overnight, dramatic shift in behavior. Instead, work smoothly toward the culture you think is most appropriate for your work environment.

TABLE 11–1   Cultural Artifacts Supporting a Pattern Culture

Component	Example
Norms	The primary norm to reinforce is the *use* of patterns in problem solving. Thus, whenever you find a solution that *could* have used a pattern but didn't, gently tell the developer(s) of the preferred pattern solution. In other words, remind him or her (or them) "We use *patterns* here!"
	Encourage developers to talk about patterns during meetings.
Rituals	Managers: Give each developer the "Gang of Four" book ([Gamma 1995]).
	A major component in developing a pattern is documenting it in a way others find accessible. Organize a biannual writers' workshop and encourage developers to submit patterns they have discovered. The purpose of the workshop is to improve the ability of developers to write patterns that can be used effectively.
	Have a square dance (think about it . . .).
	Look for patterns in code reviews. Go one layer higher: Have a *pattern* review.
	Managers: Send one or two of your most prolific writers to PLoP (or some other pattern conference) and have them write a trip report.
Symbols	List each pattern used in an application in the "About . . ." dialog describing the system (e.g., "This version of SalesWhiz was created using the Strategy and Singleton patterns"). When a certain number of patterns have been reached, award each member of the team the coveted "pattern symbol" (e.g., T-shirt, mug).
Stories	Invite an influential person in the pattern movement to share his or her personal story of how he or she became interested in patterns. Alternatively (or at the same time), as members of the team learn patterns, ask them to informally share their experiences with the team. An ideal story begins, "I remember the day I applied my first pat-tern. I was faced with this tricky problem of instantiating objects coming in from a network socket and I thought the Abstract Factory might help. And it did! . . ."
	Share "pattern" stories with new team members.
Shared Language	As mentioned above, changes in language are among the most easily identified component of a culture adopting the use of patterns. The names of patterns appear not only in analysis and design sessions, but they also appear in general conversation in the group. You can encourage this by explicitly referring to patterns whenever possible. (A little balance, please! I don't want people to reach for the air sickness bag every time they hear the word *Observer.*)
	Put patterns on 3" × 5" cards for easy reference. Such cards represent a symbol, but also serve to reinforce the shared language of the team.

ADVICE TO MANAGERS

As a formal leader, you should have more influence over the culture of the development team than any single developer.[1] By choosing to emphasize certain norms, by instituting and reinforcing selected rituals, and by sharing and promoting cer-

[1] Managers represent one kind of leader. Certainly, numerous informal leaders exist within any team, and these people have substantial influence in the shaping of culture. By *formal,* I refer to individuals having the authority to do such things as set policy or discipline others for inappropriate behavior. Such people are usually the managers of the group.

tain stories and symbols, you will shape and guide a particular culture. Of course, *directly* changing the culture of a group is not possible. At best, you can *indirectly* change culture. That said, there are some specific actions you can take to shape culture.

Don't underestimate the power of your personal style.

Promote a consistent group norm of time.

Use new members to help change culture.

Tell their stories, not yours.

Attend rituals.

Foster a climate of creativity.

Reinforce values through recognition.

Use symbols for more than just recognition.

Integrate ethnically diverse team members through rituals.

Don't underestimate the power of your personal style.   Your personal style will have more to do with the shaping of culture than any other single factor, for subordinates take their cues on what is appropriate behavior from you. For example, a team known for taking an innovative approach to problem solving will likely have a manager encouraging a culture where risk taking can flourish through his/her own behavior, even if the larger culture is one of staid conservatism. Similarly, a manager known for honest communication will foster a similar culture within the team. In general, these effects are inversely proportional to size. The most direct influence on a team's culture is through their most immediate manager.

Promote a consistent group norm of time.   In studying the differences of time perception within organizations, Vinton [1992] has uncovered several differences among group norms with respect to time. Specifically, she found that perceptions vary with respect to such things as punctuality or the margins for error on completion of tasks by stated deadlines. Imagine the tension if you value punctuality and I do not. When I'm late for a meeting, you might perceive me as lazy, apathetic, or irresponsible. When you express your displeasure, I'm likely to think of you as rigid and anal-retentive. Neither of us is likely to think the cause is a simple difference in temporal style. Establishing a consistent group norm of time will reduce or eliminate such unnecessary impediments to teamwork.

Use new members to help change culture.   When considering a candidate for the team, reflect on how their personality and values can influence culture. For example, consider searching for an innovative person if you feel the culture of your team relies too heavily on rigidly defining and following structures. Similarly, if your team is known for missing meetings, you might look for a highly punctual person to influence the team to establish more appropriate ground rules for meetings. Of course, it is inappropriate to place the burden of changing an entire culture on a single developer—but they *can* help.

Tell their stories, not yours.   The power of a story is largely based on the degree to which the listener can identify with the story's characters and underlying theme. The most powerful stories are those whose leading characters are members of the team or well-known members of the larger organization. One of my all-time favorite stories is about the FedEx employee who forget his keys to a drop-box. Going back to the office would have taken too much time, and leaving the packages would have meant they wouldn't be delivered on time. He solved the problem by unbolting the entire drop box and throwing it in the back of his truck! Every FedEx delivery person can directly identify with this story.

Because of this, you should resist telling stories of previous teams, as these stories will have slightly less impact. You should be especially careful about stories in which you are the focal character. Such stories can easily be misinterpreted as bragging about past accomplishments.

Attend rituals.   Sadly, many managers do not attend or participate in rituals. This is a mistake. As noted before, rituals enable the team to engage in actions or express behavior often prohibited by norms. Especially important are rituals associated with the completion of a project (e.g., luncheons, dinners, and so forth). *Never* skip these rituals. They represent a critically important mechanism for showing in a very real and visible manner you appreciate the efforts of your team.

That said, it is now time to present the other side of rituals. It is inappropriate for you to assume you should attend *every* ritual. Many rituals are created by the team for *the team*. They may not want you to attend. The important point is to think carefully about a ritual before blinding attending it.

Foster a climate of creativity.   Creativity within a development team can only flourish in a culture supporting and promoting it through special structures and processes. One especially powerful idea is the "special rooms" proposed by Tropman [1989:152]. The motivation for the special rooms is that too often software development cultures prematurely reject good ideas. Creating the right structure enables creativity to flourish. Here's how.

In the beginning of a project designate a special meeting room for idea testing and challenging. When an idea is to be challenged, hold a "Devil's Advocate Session." In such a session anyone present—including the inventor of the idea—knows the purpose of the gathering is to challenge, critique, kick, shake, jiggle, and otherwise stress the idea to see how it holds up under pressure. When it is to be supported, hold an "Angel's Advocate Session." This session is the exact opposite of the Devil's Advocate session: Everyone present goes to extraordinary lengths to see how the idea can be made to work—what's good about it, what are good extensions and side points, and so on.

Two rules hold. First, all ideas must go through both sessions. Second, the Angel's Advocacy session must happen *first*. This prevents early criticism from prematurely killing an idea. In the ideal evaluation process the two sessions are alternated, with the feedback from each session clarifying and solidifying the idea in the minds of everyone present. The end result is an idea transformed into something having greater support and far fewer implementation problems than usual.

Reinforce values through recognition.   Explicitly recognizing contributions through a carefully selected symbol provides one of the best ways to reinforce values. Such symbols form a strong foundation for building a beneficial culture, especially when they seem a bit obscure to "outsiders."

Symbols don't have to be big, expensive, or ostentatious. They should be fun, simple, and meaningful, both to the individual receiving the symbol and the team. Two of my favorite symbols are a Swiss™ Army knife (dependability) and juggling bean bags (the ability to work successfully on multiple projects). One group of developers rotates a "dunce cap" during code reviews to remove the sting associated with criticism.

The amount of money spent on the symbols is not nearly as important as the symbol itself. Quite often an extravagant symbol may actually detract from its purpose, as individuals begin to concentrate on the symbol instead of the meaning behind it.

Use symbols for more than just recognition.   Many managers use symbols for recognition purposes only: At the end of a complex or lengthy development, each developer is given one or more visible symbols (e.g., a plaque, a pen and pencil set, and so forth) to commemorate their role. While this has undeniable benefits—most people, developers included, take pride in a work area filled with visible contributions to the corporation—using symbols only as recognition significantly diminishes their ability to shape the culture of the team. Expand your use of symbols within the team and use them to inject changes into the culture.

One development team I inherited had a serious morale problem: They felt their contributions, which were substantial, were underappreciated. Moreover, other departments in the company often received visible symbols of their contributions, and it had been quite some time since this team had been given similar recognition. The biggest antagonist was the sales department, whose manager lavished his team with trinkets. It was easy to see how the development team could perceive themselves as underdogs. They also told me they felt I didn't appreciate their efforts or consider them excellent developers, because I had indicated their development processes were unacceptable and I was in the process of making several rather substantial changes.

As a contributor to the problem, I felt I had to find a solution. And, the solution had to be cheap, because I had no additional money in my budget, and any action would have to come out of my own pocket. I also felt the work environment had become much too serious. As I like to have a little fun at work, I felt something a bit "corny" would be appropriate (it was a few days before Halloween). I discussed a few ideas with my administrative assistant because I needed her help in making everything work and settled on purchasing a red vinyl cape for each developer.

A special meeting was announced, with mandatory attendance. No reason was given for the meeting, and no agenda was prepared, which made it somewhat suspenseful. Before the meeting my assistant and I wrote the name of the company, a big "S," and the date of the meeting on each cape. During the ceremony, I gave a cape to each developer, letting them know I thought they were "super developers." At the end of the ceremony (which turned out pretty crazy!), pictures were taken and shared, and the team had quite a few laughs. Overall, I think the capes did have the desired effect: Most members of the team appreciated them, and morale did improve. I even saw them displayed in their cubicles to, as one developer put it, "Protect me from the sales team."

Unfortunately, not every aspect of this story can be considered positive, for like every managerial action, there were unintended side effects. A few weeks later it came to my attention certain members of the team were upset about the capes because they felt it was inappropriate to spend company money on such frivolous items. In their view, such money would be better spent increasing salaries or providing bonuses. Upon hearing this I was naturally a little upset, because no company money was spent on the capes (other than the time invested in purchasing the capes and attending the meeting). At first, I ignored the comments, hoping they would die down, but after a few of the more vocal members of the team continued to cause problems with their opinions of the capes, I told them the truth in order to minimize the damaging effects of their comments. This does not mean I think it is inappropriate to allocate company funds to symbols. Quite the opposite is true, and the wise manager will search for symbols appropriate for his or her team and budget accordingly.

Integrate ethnically diverse team members through rituals.   Ethnically diverse teams can be especially difficult to manage. Cultures from around the world hold different views on many, many different things. One way to integrate ethnically diverse members is to create and/or modify rituals supporting native cultures. Suppose you sponsor a special dinner for every release of the system. One way to increase respect for other cultures would be to explicitly choose a different restaurant for each release, each restaurant representing the food from one culture. This would be a fun, nonthreatening, and low-cost way to increase team unity and multicultural awareness.

One of the most challenging assignments for any manager is assuming leadership of an existing team. As the "new" manager, it is likely you will want to modify the existing culture to suit your managerial style. One way to do this is through the introduction of cultural artifacts.

> Create rituals.
> Create stories.
> Create a team motto.

Create rituals.   As the new manager you have the opportunity to create new rituals promoting values you consider important. Consider Lisa. She was given a team who just didn't work well together. Everyone took delight in finding the faults of everyone else. Code reviews, when they were done, were especially humiliating, having become the preferred event for public humiliation. How might you change this culture?

Lisa did it by instituting a new ritual. She would select an outcome prepared by someone on the team and praise it for roughly ten minutes in the weekly team meeting. She continued to do this until everyone had an opportunity to feel the warm sunshine of praise rather than the harsh sleet of criticism. Then, she began to ask other developers what they felt was good about the outcome she had selected. Over time, she no longer had to select the outcome: Developers spontaneously began to bring outcomes prepared by *other* people to the meeting! By instituting a ritual explicitly based on positive behaviors, Lisa was able to change the culture.

Create stories.   Old stories support the old culture. And, if the existing culture is poor, you can be certain the old stories accentuate the negative. Change this by creating new stories—stories supporting the culture you wish to create.

For example, suppose you want the culture to become more focused on the customer. Hold a meeting with yourself, one or two members of your team, and the customer regarding a nonvolatile but nonetheless important topic. During the meeting, guide the conversation to a mutually agreeable outcome. Once finished, you have the foundation for a successful story emphasizing both a strong focus on the customer and teamwork among your developers (one of your developers suggested the outcome found desirable by the customer, not you, right?). Sharing this story with other developers will not only promote a new culture but will also instill pride among the participants in the meeting who become characters in the new stories.

Create a team motto.   One of the most powerful rallying symbols and a strong and visible component of a team's culture is a team motto. As Tropman stated:

> When one is forced to say in a few words the essential focus of . . . effort ("Quality is job one"—"The mark of excellence"—"Better things for better living"), it stimulates and gives concrete reality to thought. It forces [teams] to answer the question "What business are we in" and "how can we communicate this fact." Communication via the motto is first and foremost to the [team] itself and serves as an economical reminder of what the [team] stands for and promises. [1989:129]

ADVICE TO DEVELOPERS

The majority of culture is created through two mechanisms. The first is through the direct actions of management as they introduce and/or support cultural artifacts (e.g., symbols or rituals). The second, and by far the most important, is through the social interactions among members of the team. You have great power in supporting and creating culture based on the norms you choose, or choose not, to follow. You also shape culture through your support of rituals, symbols, stories, and shared language.

> Resist dysfunctional norms.
> Display your symbols.
> Be careful of displaying the symbols of previous employers.
> Avoid criticizing the culture of another team.

Resist dysfunctional norms.   Dysfunctional norms require more effort to perpetuate than positive, functional norms. Because of this, you can change a team by standing up for what you think is right. Kahn [1994] relates the story of how one team continually blamed other teams for a problem *they* had created. In every meeting substantial energy was spent finding ways to support the story they had invented rather than accepting the problem as their own and working to find a way to solve it.

The dysfunctional norm was the failure to accept a problem they had created. This norm continued to exist until a new member joined the team and rejected the accepted conclusion. By forcing the team to reexamine the problem and by refusing to support the dysfunctional norm, this individual succeeded in changing the culture from one of failure-avoidance to one of failure-acceptance. In the case of a well-known problem, it can be a simple matter to generate enough resistance to keep the team's attention focused on the matter at hand.

This advice should be followed with some amount of caution, especially if you are a new member on a team that has expended a great deal of energy covering up a problem. First, you risk significant backlash from existing team members if they perceive you as attacking them and not the problem. Second, you cannot assume your manager is unaware of the problem—s/he may not only be aware, but may also condone the dysfunctional behavior in an attempt to protect his or her own job! Indeed, Kahn found that even a strong-willed member could not always change dysfunctional norms. Sometimes they were simply too firmly entrenched.

If you decide to resist norms you feel to be incorrect, remember to take it slowly and concentrate on the problems, not the people. While you may not agree with their behavior, remember there is usually a reasonable motivation for it. Even dysfunctional norms often have reasonable motivations—if everyone fears losing their job because the system won't be completed on time, no one will be motivated to inform the customer. Dysfunctional? Certainly. Understandable? Yes.

Display your symbols.   The symbols given to you in recognition of your accomplishments were designed to support and share the culture and to show visible appreciation for your contributions to the company. While an ostentatious display announcing all of your accomplishments promotes your ego instead of teamwork, you should take pride in displaying, in an appropriate manner, the visible symbols of your hard work.

Be careful of displaying the symbols of previous employers. Symbols are given for a variety of reasons: to promote identity, recognize and reward teamwork or individual contributions, and so forth. Be careful about displaying symbols given by your former employer at your new job.

Avoid criticizing the culture of another team.   There is no beneficial outcome to you, your team, or the larger organization when you criticize the culture (i.e., the norms, symbols, rituals, stories, or special language) of another team. Indeed, the only outcomes are detrimental: negative feelings, cynicism, and a lack of trust between you and others.

11.3 GOALS

Of the three components of the integrated framework presented in this chapter, goals are the easiest to explicitly identify and "manage." To see why, first compare goals with values and then culture. Values are largely subjective, difficult to measure directly. Well-defined goals are objective and directly measurable. The same can be said for culture. While we can identify aspects of culture and work to change them, we can't really do so directly.

Webster's dictionary defines a *goal* as "an end that one strives to obtain." One aspect of a well-defined goal is the ease with which we can measure our progress in obtaining it. If we can't measure progress, then something is wrong—our goal is poorly defined. Values and culture do not share these qualities. A deeply held value is not an end. It is a "thing" guiding our behavior and motivating us to create goals consistent with the concept it represents. Culture is also not an end. It too is a thing, dynamic, more process than anything else. Certainly culture changes over time, and we can define desirable changes, but it is not itself a well-defined end.

What can make goals a bit tricky to understand is that well-defined goals share many of the same desirable aspects of both values and culture. Like values, goals can aid in conflict resolution and help ensure that people act in compatible ways. Like culture, goals serve as a unifying force within the team. When everyone is focused on achieving the same goal, everyone seems to just work more effectively with each other. Indeed, a particularly challenging goal can spawn a culture devoted to achieving it. Just listen to the language of a team pursuing a hard—but achievable—goal. Finally, clearly defined goals help team members focus on what tasks are considered important. Doing so helps make certain each task contributes to the attainment of the goal.

ADVICE TO MANAGERS

While you have little direct control over values and culture—changes to these are primarily made indirectly—goals are an entirely different manner. In general, one or more goals of the team are under your direct control. Creating well-defined goals—

and managing to them—enables you to guide the team as they prepare outcomes meeting these goals. Understanding these outcomes, in turn, helps you select the structures and processes necessary to achieve them.

Establish goals.

Make certain goals reflect the core purpose of the team.

Define goals carefully, as developers will try to achieve them.

Provide feedback.

Avoid defining extremely specific goals as they can inhibit creativity.

Define goals that are both challenging and feasible.

State explicitly the relationships between structures and goals.

Use a mission statement.

Use goals to find the right people.

Establish reward systems supporting goals.

Avoid overload.

Establish goals.   Teams need goals to explain and guide behavior. Teams need them so badly they invent them or accept them from others. Herein lies the problem, for when this happens the goals the team pursues are often contradictory or just plain confusing. It works like this. In the absence of clearly stated goals, certain (or all) members of the team will invent them or find them from others as a means of explaining and guiding behavior. Working toward these false goals makes them real. This is the process of enactment, when we cause something to exist by acting as if it really did exist. Confusion occurs because everyone is likely to invent or identify slightly different goals. Over time, the efforts of the team become increasingly disoriented and fragmented. Surprisingly, managers often fail to define goals for their teams. I'm not certain why. Maybe goals are perceived as difficult to create. Maybe they are perceived as unimportant. Both statements are untrue. One of your most important responsibilities as a manager lies in establishing appropriate goals.

Make certain goals reflect the core purpose of the team.   Well-defined goals match the core responsibilities of the team and are consistent with the expectations of other teams.

Define goals carefully, as developers will try to achieve them.   Development teams strive to achieve the goals outlined by their manager or defined by the project. This result was established by a well-known experiment conducted by Weinberg and Schulman [1974], who asked five different teams to achieve the same basic requirements with slightly different goals (e.g., one team was asked to minimize size, another to minimize memory, a third to minimize errors, and so forth). Summarizing their results, they found

♦ If you *tell* development teams what you want, you're quite likely to get it.

♦ If you *don't* tell them what you want, you're quite *unlikely* to get it.

As such, goals should be defined rather carefully: What you ask for is what you will get! Does this mean you can specify every goal and have your team pursue all of them? Not likely. Remember the principle of bounded rationality?

Provide feedback.   Goals are most effective when clearly visible feedback is provided to the team letting them know exactly how they are doing toward achieving the goal. We've all seen examples of feedback during fund-raising drives for local charities. A thermometer is drawn on a big piece of cardboard. As more money is raised, the "temperature" of the thermometer becomes higher. Feedback towards the goal is visible, accessible—even fun.

Trying to provide similarly visible feedback is a worthwhile exercise. Consider a team in a system test. How about a large graph showing the number of errors found in the system over time? Fairley [1985] refers to such a graph as a *trend plot*. Establishing a "zero-defect" goal means there are no known errors in the system (or, at least, errors are well known). Watching the graph approach this goal lifts spirits.

Avoid defining extremely specific goals as they can inhibit creativity.   Setting a goal of building a new PC-based system in C with a specific compiler and set of libraries removes a substantial amount of creativity from your development team. By broadening the goal (implement the system in a PC in this time frame, you pick the implementation vehicle), your developers may instead decide an entirely different language is more appropriate. An overly specified goal allows no freedom in how it is realized, resulting in reduced creativity and less support.

Define goals that are both challenging and feasible.   For a goal to have maximum effectiveness, it should be both somewhat difficult to achieve but still well within the abilities of the developer. Bradford and Cohen found "leaders of a high performing department set higher standards for members than members would set for themselves" [Bradford 1984]. A team given a challenging goal will often find creative ways to implement the system or utilize new technology in order to meet it. Indeed, when given a challenging goal, brainstorming to determine how to achieve it can be just as motivating as realizing the actual goal!

Of course, you should be equally careful of setting impossible or infeasible goals. Establishing a goal thought to be impossible only alienates your team and drives motivation to zero. Determining the right level of difficulty is what makes establishing challenging goals difficult. Too easy? Low motivation. Too hard? Low motivation. Hard but not too hard? Motivating!

State explicitly the relationships between structures and goals.   It is not always clear how the structures you have established can lead to the realization of the goal. As a test of both the validity of the structures you have defined and to obtain buyin for operating within their constraints, make explicit the connections between structures, the outcomes they will create, and the goal. The validity test is this: Unless you can show how the outcomes eventually achieve the goal, you have a problem. Too often, we assume these relationships are obvious, when they aren't.

Use a mission statement. When a project requires expertise and input from multiple departments, goals are sometimes expressed as a "mission statement" [Scholtes 1988]. A mission statement is a concise summary of the goal(s) of the project, including:

♦ What is to be accomplished
♦ Boundaries and limitations
♦ High-level schedule

Among other benefits, the creation of a mission statement facilitates coordination and interaction among different teams and helps establish close working relationships among teams with different subgoals. In general, the larger the team the greater the need for a mission statement. Why? Large teams generate more coalitions. Unless each coalition can clearly identify how their outcomes fit into the long term plan they will find it difficult—if not impossible—to work toward the same end.

Use goals to find the right people. Like values, clearly stated goals are a significant aid in the selection process for everyone involved. Would you be eager to join a team whose goal you find uninspiring?

Establish reward systems supporting goals. No matter what goals have been established, our behavior naturally gravitates toward that which is rewarded. As an example of the wrong way to do things, consider a manager who sets as a goal a very low defect rate (which tends to increase development time) but establishes reward systems for completing the project on an extremely tight schedule (e.g., a bonus if the project is completed on time).

In this case, developers will naturally tend to focus their efforts on completing the product on schedule. Quality, while important, will not be the primary consideration in their activities. This, in turn, can create substantial strife within the development staff: If the project begins to run late, they may be motivated to remove items known to contribute to a low defect rate (such as outcome reviews and regression testing) from the schedule. When the product is delivered and the defect rate does not match previously stated goals, management can absolve themselves from blame ("I didn't tell the developers to remove outcome reviews!") and instead place the problems associated with the high defect product on the development staff, perhaps even removing their promised bonus in the process!

As a component of overall compensation, a complete discussion of reward structures is beyond the scope of this book. However, before you establish a reward structure, take the time to explore its effects on the behaviors and outcomes required to achieve the reward. Specifically ask yourself: What activities contribute to the attainment of the reward? Are these activities consistent with the goals of the team? The results are not always clear, and reward systems that on the surface contribute to stated goals may actually promote the opposite behavior.

Consider a manager who establishes a reward structure to improve quality by offering a bonus if all code passes a code review. While this appears to support both organizational values and goals, all code may pass the review process simply because other developers don't want to have *their* code fail a review (thereby removing *their* chance for a bonus). To correct for this deficiency, this manager might establish a system to keep track of code incorrectly accepted in the review process and "charge" this to the reviewers, but this itself is fraught with complexity and managerial overhead.

Because developers are highly intelligent, explicit compensation systems are extraordinarily difficult to create and can easily become a management nightmare. While there are certainly no hard and fast solutions to these problems, explicit compensation systems can be created if they are designed carefully, thoughtfully, and within the right environment (Constantine has an excellent discussion of rewards with respect to reuse; see Constantine [1995:123–7]).

> *I cannot think of a good manager who has not agonized over the creation of appropriate compensation structures. My ideal structure consists of three components: a base salary, an individual performance bonus, and a team performance bonus. (As you read this, think of the compensation structures of a professional athlete.) The base salary would be appropriate for the skills, ability, experience, and job of the developer. The individual performance bonus would be appropriate for individuals who truly perform above and beyond the call of duty. Needless to say, it must be crystal clear to everyone involved exactly what behaviors contribute to the bonus. Finally, the team performance bonus should reward the attainment of goals specified at the level of the team.*

> *Of course, even this simple system is far from perfect. Each component requires careful modification for any specific environment. There are numerous other opinions on compensation structures. Moreover, managers are often highly constrained by the larger organization in such matters. Because of this, I anticipate most performance-based compensation structures will continue to be based on the subjective opinion of the manager. Ultimately, in this kind of system, the likelihood a developer will perceive a bonus as "fair" will be based primarily on the degree of trust between him and his manager. More specifically, I am happy with a $500 bonus if I trust my manager to treat me fairly and unhappy with a $1,500 bonus if I believe otherwise.*

Avoid overload.   When your staff is working hard pursuing their primary goal, there is often no energy left over to pursue additional, smaller goals. Although you may mean well, be careful of "goal overload," a condition in which *none* of the goals you establish are pursued because there are simply *too many* of them!

It is distressingly easy to create far too many goals. On one assignment, I inherited a group whose source code was among the worst I have ever seen! To illustrate, their aver-age number of lines of source code for a single function was well over 1,000. The record was held by one function that was an incredible 4,000 lines in length! No matter how you count lines of source, 1,000 is just too many of them! And, this was not an isolated occur-rence. Most of the code written in any language in this shop was unacceptable.

To correct this situation, I planned an elaborate metrics program. It was going to be great! We were going to implement McCabe's measure of cyclometric complexity. We were going to keep track of production errors and reviews. To make certain every as-pect of the code was improving, I set numerous goals, from source code production to code reviews to standards. You could almost feel the quality ooze from the goals.

The program was a complete and utter failure. Can you guess why? Yes, it was goal overload. I simply set far too many goals. The staff could not deal with the administra-tive overhead of tracking all their activities with respect to the goals while simultane-ously improving, maintaining, and extending the system. So, I started removing goals, one after another. In the end the team was left with a single, universally attainable goal: "Leave the code better than you found it."

ADVICE TO DEVELOPERS

While the goals of the team may be established primarily by your manager, they can be achieved only through your efforts. With this in mind, there are several specific things you can do to help achieve team-related goals and increase your overall job satisfaction at the same time.

> Use goals to stay focused.
> Choose the best alternative leading to the goal.
> Pursue goals with enthusiasm.

Use goals to stay focused.   Software development provides rich ground for distractions: It is easy to get wrapped up in the exploration of a new language fea-ture or the search for the most "optimal" or "elegant" solution. The Web is particularly seductive. Use team and project goals to help you stay focused on the task at hand by asking yourself: "How does this behavior contribute to achieving these goals?"

Choose the best alternative leading to the goal.   During problem solving it can be difficult to select between one or more seemingly good alternatives. Using the hill climbing technique described in Chapter 7, simply choose the alterna-tive you feel leads toward achievement of the goal.

Pursue goals with enthusiasm.   Pursuing goals with enthusiasm can have wonderful effects on your work! First, it imbues your work with a sense of fun.

Instead of leaving the office tired, you feel energized. Second, enthusiasm really is contagious. Those around you can "sense" your enthusiasm and "catch" it.

Of course, there is a slight downside to the enthusiastic pursuit of goals. Members of your team, or those around you, may mistake your enthusiasm for inappropriate behavior or technical incompetence. At one time or another I have been labeled a "cheerleader," described (to my face) as "technically incompetent," told I "didn't care about the customer," informed "you shouldn't have fun at work," and warned "pursuing goals enthusiastically will harm my career." Sheer rubbish. Pursue goals with ebullience. The benefits derived far outweigh any negatives.

12

ORGANIZATIONAL ENGINEERING

"Engineering" is one of the best words in the English language, for it can be used to describe in a concise manner those aspects of human endeavor somewhere between art and science. To illustrate, consider the definition of structural engineering reprinted by Henri Petroski in his marvelous book *To Engineer Is Human*:

> *Structural engineering is the science and art of designing and making, with economy and elegance, buildings, bridges, frameworks, and other similar structures so that they can safely resist the forces to which they may be subjected [Petroski 1985:40].*

Here, "engineering" is used to unite normally dispassionate objects such as bridges and buildings with such passionate words as art and elegance. It works. A well-designed bridge *is* elegant, and the most breathtaking buildings capture our imaginations for the fine works of art they are. "Engineering" can unite more than art and science. It can unite the precise and the imprecise, as evidenced by the following definition of software engineering:

> *Software engineering is the technological and managerial discipline concerned with systematic production and maintenance of software products that are developed and modified on time and within cost estimates. [Fairley 1985:2]*

Here, Fairley uses the word engineering to bridge the gap between the imprecise (estimate) and the precise (software products), the skillful (management) and the routine (systematic production). It is within the background of art and science,

precision and imprecision, skill, ability, and knowledge, I offer the following definition of organizational engineering:

> *Organizational engineering is the ongoing activity of creating, optimizing, and chang-*
> *ing with economy, elegance, and aesthetics the structures, processes, values, culture,*
> *and goals that enable a software development team to be maximally effective in the cre-*
> *ation of desired outcomes.*

Organizational engineering is organic and holistic. We cannot define a static, one-
size-fits-all approach for our organizations. Nor should we. The creation of strong
organizations is much like the creation of strong bones, which continually renew
themselves from within throughout our lifetime. The ongoing process of organizational engineering is conducted within the context of the current integrated framework of the organization, and individuals engaged in engineering the organization do
so within the constraints and supports provided by their existing frameworks for this
very process.

The creation of software systems has given rise to new ways of thinking about
organizations, for organizations can be modeled, analyzed, and engineered for maximum effectiveness using many of the same concepts we find beneficial in software
systems. This chapter explores how the engineering techniques we have learned in
the creation of successful software systems can be applied to organizations. The
study of organizations, in turn, provides insight into how we can engineer them to
create more software systems more effectively.

Chapter Overview

The chapter begins with a discussion of coupling and cohesion, two of the
most important and well-known attributes describing software systems. Like software systems, we want teams to be engineered with a minimum of coupling and
maximum cohesion. Or do we? Read Section 12.1 to find the details.

Engineers must routinely deal with complexity on multiple levels. The goal, of
course, is creating solutions with the right amount of complexity. These and other issues associated with complexity are described in Section 12.2.

The two single most important structures associated with the system are the
system architecture and the organizational topology. We know they become intertwined. But what have we *learned?* How can we *apply* what we have learned? These
issues are addressed in Section 12.3.

Are architecture and topology the only structural influences on the team? Of
course not. One critically important structural influence are roles. Two specific kinds
of roles are discussed in Section 12.4: roles associated with teamwork and roles supporting system architecture.

Teams, organizations, and software systems are not static "things." They are
dynamic in ways often mystifying their creators. Although structure prescribes and
supports process, Section 12.5 will challenge you to think of structure *as* process. It

will define what it means to have "more" or "less" structure and provide guidance on making this determination.

12.1 COUPLING AND COHESION

Coupling refers to the degree of interdependence among different components in a system [Page-Jones 1988]. Loosely coupled systems are easier to understand, modify, and reuse. In software, the ideal is for each component (i.e., a module or object) to interconnect with other components only through well-defined interfaces. In organizations, the ideal is for each developer to communicate through well-defined and completely understood outcomes.

Cohesion describes how closely the activities within a single component or among a group of components are related to each other. A highly cohesive component means the elements within the component are strongly related to each other. We give the highest marks for cohesion to those modules whose elements contribute to one and only one task. In a similar manner, we can describe a team as highly cohesive when they are organized to accomplish a specific well-defined task. In a way, this section returns us to the original use of the word, for Larry Constantine borrowed the term cohesion from sociology to describe modules as early as the mid-1960s.

The remainder of this section is as follows. First we'll take a look at coupling: its definition in software and organization, why loose coupling is beneficial, when too loose a coupling can cause problems, and how to engineer systems with the right degree of coupling. Then we'll take a similar look at cohesion and how one can work to engineer highly cohesive teams.

12.1.1 Software Coupling Revisited

The software methodologists of the late 1960s and early 1970s who devised the term coupling created an entire taxonomy to precisely explain the "strength" of the connection between modules [Yourdon 1978]. Rather than list all the different types of coupling, I'll restrict myself to briefly describing the most important kinds.

Normal coupling between two components (e.g., functions, modules, objects, etc.) implies any information passed between them is strictly through the use of parameter lists. The parameters themselves can be simple flags or complex structures. The main design goal is to minimize the passing of unnecessary information. Each component should exchange a minimum number of parameters, and each component should exchange parameters required by the other component to perform its functioning.

A less desirable form of normal coupling is *control* coupling, which occurs when one component explicitly controls the internal processing logic of another through parameter lists. Control coupling is detrimental because it requires the calling module to know the intimate details of the module being called. As Page-Jones

[1988] points out, control coupling is usually an indication of more serious design problems.

Global coupling occurs when two or more modules reference the same common information area. Its chief disadvantage is the delocalization of processing logic and reliance on the format and content of the global area [Soloway 1988]. "Delocalization" means that to understand a global area you must understand *all* the modules referencing it. If these components are spread across multiple files, the complexity of your task has increased dramatically! Global coupling also makes change more difficult: If the global area changes, then every module referencing this area may require change. It is important to note every global variable used in a program exhibits global coupling, regardless of the implementation language.

Content coupling occurs when one module uses code or directly refers to data contained or defined within another module. Content coupling pretty much violates every rule of modular design. It is the quintessential misuse of the GOTO statement—jumping from one place to another or directly referring to data in one routine from another. Fortunately, most modern programming languages have scoping rules making it difficult or impossible to create systems with content coupling (although, sadly, it sometimes appears developers try!). This is not to say modern languages have entirely removed content coupling. Object-oriented languages introduce a special kind of content coupling: inheritance. To see why inheritance is a form of content coupling, consider what happens when you reorder the data in a superclass. In general, the advantages of carefully designed inheritance hierarchies outweigh their disadvantages.

12.1.2 Three Types of Organizational Coupling

Although no clear taxonomy of organizational coupling exists, there has been research studies studying this phenomena and its effects [Weick 1979; Orton 1990]. This section outlines the three forms of coupling that exist in the SPO framework, providing examples of each (see Fig. 12–1).

Outcome coupling is the most common (and loosest) form of coupling among organizational entities and occurs when the work activity of two entities can be completely synchronized through a minimum number of formal outcomes. A maintenance

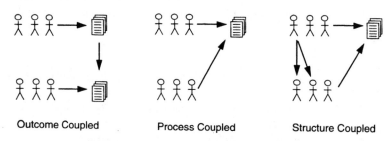

| Outcome Coupled | Process Coupled | Structure Coupled |

Figure 12–1   Forms of Coupling within Organizations

team is outcome coupled to the customer service team if the maintenance team fixes the defect(s) identified and described by the customer service team through a Customer Service Request (CSR). In this case, the outcome synchronizing the teams is the CSR.

Outcome coupling is analogous to normal coupling in software modules, with outcomes being roughly equivalent to parameters passed between subroutines. As the "loosest" form of coupling, outcome coupling enables each entity to work as independently as possible from others but is dependent on the degree of shared understanding built among the entities using the outcome to support interaction.

Process coupling occurs when the processes of two or more teams are codependent. Consider a slight (albeit negative) redesign of the work processes of the teams described above. Assume the customer service team is required to respond to the customer with a CSR tracking number for future reference. Now, let's confuse things by giving the responsibility for generating these numbers to the maintenance team. Thus, the work processes of the customer support team (identify the problem, fix if possible, if not, generate a CSR, wait for the maintenance team to formulate a CSR number, contact the customer with the number) are coupled with the work processes of the maintenance team (work on fixing problems documented by CSRs, periodically responding to interrupts to review the input queue of CSRs and assign them numbers). Process coupling in organizations can be related to both control and global coupling in software.

The third form of coupling is *structure* coupling, in which organizational entities are structurally bound one to another. This can occur within the same team or between teams. To illustrate, assume each maintenance developer is "assigned" one or more customer service representatives, such that they are the only developers allowed to service requests from these particular representatives. Imagine the impact to the customer should a developer call in sick! The parallels to software coupling include control, global, and pathological coupling.

Organizations with abnormal or inappropriate amounts of coupling are overly bureaucratic, filled with endless red tape and wasted effort. There is no joy in working in such organizations for developers or their managers as you rarely get the opportunity to identify how the specific outcomes you create materially contribute to the construction of the software system. Other negative effects of inappropriate coupling include feelings of helplessness and a lack of ownership, as entities (developers or teams) cannot identify any single aspect of a shared task that is "theirs."

12.1.3 Benefits of Loose Coupling

Why are loosely coupled systems easier to understand, modify, and reuse? More importantly, what might be the benefits of loose coupling?

The first benefit of loose coupling is cognitive. Loosely coupled components are easier to understand because all of the information needed to understand the component is located in one place (this is also referred to as "single-point control"). As described earlier, this argument shows why it is generally easier to understand code minimizing or avoiding entirely the use of global variables. A module is easier to understand when all the information it requires is passed through a well-defined parameter list. Similarly, the operation of a team is easier to understand when it is governed by well-defined outcomes.

The cognitive argument provides direction as to how we should create interfaces to components. Short parameter lists are better because they are easier to understand. Simple parameters are better than complex parameters. Unnecessary information increases the amount of time necessary to understand the module (i.e., we waste time trying to determine *why* specific information is passed and become frustrated when we realize it is not used for anything!). Of special importance are parameters indicating one module is control coupled to another. While such a component may appear loosely coupled—it is, after all, using a parameter—it is not. To understand the operation of the component, you must understand the parameters. This increases the cognitive burden on the developer.

Similar arguments can be made for the outcomes shared among organizational entities. Requirements documents should be clear, concise, and to the point. E-mail should communicate clearly and effectively. Change logs should describe the fundamental operations made in the file, no more, and no less, and so forth.

The second benefit of loose coupling deals with change. Because loosely coupled components are isolated, they can be changed without affecting other components, sometimes in quite dramatic ways. One product developed internally at ObjectSpace was able to swap one database for another in *one day* because the database was carefully decoupled from the rest of the system! More common changes to loosely coupled components include changing the representation of data from one representation to another or replacing one algorithm for a functionally equivalent but faster one. In effect, loosely coupled systems "seal off" changes.

Ease of change is as important for organizations as it is for software systems. Consider a maintenance team of eight developers responsible for 12 systems. The manager of this team should be free to assign responsibility of specific systems to any of the developers without undue external influence from other teams. This quality is known as *behavioral discretion*—the ability of a team to select their most effective manner of working free from external influence. It is analogous to a black-box approach to module design. By thinking of other modules as "black boxes," each developer is free to concentrate on his or her work and is freed from knowing the complexities of the inner workings of other components.

Loosely coupled components are easier to reuse precisely because they have less "baggage" to carry with them. Consider a page format routine in a report generation program relying on a global information structure describing paper parameters. Such a routine is less reusable than a similar routine communicating the same information via a parameter list. Why? To reuse the globally coupled routine, you must also create a global variable of the same name. Such coupling dramatically decreases the potential for reuse.

The same thing can happen with organizations. One goal of most organizations is to systematically identify best practices and then work to ensure these are documented and shared with other teams. This allows these practices to be reused for competitive advantage. If such practices are ridden with unnecessary coupling, they are difficult, if not impossible, to reuse.

Loose coupling also contributes to parallelism. Consider an organization with development teams scattered across the United States. It is easy to imagine teams at each site evaluating the same language or system, each unaware of the work of the other. To prevent some of this (apparent) unnecessary work, organizations may try to form tighter couplings by centralizing evaluation and decision-making authority. However, such tighter couplings are likely to slow down the decision-making process for any single team. Moreover, such coupling is based on a very tenuous assumption: A single technology can apply equally to every development team. By explicitly decoupling the decision-making authority, multiple teams find it easier to meet their needs.

Because organizations are comprised of humans, there are additional benefits to loosely coupled teams. The first is *adaptability*, the ability to self-correct for perceived problems in the environment. When one team is loosely coupled with another, they are able to act in novel ways in response to novel conditions. For example, a team could decide to temporarily increase coupling with another in order to resolve a particularly vexing problem. Alternatively, they may decide to change their internal processes to modify the outcomes shared with other teams. If the surrounding culture is supportive and the receiving team perceives the adaptation as beneficial, it may continue the process, spontaneously modifying itself in response to the new outcome.

It is interesting to note that the evolution of many software languages moves them toward greater adaptability. I can envision the day when software components will be able to respond to changes in their environment with minimal intervention by developers. For example, databases could dynamically reconfigure the organization of their data to more efficiently match access patterns, just as languages could reconfigure parameter lists to create more easily maintainable systems.

Arguably the most important benefit of loose coupling within organizations are the feelings of satisfaction and enjoyment each of us feels when we have control over the outcomes we create. Loose coupling means I have behavioral discretion. I am *responsible* for "something." When that "something" can be put into the context of the larger system, I've increased my satisfaction with the entire process.

Finally, loose coupling within organizations can reduce the conflict among development groups who are operating under different time constraints or relying on different structures and processes in the preparation of outcomes. Synchronizing efforts through outcomes minimizes interactions, reducing unnecessary communication.

12.1.4 Drawbacks of Loose Coupling

Given all the benefits of loose coupling, should any system be explicitly engineered around "tighter" forms of coupling? In other words, should all systems be as loosely coupled as possible? The answer is no. There are times when tighter forms of coupling are both appropriate and necessary.

In organizations the loosest form of coupling is outcome coupling. Outcome coupling, in turn, is based on the shared understanding that exists between organizational entities who use these outcomes as the basis for their interactions. If outcomes are not understood—if they are unclear, ambiguous, or equivocal—then outcome coupling will not be an effective approach. Stronger forms of coupling will be required for effective interaction.

Consider two software projects, both of which are involved in a major enhancement to existing systems. Each project is organized into two teams: a requirements team and an implementation team. The first project is basing all interactions between the two teams solely on outcome coupling. That is, the only form of formal communication between the requirements team and the implementation team is through the system specification produced by the requirements team.

The second project is structured differently. In this project, one of the implementation developers has been structurally coupled to the requirements team. Specifically, this developer splits her time equally between normal development activities and requirements determination.

Which project is likely to be more successful? Don't even kid yourself on this one. All other factors being held reasonably equal, the second team is bound to be significantly more successful, *precisely because the outcome created by the first team is likely to be somewhat unclear, ambiguous, and equivocal.* Structure and process coupling are effective managerial tools to solve these problems. Specifically, the link formed between the two teams of the second project through structure coupling is a *conceptual* link. This conceptual link dramatically increases the opportunity to create a shared understanding within the team.

Outcome coupling can also contribute to a lack of unity among developers. Designing an organization solely around outcomes does not take into account the very real need for human interaction in the development of the system. Most humans have a basic, innate, and perhaps fundamental need to work with others. By design, outcome coupling minimizes such interactions.

Finally, teams designed solely around outcome coupling will find it difficult to adopt an iterative-incremental development process. Why? The outcomes associated with iterative-incremental processes tend to be more ambiguous and equivocal than outcomes associated with other process models. This is not usually an issue, as the primary motivation *for* iterative-incremental processes is the realization that outcomes are ambiguous and equivocal and that humans have bounded rationality. Thus, teams using such processes tend to be more structurally and procedurally coupled.

While I have concentrated thus far on organizations, tighter forms of coupling can be helpful in software as well. Sometimes global data are appropriate because the data apply conceptually across the entire program, much the way a single directory service number in a company makes it easy to locate individuals. Even the dreaded GOTO statement can substantially improve the quality and clarity of code in modules involved in extensive error processing or complex resource management [McConnell 1993].

The changing nature of the software development task and the complex adaptive nature of individuals and teams mean there can be no single, static approach to engineering the right degree of coupling. The right amount of coupling changes over time depending on the task, the individuals involved, and the outcomes chosen as the means of formal communication. Although the lowest forms of coupling are preferred in any system, the actual degree of coupling is based on a careful and critical examination of these factors.

12.1.5 Achieving Loose Coupling

The general rule of thumb should be clear: Minimize coupling as much as possible. But how? This section identifies two techniques for reducing coupling.

The first and most important technique is to make certain outcomes are understood by all entities using the outcome for coordination. In organizations, this means making certain developers are properly trained in the structure (e.g., the notation used in data models) and contents of outcomes.

The second is to rely on information hiding, the time-honored technique of design that has proven time and again its value in practice [Parnas 1972; Boehm 1987; McConnell 1993]. *Information hiding* is a design technique emphasizing hiding the inner working of a component. Specifically, the algorithms, states, data structures, and so forth of the component are hidden from external components. The only means whereby a developer can ascertain the working of the component is through its external specification. By definition, the use of information hiding contributes to looser forms of coupling in both software systems and organizations.

12.1.6 Cohesive Components and Teams

Recall that cohesion describes how closely the activities within a single component or among a group of components are related to each other. Stevens, Constantine, Myers, and Yourdon [Stevens 1974; Yourdon 1979] defined several categories of software cohesion. Table 12–1 presents these terms as originally developed for software, extending (and at times tweaking them a bit) for teams. Arranged from most desirable to least desirable, these categories should provide insight into what we commonly think about regarding cohesion.

The line in the middle of the table separate acceptable and unacceptable forms of cohesion. Because there is no standard terminology for describing a routine, a function, a module, or a class, I've adopted the following convention for Table 12–1. A *component* is a function or routine in a language such as C or FORTRAN or a class in an object-oriented language such as C++ or Smalltalk. A *module* is a group of functions or classes [Fairley 1985; McConnell 1993; Page-Jones 1988].

12.1.7 Determining Cohesion

While the cohesion taxonomy presented in the previous section is useful, it can also be overkill. A group of components (software or organizational) will either

TABLE 12–1   Cohesive Components and Teams

Cohesion "Level"	Component/Module	Individual/Team
Functional	A component performs a single operation. Example: A function computing the sine of an angle or a die object in the game of Monopoly.	An individual performs a minimum of well-defined tasks. Example: Brian is asked to prepare the examples for the coding standard.
	A module provides a set of services that clearly belong together. Example: A well-defined math library.	A team is asked to perform a specific activity in the development of the system. Example: The requirements gathering team.
Sequential	A component or module containing operations performed in a specific order, sharing data in specific processing steps, and not contributing to a complete operation when done together. (This is why it is not "functionally" cohesive.)	A single team is responsible for two or more sequentially related activities in a method. Typically, the split is arbitrary. Example: A team that designs and implements, or verifies and packages.
Communicational	A component or module performing a set of operations on the same data where the operations are not related in any other meaningful way. Example: A function that given two rectangles returns both their intersection and whether or not both rectangles are square.	An individual or team asked to perform two or more unrelated activities on the same outcome. Example: A developer who is asked to both determine the performance of a routine and evaluate the source to see if it adheres to standards.
Temporal	The operations of the component or module are bound only through time. Temporal cohesion is acceptable when used for initialization or finalization of a system and unacceptable otherwise.	Forcing a development team to follow the processes prescribed by a method *every* time, in the order in which they are defined, regardless of the specific needs of the project.
Procedural	A component or module performs different and possibly unrelated activities which are organized in a specific order. It is not sequential, because no data are shared. Example: Loops performing unrelated activities.	Development responsibilities split among two or more individuals or teams based on an arbitrary sequence of activities. Example: An individual wants to update the project repository, so he or she obtains the index and add a new entry. He or she then must give the entry to another person who adds it.
Logical	Several operations are stuffed into the same routine or module because they "logically" relate to the same generic operation. The actual operation is selected via a flag passed from the outside. Example: A routine enlarging, reducing, or deleting memory based on a flag.	A single team asked to perform job duties in completely unrelated ways because the job duties "sound" similar. Example: A maintenance team given responsibility for unrelated or antagonistic systems (e.g., one written in COBOL and the other in PROLOG).
Coincidental	There are no apparent relationships between components or modules.	An individual or team given completely unrelated job responsibilities.

appear to be cohesive or not. When in doubt, you probably have less cohesion than you think.

However, it can be beneficial to determine the level of cohesion, for understanding the existing level of cohesion provides clues on how to improve it. The original technique for determining cohesion provided by Constantine was to briefly describe a component (again, software or organizational) and examine the statement carefully. One or more compound statements indicates the component is performing more than one function and therefore has sequential or procedural cohesion. Statements containing temporal words such as "when," "after," or "before" are likely to have sequential or temporal cohesion. If more than one data element is involved, you are likely to have logical or functional binding.

Because of the ambiguity of writing statements, I prefer the decision tree developed by Page-Jones and shown in Figure 12–2 [Page-Jones 1988]. Use the decision tree by beginning at the left and moving toward the right answering specific questions about the component along the way. When finished, you will have the cohesion of the component.

Is it worth it to take the time to determine the level of cohesion and work toward creating more cohesive organizations? One way to answer this question to examine the empirical data associated with software. Specifically, are software systems whose components are highly modular easier to maintain? The answer is yes. Several studies have shown cohesive modules are in fact easier to maintain [Glass 1981]. Practical experience demonstrates cohesive teams are simply more effective.

12.1.8 Structural, Procedural, and Outcome Cohesion

Cohesion in terms of the SPO framework can be thought of as a range of positive to negative values. Positive outcome cohesion means that individually produced outcomes contribute directly to a shared outcome. There are no wasted outcomes and nothing to unnecessarily slow down the team. This equates most

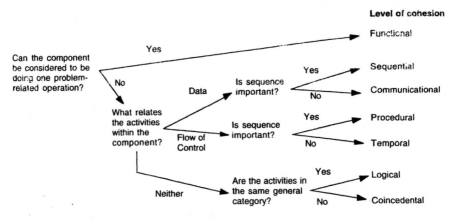

Figure 12–2 Decision Tree for Cohesion

closely to functional or communicational cohesion. For special teams formed for *very* specific purposes, it can be thought of as temporal cohesion. Negative outcome cohesion means the team is producing a variety of unrelated outcomes unlikely to materially contribute to the completion of the system. This equates to coincidental or logical cohesion.

Positive process cohesion occurs when individually produced outcomes "flow" naturally among members of the team, each extending the outcome as appropriate. An example of this is structured brainstorming, where a piece of paper is passed around the room. As you receive the paper, you quickly write down your idea and hand it to the next individual. When the exercise has been completed, the final outcome represents the ideas of each participant. This equates to sequential cohesion. Negative process cohesion occurs when the processes shared in the team are unrelated or in conflict, mirroring the effects of procedural cohesion in software.

Finally, positive structure cohesion means the multiple structures supporting the work of the team are mutually cohesive and reinforcing. (Think of a well-defined and executed strategy, as described in Chapter 8.) There is no direct relationship between positive structure cohesion and software modules; the closest is likely to be functional cohesion. Negative structure cohesion relates once again to coincidental cohesion.

12.1.9 Being Cohesive

The bottom-line advice for both software and organizational engineering is to distribute tasks so "components" perform one and only one operation. In a sense, creating cohesive components, modules, and teams is the mere application of common sense. Of course, common sense is not necessarily common, and the following techniques all contribute to creating more cohesive organizations.

First, reread Chapter 11. A shared set of values, a culture binding the team, and challenging but achievable goals all serve to give a cohesive focus to the efforts of the team. Being cohesive means our activities are related; we are working together to accomplish the same goal. You probably have problems with cohesion if the activities of the team fail to contribute to a well-defined goal.

Second, think in terms of responsibilities when distributing activities, both in software and in organizations. It would be absurd to ask the engineering department for a detailed cash flow analysis of last quarter's results, just as it would be absurd to ask marketing to design the control logic for a telephone switch signaling system. Here, *naturally* refers to the principle that the most logical locus of control is the component (in this case, the team) having the knowledge and skills necessary to perform the operation.

Third, organize work so it can be completed by a minimum number of people. This technique is described in further detail below and has the added benefit of reducing coupling between teams.

Finally, match the responsibilities of the team to the system architecture. This topic is so important it is covered later in this chapter as a separate section.

ADVICE TO MANAGERS

The primary source for the material presented in this section has been the field of structured systems design, which gave us the terminology associated with coupling and cohesion. Although we've seen how to apply these concepts in the SPO framework, actually putting them to good use to reduce coupling and increase cohesion can require some creativity.

Obtain support from other managers when changing coupling.

Use workflow diagrams to locate inappropriate coupling.

Use behavioral discretion to create looser coupling and higher cohesion.

Redesign work so one entity can complete the whole task.

Beware of excessive meetings and memos.

Watch for unrelated inputs.

Reorganize when necessary.

Obtain support from other managers when changing coupling.
You are likely to find only partial success in experimenting with different forms of coupling unless you obtain the support of other managers first. Why? The most common form of coupling is between teams working on the same problem. Changing coupling (e.g., placing a test engineer on the requirements team) means changing the structural and procedural relationships within and between both teams. This change is most easily accomplished if the manager affected by the proposed change agrees to it.

Use workflow diagrams to locate inappropriate coupling. A *workflow diagram* is a model showing all the entities and process steps associated with the production of an outcome. It can be used to identify inappropriate coupling in the following way. First, prepare a workflow diagram. You don't need a fancy drawing package—a pencil and a piece of paper should work just fine. Second, examine the diagram. How many people are associated with the preparation of the outcome? Is this number reasonable? Is this number necessary? Is each intermediate outcome required? How many times are intermediate outcomes transmitted between two or more people? Are there any processing steps where one team must wait for another? Does this wait make sense or is it a sign of inappropriate process coupling?

Use behavioral discretion to create looser coupling and higher cohesion. Behavioral discretion is a powerful concept. It is both an enabler of loose coupling and an identifiable benefit of the same. One way to achieve behavioral discretion is through delegation. Assign a task and let your team determine the best way to solve it. Specifically, assign the creation of a specific outcome and then let your team choose the best process for generating it.

When actually creating the outcome (engaging in the process), the team is likely to discover one of several things. They might find they have to work more closely together (increasing cohesion). Alternatively, they might find completing the task requires coordination (i.e., coupling) with another team, which is an opportunity to determine which kind of coupling is most appropriate.

Use this technique with some caution, for it won't work for every team. Newer teams (e.g., recently formed teams) may not know each well enough to determine how to work together. Teams of inexperienced developers may also find delegation troublesome as they don't have enough experience on solving the problem. Both of these cases require more direct forms of intervention and less use of delegation.

Redesign work so one entity can complete the whole task.   One goal of business process reengineering is the redesign of work processes to minimize the number of individuals or teams needed to create outcomes [Hammer 1993]. Such efforts substantially reduce the degree of coupling between organizational entities, usually increasing both cohesion and job satisfaction at the same time.

Beware of excessive meetings and memos.   If you have too many meetings, too many memos, or memos with dozens of names on the distribution list, you are likely to have excessive coupling. A well-designed system does not distribute all information globally or equally but instead distributes information to the individuals requiring it and makes it available to those who need it.

Watch for unrelated inputs.   Examining the inputs to a team helps determine if the team might be suffering from negative outcome cohesion. To understand why, think of a team like a black-box software module transforming inputs into outcomes. Generally speaking, the more inputs, the more outcomes. The more unrelated the inputs, the greater the chance for unrelated, negatively cohesive outcomes.

Reorganize when necessary.   Part of creating a great software system is a real desire to reduce unnecessary coupling at every opportunity. Are you passing a complex record structure to a function that doesn't make good use of all the data? Change it. Pass only the information you need. Using a global variable to "quickly" share information between two components? That's a hack, and you know it. Fix it. Don't know where to put a new function? Adding it to an existing module, even though it is somewhat out of place, will get the job done but reduces cohesion in the process. Either find the right module or create a new one.

The same thing can happen in development teams. When the project begins, the preliminary architecture and distribution of responsibilities seem clean. Over time, changes in the requirements, an increased understanding of the system, and an evolving architecture stress the originally clean design of the team. Eventually, the well-designed, decoupled, and cohesive team becomes poorly coupled and uncohesive. As we periodically reorganize software, so too should we periodically reorganize our teams.

ADVICE TO DEVELOPERS

The best form of coupling enables you to accomplish your assigned tasks easily and effectively but is also flexible in allowing change. This is most often achieved through outcome coupling but can sometimes be accomplished through process and even structure coupling. Using the principles of adaptability and behavioral discretion, you can actively work to achieve the most appropriate coupling given your current assignment.

> Avoid excessive reliance on a single individual in another department.
> Don't confuse coupling with friendship or networking.
> Don't be overly concerned about reorganizations.

Avoid excessive reliance on a single individual in another department.   It is perfectly natural to establish direct ties with individuals within other departments. Quite often it is simply the best way to get things done in large organizations. However, we take this too far when *they* are promoted and we look to them for assistance in their *old* job. This problem is especially pervasive when a skilled developer moves from one position to another: Former colleagues make inappropriate requests for help!

Don't confuse coupling with friendship or networking.   Friendships and networks not only make work more enjoyable; they also provide a wonderful opportunity to grow our skills and help others increase theirs. The difference between friends and networking and inappropriate coupling deals with the nature of the communication, the relationships among the individuals, and the problem. Preferring to interact with a particular individual in another department may be a sign of friendship. Sharing a magazine article on a new development technique is networking. Dependence on a single person in another department is a sign of inappropriate coupling.

Don't be overly concerned about reorganizations.   Many developers become anxious when they learn of an impending reorganization. Sometimes this is for good reason. Many corporations use the word "reorganize" to mean "We are going to fire a bunch of developers but we are going to call it a reorganization." If you work in such a company perhaps you should consider looking for a new job before you get "reorganized" out of your present job.

However, not all reorganizations are bad. One good motivation for reorganizing (i.e., restructuring the organizational topology) is to compensate for the negative effects of inappropriate coupling. Like software, small, modular, loosely coupled teams can over time exhibit a bewilderingly complexity of interconnections. As developers, we respond to this in software by redesigning one or more aspects of the system, changing existing components or creating new ones. Such reorganization of a software system also occurs naturally as we learn more about the problem domain and the best way to solve it.

The same is true with organizations. Ideally, a reorganization often means nothing more than your manager has learned more about the environment and the problem and thinks that a different structure will enable the team (or entire organization) to utilize resources more effectively. Reorganizations are so important, especially when considered with respect to the system architecture, that they are discussed in greater detail in subsequent sections of this chapter.

12.2 COMPLEXITY AND VARIETY

I'm often asked: "How do I know if my system is too complex?" My standard answer is: "That depends. What problem are you trying to solve?" To illustrate, suppose I asked you to print out and compare the source code for Microsoft Notepad, WordPad, and Word to determine which source code was more "complex." What do you think you would find? Not surprisingly, you'd find the source code for Notepad was far less complex than Word, with WordPad somewhere in the middle. But is any *too* complex?

The answer lies in what we mean by "complex." Brooks [1995] has identified two kinds of complexity associated with any system. *Essential* complexity is the complexity needed to solve the problem correctly. *Accidental* complexity is unnecessary complexity introduced as an artifact of the problem-solving process based on human frailty (i.e., bounded rationality).

Thus, a trivial program counting the number of vowels in a text file will have a simpler structure than a program scheduling production schedules in a factory. If the vowel counting program is too complex, it is likely to *contain* errors, and if the production scheduling program is too simple, it is likely to *cause* errors. The goal is to minimize accidental complexity while effectively managing essential complexity.

Organizational theorists use the term *variety* in much the same way developers use the term complexity. Specifically, an organization has *requisite variety* to the extent it can accurately deal with its environment. The more complex the environment, the more varied the organization needed to support it. The principle of requisite variety motivates the need for diversity, because it is through diversity that organizations can detect and respond to changes within their environments. Although I am using the term *requisite variety* to describe teams and/or larger organizations, the term can be used just as easily to describe individuals. Requisite variety means that to solve a complex problem you need a diverse (complex) person—to manage a complex project, you need a complex manager.

Complex environments, in turn, have an interesting effect on the organization: Highly complex environments tend to promote loose coupling, as managers attempt to cope with the complexity through decentralization and autonomy [Mintzberg 1992]. Loose coupling, in turn, enables the organization to obtain the needed requisite variety by allowing individuals greater behavioral discretion in interacting with the environment, both within and outside the organization.

To give a more concrete illustration of requisite variety, assume you are asked to assemble a team of developers to create a GUI-based front end to an existing legacy system. It is expected the system will require some distributed data management and may have to run on more than one hardware platform. The principle of requisite variety states the team you create must be diverse enough to address the complexities of the given problem in order to solve it correctly.

You would probably want individuals experienced in GUI design, mainframe database management, interfacing legacy code with newer languages, and so forth. If you cannot create such a team, the principle of requisite variety states the system you create will not solve the problem effectively. Your team will ignore, avoid, abstract, or simply fail to identify critical aspects of the problem and create an incomplete, inappropriate, or just plain wrong system. Of course, one can explicitly reduce the complexity of the input as a response to a complex environment, a practice that tends to happen anyway in production environments (i.e., certain features of the requested system are foregone).

ADVICE TO MANAGERS

The principle of requisite variety motivates two questions. Is your team sufficiently varied (i.e., diverse; complex) to solve the problem they are given? Are they too varied?

Use volume and intricacy to measure complexity.

Staff one journeyman for important projects. Staff one master for mission critical projects.

Staff one realist for every three optimists.

Balance personality.

Use volume and intricacy to measure complexity.   A mechanical watch that can accurately keep the time and date is complex because it is *intricate*. A skyscraper is complex because it is *big* even if it can be described in a simple and regular manner. These simple conceptual tools for measuring complexity can help you select, prepare, and guide projects.

An intricate system performs complex processing tasks. As intricacy increases, the need for skilled and experienced developers increases. A voluminous system performs many processing tasks. As volume increases more developers are needed. The most complex systems are both large and intricate, requiring the dedicated efforts of many skilled developers.

Staff one journeyman for important projects. Staff one master for mission critical projects.   Remember the skill levels defined by Meiler Page-Jones in Chapter 6? They are also useful for understanding the kind of requisite variety (i.e., individual complexity) needed for projects. Specifically, just about any project will require at least one developer at the level of journeyman (e.g., their cognitive library contains enough plans to enable them to assist others). Projects can be successful with developers of lesser skills (e.g., two good practitioners), but as the project becomes larger or more complex it becomes increasingly difficult to ensure they are skilled enough. A mission critical project should have regular access to a master. If the project is important or large enough, it should have even more than one master.

Staff one realist for every three optimists.   One common mistake in selecting developers is to include too many with the same basic orientation or personality. This results in insufficient variety and can cause serious problems. Consider optimism, the belief "things will go well," versus pessimism, the belief "things will go poorly." In general, developers tend to be optimistic: "This time the program will run correctly," or "I know my interface is simple and intuitive" [Brooks 1995]. More often than not, they are incorrect, and they must debug the program one more time, or rework the interface to make it simpler and easier to use.

Yet, it is hard to deny the positive effects of the optimists. Optimism in and of itself is a good trait, for without it, most programmers would find the long hours of debugging code and reworking existing code into new solutions insurmountable. Yet, when staffing a project, dangerous things can happen when too many optimists work together. Since they believe they can get almost any piece of code to work correctly, they tend to be less rigorous in evaluating designs before implementation. Worse, they tend to be great salespeople, striking a common chord in other optimists who review their work and share their same basic enthusiasms.

A pessimist, on the other hand, refuses to think the system will work or be a success, which can have an even more detrimental effect. Their tendency to focus on the negative aspects of life can drain the energy from the team. A pessimist simply cannot be convinced testing was adequate and instead makes gloomy predictions about the impending doom when the system is released. Pessimists are not the appropriate balancing mechanism for the team.

How can you provide the variety needed to balance the optimists? Use a realist, someone who has a healthy disdain for most solutions proposed by the optimists. A realist is not a pessimist, for the realist shares with the optimist many of the same basic values and joys in building systems. Realists provide the necessary balance. They aren't as easily convinced the design is all that great. They would prefer the testing suite be reviewed just like any other outcome to ensure it is appropriate and accurate. They are perpetually convinced there are better ways to do things and are willing to expend energy in looking for them, even though the team may appear to be doing "OK."

Experience demonstrates *both* optimists and realists are needed for the successful operation of the team. The optimists provide the juice, the power, the zeal. Realists provide the discipline—brakes, if you will—needed to ensure the solution is correct before implementing. Together they provide enough variety in their predisposition to ensure the project is a success. However, because any one realist can easily overpower an optimist (it is much easier to demonstrate the problems with a proposed solution than its benefits), to achieve balance you need three optimists for each realist.

Balance personality.   Recall from Chapter 4 each of us solves problems and processes information in a slightly different manner based on our basic personality. Capitalizing on the variety in personalities is important over the life of the team, as different personality styles are more effective in different stages of the project [Weinberg 1994; Kirton 1994].

In the early phases of the project NT "visionaries" and KAI "innovators" are needed to help establish direction and get the project moving in the absence of well-established structures. Later, SF "cooperators," NF "catalysts," and moderate KAI "innovator-adaptors" are needed to make certain the project is working smoothly. Finally, ST "stabilizers" and more extreme KAI "adaptors" are needed to ensure the project reaches completion. Of course, I don't mean to suggest the only criterion for adding an individual to the project is their personality type. The point is each personality type brings one or more strengths to the project, and the most effective teams have a variety of personality types.

ADVICE TO DEVELOPERS

Every time you feel stretched by a complex new problem, the principle of requisite variety is at work, for to handle a complex problem you must be a complex person. Thus, the most important advice to glean from the principle of requisite variety is this: Complicate yourself!

> Complicate yourself.

Complicate yourself.   A complicated person is one who knows when to question, when to move forward. A complicated person cannot only generate more than one solution to the problem, but they can also correctly determine the criteria by which the alternatives are to be judged, thereby selecting the right solution for the right reason. A complicated person is able to play multiple roles within the team: An optimist, to balance the realists, and a realist, so important concerns are made known to all members of the team. Weick eloquently summarizes the value of complicating yourself: "to be complicated is to take pleasure in the process rather than pleasure in the outcome" [Weick 1979:263].

12.3 SYSTEM ARCHITECTURE AND ORGANIZATIONAL TOPOLOGY

Recall from Chapter 7 that a system architecture defines the basic "structure" of the system while the organizational topology defines the basic "structure" of the team. Conway's law [1968] states: "Organizations which design systems are constrained to produce systems which are copies of the communication structures of these organizations."

OK. So we know architecture and topology will become, as Brooks put it, "intertwined" [1995]. But what have we really *learned* about the interplay between architecture and topology that *enables* us to design and build better systems? Sadly, it often appears the answer is "not much." The role of topology in support of systems development is often misunderstood and inappropriate topologies are a major impediment to creating appropriately architectures.

Too often we allow existing topologies to drive the design of new systems. In the long run, this is counterproductive, as the old topology inhibits the creation of a new system. Alternatively, because we don't systematically apply sound principles of architectural design, we don't have a good starting point from which to structure the topology. The ideal approach, and the one described in this section, is to take proven architectures, tailor them to the needs of the project, and then expend every effort to create a topology explicitly supporting this architecture. Of course, you can't focus solely on these two things, and along the way we'll have to deal with long-term growth, modularity, and other factors impacting both the human and the technical elements in the system.

This is a tall order, but it can be done by integrating four specific concepts into a unifying whole. The first is system architecture, and the principles by which they are created. The architectures presented herein are admittedly biased toward the development of object-oriented systems, the application technology with which I am most familiar, but can be easily extended to other technologies. The second is organizational topologies, and the motivations for their use. The third is organizational paradigms, which are expectations of communication within a group. The fourth is the initial size of the team, the projected size, and the rate of growth. This section concludes with some specific advice on how to put everything together.

12.3.1 System Architecture

We've already covered some of the most important principles associated with the design of good architectures: coupling, cohesion, and complexity. But what really goes into making an architecture good? The essential activity of architectural design (its design because we are creating something in response to a requirement whose outcome is evaluated on predominantly subjective criteria) is the partitioning of work into identifiable components. Here I'm using the term "component" to mean a subsystem built (or purchased) in order to solve a specific or related set of problems.

Suppose you are asked to build a software system for an airline to perform flight scheduling, route management, and reservations. What kind of architecture might be appropriate? The most important architectural decision is to separate the business domain objects from all other portions of the system. Quite specifically, a business object should not know (or care) how it will be visually (or otherwise) represented. This is illustrated in Figure 12–3, which shows a basic architecture.

Note how the domain objects, the heart of the system, are decoupled from any specific representation. This means, for example, we could replace the screen presented to a service agent with an interactive voice response system or a dynamic

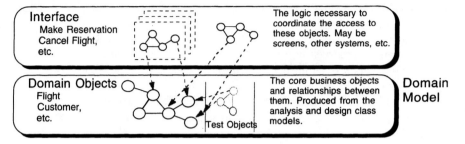

Figure 12–3   Basic Architecture

Web page. Think carefully about what this means. It means, for example, that all business rules (e.g., validating of input) should be done in the domain layer, and not in the user interface. It also contributes to cohesion: Each layer of the architecture thus far is responsible for a specific set of related operations.

But is this architecture sufficiently complex? The answer is quite likely no, for two reasons. First, most business operations require sophisticated application management procedures. Consider the operations involved with changing a flight or canceling a reservation. Data may have to be collected from multiple screens, and the like.

Second, most applications utilize some form of persistent storage, usually in the form of a database. Directly connecting the domain information to the database unnecessarily couples the conceptual model of the system with the physical model of the database. This is made even more difficult in most object-oriented applications, which must often connect to nonobject-oriented legacy systems. Such connections are often frightfully complex, as these legacy databases do not store objects as objects, but instead as records that must be converted to objects. Applying the principles of cohesion and coupling in the context of essential complexity leads us to the more general "four-tier" (or five, depending on how you count them) architecture shown in Figure 12–4.

As a "generic" architecture, Figure 12–4 provides a consistent starting point for the design of loosely coupled, highly cohesive systems with the essential complexity necessary to effectively handle many different problems. Figure 12–4 is not perfect: Distributed computing changes the picture, as does the need to connect new systems with legacy code. However, each of these can be added as separate tiers of Figure 12–4 extending it in a *specific* problem context. The overriding engineering principles of loose coupling, high cohesion, and appropriate complexity drive the design of the architecture.

After the basic tiers of the architecture have been defined, the focus turns to the identification of subsystems within the tiers representing cohesive units of work. The best subsystems are taken directly from the problem domain. In this case, subsystems would include fleet management, route management, and reservations. Each subsystem should be thought of as a vertical "slice" through the tiers.

Another mechanism for creating subsystems is to identify common and consistent behaviors or responsibilities between the objects comprising each layer. Such

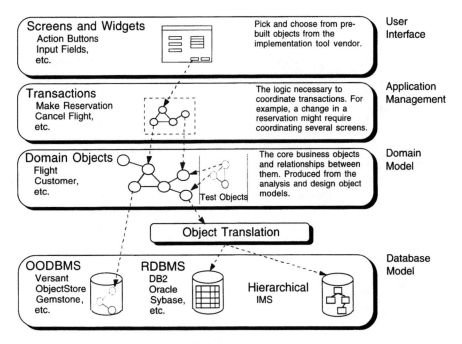

Figure 12–4   Four-Tier Architecture

an approach would deem "testing" methods (or functions) as a separate identifiable subsystem. I'm not in favor of this approach, as it eventually motivates inappropriate structure coupling in the teams building the system. However, when major changes need to be made very rapidly, such an approach may prove effective.

12.3.2 Traditional Topologies

Like the system, the developers involved in its construction must be appropriately partitioned. Some of the most common ways of partitioning organizations (and creating topologies in the process) are presented in Figure 12–5 [Mintzberg 1992; Tropman 1989]. As with the system architectures presented earlier, these topologies represent ideals; few, if any, organizations are structured *exactly* as shown in Figure 12–5.

Because the hierarchy and matrix represent two common topologies already discussed in Chapter 7, they are not discussed in further detail here. Instead, I'll focus my discussion on the orbit and cluster, two more-or-less novel topologies.

To construct an orbit, first create a single organizational circle by linking together each node at the bottom of a functional area in a pure hierarchy, placing the *responsibilities* associated with the functional area in the center. Repeat this process for each functional area, adding their responsibilities to the center. If the teams have initially been well structured, the center will represent all the activities required in

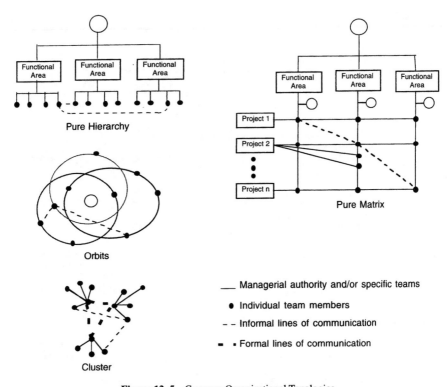

Figure 12–5   Common Organizational Topologies

the development of the system. Consider a department organized into three teams: technical support, new product development, and maintenance. By placing the product in the center, a single orbit would be created for each of the functional areas.

The advantage of the orbit as a topology is its emphasis on the unity of different functional areas: Everyone is directed toward the center. The changing influence of different functional areas (and individuals within those functional areas) is represented by the "distance" of the orbit from the operating core. As the organization begins development on the next release of the product, the new development team's orbit would gain in prominence.

As the next release of the system is being prepared, the testing orbit increases in prominence. In the terms of planetary motion, the testing orbit is at perihelion, the position closest to the larger body governing the orbit. After the next version is released, the testing orbit moves from perihelion to points farther away, and the requirements and analysis orbits gain in prominence (themselves moving to perihelion).

Clusters represent small teams of individuals "clustered" around a specific unit of work. Clusters are especially useful for managing rapid growth. Specific teams working on one aspect of the system stay as small as possible and continue to grow team members until it is appropriate to split into two more clusters. As each cluster splits, the technical leads from the previous cluster are expected to remain in close communication through formal means. This most directly supports the goal of keeping teams as small and as focused as possible. Applying this process in reverse to the cluster in Figure 12–5, we can see the original project team consisted of three members, which subsequently split over time into three clusters. The importance of the original project members should be reinforced through as many additional structures as possible. For example, they might have a weekly meeting to discuss the architecture and make certain the initial design they created is followed.

Readers familiar with organizational topologies may wonder why the cluster is any different than the traditional hierarchy: Simply rearrange a few nodes and the cluster is transformed into the hierarchy (and vice versa). While this may be true on paper, in an abstract, theoretical way, I do not think this is true in practice. The moment I made the decision to organize via a cluster, I have structured everything—including how I think about the system—in a different way. Once this is done things will never be quite the same again.

12.3.3 Organization Paradigms: Working within the Topology

Topologies are important for the manner in which they influence communication. Constantine [1993] characterizes the implicit assumptions made regarding how we interact with others as an *organization paradigm*. Specifically, he identifies four paradigms, as outlined in Table 12–2 (Adapted from Constantine [1993]).

An organization paradigm defines more than just how we operate in a given topology. It touches on communication (e.g., contentious debate versus previously agreed upon understanding), culture and personality (e.g., some of us are just plain happier in a closed environment). Organization paradigms are included here because topologies influence paradigms. Paradigms, in turn, are selected to support the perceived issues associated with a given architecture. If you are working on an entirely new architecture, you might consider using a random paradigm explicitly supported by an orbit. Of course, the random paradigm and circle topology are probably inappropriate for a maintenance team working on an existing system. In this case a more appropriate paradigm might be the close paradigm supported by a traditional hierarchy.

12.3.4 Addressing Size and Growth

There are two approaches to understanding the issues associated with the initial and projected size of the team and the rate at which new developers are added. The first is to derive mathematical models from empirical data collected from real projects and use this to predict the performance of future projects. The second is to create a dynamic model of systems development.

Both approaches have advantages. Empirically based mathematical models enable us to develop an understanding of the basic curves associated with successful

TABLE 12–2 **Organizational Paradigms**

Paradigm	Characteristics	Strengths	Weaknesses	Topology
Closed	Centralized decision making and leadership enable the efficient production of standardized outcomes.	Efficiency in using known structures and processes in creating known outcomes.	Poor at creating new structures, processes, or outcomes.	Hierarchy; matrix
Random	Individual and independent decisions are partially controlled through creative chaos.	Minimal structure allows multiple processes to create numerous diverse outcomes.	Inefficient and unstable structures make producing outcomes difficult.	Clusters or orbits
Open	Adaptive collaboration through open discussions on the goals of the project and the best means to achieve them.	Agreed-upon structure emphasizing communication processes and the critical examination of potential outcomes.	Lots of communication means work output is slow.	Orbits; matrix
Synchronous	Minimal communication among highly efficient work teams.	Well-known processes enable developers to produce outcomes with a minimum of communication in a harmonious manner.	Unresponsive to innovations; heavy reliance on shared outcomes and the collective mind makes the socialization of new team members difficult.	Self-adapting clusters

projects. Substantial deviation from these curves means we should proceed with caution with our current plans, if at all.

Dynamic models enable "what-if" analysis of the many factors associated with size and growth. Can we increase net productivity by reducing the training time for new staff? If so, by how much? By using different parameters to well-known factors, we can simulate multiple scenarios.

Detailed discussions of both of these approaches are beyond the scope of this book. Instead, this section briefly reviews some of the results associated with these results in order to find guiding principles. Beginning with DeMarco's [1982] extensive discussion on mathematical models, we find

1. The rate of staff buildup resembles a Raleigh curve, reaching the maximum number of staff members around the time of system testing and product release. (A slightly different curve represents projects where some staff is already working on the project.)

2. In turn, the Raleigh curve shows starting off with too many developers is a waste of time but not adding them fast enough strains resources.

3. There is a definite limit on the rate at which you can grow the team. Faster growth rates may result in the project being completed more quickly, but overall productivity will be lower. The absolute limit of growth is what Boehm refers to as the "impossible region" [Boehm 1981].

4. Reducing functionality increases productivity nonlinearly.

The advantages of these equations give us a "feel" for how we should add developers and shows us the limits on the rate at which this can be done. But what are the real implications for doing this? The dynamic models of Tarek Abdel-Hamid and Stuart Madnick [1991] to the rescue!

To increase understanding of software development projects, Abdel-Hamid and Madnick created a dynamic model of a "typical project." By experimenting with the parameters in the model associated with staffing policies (e.g., the hiring rate, the average delay from adding a developer until they become completely productive, the rate at which people leave the project, and so forth), they performed extensive "what if" scenarios on the size and growth rates of successful teams. The following results and variables seem especially relevant.

1. There is a difference in productivity between newly hired developers and experienced developers. The time it takes to become a productive developer is measurable *and almost never zero.*

2. Inexperienced developers place a measurable productivity loss on experienced developers.

3. The desired work force level changes dynamically throughout the project and often cannot be specified in advance.

4. Brooks's law can be cheated provided you add manpower carefully. In general, their model shows adding manpower earlier in the project is far better than adding manpower later. Why? No matter when you add manpower, they will have a negative effect on productivity because of training and increased communication costs—Brooks's original argument. The model shows the ramifications of this decreased productivity is far greater at the end of the project than at the beginning.

12.3.5 Putting It All Together

Armed with an understanding of basic architectures, topologies, paradigms and growth rates, we are now ready to put everything together. Briefly, architecture defines the structure of the system. Topology defines the structure of the team. Paradigms guide communication style. Growth rates define how quickly we can and/or hope to acquire the resources needed to complete the project.

There is one final assumption. You are adopting an iterative-incremental process model, where the system is grown through a series over a well-defined series of cycles. This, in turn, motivates adding developers on well-defined iterations of the system. Of course, I am not suggesting this is easy to do—finding the right people with the right skills *exactly* when you need them is never easy. It is, however, a worthwhile goal.

Putting it all together isn't obvious or straightforward. It is certainly not easy. Each of the "variables" described above is interdependent on the other. Changing one *eventually* motivates changing the others. And each will change. The goal is to achieve points of stability during development so the team has to deal with a minimum of changes at any one time.

The first variable to address is initial size. Choose the absolute smallest team feasible for your project based on the complexity of the system. If you can get away with four developers, one assigned to each layer, do it. Six is acceptable and ten is the limit. Be especially careful in the transition from six to ten. Six to ten developers will require additional support staff and a project lead separate from the rest of the team. Why start with a small team? First, communication patterns are far simpler, as described in Chapter 10. Second, achieving a shared understanding of the system (what Brooks [1995] refers to as "conceptual integrity") is easier when there are fewer people.

The primary purpose of this initial team is to define the architecture of the system and then create its first implementation. This may mean the team does requirements gathering and a substantial amount of analysis *before* defining the architecture, as both these outcomes are necessary prerequisites required for architectural definition.

The next variable to address is topology. Although a small team can be effective using almost any topology, two specific topologies stand out as most beneficial. The first is the hierarchy as realized by a chief programmer team (described further below). The second is the circle—a "team of equals." The specific selection of topology is based on the influencing variables of previously established outcomes (e.g., requirements specifications, analysis models, and the like), domain knowledge, and previously established system architecture.

If there are no previously established outcomes (i.e., the team is involved in the earliest stages of a *brand new* project), then the team must engage in the process of requirements gathering to produce the requirements specification (and potentially other outcomes). Use a slightly modified circle for this process. The modification is to establish one developer as the "leader among equals" responsible for resolving potential disputes. Because requirements gathering requires skilled communicators, consider assigning this task to a person with demonstrated communication ability.

Once the requirements specification exists, the team can focus on the system architecture. If domain knowledge is low or the architecture is tentative or nonexistent, use a circle in support of the open paradigm. Once again, establishing a "leader among equals" will be helpful to resolve disputes. This time, however, assign this responsibility to your most technical developer. If the architecture is truly nonexistent (i.e., the team is in the next phase of a *brand new* project) establish a *preliminary* architecture using the basic architecture presented in Figure 12–4 as a starting point.

It is worth emphasizing this architecture is *only* a starting point. It needs to be customized. Customization, in turn, requires lots of intense communication—meetings, reviews, and so forth. These are best supported by the open paradigm. The open paradigm, in turn, is best supported by the circle. Once the preliminary architecture has solidified, the team should be converted to a sequence of clusters where each cluster is focused on a specific aspect of the architecture. In this approach a "cluster" can be as small as one developer.

A traditional hierarchy as realized chief programmer team is effective when a small team of inexperienced developers is being led by an experienced developer. The senior developer takes the role of chief architect, designing the architecture and allocating work to the other developers according to architectural layers. Each developer is assigned responsibility for a specific layer. Some developers may have general responsibilities. Brooks [1995] recommends adding additional people to manage documentation (e.g., the "mercenary analyst" proposed by Coplien [1995]), a toolsmith to craft necessary supporting tools, and a program clerk for managing configurations and shared information.

One important change to make in the use of the chief programmer team concerns the distribution of assignments and staff responsibility. These *must* be done in direct support of the architecture. The chief architect has the unified view of the system; everyone else is *structured through topology* to realize it.

Because the chief architect is given responsibility for ensuring the architecture can support growth and change over time, they also play a vital role in growing the team. Specifically, the chief architect provides input to the project manager as to what resources are needed and how they should be placed. As resources are added, the topology will change. As described in more detail later in this section, the topology should move from the chief programmer team hierarchy to architecturally motivated clusters. If growth continues, the final topology will be an architecturally motivated matrix.

Even though a chief programmer team is a form of hierarchy, I prefer to think of chief programmer teams as being organized into clusters, where again a cluster can be as small as one developer. Why the push to organize as a cluster as quickly as possible? The primary reason is handling growth. Ideally, developers are added to the project in a reasonably controlled manner in order to address tasks beyond the abilities of the current team. What is motivating growth? The complexity of the problem as based on *volume.*

A team of five great developers may have the necessary requisite variety to build an intricate system but cannot handle the volume required by a large system. Think of a house compared to a skyscraper. Five people could refurbish an existing house (e.g., new electrical and plumbing systems, interior paint, and so forth) in a reasonable amount of time. Five people, no matter how capable, could not similarly refurbish a skyscraper in a reasonable amount of time.

In a like manner the five best developers in the world cannot build the complete airline management system described earlier. While an initial team of five developers can capably *specify* the architecture, they cannot build it. The project is simply too large. Thus, more developers must be added. Adding developers effectively means knowing *where* to add them. Clusters support the addition of new developers effectively because clusters are easily split when they become too large. By adding developers to and then splitting teams on architectural boundaries, architectural integrity is preserved.

In practice, this tends to happen anyway. Suppose the five developers building the prototype for the airline management system were organized as a circle and they add three new developers. Where will they be added? Typically, they will be added (i.e., given specific assignments to complete specific tasks) within some aspect of the architecture. This approach is simply made easier if the addition occurs within a previously created cluster.

The only alternative to the cluster for smaller teams (< 20 developers) is to use one or more orbits. Two things must hold for this approach to be effective. First, as described above, the team must be working on a *very* complex or breakthrough type problem and should use the orbit to institute multiple random or open paradigms (one within each orbit and a "meta" one for intercommunication between orbits). Second, although each developer will ultimately be assigned to a specific role, they must be willing and able to change roles as necessary.

As developers are added to the project, the effectiveness of the cluster approach begins to taper off: There are simply too many people in one group. The lack of management structure begins to impede progress rather than support it. Alternatively, the clusters are reduced to simple hierarchies because they are easier to manage directly. Eventually, the lack of management structure makes it impossible to achieve coordinated work. The first step to address continued growth is to continue to split the team into clusters, but add middle managers (or technical leads) to each cluster to add the necessary structure to the team.

Clusters continue to be a viable approach for teams up to 25 people. Consider a four-layer architecture. Create one cluster for each layer with 5 developers in each cluster. Add a project manager, 2 developers for system testing, a mercenary analyst, and 1 support staff. (One support staff may not be enough.) The total is 25 developers with 1 formal manager and 4 technical leads, one for each layer. The technical lead of the domain should retain the title of chief architect.

Multiple clusters do not support the needs of very large teams working on very large systems. Specifically, there is not enough structural support for organizing the communication between developers working in different architectural boundaries. For large teams (> 25 developers) the best approach is to create an architecturally motivated matrix organization as shown in Figure 12–6, which shows a team of 42 *developers*. Additional support staff and necessary managerial layers are not shown in Figure 12–6. (The matrix structure proposed here is far different than the matrix structure proposed by Page-Jones [1985]. In his approach, horizontal layers represent specific "assembly lines" and their associated products, while vertical layers provide the staff necessary to complete these projects [refer again to Figure 12–5]. This does not mean the two approaches are antagonistic: Page-Jones is focused on organizing a complete *department,* while the matrix I propose is for a *single project.*)

Horizontal layers of developers represent equivalent layers of the architecture. Organizing developers in this manner contributes to cohesion of technical skills

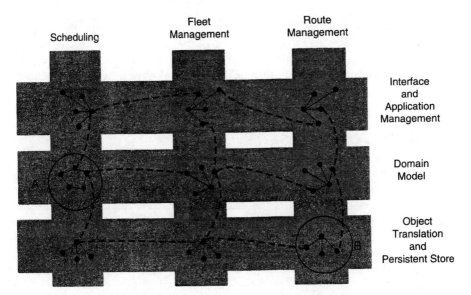

Scheduling
Fleet
Management
Route
Management

Interface
and
Application
Management

Domain
Model

Object
Translation
and
Persistent Store

Figure 12–6   Matrix Management in Large Teams

within a layer. Vertical "slices" represent related aspects of functionality in the delivered system and contribute to cohesion of domain knowledge. Vertical slices and horizontal layers are loosely coupled, further contributing to growth and ease of change within each. Additional teams needed to solve specific technical needs of the project (e.g., interfacing to a legacy system or establishing a reuse repository) are not shown in Figure 12–6. These teams should be internally structured according to their own needs and specifically decoupled from the architecture.

Two more issues must be resolved in evolving into the matrix structure. The first is authority. Specific managers must be created for *both* vertical business slices and horizontal architecture layers. The vertical business slice manager is responsible for ensuring the appropriateness of the system in meeting stated requirements and objectives. Practically, this means their staff (which are *not* shown in Figure 12–6) will be larger in the beginning and end of the project due to requirements gathering and acceptance testing and somewhat smaller during system development. Ultimately, the vertical business manager is responsible for ensuring the *right system* is built.

The horizontal architectural layer manager is responsible for ensuring the technical correctness of the solution developed within that layer and for sharing processes and outcomes as appropriate among these layers. Ultimately, the vertical business manager is responsible for ensuring the system is built the *right way*. Clearly, both horizontal and vertical managers need to buy into this approach and work closely together. This can be accomplished through another structural device: the overall project manager, who works to make certain the other managers are working together in an appropriate manner.

There is no requirement that each subteam within the matrix use the same topology. Indeed, striving for this is likely to be ineffective, as different teams have different operating needs. This is illustrated in Figure 12–6 by the two circled teams A and B. A has chosen to structure themselves as a circle, while B has chosen a hierarchy.

ADVICE TO MANAGERS

There are many different kinds of managers associated with a project. Some are technical managers, responsible for ensuring technical correctness and managing developers. Others are project managers, making certain resources, scheduling, and appropriate administrative details are properly handled. Regardless of the specific managerial role you play in the project (and there are other roles than those described above), the architecture, topology, and growth rate are your responsibility. Understanding the basics of each will go a long way to improving your success in building systems.

> Go graphical with the architecture.
>
> Show developers how the topology supports the architecture.
>
> Avoid direct mappings between topology and architecture.
>
> Establish clear lines of responsibility and authority.
>
> Construct the domain first.
>
> Acquire the best possible resources whenever you can.
>
> Respect architectural boundaries when creating assignments.
>
> Put yourself at the bottom of the topology.

Go graphical with the architecture.   The architecture is a critical vehicle for creating a shared understanding of the system. If *every* member of the team can't draw it, you've got a problem. If the drawing can't fit on one page, you've got a problem.

Show developers how the topology supports the architecture.   It may be crystal clear in your mind how the topology supports the architecture, but if it isn't clear to your developers, they will probably fail to utilize the topology to its fullest potential. It is worthwhile to make certain each developer understands the architecture, their specific role in creating it, and the nature in which the topology supports both.

Avoid direct mappings between topology and architecture.   There is rarely a direct mapping between architectural subsystems and development teams. First, this is often overkill. On a small project, it is entirely reasonable to place the issues of connecting to a simple remote database, a legacy system, and a special hardware device in a "technical implementation" team. This team is now responsible for three "layers" of the architecture. Exercise *some* caution in this approach. The team responsible for more than one layer needs to have enough discipline to maintain architectural integrity even if they are not specifically structured to do so.

Second, there is usually some mismatch between architectures and topologies. Both evolve slightly (sometimes greatly!) over the life of the project. It is rare each will evolve at the same rate. Immediately propagating changes in one to the other is counterproductive.

Establish clear lines of responsibility and authority. Every team needs to know who is ultimately responsible for the creation of the outcomes. This means each team has a specific developer responsible for each outcome. It means each layer has an individual responsible for that layer. It means the system as a whole has one individual responsible for the system. And, it means each person given responsibility for the layer is also given the authority to enact decisions necessary to preserve architectural integrity.

Construct the domain first. Successful projects rarely concentrate on building all layers of the architecture at the same time. Instead, they focus first on the domain, for it represents the heart of the system. Get the domain right and it is far easier to get the rest of the architecture right. Get the domain wrong and very little can save the project. After the domain has been validated the project can proceed to construct other layers.

Address high-risk layers next. These could be interconnections with legacy systems, distributed technologies, and so forth. Personally, I prefer to address the user interface immediately after the domain, as customers and users always want a good user interface. (A brief definition of "good" for the user interface is as follows: A user interface is good to the extent that it enables a user to accomplish their tasks efficiently and enjoyably with a minimum of errors.)

If there are sufficient resources, many layers of the architecture can be addressed in parallel. The key to this approach is to establish the architecture early, make certain each layer is addressing similar vertical slices, and integrate frequently (as described in Chapter 10). If you are going to attempt parallel development of each layer, make certain each layer agrees the domain is the key driver of the other layers. Changes to the user interface *should not* motivate changes to the domain. The converse does not hold: Changes to the domain *are likely* to motivate changes to the user interface.

Acquire the best possible resources whenever you can. The mathematical models tell you obtaining resources before you need them is wasted effort. Still, you've just interviewed an awesome developer but don't really need her for another two months. What should you do? Ignore the models and hire her, of course! Now you've got her, what do you do with her? Lots of things. Have her build test cases or review requirements. Send her to training. Have her clean up existing code. The list is endless, but the point is clear.

Respect architectural boundaries when creating assignments. There are very few developers who can handle tasks spanning multiple layers of the architecture. Review each task with respect to architectural boundaries. Change any assignment crossing architectural boundaries to respect them.

There are three exceptions to this rule. First, the system architect has, by definition, a boundary spanning assignment. Second, the quality assurance group is also exempt by the nature of their work. Third, reviews and inspections *should* cross boundaries as a way of ensuring correctness and increasing knowledge of the system.

Put yourself at the bottom of the topology. Managers have a distressing tendency to forget their primary function is to serve the team. By putting yourself at the *bottom* of the organizational topology, rather than the top, you can further remind yourself of two important things (refer to the very first figure in this book located in the preface). First, your primary function is to serve the team. This becomes more visual when you place yourself at the bottom. Second, a significant portion of the communication on the team *does not* need to "flow" through you. By putting yourself at the bottom, you are less likely to create barriers to effective communication.

ADVICE TO DEVELOPERS

The complex interplay of architecture and topology bottoms out in the exact tasks you are given in the creation of the system. Your objective is to work within the topology to create the system as defined by the architecture.

> Respect architectural boundaries when solving problems.
> Use software patch panels to create flexible architectures.

Respect architectural boundaries when solving problems. It is often surprisingly easy to violate the boundaries of most architectures. You could, for example, inappropriately couple the user interface to the domain by placing validation rules inside the user interface instead of the domain. To see why this is a mistake, ask yourself what happens when the user interface changes. Or you could put the knowledge of how to translate information from the domain to the persistent store into the domain, thereby inappropriately coupling the domain to the persistent store. To see why, ask yourself what happens when you want to migrate to a new persistent store. Keep the domain layer focused *solely* on business logic.

Use software patch panels to create flexible architectures. Most poor decisions made concerning the architecture are not done out of malice but out of inexperience or a misunderstanding of what aspects of the system may change. Fortunately, early in my career I learned a hardware technique that continues to be the single best technique I know for creating loosely coupled and flexible architectures: software patch panels. Let me explain.

> *My first job at EDS was pulling cable underneath raised floor in an EDS Information Processing Center (IPC). Although this may seem like a pretty "low" job, I didn't mind. My manager was awesome, my colleagues patient teaching me what I needed to know, and in the process of pulling cables I learned a great deal about computer networks.*

> *One day, my manager came into my office and said we were going to create a patch panel. "What's a patch panel?" I asked. He explained that because network terminals were directly connected to their controlling devices (see the left side of Figure 12–7, a substantially simplified representation of an IBM SNA network), it was difficult to re-configure the network topology. Specifically, anytime the network changed, cables had to be completely rerouted.*

> *A patch panel, on other hand, consolidated change in one location. Now, whenever there was a change in the network configuration, you merely had to swap two simple wires in the patch panel. I've learned to apply this simple idea to every aspect of a software system: Ruthlessly identify those aspects of the system likely to change and provide for that change through a software patch panel.*

I'm certainly *not* the first person to think of this approach. Perhaps the most influential person in the software field recommending this approach is David Parnas [1976; 1979], who has so strongly advocated the use of information hiding discussed earlier. Parnas provides a simple and easy test for helping to determine when a software patch panel might be needed. Simply ask yourself "Could this aspect of the architecture change?" If the answer is yes, you need a patch panel. Note how easily the generic architecture proposed in Figure 12–4 supports such change *if* you adhere to its boundaries. What happens when there is a change in the user interface? You can also apply this process recursively within a layer as necessary. Within the user interface, what happens if you change platforms?

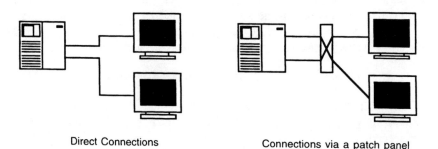

Direct Connections   Connections via a patch panel

Figure 12–7   Patch Panels

12.4 ROLES

A *role* is a set of formal and/or informal expectations held by an individual and other members of the team about how that individual should act in a given situation and the implicit and/or explicit responsibilities that individual has been given with respect to the proper functioning of the team [Mintzberg 1992; Quinn 1990]. I've already addressed roles implicitly: Remember the discussion about optimists and realists or the manager of the repository? The purpose of this section is to further define the concept of a role and show how certain roles can directly contribute to project success.

12.4.1 Implicit versus Explicit Roles

Implicit roles exist within any team. They are formed as members of the team naturally gravitate toward certain sets of behaviors consistent with their basic personality. They are also created and reinforced through interactions with other members of the team, sometimes to our surprise (or dismay). Implicit roles routinize interactions and help the team form the collective mind discussed in Chapter 7.

Explicit roles are created when there is a well-known task to accomplish (e.g., the "manager" of the repository or the system architect). While some texts equate the role of the individual to the set of tasks they have been assigned on the project, an explicit role is more appropriately thought of as a set of behaviors needed across many tasks or the duration of the project. This viewpoint helps us separate the motivation of the explicit role from the person fulfilling it and gives managers slightly greater flexibility in meeting the needs defined by the role. It also provides the developer with some behavioral discretion in how the role might be fulfilled.

Special roles often exist within a software development team, and certain organizational topologies (e.g., the surgical team proposed by Brooks [1995]) are based on the formation of these roles. For example, many teams create the role of a toolsmith, an individual who is responsible for creating reusable components for other members of the team.

One final point of differentiation exists between implicit roles and explicit roles. Implicit roles generally find their support in implicit structures and processes. Thus the outcomes influenced by implicit roles may not be easily traceable to the formal goals of the team. Explicit roles, on the other hand, require formalized structures and processes to ensure the outcomes associated with these roles meet the goals leading to their formation. Indeed, one way to distinguish between implicit and explicit roles is by the amount of explicit structure associated with the role.

12.4.2 Roles in Support of System Architecture

It is developers who ultimately build the system according to the architecture and topology engineered for the team. The question now is this: What specific skills are needed in support of architecture? What specific responsibilities are given to layers within each architectural layer (see Figure 12–8)? The assignment of responsibilities along architectural boundaries establishes explicit roles. Knowing these roles

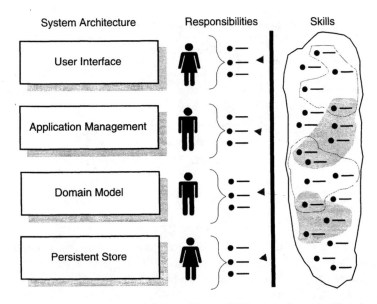

Figure 12–8   Distribution of Skills and Responsibilities According to Architecture

enables the team to have appropriate expectations of the knowledge and behavior of other developers. The remainder of this section discusses architecturally motivated roles (see Schultz [1995] for a similar description of architecturally motivated roles).

Senior Architect.   The senior architect (see Table 12–3) is the most important person on the project team. This person should be intimately familiar with the problem domain, and have experience in at least two to three other projects of similar size and complexity.

TABLE 12–3   Skills and Responsibilities of the Senior Architect

Characteristics	Skills/Knowledge Base	Responsibilities
Broad-based thinker	Broad familiarity with each	Establishes and maintains
Open minded	technology to be used on the	"conceptual integrity"
Capable of clearly envisioning	project	Directly selects and/or
the entire system. Able to	Deep understanding of the core	approves all major technolo-
communicate and explain this	implementation technology	gies on project
vision to others	Understanding of project man-	• implementation language
Able to balance technical and	agement and scheduling consid-	• databases, etc.
nontechnical aspects of the	erations	Oversees technical plans
project	Experienced with iterative-	• testing, metrics, reviews
	incremental development projects	Arbiter of technical decisions
	Extensive domain knowledge	• subsystem factoring
	Ability to span architectural	• development standards
	layers.	• etc.

TABLE 12–4   **Skills and Responsibilities of the User Interface Developer**

Characteristics	Skills/Knowledge Base	Responsibilities
People oriented	Widgets (when and how)	Usability
Recognizes and can correct awkward user interfaces	Window design	Economic analysis of user interface (as necessary)
Innovative	Usability testing	Selecting user interface metaphor
Knows who Don Norman is!	Limits of human cognition	
	Platform standards	Designing windows, etc.
	Task analysis	Inter- and Intraapplication consistency
		Address physical and environment constraints

User interface developer.   The essential responsibility of a user interface developer (see Table 12–4) is to create a "good" user interface. Recall that a "good" user interface enables a user to accomplish his or her tasks efficiently and enjoyably with a minimum of errors.

Transaction management and domain mode developers.   From the very earliest stages of the project, these individuals make certain the "guts" of the system are done the right way. Table 12–5 is organized into three sections. The first

TABLE 12–5   **Skills and Responsibilities of Transaction Management and Domain Model Developers**

Characteristics	Skills/Knowledge Base	Responsibilities
Technical	Implementation technology	Translate method outcomes into code
Can correctly differentiate between method activities	Method-defined processes and outcomes	Following project and corporate standards
Respects architectural boundaries	Coding/Debugging	Participate in software engineering and quality assurance processes
	Business logic	
	Software Engineering: Reviews/Metrics, etc.	May participate in generating method outcomes
	May be a novice or veteran with respect to any of the above	
Patient	Deep familiarity with the implementation technology	**Performance tuning**
Detail oriented	Computational complexity	
Distrustful of outcomes (not people)	Black- vs. white- box vs. gray-box testing techniques	Testing
Delights in demonstrating problems with solutions	Testing tools:	Map from outcomes to test plans
Pessimistic	• Coverage analysis	
	• Testing frameworks	

TABLE 12–6   **Skills and Responsibilities of Database Model Developers**

Characteristics	Skills/Knowledge Base	Responsibilities
Very detail oriented *Very* technical—ultra "geeks" Decisive	Extensive knowledge of the method notation Modeling Capacity planning Specific database(s) as determined by the architecture	Define the logical and physical mapping between representations Maintain single, unified model Representation translation Consult on design decisions from senior architect impacting this layer

details the skills of a general developer for either layer. The second addresses developers responsible for performance tuning. The third addresses developers associated with testing.

Database model/persistent store developers.   Developers associated with the database model (see Table 12–6) tend to be somewhat "schizophrenic" as they must bridge the gap between multiple worlds. Specifically, in an object-oriented project, the representation of objects within the system does not often correspond to their representation within a database. They must be translated from one representation to another. This translation, in turn, requires multiple kinds of knowledge and skills at the same time.

Reuse team/reuse librarian.   A large number of developers require separate teams to support the reuse of outcomes. Smaller teams can establish a single person with the characteristics listed in Table 12–7.

Project manager.   The roles and responsibilities of the project manager on an object-oriented project are largely the same as on traditional projects, as shown in Table 12–8.

TABLE 12–7   **Skills and Responsibilities of the Reuse Team Developers**

Characteristics	Skills/Knowledge Base	Responsibilities
Good communication skills Ability to create abstract components from concrete components Ability to modify systems with a minimum of adverse effects.	Library science—the storage and retrieval of information	Establishes and maintains the project and reuse repository Provides assistance in finding reusable assets Ensures quality of managed assets Updates interested parties on modifications/updates to managed assets

TABLE 12–8   Skills and Responsibilities of the Project Manager

Characteristics	Skills/Knowledge Base	Responsibilities
Can balance many competing demands	Technically competent in all aspects of the project[2]	Everything!
Internally and externally congruent	Scheduling	
Willingness to navigate the corporate bureaucracy	Coordination and people management within the organization	

12.4.3 Roles Associated with Teamwork

While establishing a well-defined set of architecturally motivated roles and then "fitting" developers into these roles helps the team succeed, it is still not enough to produce a highly successful team. Other implicit and explicit roles are needed, such as the developer who reduces group tension through humor and a generally positive attitude. These roles help the team in *how* the task is accomplished.

The work of R. M. Belbin provides a simple foundation for understanding nonarchitecturally motivated roles needed for a highly successful team. Belbin based his approach on psychological profiles such as the MBTI (described in Chapter 4) as well as other aspects of personality (e.g., anxiety versus stability). In all, Belbin's research showed highly successful teams have eight clearly identifiable roles as described in Table 12–9. This does not mean a team must consist of eight members, as a member of the team often assumes more than one role. One way to visualize these roles is shown in Figure 12–9.

Belbin's theory has widespread empirical support in predicting unsuccessful teams. Specifically, it has been shown that teams with all eight roles are much more likely to be successful than teams without. Teams with few of these roles are almost always failures. It may appear simple, but the most effective teams are not created by

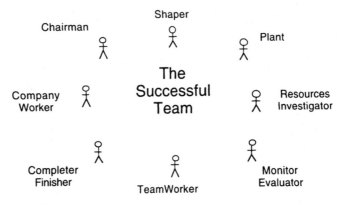

Figure 12–9   Roles Associated with Successful Teams

[2] Technical competence does not mean the project manager is the *expert* in every aspect of the project. It does mean they can't be easily fooled.

TABLE 12–9   Roles Associated with Teamwork

Role	Description
Company Worker	Turns concepts and plans into practical working procedures.
	Enjoys carrying out agreed upon plans systematically and efficiently.
Chairman	Controls the way in which the team moves toward team goals by making the best use of team resources.
	Identifies the strengths and weaknesses of the team and works to ensure the best use is made of each team member.
Shaper	Shapes or molds the manner in which effort is applied within the team.
	Directs attention to the setting of goals and priorities.
	Seeks to impose structure on group discussion and on group-related outcomes.
Plant	Advances new strategies and ideas, especially with respect to major issues faced by the team.
	Looks for ways around the roadblocks faced by the team.
Resources Investigator	Explores and reports on ideas, developments, and resources outside the team.
	Creates external links with other teams; conducts negotiations with other teams.
Monitor Evaluator	Analyzes problems.
	Evaluates suggestions and ideas offered by the team.
	Assists the team in making decisions based on these evaluations.
Team Worker	Supports other team members by building on strengths and underpinning their weaknesses.
	Improves communication within the team and fosters team spirit.
Completer Finisher	Ensures the team is protected as much as possible from mistakes of omission and commission.
	Identifies aspects of work requiring additional attention.
	Maintains a sense of urgency and makes certain assignments are completed.

simply taking a bunch of experts and placing them on the same team. Instead, the most effective teams are comprised of individuals who can balance their efforts with respect to the eight roles just defined. Table 12–10 details which of Belbin's roles lend themselves to implicit versus explicit assignment.

> *Knowledge of human physiology motivates another, but considerably simpler, theory of the roles on a project. Recall muscles are physiologically designed to perform one and only one operation: contraction. These contractions are subsequently used for one of two functions: movement or stabilization. Movers contract to move a body part through a range of motion. Stabilizers contract to hold other body parts stable during movement. At times, a stabilizer is "opposite" the mover, in which case the mover is called the antagonist and the stabilizer is called the protagonist. Most muscles are both movers and stabilizers and assume these "roles" depending on the kind of movement being performed. In very complex movements a muscle can rapidly alternate between movement and stabilization.*

TABLE 12–10   Implicit/Explicit Roles for Teamwork

Role	Implicit/Explicit	Notes
Company Worker	Implicit	Examine the impact of the method on the company worker. Following the structure provided by the method is a key aspect of the company worker.
Chairman	Explicit	Could be the senior architect or project manager.
		Multiple "chairmen" may be needed for large teams (e.g., horizontal layer managers are chairmen for people; vertical slice managers are chairmen for determining development priorities.
Shaper	Implicit	While the chairman explicitly allocates resources, the shaper works to make certain these resources remain focused on the task at hand.
		Shapers tend to believe in and rely on structure.
Plant	Either	An explicit plant is useful for addressing specific risks faced by the project. Such an individual tends to be very technical.
		An implicit plant assists by identifying and solving problems before they arise. This requires experience.
Resources Investigator	Either	An explicit resources investigator (RI) is useful when a project is exploring the use of a new technology. They possess a balance of technical and business skills. An explicit RI is also helpful when the project must interface with multiple groups. The role is essential when these groups may be pursuing multiple objectives.
		An implicit RI is like the developer who spends time at home surfing the Web looking for new tips and techniques.
Monitor Evaluator	Either	Establishing an explicit monitor evaluator is useful on large projects where they can "float" as necessary between work groups assisting with any issues faced by these teams.
		An implicit monitor evaluator is often skilled at following the processes dictated by the method.
Team Worker	Implicit	Cheerleaders, motivators, and similar individuals are all included in the role of team worker.
Completer Finisher	Either/ Explicit	While implicit completer finishers are acceptable, it is best to explicitly create this role. Establishing specific responsibility for the production of outcomes contributes to both explicit completer finishers.
		Ultimately, the explicit role of completer finisher is fulfilled by the project manager.

Successful teams are comprised of both movers and stabilizers who can alternate between these roles as necessary to benefit the team. During a design meeting the mover might be the individual presenting a design, while the stabilizers are those teammates who provide support and encouragement as new ideas are presented. These roles can be immediately reversed after the idea is presented as the stabilizers begin to critique the design. In some physical movements, certain muscles are considered to be inactive or not directly contributing to the movement. This too has some parallels to software development, as certain members of the team will appear to be inactive in certain phases of the project. However, all muscles are eventually needed if the movement is sufficiently complex, just as in a complex project the skills of all members of the team are needed to implement the system correctly.

12.4.4 Problems Associated with Roles

Two problems are often associated with roles. The first is role ambiguity. *Role ambiguity* occurs when an individual is unsure about the role they have been explicitly given or have implicitly assumed. It is commonly experienced among new employees when they are unfamiliar with what is expected from them on their job. This can happen most easily when the new employee was selected as a "replacement" and existing team members frame their interactions with the new person based on the role(s) of the former team member. Experienced employees are also susceptible to role ambiguity when they transition from one job to another where the implicit and explicit roles are new (e.g., moving from development to management).

The second is role conflict. *Role conflict* occurs when expected roles require contradictory actions and/or behaviors. Conflict is greatest when the individual does not have the authority and/or experience necessary to resolve the conflict and in extreme cases can be debilitating. One source of role conflict in software development occurs when developers receive contradictory information about system requirements and are given insufficient information to resolve the conflict. Managers can experience role conflict when their superiors make inappropriate demands on their subordinates. Individuals who play multiple roles often experience role conflict because many roles have competing demands. Consider, for example, the completer finisher and the resources investigator. Working to complete the project is at odds with working to find new ways to do things.

ADVICE TO MANAGERS

Every member of a team has a need to know how they "fit" into the project. Roles, especially explicit ones, help accomplish this goal.

> Use Task-Relevant Maturity (TRM) in establishing roles.
>
> Ask your staff what role they want to fulfill—the results may surprise you!
>
> Help your staff understand the implicit roles they fill.
>
> Avoid defining a multitude of narrowly defined roles.
>
> Don't force new team members into old roles.
>
> Rotate desirable and undesirable roles.
>
> Ask your staff what roles they expect you to fulfill.

Use Task-Relevant Maturity (TRM) in establishing roles. Simply deciding the "role" of a senior architect is needed and then assigning someone to it is hardly a formula for success. Instead, you need to take into account something Andrew Grove [1983] has referred to as task-relevant maturity. *Task-relevant maturity is the ability, desire, and motivation to take on the responsibility of an explicit role.*

TRM is based on many factors, including education, training, and experience, and is usually specific to a particular kind of role. The presence of our cognitive libraries and various competency levels (described in Chapter 6) means we have multiple levels of TRM: high in the areas we "know," and low in the areas we don't. Our TRM can be assessed be determining the depth of competence we exhibit with regard to formal training and/or our proven ability to perform a job. Knowledge of a developer's TRM enables you to adopt a management style appropriate for that person as they assume a role. Specifically, individuals with low TRM require greater direct supervision, requiring increasingly less supervision as they achieve competence.

Ask your staff what role they want to fulfill—the results may surprise you! Managers are often faced with the following dilemma: A well-established role exists, but we are not certain which member of the team should be assigned to fill it. One way out of this dilemma is to simply *ask* our staff which roles they wish to fulfill. Armed with this knowledge, we can try to assign roles according to individual preferences.

> *One good piece of advice often given to managers is "don't make any quick changes when given a new assignment until you know the organization." In general, a good rule of thumb is to wait anywhere from two to six months. This time frame enables the new manager to thoroughly learn the existing structures, processes, and outcomes of the team before making any changes. Sometimes, however, drastic changes are needed immediately.*

> *In one assignment I was given a development group with no formalized production support team. Instead, all developers within the organization were expected to share the duties of production support through a weekly rotation. It was a disaster. When a production problem reared its ugly head, it was fixed, but no schedule extensions were given to acknowledge the effort spent in fixing the problem. Thus, production support problems were fixed poorly, if at all. If you didn't fix the problem during your week of production support, you could hand it off to the next developer in the weekly rotation.*

> *Moreover, some developers worked harder than others because they had developed special knowledge of the primary systems. The net effect was an uneven distribution of work, and general feelings of ill will throughout the team. Analyzing the team from the standpoint of cohesion and coupling, it is easy to see the separate functions of production support and new product development were too tightly coupled within the same team. This actually prevented cohesion among the developers assigned to these tasks.*

To rectify this situation, I announced I would split the single development team into two separate teams, one devoted to production support and the other devoted to new product development. During the meeting, I also announced the final composition of this team was not yet set, and a subsequent meeting would detail the members of the team. I then explained the reason for the delay, and for the present meeting, was to solicit "volunteers" for the production support team. I much preferred to staff the team with people who wanted to engage in production support activities. At the same time, I requested that any developer with an extremely strong aversion to production support come talk with me in person, so I could better understand their point of view. I assured everyone I would try and take their wishes into account as I defined the final composition of the team.

What I expected from this announcement was a steady stream of developers walking into my office telling me how much they disliked production support, and how they didn't want to be on this team (primarily because I don't like production support). To my surprise, during the next week three of the top developers within the organization stopped by my office to volunteer for membership in the production support team. They each had their own reasons ("I enjoy going home at the end of the day knowing I fixed a problem"; "I am tired of working on long-term development projects and would prefer to work on shorter term projects"; "I know more of the problems in the system than anyone else—give me the opportunity to fix them!"). By the beginning of the next week I had three of the six people I needed for the team, simply by asking!

A few people did stop by my office to state they did not want to be a member of such a team. They too had good reasons. Unfortunately, I was forced to place one of these individuals on the production support team because she possessed a unique level of knowledge on a crucial subsystem. She reluctantly accepted the assignment, but asked if I would try to move her off the team as soon as possible. Over the next several weeks I looked for ways to "trade" her from the production support team, and within two months she was happily working on a new development project (this two-month time frame included the necessary transfer of knowledge to a new candidate).

The formation of the two groups enabled both teams to operate more effectively. Coupling among the activities between the teams was substantially reduced, while cohesion increased by a similar amount. These results are consistent with the general effects of low coupling: Low coupling among teams allows each to become more cohesive. While this scenario took place in the context of a major reorganization of the team, its underlying principles are applicable in any project. Indeed, it is appropriate to ask this question periodically on very long projects. Perhaps an individual changes his or her mind about his or her current assignment and would rather try something different. Or, perhaps they are a little tired with what they are currently doing and just need a change of pace. Regardless of the reason, you can often find roles people enjoy fulfilling by simply asking.

Help your staff understand the implicit roles they fill. Developers (and managers) often fail to take advantage of their implicit roles because they fail to see themselves within that role. For example, informal leaders often have difficulty realizing their influence. Because of this, they fail to realize the full use of their power in shaping the team in beneficial ways. Helping your staff identify their implicit roles helps them use these roles to their greatest advantage.

Avoid defining a multitude of narrowly defined roles.   It is far better to gather a number of activities into a single broad role that can be subsequently split over time into more narrowly defined roles than it is to define many separate roles and later attempt to collect these disparate activities into a single, more comprehensive role.

Don't force new team members into old roles.   When a senior member of the team leaves it is tempting to try to fit a new team member into the recently vacated role(s). In general, this is a mistake for at least three reasons. First, other members will naturally expect the new team member to perform this role as effectively as the former team member. Unfortunately, the new team member may not have the TRM necessary to perform in the role as effectively as the departing team member. Second, establishing a new team member in an old role makes it extraordinarily difficult for the new team member to establish his or her own identity within the team. There are simply too many expectations established within the minds of older team members as to how he or she "should" behave. Third, an existing team member may have viewed the departure as an opportunity to obtain the role of the departing individual, and immediately placing a new team member in this role can prevent growth among existing team members.

Rotate desirable and undesirable roles.   Rotation of roles provides the team with cross-training and can alleviate problems when a backup is required. Needless to say, some roles are more desirable than others. Rotating desirable roles can increase job satisfaction and provides a renewed enthusiasm for the developer assuming the desirable role. Rotating an undesirable role can alleviate the burden and "share the pain."

Rotating undesirable roles can be extraordinarily difficult: The reason a role is "undesirable" is because no one wants to do it! The best approach is to address the issue squarely. *Tell* the team each member will be rotated through these roles in a timely and consistent fashion. Once you have made the commitment to rotate individuals, stick with it. You will always get a fair amount of resistance, but this will fade as developers realize you are serious about rotating roles fairly.

Ask your staff what roles they expect you to fulfill.   Managers sometimes lose sight of the fact they also have explicit and implicit roles. One way to make certain you are performing the right roles is to ask your subordinates the kinds of roles they expect you to fulfill. Some of the responses will be outrageous, some inappropriate, but you are likely to find most represent reasonable expectations of a manager. Table 12–11 provides some ideas to help get you started. (See Quinn [1990] for a detailed discussion of managerial roles along with specific exercises designed to improve performance with respect to these roles.)

TABLE 12–11   Common (or Uncommon) Managerial Roles

Managerial Role	Notes/Examples
Enforcer	Ensures coding standards are being followed, individuals are preparing for outcome reviews in an appropriate manner, and rules for meeting etiquette are followed.
Motivator	Encourages developers to work toward the objectives of the project. This is *not* "Do it or else" motivation.
Planning/Controlling	Creates plans for the team and monitors performance with respect to these plans.
Developer *of people*	Works with subordinates to create development plans. Monitors achievement with respect to these plans. Provides appropriate feedback when behavior is not consistent with the plan.
Conflict Management	Ultimate arbiter of disputes within the project.
Information Distributor	Distributes needed information in a timely manner.

ADVICE TO DEVELOPERS

As described above, there are a variety of implicit and explicit roles you can fulfill. Indeed, chances are good you will fulfill *more* than one role over the life of the project.

> Select implicit roles consistent with your personality.
> Ask for the specific roles you desire.

Select implicit roles consistent with your personality.   We tend to select implicit roles consistent with our basic personality. I have a colleague who is quite innovative. Although he does not realize it, he has assumed the role of resources investigator. Another is impatient. His role is completer finisher. A third is detailed and meticulous. She has assumed the role of company worker. Which of Belbin's eight team roles described in Table 12–9 are consistent with your personality? Which are weak or nonexistent on your current team? Can you begin to act in this role?

Ask for the specific roles you desire.   Your manager may not have had the luxury of reading this book and as such may not think to ask you what role you would like in the team. However, there is nothing stopping you from asking for a specific role. To enhance your chances for success, consider your request as a mini job interview. View the role you desire as a job and approach your manager as the most qualified candidate for the position. While you may not obtain the role you want, you will have made certain your manager knows and understands your desires to pursue a different role. This can provide unexpected dividends in the future (e.g., your manager could learn about a similar role in a different team and offer your name as a potential candidate).

12.5 STRUCTURE AS PROCESS

The definition of structure as "relatively stable" in Chapter 7 implies the structures of the team change over time. They do. Structures appropriate in the beginning of a project may not be appropriate at its end. Structures forming the foundation for success in one context may sow the seeds for failure in another. And, the presence of feedback loops between the three elements of the SPO framework all indicate structure *will* change. Determining, guiding, controlling, and otherwise managing the structures associated with the project are of central importance to successful software development.

12.5.1 The Impact of Structure

Engineering a "relatively stable" structure is a decidedly tricky business. Structures outlast their originators and are relatively impervious to modification, even by those individuals who may have been given the task of making changes.

Think of organizational structures as a parking garage made from concrete. When the garage is under construction, special structures are used to support the concrete as it sets. Once the concrete has cured, these structures are no longer needed and they are removed. Over time, the garage becomes weak and needs to be renovated. The renovation process usually requires adding temporary structures to once again support the garage. Similarly, more or less structure may be needed at any time during the life of a project for the successful functioning of the team.

Experience has shown successful teams can succeed despite poor structures. For example, the waterfall model is a poor structure for supporting the process software development. It delays feedback about outcomes, is based on the idea that outcomes are stable and complete at the completion of every process stage (at best, wishful thinking), and inhibits reuse. Yet, many successful software projects have been created using the waterfall structure, and it is likely many future projects will find success using the waterfall despite its shortcomings. Ultimately, the mixture of individuals involved in developing the software, from the customer to each developer, is more important than any specific structure.

While it is true a team can succeed despite inappropriate structures, it often takes an exceptional team. More importantly, achieving success in this manner extracts a large cost from everyone involved. Unfortunately, managers (and developers) tend to rely on the past successes of exceptional teams and fail to critically examine the structures associated with the team contributing to or inhibiting performance.

12.5.2 More or Less Structure

What do I mean by "more" or "less" structure? Actually, I mean many things at the same time (see Figure 12–10). In general, more structure implies each process step prescribed by the structure is closely followed, there is more rigidity in form and content of outcomes, communication is formal, and there are more checks and

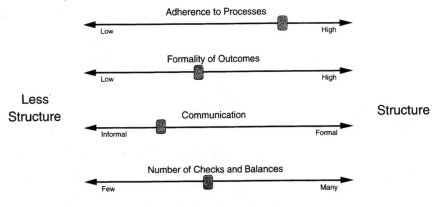

Figure 12–10   More versus Less Structure

balances of the processes and outcomes defined by the structure (e.g., more inspections, which themselves constitute an SPO framework).

A team having a high degree of structure is one that could easily be defined as a team producing all the outcomes necessary, following *all* the process steps, and having appropriate—and perhaps elaborate—checks and balances to *ensure* they do so. The idea of more or less structure is orthogonal to the issue of topology: A cluster can exhibit far more structure than a hierarchy. It is also orthogonal to architecture, for although architecture *defines* a structure, the team building it may not adhere to it.

Some readers may argue that following a process more completely and formally is more process, and not more structure. Such a view is inaccurate for two reasons. First, process formality exists only to the extent the structure prescribes, defines, and supports the process in a formal manner and is engaged as such. Second, and more importantly, all processes are engaged in the context of some structure. Ad hoc or informal structures cannot support elaborate and formal processes.

12.5.3 How Much Structure?

What makes organizational engineering such a "decidedly tricky business" are the number and complexity of the variables involved in the selection and establishment of an appropriate structure. Among them are the degree of experience among the members of the team, the size and age of the organization, and the perceived difficulty of the problem as determined by its volume and intricacy. It helps to visualize these variables as a series of controls helping you "pick" the right amount of structure (see Figure 12–11). The meanings behind these variables are explored below.

♦ *Experience.* In general, as experience increases the need for structure decreases for three reasons. First, to have "experience" means the developer has many cognitive plans enabling them to solve problems efficiently within a problem domain. Thus, less external structure is needed because there is far more internal structure. Second, experienced developers have internalized the

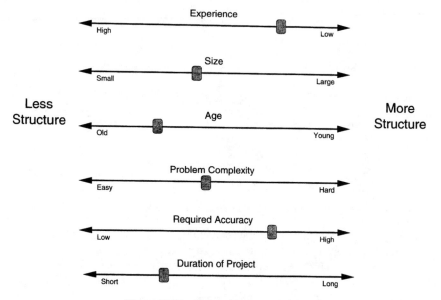

Figure 12–11   Variables Influencing Structure

structures and processes necessary for communication and coordination within the team, thus reducing the need for external structure.

Third, greater experience often implies greater discipline, the process whereby structure is modified from externally given to internally motivated. However, experience does not necessarily mean individuals or teams will engage in the discipline necessary to use structure effectively; paradoxically, individuals or teams with a great deal of experience may in fact require more structure to use their experience effectively.

♦ *Size.* Size is perhaps the most difficult variable. Changing size changes topology, architecture, communication structures, coordination structures, and a host of other things. The bottom line is this: No matter how good each individual is, larger teams require more structure in the problem-solving process for two reasons. First, communication, coordination, and integration complexity increase nonlinearly. Second, outcomes must be prepared with more formality and clarity as the potential for divergence is far greater.

♦ *Age.* The age of the team is how long they have been working *together*. Young teams tend to start with minimal structures and grow them over time as needed to solve specific problems encountered within their environment. Less structure also enables young teams to have the latitude necessary to try different outcomes, searching for those most appropriate. This is not to say less structure is optimal for a young team. In fact, more structure is often beneficial, as it enables a young team to focus more effort on solving the problem (as opposed to solving the problem of how to solve the problem).

The key influencing variable on age with respect to structure is experience. A young team of inexperienced developers requires far more structure than a young team of experienced developers.

♦ *Problem Complexity. Large* problems require more structure because there are more developers associated with the project. *Intricate* problems require more structure because skipping a process step dramatically increases the chances for error. Generalizing, as problem complexity increases, the need for structure increases.

♦ *Required Accuracy.* Highly accurate solutions require more structure (e.g., more testing, inspections, formality in outcomes) during *every* phase of development.

♦ *Duration of Project.* Short projects require less structure than long projects, typically because they are focused on short-term, tactical problems.

The creation of an appropriate structure for the team is an ongoing process beginning with the creation of one or more initial structures. These are evaluated in the context of use by how well each supports the team in problem solving. This evaluation must focus on the outcomes generated through the processes prescribed by the structure. If the outcomes are appropriate and can be prepared with ease, the structure is "good." If not, the structure must be changed.

The goal is to achieve an organizational structure which is *stable*, in that it supports the team as they engage in the processes necessary to generate appropriate outcomes, and yet *flexible*, in that it also supports changes to the processes, outcomes, and even the members of the team engaged in the work.

12.5.4 The Dangers of Too Much Structure

Imagine taking every control in Figure 12–10 and moving each far to the right—is this amount of structure what your project needs? For the vast majority of projects, the answer is a clear and resounding "no." An overly structured project results in Byzantine or overly bureaucratic processes; excessive, redundant, and often unnecessary communication, increased development costs, reduced time to market, and increased dissatisfaction and frustration within the team building the system.

Creating the right amount of structure is an engineering decision based on the variable presented in Figure 12–11. As such, we have to balance the amount of structure given to the team and remain sensitive to when too much structure (or too little) cause problems.

ADVICE TO MANAGERS

It can be easy to think any given structure is static. However, this is not the case, and adopting a view of structure as process enables you to respond and even anticipate the needs of the team.

> Avoid creating formal structures you are not willing to support.
>
> Small teams do not equate to no structure.
>
> Simplify, simplify, simplify.
>
> Structure is like spice: A little goes a long way.

Avoid creating formal structures you are not willing to support. As structures become more formal, they require more managerial effort to maintain and enforce. Establishing any structure is pointless unless you are willing to expend this energy. Consider Ralph, a manager who read an article on the SEI-CMM and suddenly decided metrics were to be gathered for every project. So, Ralph sent an e-mail to his team detailing six specific metrics they were to collect for their project. At first, developers complied with his request and began to collect metrics. Over time, they stopped, as they realized Ralph wasn't doing anything with the results. Unfortunately, Ralph failed because he didn't create an appropriate structure for gathering, storing, and subsequently analyzing the metric results.

Small teams do not equate to no structure. Although small teams can be successful with substantially less formal structure than large teams, it is a fallacy to think they require no structure. For example, smaller teams tend to require less formality in outcomes, mostly because differences in shared understanding can be resolved quickly through face-to-face communication, something impossible in larger teams.

However, some structure is needed no matter how small the team. Fortunately, you get a break with respect to structure on small teams: Even if you don't create the necessary structures, small teams are often surprisingly quite adept at creating their own structures *as long as* there is someone on the team with the experience and skill necessary to do this. However, relying on this is risky, and it is usually far better to work on creating the appropriate structures for even small teams.

Simplify, simplify, simplify. As structures change over time, they tend to become more complex. Be careful of this. Watch for it. Simplify.

Structure is like spice: A little goes a long way. Food is most enjoyable when the cook adds enough spice to enhance the dish, not overpower it. More importantly, we can easily add spice but cannot easily remove it. Structure in teams is like spice in foods. It is easy to add, hard to take away, and a little goes a long way. Like food, work is most enjoyable when structure enhances and supports but does not overpower.

ADVICE TO DEVELOPERS

Defining a completely perfect and stable structure is impossible: There are simply too many variables and each is subject to change over the life of the project. Perhaps the most important advice is to remain flexible, working within structures as best you can. Alternatively, when the appropriate structures do not exist, work to establish them (see Chapter 3) as necessary and appropriate.

> Take structures seriously.
> Set a good example.

Take structures seriously.   Many structures created by managers fail for quite a simple reason: The development staff did not think the structure was needed or appropriate. Because the staff did not believe in the structure, they ignored it, challenged it, circumvented it, and did everything but follow it. Any structure, no matter how stringent, requires your support for effectiveness. Only by working within the bounds of a structure can you learn its limits, and only by knowing the limits can you make appropriate extensions.

The need for structure increases dramatically in certain environments, a concept military organizations have long realized. Imagine you are responsible for helping to land an F-16 on an aircraft carrier in rough seas. Unless you adhere to *every* part of the structure designed to accomplish this objective several lives could be lost. While I concede that few projects (but not all) in software development require military-style structures, following structures consistently and faithfully does contribute to higher performance.

A good illustration of the need to adhere to the structures is in the practice of configuration management. In the classes I teach covering this topic, I always try to stress the importance of adhering to the structures of configuration management systems in both "spirit" and "law." During one class, however, my students challenged me on this point. They said they currently use a configuration management system, but in the spirit of open teamwork and to achieve greater efficiency they regularly shared passwords (thereby violating one of the most important structures of good configuration management).

As I questioned them further about the effectiveness of this decision, individual developers started to voice many specific examples where this approach caused significant problems, especially during integration testing when the team needed to track specific modifications to the system. By the end of the class, the team had agreed to give my approach (follow the structures as faithfully as possible and do not share passwords) a try and to let me know if indeed this helped the team be more effective. About six weeks later I sent an e-mail to the individual in charge of the configuration management procedure to see how things were going. The response? "Much better."

Set a good example.   As new developers join the team, they learn to adhere—or ignore—structures based on the behaviors of existing team members. In other words, your adherence to structure is part of the culture of the team. Thus, if you consistently violate a structure, you will effectively propagate that behavior within new team members. Others are watching. Do you really want new developers to ignore structures established to support the team?

13

TECHNOLOGICAL AND ORGANIZATIONAL CHANGE

Software developers are more accustomed to change in their work than individuals in many other professions. New forms of hardware unthinkable just a few years ago find their way to our desktop, laptop, palmtop, shirt pocket, eye, ear, or hand. New programming techniques and languages continue to be introduced at a dizzying pace. Who among us has not had their work habits—and sometimes, their entire career—changed forever by some new technology?

For many of us, change is part of the fabric of our lives, and the idea that others around us may not embrace and perhaps even look forward to such continual change is strange, at best. Yet, even the most future-oriented individuals can find certain aspects of change difficult, such as when a successful project team is disbanded and they must become a member of a new project team. Ultimately, change is inevitable. Feedback loops predict it. The external environment requires it.

The purpose of this chapter is to provide a foundation for understanding and managing change. It deals with two kinds of change. The first is *innovations*, which are tools, techniques, and/or outcomes perceived as new, and *reorganizations,* which are changes in and among members of the team over time. Strategic change, which simultaneously affects all the components of the integrated framework, involves both innovations and reorganizations.

Change begins by impacting one or more components of the framework. And, due to the interrelated aspects of the framework and the presence of feedback loops, changing one component eventually changes them all. Indeed, after the change has been successfully introduced, the exact "thing" that changes may be difficult to find. To see why this is so, consider the long-term effects of a new manager (a reorganization) or programming language (an innovation). At first, both are considered quite new. Over time, they become assimilated into the working environment (and the working environment restructures itself to accommodate them). The remainder of this chapter explores these ideas in greater detail.

Chapter Overview

The chapter begins with general discussion on many factors influencing change in Section 3.1. Section 13.2 follows by addressing innovations. Section 13.3 addresses reorganizations.

13.1 GENERAL OBSERVATIONS ON CHANGE

Both innovations and reorganizations require individuals within the organization to deal with *change*, something perceived as new or different. In this manner, both kinds of change share the following observations with respect to how individuals perceive, enact, and manage change.

- ◆ *Change can be tough!* The process of change can be tough. Not every member of the team may perceive the need to change. If people agree a change is needed, not everyone may agree with the proposed change. Effective, long-lasting change is not easy. It requires real work to assimilate new structures and processes. Motivation is a key factor here, and making a change means sustaining motivation through the process of change until the desired objective is realized.

  Even if you are motivated to change, it can still be tough, especially when the change involves an ingrained behavior. An athlete suffering an injury may have to relearn how to perform the same movement in a new way. Such a change is exceedingly difficult because complex physical movements take time to learn, and once learned, are not easily forgotten. In this respect our mental structures mimic our physical structures. Changing patterns of thought and/or behavior are difficult. In general, the more difficult the perceived change, the more important motivation becomes in the change process.

- ◆ *Continuous versus discontinuous change.* Innovations and reorganizations can be further classified along two dimensions: continuous or discontinuous (see Figure 13–1). *Continuous change* consists of making minor modifications to existing structures, processes, and outcomes. Such change often occurs implicitly, through learning and/or experimentation on current practice. *Discontinuous change* is a replacement of one or more existing structures with a new structure. It is, by its very nature, explicit.

  Paradoxically, it is often easier to achieve discontinuous change than continuous change. The wholesale replacement of a given structure with a new structure forces one to deal with the new structure. It is easy to ignore making

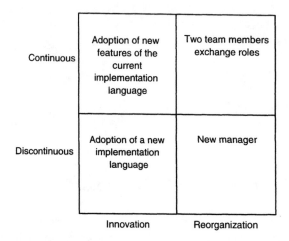

Figure 13–1   Dimensions of Change

minor modifications to existing structures even though these modifications are desirable. Many organizational structures support slightly diverse processes. Making minor modifications to a process within a given structure is often the most difficult change of all.

To illustrate the difference between continuous versus discontinuous change, imagine you are the captain of a merchant ship carrying spice from the West Indies to France in the seventeenth century. Your only guide is a sextant, which you consult regularly to stay on course. Stopping for supplies along the way, you learn Britain has just declared war on France, and any ship traveling to France could be attacked by the British. Seeking to avoid such unpleasantries, you decide instead to set a new course to Portugal, where you can safely unload your cargo. Continuous change can be thought of as the small corrections made to your course when traveling to France. Discontinuous change is the entirely new course set for Portugal.

◆ *Willingness to change.* Individuals differ substantially in their basic attitudes toward change. Some of us thrive on change. Others tend to avoid it. Teams, because they are comprised of individuals, exhibit similar differences. Finally, entire organizations are often characterized by their willingness to change. Our willingness to change is greatly influenced by the perceived beneficial effects of the change. If the perceived benefits are strong enough, even the most reluctant of us will enact the change.

◆ *Known outcome.* Change is most effective when there is a clear expectation of the desired effects of the change. Put another way, any trip is easier if the destination is known. One way of doing this effectively is to state the effects of the change—and the change itself—as a goal to be accomplished. This, in turn, enables us to monitor progress toward the desired change.

♦ *Known impact.* All change impacts one or more components of the framework immediately and all components eventually. Considering the impact of change in the context of the SPO framework enables the team to prepare effectively for the effects of change in *each* component. ·

♦ *Communication.* Communication is essential throughout the change process. Initially, communication about the change establishes the context and motivation for the change. While the motivation for change can appear "obvious" to the proponents of the change, this understanding may not be shared by every member of the team. During the change process, communication about the change maintains motivation and keeps the team focused on the objective.

♦ *Education.* The need for explicit education is most easily identified with innovations: A new structure or process requires education in its use. Explicit education is less often a component of reorganizations, although education is often required here to teach skills relevant to new roles.

♦ *Time.* While the decision to change can happen immediately, the actual process of making a change can take substantial amounts of time (did you really expect your Monday morning memo would result in the team following a new process by Friday?).

♦ *Increasing entropy.* Changes made to a software system tend to increase the entropy and complexity of the system. Eventually, the system becomes so complex it can no longer withstand the change, but must instead be redesigned. The same is true of change within organizations. Innovations and reorganizations can easily increase entropy unless they are designed and implemented with care.

♦ *Distribution of power.* Innovations and reorganizations affect the distribution of power in the team. Quite naturally those in positions of power prefer changes allowing them to retain their base of power. Quite often they will actively work against change if it is perceived the change could cause them to lose power.

♦ *You are never "there."* Once you have identified the need for a change, whether it is an innovation or reorganization, by definition one or more of your current structures, processes, or outcomes are inappropriate. Where you want to be is in the future. Once you get there, the environment has changed, and the change you thought was appropriate can only sustain you for a short while until the change process begins once again. The focus of change is the future; current practice is, at best, in the present.

ADVICE TO MANAGERS

Before becoming too concerned about managing specific kinds of change, it is helpful to have a more general foundation for leading change within the organization.

> Avoid crises through continuous change. Fix them through
>   discontinuous change.
>
> What will remain constant during the change?
>
> The more discontinuous the change, the greater the need for your
>   involvement.
>
> Reorganization may be required for *any* change.
>
> Make discontinuous change fast.
>
> State and then evaluate the proposed change.
>
> "What have you learned or done new this week?"

Avoid crises through continuous change. Fix them through discontinuous change.   Starbuck and colleagues define a *crisis* as a severe threat to the existence of the organization [Starbuck 1978]. He identifies two sources for crisis: substantial changes in the external environment and managerial structures held in place too long. Although you can't avoid all forms of crisis (e.g., a competitor announces a revolutionary new product), you can minimize the number of crises you must face through appropriate, controlled, and predominantly continuous change.

This is not to say that discontinuous changes are bad, for they are the primary vehicle to use in getting out of a crises. Consider Raymond, a manager who has just assumed management authority for a project that is on its last legs. You see, the project is continually missing deadlines, has produced buggy products, and is losing market share rapidly. Unless things are turned around, the product will be removed from the market and the team disbanded. Raymond is faced with a crisis. Continuous change to existing managerial structures is not going to work. Instead, Raymond must carefully examine the current structures and make the discontinuous changes necessary to get out of the crisis.

What will remain constant during the change?   Our willingness and ability to enact a change are based on many factors. One important factor is the comfort in knowing some portion of the environment will remain stable during the change. It is important to differentiate and communicate what aspect of the environment will remain stable during the change.

Consider a team adopting object technology. Adopting object technology effectively requires *substantial* changes to all aspects of software development. There are new programming languages, methods, configuration management tools, and a whole host of other new structures, processes, and outcomes. One way to manage all this change is to place it in the context of the prevailing values and culture. Another is to use known topologies during the change. By assuring everyone these aspects of the environment are *not* changing, you provide a hook—an anchor—to a stable aspect of the work environment. Rarely, if ever, should individuals be subjected to major, simultaneous change in all aspects of their environment.

The more discontinuous the change, the greater the need for your involvement. Discontinuous change means the team, and quite possibly yourself, are moving to new, uncharted territory. As a leader, don't provide the team with a goal and a map and then walk away from the journey. Take the journey with them.

I regularly work with teams faced with the task of moving from mainframe COBOL-based applications to client-server applications based on Smalltalk or C++ and graphical user interfaces. This is a highly discontinuous change. My experience indicates that managers who become actively involved in the change process by learning about the technology navigate the new territory significantly more effectively than those who only pay lip service to the change and leave the major aspects of the change to their teams.

Reorganization may be required for *any* change. Regardless of the willingness of each individual on the team to make a change, mutually reinforcing patterns of interaction and expectations among members of the team may make real change impossible without a reorganization.

Make discontinuous change fast. The more discontinuous the change, the greater the need to implement the change rapidly and decisively. Trying to achieve discontinuous change slowly decreases your chances for success for at least three reasons. First, when discontinuous change is slow, those most affected can easily build resistance to the change by pointing out what is wrong with it. If given enough time, they can build enough resistance to permanently damage the desired change. Second, adopting a discontinuous change often means adopting entirely new structures, processes, and outcomes. Maintaining multiple frameworks requires an extraordinary amount of energy. You and your staff will find it easy to slip back into well-known (but undesirable) patterns of behavior. Finally, making discontinuous change quickly demonstrates your commitment to the change. If your staff has no reason to question your commitment they will more readily accept the change.

State and then evaluate the proposed change. Enacting a change is not possible if you don't know the change you seek and how it will affect your team. Table 13-1 provides a structure for evaluating and implementing a proposed

TABLE 13-1   Evaluating The Change

Desired Outcome	Motivation	Modifications to Current		Monitoring Mechanism
		Structures	Processes	

change. Begin by placing the desired change in the first column as an outcome to be achieved. In the second column describe your motivation. This will help you in communicating the change to those most affected by it. In the third and fourth columns state the modifications to current structures and processes. In the fifth column, state the mechanism you will use to monitor progress toward achieving the change. Avoid instituting *any* change until you have determined how you will monitor progress.

Table 13–1 focuses on structure, process, and outcome because these components of the framework are most easily changed by managers. However, this table can be modified to address changes in other components of the integrated framework (i.e., values, culture, and/or goals). Simply add one column for each aspect of the framework you wish to modify.

Using this table doesn't have to take a lot of time or be burdensome. To illustrate, here is a sample table regarding a change I enacted at ObjectSpace. When I was first promoted to my present position, ObjectSpace courses did not have instructor guides detailing how each course should be taught. This was not a problem, as there were only two other instructors, and we could easily share such information directly. However, such an unstructured approach could not effectively support the growth goals of the company. Therefore, I decided to introduce the following "change": the preparation of an instructor guide for all ObjectSpace training classes. The table describing this change is presented below. You might notice that some of the structures, processes, and outcomes listed in this table are changes to existing structures, processes, and outcomes, and some are entirely new. This is generally the case with any change, and you may find it useful to organize your table so that changes to existing SPOs versus the creation of new SPOs are differentiated.

Desired Outcome	Motivation	Modifications to Current		Monitoring Mechanism
		Structures	Processes	
All ObjectSpace courses have instructor guides.	1. Provide better value to customers by improving the consistency of course delivery. 2. Share "best practices" among instructors.	1. A template for the contents of an instructor's guide.	1. Modify course creation process to include the creation and review of the manual. 2. As each class is taught, instructors will take notes to "build" instructor guides in an iterative-incremental fashion.	1. Template defined. 2. Instructor guide exists for each course.

"What have you learned or done new this week?"   All too often, we concentrate on the "big win," the dramatic and decisive change "guaranteeing" project success. Brooks [1995] refers to this approach as searching for a magical silver bullet. Your team wins when they are focused on continual improvement, something the Japanese call *kaizen*. This simple question can go quite a long way to promoting an atmosphere of continual, but focused, change.

ADVICE TO DEVELOPERS

It can be easy to feel change is not done *by* you, but instead *to* you. In some cases, these feelings are entirely accurate, and you may have little, if any, input in the change process. At other times, you can have a rather substantial impact, effectively implementing the desired change or killing it. By focusing on the positive benefits of change, you can make certain all forms of change enhance you and the team. The first step is to embrace change.

Embrace change.

Do not die for the cause.

Capitalize on the opportunities presented by change.

Question the motivation for a change.

Embrace change.   "The only constant is change" may be a cliché, but it is still true. Change is inevitable. Learning to embrace change is part of learning to be a professional. I particularly like the description of change provided by John Enright [1984], who compares our receptiveness to change to two twigs floating in a river. The first floats effortlessly in the waters of the spring runoff, occasionally bumping into a rock but slowly and surely gliding toward the future. This twig, and people like it, are comfortable in face of constant change. In contrast, the other twig has become wedged in a rock. Buffeted and battered by other debris and the fast moving current, this twig experiences change as endless pressure. If a person, it would experience severe pain and distress. Which twig best describes your attitude toward change?

Do not die for the cause.   Some changes you support while others you resist. Some you initiate and others you pursue with great passion. What happens when others resist your wonderful idea? One alternative is to wait a bit, until they have had time to support the change of their own volition. Another is modify how you are presenting or proposing the change to gain wider acceptance. A third is to just push harder. This third option is not recommended. Pushing too hard puts you at risk of serious damage to your career, your credibility, and (in extreme cases) your job. Sometimes you just have to accept others are simply not ready or willing to make the change you advocate.

Capitalize on the opportunities presented by change. Change often presents us with opportunities, but these opportunities often have a finite window. Be careful of thinking the opportunities presented by change will always be there—they won't. Sometimes, you may have to embrace a change more quickly than desired to take advantage of the window even though you may feel you are not "ready" for the change. The opportunity will not last forever.

Question the motivation for a change. You have a right to understand the motivation for the change—so ask! You may not agree with the rationale, but you have a right to know.

13.2 INNOVATIONS

Much of the research studying the process of change within organizations has centered on the diffusion of innovations [Rogers 1983]. The goal of these studies is to identify how an individual or organization becomes aware of an innovation and how and why they choose to either adopt or reject it. While there are some differences in how different authors characterize the process by which innovations are diffused, most agree on the basic ideas presented in this section.

> *I became interested in the ideas presented in this chapter when I experienced extraordinary resistance to innovations I had proposed. In general, I mistakenly thought the "benefits" of my "superior way of doing things" would be "obvious." This is probably the most common fallacious belief of change agents (people who advocate the adoption of an innovation), and one that took me a long time to overcome. By reading this section you will gain an understanding of how innovations are diffused. This will increase the likelihood that the innovations you propose are adopted.*

13.2.1 Innovation Structures

Perhaps the most important structure with respect to innovations within organizations is the degree of centralization or decentralization of the innovation process. In a *centralized* approach overall control for deciding which innovations are selected and how they are diffused is centralized in a small number—ideally one—of well-defined teams. In *decentralized* approaches the opposite holds and individual teams decide on their own about which innovations to pursue.

Each approach has distinct advantages and disadvantages. Centralized structures can evaluate innovations quickly by focusing dedicated resources. They can seed the innovation and coordinate the efforts of multiple groups. They can also serve as an essential linking mechanism between groups that may otherwise not communicate. Centralized systems suffer from an inability to encourage the slight modifications to innovations known as *reinventions* often required before an innovation is considered successful. This is an especially important consideration in the computer industry, as software developers are much more likely to accept an innovation if they perceive they have had some control in the decision to adopt it.

Decentralized structures are often more effective at finding innovations and reinventing them as needed. A centralized and usually corporately supported team does not face the project pressures of a decentralized team. Because of this, the decentralized team often discovers innovations out of sheer necessity. Such teams have a vested interest in making the innovation work. Decentralized structures suffer from a lack of sharing of information and often needlessly duplicate work. While they are on opposite ends of the spectrum, both structures have been found to be effective in fostering the adoption of innovations. A combination of both approaches is ideal.

The second most important structural aspect relating to innovation are the communication structures educating and influencing individuals to adopt (or reject) the innovation. These structures include the communication channels by which the individual first becomes aware of the innovation and the ongoing communication structures by which the individual increases their awareness of the innovation. Of course, the centralization or decentralization of the diffusion process forms one kind of communication structure, but there are others.

Of special importance is the degree of homophily versus heterophily in the communication structure. *Homophily* is the degree to which individuals share attributes such as beliefs, education, social status, and the like. *Heterophily* means the opposite: Individuals don't share as many attributes. One particularly interesting finding in diffusion research concerns communication effectiveness. In general, while more effective *communication* occurs between individuals who are homophilus, more effective *diffusion* occurs between individuals who are heterophilus.

This makes sense. Homophilus people tend to read the same magazines, surf the same Web sites, and value the same things. Heterophilus people read *different* magazines, surf *different* Web sites, and value *different* things. Heterophilus communication has the greatest potential for exchanging *new* information. The greater the difference, the greater the potential.

The accessibility of opinion leaders and change agents is another important structural aspect of innovations. Respected leaders have a significant impact of the decision to adopt or reject an innovation. Similarly, interaction with change agents (e.g., sales engineers from vendor companies, people who believe in the innovation, educators, or writers) can provide substantial influence in the adoption process. The greater the number of people who tell us an innovation is wonderful, the greater the likelihood we will believe them and adopt the innovation. This effect is magnified when we trust their opinion of the innovation.

Communication channels are not the only aspects of structure impacting innovations. Structures can also be created to ensure individuals and organizations evaluate the innovation in a thorough manner. Examples of such structures can be found in the research and development groups found in many large organizations in which innovations are systematically examined in the context of the perceived needs of the organization. Through this structural device we can ensure the decision to adopt or reject the innovation is a good one.

13.2.2 The Innovation Evaluation Process

The adoption process begins when an individual first becomes aware of an innovation and ends when the decision is made to adopt or reject the innovation. It can happen quickly or slowly, but usually proceeds through the following stages (see Figure 13–2) [Rogers 1983; Mackie 1988].

◆ *Perceived problem.* An individual perceives a problem and initiates a search to find a solution. Initial awareness of an innovation often occurs as a result of this search. Knowing you have a problem is an optional step. Many of us simply read magazines looking for "new things" without necessarily understanding what problem the "new thing" can successfully solve. For example, when I was learning C++ I read about *many* powerful language features without really knowing what problems they solved most effectively. It has only been over time that I have found a good use for many of these features.

◆ *Awareness.* An individual becomes aware of an innovation through internal or external information sources. As discussed above, two kinds of structure strongly influence awareness. The first is the degree of centralization in evaluation structures. The second is the degree of heterophily in the communication structure.

◆ *Knowledge acquisition.* The individual or team engages in knowledge acquisition to obtain the necessary information to make an informed decision regarding the innovation. Several factors influence this process, including predisposition to adopt or reject the innovation, motivation to evaluate the innovation, depth of knowledge required, and amount of time allocated to the knowledge acquisition process.

◆ *Evaluation.* The innovation is evaluated along a number of dimensions, including compatibility with existing structures, processes, and outcomes, complexity, cost, relative advantage over the status quo, and ability to backtrack from the change should it prove, in the long run, ineffective. *Persuasion* is the process whereby a change agent promotes the advantages of the innovation with respect to these factors. It is an especially important aspect of the evaluation process.

◆ *Decision.* The outcome of the evaluation process is the decision to adopt or reject the innovation.

Not all adoptions or rejections are created equal. Teams often exhibit a special kind of adoption called *compliance*, in which an innovation formally thrust upon them by management is apparently adopted but little used, and, if possible, quickly discarded. This happened to Kris, a manager of a C team who unilaterally decided his team should switch to C++. His staff apparently complied with his request by purchasing a C++ compiler but in reality rejected it by continuing to develop in C.

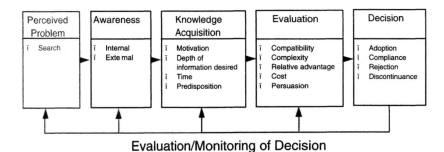

Evaluation/Monitoring of Decision

Figure 13–2   The Innovation Evaluation Process

The decision is not the final stage in the process. Feedback loops (as shown in Figure 13–2) exist from later stages to earlier stages. Even if an innovation is initially rejected, we are forever changed, for once aware, it is impossible to become "unaware" (although we can effectively accomplish this by forgetting).

Diagramming this process gives it a certain structure. This structure, in turn, provides the support necessary for effective decision making. Suppose you are interested in using a new database on your current project. Ask yourself: What problems do I have with the current database? What sources of information, both internal and external, are available to help make the decision? How much time do I have to make the decision? What are specific factors most important in the evaluation decision? and so on.

Finally, the evaluation process takes place in the context of the current values, culture, and goals of the larger organization. Organizations placing a high degree of emphasis on the adoption of innovations such as 3M or Hewlett-Packard generally experience more innovation. It is not just that such companies have more structural support for innovations. It is that innovations are supported across every component of the integrated framework.

13.2.3 Tools, Techniques, and Interrelated Outcomes

The initial adoption of the innovation should be given special consideration for it is here the impact on the other components of the frameworks can be traced. Managing the initial adoption well ensures that the longer lasting effects on existing SPO frameworks are desirable.

Tools are structural innovations. *Techniques* are process innovations. Their differences are most easily demonstrated when one first considers the initial effects of the innovation.[1] Tools impact the framework by changing the processes by which outcomes are generated (e.g., by allowing them to be created more efficiently, easily, or completely). Changes to processes in turn produce a change to outcomes, shown

---

[1] The structures, processes, and outcomes described in this section *are not* the structures, processes, and outcomes associated with the diffusion of innovations. Instead, they are the structures, processes, and outcomes *affected* by the innovation.

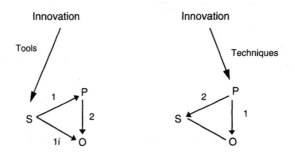

Figure 13–3   Impact of Tool and Technique Innovations in the SPO Framework

as 2 in the right side of Figure 13–3. Tools can also change outcomes, shown as 1' in Figure 13–3.

Techniques first impact the framework by producing current outcomes in new ways, usually in the context of existing structures. Once the technique has been proven successful structure is changed to support the technique more effectively. An example of a technique change is the decision to adopt design patterns. Initially, the team will use design patterns within the dictates of their current structures. In the long run, this technique will be made more effective if structures are modified or created to support it, perhaps by providing templates that developers can use to create their own patterns.

This model is based on the idea innovations are initially adopted because of perceived desirable effects on outcomes. This does not imply knowledge *of* the innovation precedes knowledge of *how* the innovation will impact the outcome. A developer can attend a class and learn a new language feature without knowing how this technique can be applied. Only later, when a tentative outcome seems appropriate for the new technique is it tried. Indeed, the outcome may not always relate to the needs of the team (e.g., a manager adopts a tool because she thinks it will enhance her power), but the model presented here states some form of desirable outcome exists before adoption of the innovation.

A tool or technique is *institutionalized* when all components of the framework have been modified to support and maintain the innovation. Institutionalization means the innovation is no longer perceived as new. It is an indistinguishable part of how the team works.

13.2.4 The S-Shaped Curve of Adoption

Suppose you invent a new technique for using C++. How quickly will the world beat a path to your door? Will every C++ developer simply begin using the innovation overnight? Of course not! We know the rate of adoption is slowed by such things as the time it takes to communicate its value, the evaluation process, and the like.

Still, understanding the rate of adoption is important for at least two reasons. First, adopting an innovation too early or too late loses money. Adopt too early and

you may fall victim to the marketing hype of the latest vendor promising the next
"silver bullet" to fix all your development woes. Adopting too late loses money. Suppose the innovation isn't the silver bullet promised by the vendor but it does help reduce development costs. The longer you wait the more money you spend.

Second, when proposing an innovation it is important to know how early you
are relative to other adopters. The earlier you adopt the less likely you can rely on
others for help. In effect, you become a trailblazer. Adopting later means you can ask
others for help.

Countless numbers of studies have found the adoption of an innovation follows the S-shaped curve shown in Figure 13–4, with consistent groupings of adopter
categories [Rogers 1983]. The curve changes shape depending on the innovation: It
can be more or less steep, more or less high. The differences between categories are
also not perfectly defined, but they do represent generalizations accurately characterizing the willingness and timing of adopting an innovation.

1. *Initiators.* The very first individuals to adopt an innovation are the initiators.
   Such individuals usually have greater contact with the inventors and the re-
   sources necessary to sustain themselves during the adoption of the innovation.
   Such resources are critically important should the innovation fail.

2. *Early Adopters.* Early adopters are the early riders of the curve. They tend to
   be more respected than the initiators for they are viewed as slightly more conservative. Early adopters are often key predictors of the success of the innovation. If they can demonstrate its utility the innovation is likely to be accepted.
   If they can't, it's likely to be rejected. Early adopters tend to be more educated
   and have a fairly high degree of heterophily in their personal communication
   networks.

3. *Early Majority.* Close on the heels of the early adopters are the early majority.
   As you can expect, these individuals are slightly more conservative than either the innovators or the early adopters. This is not necessarily bad, for this

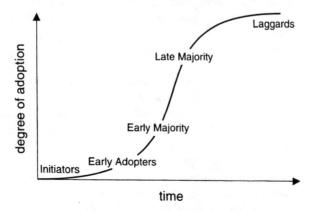

Figure 13–4   The S-Shaped Curve of Adoption

portion of the curve is often when the price/performance associated with the innovation becomes most favorable. The earliest of the early majority often finds the greatest advantage.

4. *Late Majority.* The late majority are reluctant to adopt an innovation, preferring tried and true mechanisms for dealing with problems. In fact, they may only adopt under significant economic pressure. Adopting this late in the process produces minimal competitive advantage.

5. *Laggards.* Individuals who wait the longest to adopt an innovation are characterized as laggards. In general, they have the lowest social and economic status of all adopter categories. By adopting so late they derive little, if any, economic benefit from the innovation.

What are some of the some of the reasons an individual would become an initiator rather than a laggard, or part of the early majority as opposed to the late majority? One motivation might be their general predisposition to innovative behavior as measured by the KAI. While important, our personality is less of an influence than previously thought, as Foxall [1994] found *both* innovative *and* adaptive people (as measured by the KAI) initiate the adoption process.

Still, some innovations are adopted more quickly than others. Compare the rate of adoption of Smalltalk, Visual Basic, and Java. While these languages are generally targeted toward different kinds of applications, there has been a substantial difference in their rate of adoption. If KAI cannot explain the difference in their S-shaped curves, what can?

Several things. First, innovations are adopted primarily because of their perceived effects on current problems. You might quickly adopt a new release of your favorite compiler in the middle of a project, especially if this compiler provides a much-needed bug fix or new feature. If the new release fails to address any specific problems, it is far safer and cheaper to stick with the current compiler.

Second, innovations (by definition) change existing structures, processes, and outcomes. Even the most innovative (as measured by the KAI or otherwise) team cannot withstand a continuous stream of new structures or processes: Outcomes will vary widely out of control.

Third, we cannot discount the impact of marketing hype. Some innovations, such as a new language, are adopted far more quickly than others because they receive more press. Alternatively, the cost to adopt the innovation may appear particularly small, thus enhancing the likelihood of adoption.

Fourth, adopting certain kinds of innovations requires substantial amounts of capital. Every developer I know, and all of their management, would *always* like to have the absolutely fastest machine on the market. Few of us rarely do, for continually purchasing the very fastest machine would put most companies out of business!

This last point brings out one of the most interesting results of classical diffusion research currently undergoing substantial reexamination in the computer industry. Generalizing substantially, most diffusion research shows the economic benefits accruing to the initiators and early adopters creates a self-perpetuating cycle. Adopt-

ing early provides a significant economic advantage, which provides the capital necessary to adopt future innovations, and so forth. However, this cycle does not quite
apply in the computer field, especially with respect to hardware. Adopting somewhat
later allows you to obtain more favorable price/performance characteristics.

Consider the price of personal computers, where rapid price drops following
the introduction of innovative new technologies are commonplace. It is often more
cost-effective to purchase the technology *one* cycle *behind* the bleeding edge. The
same effect can be noted in the software field for different reasons. Adopting too
early may put you at too much risk (e.g., buggy compilers, immature tools, and so
forth). Being an initiator means there are fewer well-known structures supporting
you in using the innovation.

The innovativeness of the team cannot be examined outside the context of the
current project and larger organization. Even the most innovative team is ill advised
to adopt a major innovation (such as a new programming language or method) in the
middle of a project. The simultaneous change to structures, processes, and outcomes
is too great a shock to the system. Taken together, this suggests an effective strategy
is to examine innovations as early as possible but adopt when appropriate.

13.2.5 Making Innovations Happen

The innovation process described thus far has focused on making the decision
to adopt or reject an innovation. Suppose you decide to adopt. What do you do
know? One option is to simply push the innovation on others. As a manager, you
could unilaterally mandate everyone adopt the new tool or technique. As a developer, you could rant and rave about the innovation, cajoling, pressuring, and coerc-
ing others to adopt. Unfortunately, pushing the innovation will generate resistance.
Push hard enough and long enough and those around you will universally reject any
change your propose.

Is there a better alternative? Certainly. The adoption of an innovation, as described earlier, is facilitated by education, communication, general predisposition, a
known (or at least desired) outcome, and a plan for getting there. Of all these, the
most important first step is a clear understanding of *why* you are adopting the innovation (or making a reorganization, as described in the next section). I'm not looking
for a long-winded justification. I am looking for a simple and concise statement of
your motivation.

The next step is to create a plan for adopting the innovation. The complexity of
the plan should match the perceived magnitude of change. Purchasing ten licenses of
a new compiler requires a much simpler plan than adopting a CASE tool. Recall
from Chapter 3 that future perfect thinking helps in the planning process. Apply the
technique by imaging a fully institutionalized innovation: What steps were necessary
to make this happen?

The final step is enacting the plan—the actual adoption of the innovation. Be
prepared to accept some glitches in the process. Remain committed to your decision, but be willing to make midcourse corrections. Ideally, the evaluation process

identified the major glitches, but it probably didn't find all the minor ones. Put another way, expect some surprises, but no shocking revelations!

ADVICE TO MANAGERS

The problem isn't finding innovations—simply read any popular computer magazine and the number of innovations will startle you. The problem is balance: incorporating innovations rapidly enough to keep your team maximally effective without overloading them with change.

> Perform an economic analysis.
> Hire people who like change if you want change.
> Time innovations to match project milestones.
> Start small.
> Encourage reinventions.

Perform an economic analysis.   As described above, adopting an innovation too early or too late can cost you. Your goal should always be to adopt when the innovation is most economically feasible given the context of your work environment. This is tempered by two things: your personal preference for structure as measured by the KAI and your personal preference for change. More adaptive individuals tend to adopt innovations optimizing their current environment. More innovative individuals tend to adopt innovations substantially transforming their environment. An adaptive manager might adopt new versions of an existing compiler, while a more innovative manager might want to change compiler vendors or even change languages. But just how quickly should these changes occur? This is based on personal preferences for change. Just because you are innovative does not necessarily mean you are comfortable with a fast-paced, continually changing environment.

By now, I hope I've got you thinking: Am I being too adaptive? Too innovative? Am I adopting innovations too slowly? Too quickly? Is there a way to help make these decisions without my personal preference being the sole driving force? I don't think there is a way to completely avoid personal preferences and I don't think you should try. However, I do think you should temper your preferences by performing a simple economic evaluation of the evaluation as part of the evaluation process. Consider the following:

- Training
- Capital requirements
- License fees
- Impact in other departments
- Opportunity cost by *not* adopting the innovation

Certainly, this is not an exhaustive list. It will, however, help you get started in making a more objective decision to adopt the innovation. Of course, any analysis is based on assumptions, and your personality and willingness to adopt an innovation will motivate your assumptions. However, by stating your assumptions in black and white, you open your decision-making process to yourself and your peers.

> *One project team I worked on used an economic analysis to obtain a much sought after outcome. At the time, we were building a Novell LAN-based client-server system using the C programming language on 80386-based computers. 80486-based computers had just been announced, and our team was dying to acquire the new technology. When first presented to management, our request was denied. The budget simply did not allow for the purchase of new computers. Rather than accept defeat, one of the members of the team timed a standard compile on an 80386-based PC and again on an 80486-based PC. He then calculated the payback period of purchasing the new computers (with depreciation, of course) based on the differences in these times. He also factored in the impact on the schedule. The results clearly demonstrated purchasing the computers more than paid for themselves in increased productivity. Of course, it certainly helped our cause to have a senior division manager who was extremely innovative (as measured by the KAI).*

Hire people who like change if you want change.   Individuals vary tremendously in their overall approach to change. If you want innovation, hire it.

Time innovations to match project milestones.   Within any project there are well-punctuated events providing ample opportunities for the adoption of an innovation. Taking advantage of such events minimizes the disruptive effects of the innovation and maximizes its benefits. The best such event is the completion of a milestone. For example, I'd be very unwilling to introduce a new compiler two weeks before the shipment of a new release, but very willing two weeks after.

Start small.   Perhaps the biggest reason innovations fail is attempting too much too quickly. Starting small provides three important benefits. First, it minimizes the overall impact of change. Second, it encourages the reinvention process, which helps make certain the innovation is right for your environment. Third, it minimizes risk. Should the innovation prove unsuccessful, starting small means it can be more easily removed. Starting small *does not* mean you are uncommitted. It means you are committed wisely.

Encourage reinventions.   The degree of acceptance of an innovation within the team is often determined by the degree of reinvention occurring in the adoption process. Encourage your staff to "reinvent" the innovation as necessary in the context of their environment.

ADVICE TO DEVELOPERS

You are constantly bombarded with innovations. The question is: What are you going to do with them? What is their impact on your career? Surfing the wave of innovations can be fun—if you approach it as part of the normal part of your career.

> Learn your personal preference toward innovations.
>
> Dress and act appropriately.
>
> Kaizen is your job.
>
> Increase heterophily in your communication network.
>
> Reskill.

Learn your personal preference toward innovations. How effectively do you embrace innovations? Answering this question in an honest, straightforward way is an important step to learning how to manage innovations effectively. Suppose you tend to be an extremely conservative individual working in a team full of initiators. More specifically, for any given innovation, you would characterize yourself as being a member of the early majority or the late majority, while everyone else seems to be far earlier on the curve. Continually resisting their behavior is taxing on both you and them. Yet, simply going along with their desire to adopt is difficult on you. Is there a happy medium? Yes. Rather than resisting innovations proposed by more innovative members of the team, redefine your role to help identify when adopting the innovation is most effective.

To illustrate, let's assume your are in the middle of a project when one of the more innovative members of your team proposes the adoption of a new programming language. (She has heard through the grapevine this language is going to be recommended by the corporate technology group and wants to get a jump on other teams.) While this may appear to be an exciting proposition to her, to you it appears as a catastrophic event! Rather than rejecting her proposal outright, instead evaluate and guide the innovation to acceptance at an appropriate phase of the project. In this sense you can act as a flywheel, dampening ill-timed innovations until they make sense while making certain innovations are introduced at a sustainable rate.

Dress and act appropriately. One of the biggest mistakes made by initiators and early adopters is to focus solely on the technical merits of the innovation. Innovations are rarely accepted or rejected purely on technical grounds. Basic human emotions play a huge part in the process. Many times an innovation is rejected because the individual proposing it is perceived as too young, brash, or harsh in their criticisms of the status quo. Any of these perceptions leads decision makers with the authority and power to formally adopt the innovation to reject it for the wrong reasons.

One way to combat this is to adopt an appearance and personal style appropriate to both the innovation you propose and the adopter audience. *This does not mean you should dress in a formal, conservative manner, or speak in some stilted, formal style.* It does mean you should represent yourself in a way appropriate to the people you are trying to influence.

I learned about the importance of appearances while watching a senior executive in charge of a research group designed to create innovations continually fail because of his personal style. Certainly he dressed well. And, he knew both the problem and how the outcomes created by his team could help solve it. The problem was his hostile style. He would effectively tell potential adopters they were stupid. His organization had invented not only a better way to solve their problems, but also the only way. The response? At best, compliance (he was, after all, a senior executive). Most of the time outright rejection (very few people I know enjoy being told they are stupid).

Kaizen is your job.   Acting as a professional requires you to continually assist your team in adopting the best possible practices for creating software. *Kaizen* is a Japanese word emphasizing the adoption of new and better techniques for creating well-defined outcomes. For example, perhaps you are a C developer and have just read an article describing how to best organize source code files for efficient compilation. If you think your team could benefit from these techniques, you should work to adopt the innovation.

A good way to do this is to privately try the techniques in the article on the existing source files to ensure they work. Once this has been confirmed, summarize how the team could benefit most from these techniques in a manner appropriate for your environment (this is the "reinvention" step referred to earlier). Then, instead of "demanding a change" because you are "right," simply demonstrate the effectiveness of the new technique to a few members of your team. Taking a low-key approach helps minimize resistance to the change. The whole process can be done informally—no elaborate meetings or four-page memos are needed.

Increase heterophily in your communication network.   One of the easiest variables to change to increase your awareness of innovations is to expand the heterophily of your communication network. For example, once a month go to lunch with someone not directly in your team or read a magazine not in your immediate line of work. Another approach is to periodically read different Internet newsgroups.

Reskill.   While keeping abreast of *all* the innovations in the computer industry is impossible, it is important that you maintain awareness of some of them, particularly in your specific field of expertise. Why? There are always specific discontinuous points of change we must decide to embrace or reject. Continual rejection is not an option, so the question becomes: When must I reskill to maintain my career? Some of the factors influencing this decision include the amount of work necessary to reskill, the perceived benefit to your career, and the availability of the tools necessary to reskill.

In some ways, this advice is a brief recap of Chapter 6. However, given the importance of staying current and the difficulty in making the reskilling decision, it should be addressed again in the context of change. Everyone faces this decision. As I was writing this book I learned of three major programming languages I had never heard of before. One of these languages seems important enough to learn, so I have decided to invest the time to do so. Did I make the right decision? Should I have instead increased my knowledge about distributed computing or object-oriented databases? I don't know. As a wise person once said, predicting anything is difficult, especially the future. More important than making any single decision is your commitment to assessing your skills in the context of the innovations of our industry and reskilling when necessary. It is easy to make a slightly less than perfect decision. The only bad decision is the decision to never reskill.

13.3 REORGANIZATIONS

Imagine you are a patron of the arts and have decided to sponsor the production of a new play. The director has been chosen. The initial cast is ready to begin rehearsal. The premiere is three months away. Consider all the things that must be done for a successful premiere. Costumes and scenery must be created. An entire marketing campaign must be initiated. Tickets and programs need to be designed and printed. But are these what make the play successful?

Of course not. The primary success of the play is a thought provoking and entertaining script performed by skilled actors. Assume the script *is* sound—it is an intense story about the effects of the Internet in looking for a mate. This means the primary success of the play is left to the director and the cast. How well they learn to work together will by and large determine the success of the play. But how will they do this? Will the cast learn to work together in a predictable manner? If so, can we prepare for and manage these changes?

Any team, from the cast in the play described above to a high school football team or your favorite software development team faces two kinds of change. The first concerns the changes in and among the members of the same team over time. The second concerns changes to the composition of the team. This section describes these two reorganizations in detail.

13.3.1 Team Life Cycles

Teams form, establish communication, coordination, and leadership patterns, and eventually dissolve in a fairly predictable manner. Collectively, this process can be referred to as the *team life cycle*. It is characterized by the following five stages [Tuckman 1965; Scholtes 1988].

1. *Forming.* The team is formed and given their assignment. Team members grapple with determining the group's focus and orientation, learning how each can contribute to the overall solution, and understanding the problem. The forming stage tends to be chaotic and can appear to be quite unfocused. Lengthy, abstract, and oftentimes irrelevant discussions are common. Feelings associated with the project at this time include excitement, optimism and pride, but also fear and anxiety about completing the project on time. Organiz-

ing the team according to familiar structures and processes can reduce the chaos.

2. *Storming.* The team deals with issues of power, control, and authority. The appropriate distribution of work is the primary issue. During this stage progress is made toward the solution, but there are many "false starts." Creativity is often highest in the earliest part of this stage as the team is unencumbered with past ways of looking at the problem; there are few structures in place, so there are few restrictions on approaches.

3. *Norming.* A team enters the norming stage with preliminary structures, leadership patterns, and knowledge of each other. Normative behaviors, including communication patterns, are solidified, helping to establish the culture of the team. The formation of the collective mind is well underway. The problem, and how it is to be solved, is relatively well understood. The team has a sense of direction: They know where they are going and have a reasonable understanding of how they are going to get there. They begin to "jell."

   With cultural issues resolved, the team works on the problem. Productivity increases sharply as assignments are identified and distributed. Promising outcomes are selected for further refinement, and structures and processes supporting the generation of these outcome become more prominent.

4. *Performing.* The team is operating at peak capacity. Energy is high, especially in projects based on an iterative-incremental process model, for by now the first iteration is working (albeit in a simple manner). The project can be characterized as "fun," and there is a close, personal attachment to the success of the team. Ideally, the iterative-incremental approach keeps the team in the performing stage for the duration of the project.

5. *Dissolving.* The team is disbanded for any number of reasons. The project is completed. It is stopped because of a loss of funds or the loss of a corporate sponsor. The team is deployed on a new assignment. Unless the dissolving stage is managed properly there is a possibility for tension and strife and a lack of closure.

Referring to the analogy of the play, when the cast is formed, their first performances are likely to be quite poor. Indeed, their performance is *expected* to be poor, even *if* the script is known and they are all accomplished actors. Why? They have not yet learned about one another well enough to engage in a command performance. Moreover, the manner in which the director wishes the actors to prepare and perform are not well known. The same can be said for any newly formed software team. Even *if* all the developers know the method, they must still learn how to apply the method on this project. And, they must learn how the project manager wants the project run. It takes time and energy for any team to achieve the potential motivating its creation.

This description has purposely focused on an ideal life cycle. This is not always achieved in the real world. For example, an especially disruptive developer can inhibit the creation of beneficial team norms or motivate the creation of a poor one. Similarly, when a team is faced with an impossible deadline, they are likely to be characterized as lethargic instead of energetic during the performing stage. Finally, only the smaller subteams of a very large team may go through these stages as a group.

The chief advantage of this model is that it provides us with a way of understanding reorganizations within any team over time. Figure 13–5 illustrates this idea graphically. When the team is first formed (on the left), any communication pattern can be said to exist. Leadership is distributed, and coalitions have not formed. Over time, leadership and communication patterns emerge. It is this emergence that enables the team to operate at maximum efficiency and capacity.

As an instructor I have the opportunity to watch the team life cycle time and time again. Given an assignment, I watch teams form, establish coordination and leadership patterns, and work on classroom projects. One interesting result is that coalitions tend not only to form around mutual interests, but also around mutual understandings. This can negatively impact performance, especially on projects adopting an iterative-incremental process model, because once a coalition is convinced they understand the problem, they usually do one of two things. First, they want to skip process steps of the method. Specifically, once the problem is thought to be understood they try to skip analysis and design and move to implementation. Second, and much worse, the coalition who thinks they understand tends to communicate ineffectively (if at all) with the coalition who doesn't. Communicating what you know is hard, especially when you think the other person just doesn't "get it."

In both the classroom and a project this can have a disastrous effect. To combat this, I ask if everyone in the team understands the intended implementation. If they answer yes, I ask a member of the coalition I think does not understand the problem and/or the proposed solution to begin coding. If they begin and proceed to a correct implementation, then I was wrong in my assessment—which is fine by me. Usually they are forced to admit they don't understand the solution (which is also OK) at which point I direct the students in the "fast" coalition to explain their solution to the "slow" coalition. In the process, both coalitions learn what the "fast" coalition overlooked, forgot, or otherwise incorrectly solved. These problems were only corrected with the aid of the "slow" coalition. More generally, this illustrates that the more shared the outcome is, the greater our effectiveness as a group.

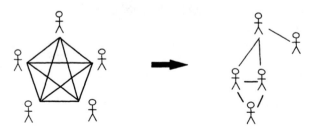

Figure 13–5   Reorganizations over Time

13.3.2 Entrances and Exits

Both managers and developers must learn to deal with the effects of a changing team membership as there is a natural buildup of personnel on most projects. As described in the last chapter, Norden [1958] found that the acquisition and utilization of personnel on research and development projects followed a Rayleigh curve. Putnam [1976, 1978] confirmed these results for software development projects and found that the maximum number of developers usually occurs during system testing and final product release. We start small in requirements and continue to add developers during analysis, design, implementation, and verification. In addition, not all developers are associated with each phase: Analysts come and go, as do other people in the project. The second major cause for changing personnel is turnover. A turnover rate of 10 percent to 20 percent is not uncommon for small organizations; for larger organizations, turnover rates of 30 percent to 55 percent have been reported [Tanniru 1981; Bott 1982]. The third major cause of a changing team membership is the termination of employment.

Just how much change in the composition of the team is normal? In other words, how quickly can you grow the team? What rate of turnover is normal? Is there a minimum turnover rate considered beneficial? What about terminations—when are they appropriate?

Answering these questions is quite difficult because they rely on so many other factors. I'll address the easiest one first. Terminations are usually the last step in a multistep process aimed at keeping an individual. In other words, most employers strive to keep an employee as long as possible and will only terminate employment for one of several basic reasons (e.g., repeated failure to perform the duties of the job even after coaching and training; repeated violation of company policy; illegal activity; extremely disruptive behavior, and so forth). The bottom line is that managers tend to keep developers far longer than we should. In the long run, this is actually good. It is far better to pull out all the stops to keep an employee rather than terminating their employment too early. While termination can have a net-positive effect, they are undeniably the singularly most disruptive reorganization.

Turnover can be neutral, normal, or abnormal. Neutral turnover has nothing to do with the project (e.g., a developer leaves because his spouse has been transferred to a new job in a different state or he retires). Normal turnover is motivated by the effects of different phases in the project or the explicit decisions made by managers as they develop an employee. An example of normal turnover occurs near the end of the project as analysts and designers are placed in new assignments. Another example includes the manager who agrees to let a star developer become the architect of a new system. In the short run the manager experiences turnover, but in the long run everyone benefits.

Abnormal turnover is a turnover caused by poor management. Examples of poor management leading to abnormal turnover include allowing incompetent developers to join the team through poor hiring practices, impossibly difficult "death march" schedules, failing to develop employees; micromanagement, and managerial incompetence.

Many developers rightly flat-out refuse to work for someone who is not technically competent.

Notice that abnormal, normal, and neutral turnover have *no correlation* to a specific turnover rate. A loss of 1 employee in a team of 100 could be any of the three. However, the specific turnover rate is a good *indication* of normal or abnormal turnover. In general, the higher the rate the greater the chance it consists of abnormal turnover.

Reorganizations associated with the growth of the team are of special importance to managers and developers given the time-tested advice found in Brooks's law [1995]. But how quickly can new developers be added to the project? Abdel-Hamid and Madnick [1991] estimate one new member can be added for every three *fully productive* full-time existing members of the team. This means if you start with two people you can *at most* safely add one new person to the team. And, if it takes six months for them to become fully productive, you shouldn't add another new team member for another six months. I'm not certain these ideals hold in the real world, and quite often the best advice for a rapidly growing team is to grab a good person whenever you can! Still, grabbing more than you need or more than the team can productively handle is a problem. Idle resources are not neutral—they can actually cause negative productivity.

A change in the composition of the team, especially those associated with adding new people, presents the following challenges and opportunities.

♦ *Socialization of new team members.* New team members must become socialized into the working practices of the team. The socialization process touches on all aspects of the integrated framework, for becoming a respected and productive member of the team means more than simply learning the structures, processes, and outcomes of the team. It also means learning values, goals, and culture.

   The socialization process is fraught with difficulties. New hires often experience surprise when they find the job they are doing is often quite different than the job advertised. Other problems include inadequate training; confusing messages from managers and existing team members; the social costs of "asking too many questions" (i.e., appearing incompetent); and the transference of the domain knowledge essential for success on any project.

♦ *Decreased productivity.* A new hire is not immediately productive. It can take anywhere between two and nine months for the new recruit to become truly useful on the project. The length of time is dependent on a wide variety of factors, including familiarity with the problem domain, the technology, and the company. It gets worse. Abdel-Hamid and Madnick [1991] estimate the productivity loss on existing members to be roughly 20 percent. Thus, the "double whammy." New people are not fully productive *and* they place a significant drain on existing resources.

♦ *Conflict between new and existing staff.* New staff often enter the team with a different set of skills, including training in what may be considered to be the latest development techniques and programming languages. They may view current structures, processes, and outcomes with disdain and try to motivate innovative change. Existing staff, on the other hand, justifiably wary of the innovations, may discount the suggestions of the new staff. After all, the new developers couldn't possibly know how to solve the problem better—they are completely unfamiliar with the problem domain!

These differences all serve to foster conflict between the new and the old members. The positive effects of this conflict include the opportunity for experts to reexamine their approach to the problem and to guide less-experienced developers in learning the problem domain. The negative effects of this conflict include the formation of coalitions between the "new" and the "old."

♦ *Relief.* The good people learn the bad fairly quickly. In their eyes, when management finally makes the decision to terminate an incompetent developer, it is long overdue. I'm not advocating managers skip any steps in the company-defined termination process. I am asserting the good people feel relief (not joy) when the bad are removed.

♦ *Reformation of communication structures.* Communication structures change both qualitatively and quantitatively during reorganizations.

♦ *Creativity.* Recall teams are often most creative in the forming and storming stages of the team life cycle. Adding a new person provides an opportunity to increase creativity by moving the team back into the forming and storming stages.

Returning to our theater analogy, individual actors and actresses come and go, and when they do, the existing members of the cast are forced to adjust. This can be a period of renewed vigor and excitement, and changing one or two members of the cast can add dazzle to a lackluster crew. Losing the star(s), however, can seriously damage the show.

13.3.3 New Organizational Topologies

As described in Chapter 12, new organizational topologies are often required to adequately support the architecture, growth, and skills of the team over time. Briefly reviewing these results, there are four common motivations for topological change.

The first deals with growth. A small team may start with a circle or simple hierarchy. As the team grows, the simple hierarchy becomes unwieldy and is changed to multiple clusters or even a matrix.

The second deals with internal promotion. It is common for technical leads or first-line managers to be promoted from within. Such an approach changes the topology of the team.

The thirds deals with a change in assignments. When a phase of the project is completed, it is sometimes beneficial to change the topology to take advantage of new assignments.

The final reason is simple: The manager in charge of the topology wants to change it. *Why* they want to change it may not be well known—perhaps they read this book and have decided to scrap the existing hierarchy in favor of a cluster. Maybe they just want to try something new. In any case, changes in topologies are common.

ADVICE TO MANAGERS

As the director in the software development play, your job is to guide your cast to a peak performance. Beginning with the team life cycle, there are specific things you can do to help ensure reorganizations achieve this goal. The basic idea is to anticipate the problems associated with each stage and prevent them from occurring.

> Share knowledge when forming.
> Concentrate on structure when storming.
> Rely on culture when norming.
> Keep the team fit.
> Commemorate dissolution.

Share knowledge when forming.   A new team on a new project lacks two important kinds of knowledge. They don't know each other. They don't know the problem. Overcoming the first problem is easier when you help them learn about each other. This is commonly referred to as "team-building" exercises. The objective is to get people together to learn more about each other. One work-related activity I have found effective is resume sharing. Distribute a copy of everyone's resume to everyone else, and organize a meeting to review the results. By reading resumes, we gain insight into the experiences influencing others. Another favorite is an off-site excursion, such as a day spent at a park with developers and their families. There are many others, and with a little effort you can easily create your own.

Concentrate on structure when storming.   The great temptation in the storming stage is to simply let people attack the problem (process) and worry about structure later. Resist this. Paying attention to the structures needed to manage the problem effectively (and support the growth of the team) provides large payoffs in the future.

Rely on culture when norming.   It is no coincidence that the most important aspect of culture—normative behavior—shares a name similar with this stage of team growth. Use all of the advice presented in the chapter on culture to ensure the creation of a progressive, supportive, and functional culture during the norming stage.

Keep the team fit.   One of the first things a fitness professional learns is fitness cannot be "stored." Instead, it must be continually regenerated through regular physical activity. In a similar manner, a high-performing team cannot "store" its performance for a future date. High performance must be continually regenerated through the life of the team. This can become difficult, especially in a project of long duration. Like the director of a play, you must remain vigilant for decreased performance, taking steps to ensure each team member and the team as a whole are operating at peak performance.

There are many clues to waning performance. Deadlines once hit are missed. Error counts show a sharp increase in testing. There is more tension. Disagreements are more difficult to resolve. Complaints about the current project or work environment increase for no easily identifiable reason. Confidence in the ability of the team begins to fade. There is little laughter; no one seems to be having any fun. Whenever you notice any of the above plaguing your team stop what you're doing and examine the situation. Remove the problem and begin again.

Commemorate dissolution.   The projects I remember most favorably had a manager who clearly and explicitly commemorated the completion of the project and the dissolution of the team. On one project it was a simple dinner at the home of the project manager. On another, it was a party for everyone—spouses included. Of course, the project team didn't leave the very next day. Instead, we stayed in place, some of us as long as two months, but we *knew* the project was *finished*. It was time to find a new project. Now I realize these events helped me, and others, reach closure. Without such closure, project members are left wondering if things are really done.

Every team undergoes the reorganizations associated with the team life cycle. Every team must also withstand their share of entrances and exits. There is often unnecessary trauma associated with adding, replacing, and removing personnel. Eliminate this trauma through effective management.

> Identify your turnover rate.
> Strive for stability.
> Add developers carefully to beat Brooks's law.
> Identify the motivation for leaving.
> Keep them as long as you can.
> Interview the right way.

Identify your turnover rate.   As DeMarco and Lister point out in *Peopleware* [1987], you are not even beginning to manage turnover effectively unless you know the rate at which employees leave your organization and the average cost to replace them. Keeping track of these things is a critical metric to improving your team.

Strive for stability.   Nothing can help the project if the team is changing so rapidly it never moves past the forming or storming stages. Stability is critical to the success of any project. Gause and Weinberg have referred to it as the "essential ingredient" for project success [Gause 1989]. The conceptual integrity Brooks describes can only be achieved through stability [Brooks 1995].

Add developers carefully to beat Brooks's law.   Your project is late. What do you do? You've thought about adding more people, but Brooks himself whispers in your ear . . . *"Adding manpower to a late software project makes it later"* [Brooks 1995:25].

While Brooks's law is generally the best available piece of advice for the manager who finds him or herself with a late project, it is, as Brooks himself admits, an outrageous simplification. Recent research by Abdel-Hamid and Madnick [Abdel-Hamid 1991] demonstrates there are many factors to evaluate when considering adding manpower to a late project, including prior experience in the problem domain, the structures, processes, and outcomes of the project, as well as prior knowledge of the current team. They conclude: "Adding more people to a late project makes it more costly, but it does not *always* cause it to be completed later [italics theirs]."

Does this mean you should pitch Brooks' law? *Absolutely not!* First, as Boehm's [1981] cost and estimation models have shown, the relationship between men and months is far from linear. Second, it is hard to add developers in a way to beat Brooks's law. Training must be undertaken, existing staff must be willing to cooperate, new people must be willing to work within existing structures and processes, and the work must be repartitioned. Perhaps the most important aspect of the new developer is finding someone who is willing to work within existing structures. Their arrival in the team is enough of a disruption. The more they want to change, the less likely they will be assimilated quickly and efficiently.

Identify the motivation for leaving.   Request an experience report from everyone who leaves. The purpose of this report is to provide important feedback for you, them, and the organization. Structurally, there are three parts to this report:

1. A summary of what they learned and accomplished. This helps them identify the positive aspects of the experience. It helps you compare what they *think* they accomplished with your own thoughts on the matter.

2. A summary of what you can do to be a more effective manager. Without such feedback, improving your skills as a manager is difficult, at best. Ideally, you will obtain some of this information during the life of the project rather than waiting until the very end.

3. What must be done to improve the effectiveness of the team?

Keep them as long as you can.   Even the most effective, high-performing team is not likely to last forever. Changes in the composition of the team are inevitable for at least three reasons. First, part of achieving high performance is the voluntary "giving up" of certain aspects of our personality. You or I don't complete the assignment on time—the team does. You or I don't make the project successful—the team does. The problem is "you" and "I" get lost. Our individual efforts—which must be considerable—are hidden to the world. Most people can only operate this way for so long before they feel the need to reestablish their uniqueness. Establishing uniqueness contributes to the dissolution of the team.

Second, high-performing teams are intense. While existing members of the high-performing team may enjoy their success, they may also tire of the intensity in the team and/or become bored with the same assignment. Finally, members of successful teams are highly attractive to other managers and companies, and they may be offered positions in other organizations simply too good to refuse.

To see these effects played out on a much grander scale, watch what happens to any professional athletic team. Winning one championship is extraordinarily difficult. Winning two is nearly impossible. Winning three is so rare only a handful of teams in a handful of sports have ever done it.

Interview the right way.   Here is a step-by-step process for hiring a developer. (See Chapter 16 for an in-depth discussion of the hiring process from the perspective of the developer.) Follow these steps *after* your human resources department has done all the preliminaries (screened the resume, contacted the candidate, and so forth).

1. *Assess technical knowledge with a test.* Beginning with simple questions, ask progressively more difficult questions throughout the test. End with questions really testing the boundaries of their knowledge. To reduce test-taking anxiety, let the candidate know the test is designed to assess a wide range of knowledge, and few people are able to obtain a perfect score.

   Customize the test for the specific position. For an implementation developer, the test would focus on the target language. For a GUI designer, the test would focus on specific aspects of usability and GUI design. For an analyst, the test would assess their knowledge of their chosen method, and so on.

2. *Ask them to solve a simple analysis and design problem.* Do they ask the right questions? Do they jump to conclusions? Make the problem harder. How do they react to increasing complexity? What aspects of their design, if any, require change? Is the change appropriately isolated? Do they follow a method? Can they differentiate between analysis and design?

   Don't use just *one* problem. Why? One problem does not provide enough data on their skills. Instead, use three to five problems, each conducted in front of pairs of developers from the existing organization. Is this expensive? Absolutely. Is it worth it? That depends on you. How badly do you want the greatest people?

3. *Review prior work.* Ask them to bring a sample of code for you to review. This lets them know you care about the details. I've had candidates opt out of the entire process on this step!

4. *Give them an implementation test.* Give them a completed problem and ask them to implement the solution in source code. Many developers can know a lot about the language and even generate good designs, but they fail when it comes to actually writing the code. Again, this test has to be customized for the position. When hiring an instructor, I ask them to teach me a specific concept, such as polymorphism or dynamic binding. If they cannot organize and present information clearly, they are probably not suitable for an instructor position.

5. *Ask the right questions.* What do they value? What do they expect? What job do they want to do? Interviewing a developer for one position who wants to do a completely different job is a recipe for disaster. Sure, they may want— even need—the job. But how long will it be before they yearn for a different position?

    As described in Chapter 6, ask how they stay current in their field. What obstacles in other projects have they faced? How were these overcome? Where do you want to go in your career? When? Why?

6. *Schedule a hiring meeting.* Put everyone who interviewed the candidate into the same room and review their performance as a group. The goal is to get as much information as possible before making the final decision. Usually, the decision is clear. Other times it isn't. The only way to make certain you are getting the best is to carefully review *everyone's* feedback.

A strict hiring process has additional benefits. First, it can motivate candidates to work hard to enter the organization. I once hired a candidate who failed his first interview but was so impressed with this process he worked hard and came back for another attempt. He improved his skills substantially and was hired.

Second, a new employee is instantly accepted by his or her peers. And every candidate rejected reinforces the value of the process. Of course this process, like any other, is not guaranteed to be perfect. Candidates will pass even this process, be hired, and then later be let go. However, if you faithfully follow this process you will find you will have to let go far fewer employees than you think, for you will have done a far better job of preventing incompetent developers from joining the organization in the first place.

ADVICE TO DEVELOPERS

Reorganizations are another aspect of the constant change we face in our daily lives. They can be continuous, as described by the team life cycle, or discontinuous, such as a new topology or member of the team. The following is designed to help you capitalize on all reorganizations.

> Participate in the team life cycle.
>
> Maintain focus.
>
> As a "newcomer," ask. As an "old-timer," explain.
>
> Avoid changing what you don't know.

Participate in the team life cycle.   Do you think you are the only person who feels anxious and excited at the beginning of the project? Of course not! All teams pass through the stages described in the team life cycle, and these feelings are quite normal. The worst thing to do is try and skip a stage. Instead, participate, for it is through your participation with the team in such things as team building that the team moves through the life cycle.

Maintain focus.   It is easy to lose focus on your job when you hear of an impending reorganization (e.g., a change in the composition of the team or a new topology). Be careful of this—while it is natural to think of the effects of such a change, it is unnatural to fixate or obsess over the change. In many cases the change is in the future and you have little control over it. It is better to concentrate on your job.

My first job was in an organization experiencing tremendous growth. My most prominent memory of those first few months is one of constant reorganization. New people were hired at a dizzying rate. We seemed to have a new topology every two weeks. I quickly learned to treat reorganizations as just another aspect of work, sometimes interfering with my real job. This was in stark contrast to my initial view on reorganizations. When I was first hired I expected each to produce substantial change.

As a "newcomer," ask. As an "old-timer," explain.   The socialization process can be made substantially easier if new developers join a culture where it is OK to ask questions about the job. This, of course, requires "old-timers" who are willing (and able) to answer these questions.

Avoid changing what you don't know.   Good maintenance developers know it is best to try and minimize the impact of changes to the system. Why? Quite often the motivations of the original designers have been lost over time and you may make a change breaking another part of the system. The same advice applies to new members of existing teams. While you may think of many wonderful new ways to do things, you should be careful of changing the structures, processes, and outcomes of an existing team and avoid changing what you don't know.

14

TEAM-ORIENTED TRAINING

Chapter 6 was devoted to a single theme: Developers should take responsibility for their training. This chapter returns to the more commonly accepted view of training as the responsibility of the organization. This view holds the organization as responsible for not only defining the training required to fulfill a task but also providing it. Defining the training required for a task has an additional benefit: By defining the training required to complete a task, you have largely defined the task. I'll begin by discussing some of the benefits of training and then move on to identifying when and for what purpose training is needed. I'll also discuss some approaches to training consistent with those discussed in Chapter 6.

Chapter Overview

The chapter begins a discussion of the benefits of training in Section 14.1. The discussion then turns to identifying when training is needed in Section 14.2. Section 14.3 reviews the issues of breadth and depth with respect to teams, while Section 14.4 addresses what specific topics and concepts are needed. Section 14.5 concludes with several different approaches to organizing training.

14.1 TRAINING BENEFITS

The primary purpose of training is to provide the skills necessary to perform job assignments. Training in the structures, processes, and outcomes associated with a task enables developers to perform that task more effectively. Consider a developer constructing an object model. First, they need the structural knowledge of what processes are involved in building the model, the order of these processes, and the form and content (i.e., the notation) of the outcomes.

Procedural knowledge is next. That is, "To construct the object model I examine the requirements specification to look, circling nouns and verbs. These are good candidates for objects and their relationships. Then, I examine each object for appropriate attributes." Training in process also contributes to the feeling of teamwork generated when everyone is not only working toward the same goal, but also working toward it in a reasonably similar way.

Training in outcomes is especially important, as they are the only means by which we can communicate. Mintzberg [1992] views training in outcomes as the central mechanism by which coordination is achieved in professional organizations.

There are two other benefits of training. Organizations modeled after military institutions are nearly fanatical about supplying high-quality training (and lots of it) to their people. Why? A soldier in the heat of battle doesn't have time to think about what to do to save his or her life: Either he knows, or he dies. I don't mean to sound overly dramatic, but it is true. Rigorous training in how to respond *immediately* and nearly *without thought* is what enables military personnel to save their lives. Without such training, they can, quite literally, die.

I doubt that this kind of training is needed in your organizations, as few software development projects put developers at risk of losing their life. Still, focusing intensely on training is important for improving productivity. Consider two development teams, one rigorously and thoroughly trained in their method, and the other significantly less trained. Which will be more effective at quickly and effortlessly communicating about the problem? Which will *know* which process step to do next? Which is more likely to implement the system on time and within budget?

Are you looking for some quantitative results? Capers Jones [1995] has found that "companies that provide 10 or more days of training per year have higher annual productivity rates than similar companies that provide none." Goldberg and Rubin [1995] found in a study of 32 projects adopting object technology only 19 were successful; of these, 14 had some form of classroom or formal training.

Qualitative results are important as well. DeMarco and Lister [1987] report organizations who invest heavily in training and retraining programs experience far lower turnover than organizations who don't. Part of this reason is the feeling of loyalty engendered in the employee ("Hmm. If they are willing to invest in me, I must be important. I think I'll stay.") On a personal note, part of the reason I spent ten years at EDS was their investment in my skills, achieved through a very creative mechanism (i.e., although I did not participate in the standard educational program of EDS, it was through their support I received a substantial amount of education).

Beyond training, which is focused on building a specific set of operational skills to accomplish a well-defined task, lies education. Unlike training, education concentrates on building the critical thinking skills necessary to know how and when to apply specific skills. Training helps us get the job done by providing the skills. Education helps us evaluate the problem and select the skills necessary. In general, training precedes education. To illustrate, recall the seven levels of competency defined by

Meiler Page-Jones presented in Chapter 6. Training is required to move from *innocent* to *aware* and is likely to be required again in the move from *aware* to *apprentice*. Once an apprentice, education (and experience) are required to acquire the critical thinking skills characterized by higher competency levels.

14.2 WHEN IS TRAINING NEEDED?

Training is required for a wide variety of reasons, some of which are listed below.

- ◆ *Innovations.* Training is intimately associated with innovations, for many times the *only* way we can take advantage of an innovation is through training. As indicated by the evidence from Goldberg and Rubin cited above, adopting object technology (and more generally, any discontinuous innovation) requires training.
- ◆ *Reorganizations.* Training associated with a reorganization focuses on developing those skills needed for a job. A promotion to a technical lead or first-line manager should include management and leadership training. A move to a different layer of the architecture requires training in the skills appropriate for that layer.
- ◆ *Socialization.* The addition of a new member is a special kind of reorganization and deserves special attention from the training perspective. Such training needs to focus on all aspects of the integrated framework, from the structures commonly used in the organization to its values, culture, and goals. Fortunately, such training is commonplace in large organizations that provide "indoctrination" programs of up to two weeks in length.
- ◆ *Performance Gap.* A *performance gap* occurs when the team fails to meet one or more objectives. The occurrence of a performance gap may indicate a need for training; repeated performance gaps almost certainly indicate such a need.
- ◆ *Growth.* Both training and education are be required to maximize the contributions of each member of the team. The former is required to broaden skills, while the latter is required to deepen them.
- ◆ *Roles.* Training in the skills supporting specific roles is essential. As described in Chapter 12, two kinds of roles are considered especially important. The first concerns the architecture. This kind of training focuses on building the essential skills on which the role is based. The second concerns teamwork. Even these roles can benefit from explicit training.
- ◆ *Periodic Reinforcement.* Periodic reinforcement in all components of the integrated framework is necessary to ensure maximum performance. An example of this is a CPR (cardiopulmonary resuscitation) certification, which must be renewed every year. Periodic reinforcement provides at least four benefits.

    First, periodic reinforcement helps keep everyone fresh by reinforcing which structures and processes produce desirable outcomes.

    Second, it gives you the opportunity to reevaluate current problems from a new perspective. I'm always glad when students tell me *during* class that they have solved a current problem by applying the techniques they've learned in the class.

Third, it provides the opportunity to build your network, get out of the office, and share experiences with other developers. Chances are good they are facing the same problems you are facing—how are they solving them?

Fourth, you get a chance to hear about the "latest and greatest" stuff from instructors who should be continually scanning the literature for just this kind of information. For example, many students take an Object-Oriented Analysis and Design (OOA/D) class *even when they know* OOA/D just to learn about patterns.

Ultimately, training and education are not a one-time occurrence. Both are an integrated aspect of the career of any developer or manager.

14.3 BREADTH VERSUS DEPTH IN TEAMS

Selecting the right amount of breadth and depth for the team is a special challenge. You want enough depth to make certain the required expertise exists and enough breadth so each layer of the system architecture is properly addressed.

Beginning with breadth, define the skills (requisite variety) needed for each architectural layer. Breadth, in this sense, is not based on the hexagonal structures used in Chapter 6. Instead, breadth is determined by the complexity of the architecture. Suppose the architecture consisted of three layers: a graphical user interface, the domain model, and a persistent store. Breadth in this example consists of developers in each layer possessing the appropriate skills.

Depth is determined next by examining those layers of the project considered high risk or essential for success. Recall that absolutely critical layers should be assigned *at least* one developer who has obtained the competency level of journeyman. Training should be provided to ensure each developer reaches the level of apprentice.

It is assumed the domain model is the most critical layer. This means each developer associated with *every other layer* will be trained in the method selected for the project. What is considered the next most critical layer is based on specific project requirements. For example, if project success required a highly usable graphical user interface, I would provide my user interface developers with more training. If, on the other hand, the project involved stringent performance requirements, I would consider advanced language classes. The ultimate goal is to match training breadth and depth to the needs of the project as guided by the architecture.

14.4 WHAT TO TRAIN

There are two main aspects of *what* to train. The first deals with the general knowledge required by all developers who are preparing to use the technology. The second deals with the specific needs of the project and/or architectural layer to which the developer is assigned. This is illustrated in Figure 14–1, which shows a recommended

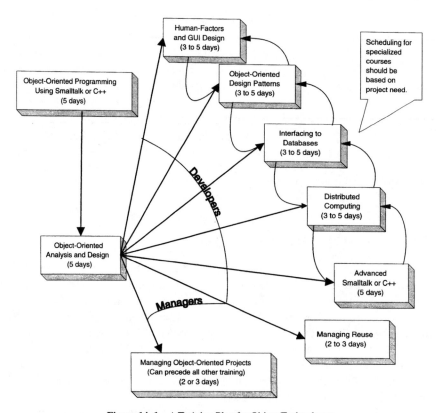

Figure 14–1   A Training Plan for Object Technology

sequence of courses to achieve a specific training objective (in this case, the adoption of object technology).

Examine Figure 14–1 carefully. *Everyone*, developers and managers alike, take the same introductory courses. These consist of the language *followed* by analysis and design. Why have everyone take both courses? Three reasons. First, training everyone—developers and managers alike—facilitates adoption of the new technology. Second, everyone associated with the project begins with a consistent foundation. Third, everyone is exposed to the same body of knowledge in a controlled manner.

Why take the language first? This is a common question. Recall the Sapir-Whorf hypothesis from Chapter 1: Language structures thought. It is impossible to "think" about objects effectively—analyze them or design them—without an internal language to express them. Teaching the language first provides this critically important structure for thought.

Following the two initial courses are courses supporting specific layers of architectures common in most object-oriented systems. There are also courses addressing higher-level, cross-project management issues, such as reuse or patterns. A similar "flowchart" can be created for every project, enabling it to address specific training needs.

14.5 APPROACHES TO TRAINING

There are several ways to organize training. Each has its own advantages and disadvantages, and each may be appropriate at different times given the specific needs of the project. The first two approaches are most appropriate for developing skills in a small number of developers in the context of a specific project.

- ◆ *Personal Initiative.* Each individual is responsible for creating a training plan ensuring the appropriate skills are obtained as outlined in Chapter 6. This approach is not generally recommended. It cannot be measured or tracked to ensure organizational objectives are achieved. Still, in the intense and busy world of software development personal initiative can be an effective *informal* technique for the development of some required skills. Taking advantage of personal initiative from a managerial perspective usually requires the creation of a special assignment exercising or requiring these skills. More generally, training programs are only one-half of the overall development process for any employee. The other half are the assignments designed to exercise skills and further develop the employee by motivating him or her to learn new skills.

  For example, one of my instructors recently expressed a desire to learn more about the Web, and HTML1 in particular.[1] needed another instructor with those skills but couldn't spare the time to develop them. By assigning her the responsibility of maintaining the ObjectSpace Web page devoted to the training department, I was able to take advantage of her personal initiative without providing an extensive amount of more formal training. The approach worked because she is a capable, competent developer. Would I take a similar approach for an entire team? Not likely. However, personal initiative is an effective approach when coupled with well-controlled job-related assignments.

- ◆ *Just-in-Time.* Training is provided for a specific project need as close as possible to the actual need for the skills. The advantage to just-in-time training lies in the retention of knowledge learned in the classroom. Specifically, knowledge decreases rapidly unless it is put to use rather quickly. The primary disadvantage of just-in-time training deals with scheduling. The training you need may not be available when you want it. This motivates seeking training from several different organizations which detrimentally impacts quality and consistency. The difficulties associated with just-in-time training are often too great to make it a viable approach.

The next set of techniques are recommended for organizations currently in the process of making a strategic change in development practices. Recall that a strategic change is the adoption of multiple SPO frameworks designed to meet specific organizational objectives, such as the decision to institute a metrics program or adopt object technology. As both of these are usually viewed as discontinuous changes,

---

[1] HTML stands for Hypertext Markup Language. HTML is interpreted by a Web browser to render a Web Screen.

there is a special need to organize training for all of the teams associated with the project or contained within the organization.

- ♦ *Sheep-dip*. Stage a series of organizationwide courses and shuffle all software engineers, project managers, and so forth, through the series. This can be an effective means for creating initial awareness, but the concepts learned in the course can be rapidly lost if not reinforced through other means (such as consultants or mentors). This analogy, suggested originally by Gerald Weinberg, comes from the approach used by farmers to rid their sheep of various infections by dunking them in a bath of disinfectant.

- ♦ *Apprenticeship*. Used in the context of a single project, a single team finds an outside expert to temporarily join them as a mentor. The mentor guides them in the application of the innovation or strategic change. The advantage of a mentor is their immediacy: They are always there to answer questions. Of course, this limits the practical size of the team, as a single mentor (no matter how skilled) can only handle about five to seven developers effectively.

  There are many potential disadvantages with this approach. The first is the mentor's doing too much of the work. In general, the more work done by the mentor, the less effective the training. The second deals with consistency and quality. Because the mentor is responsible for both formal and informal training, quality can vary substantially from mentor to mentor. Mentorship is most effective when the specific educational goals of the project are outlined as early as possible. Of course, a good mentor can assist with this process.

In addition to these approaches, one additional approach for innovations is highly effective.

- ♦ *Immersion*. A six- to twelve-week intensive "bootcamp" style program introduces a small number of students (five to twelve) to the innovation in the context of a challenging, but solvable, problem. Immersion has *numerous* benefits. Students acquire broad *and* deep knowledge of the innovation in an intensive program. The close setting means the instructor can customize material to meet the specific needs and skills of the student. The small student-to-instructor ratio ensures appropriate use of the innovation is constantly reinforced and allows students the opportunity to ask detailed questions.

ADVICE TO MANAGERS

Your role in training lies in the combination of skills needed for your project as defined by the implementation technology, system architecture, and specific roles created within the team. Because so many of these issues have been discussed in other parts of this book, this section will provide relevant pointers to those sections as necessary.

Use the training hexagon.

Support architectural roles with explicit training.

Plan—and budget—for training.

Avoid thinking of training as a bonus or perk.

Remain aware of the impact training has on overall compensation.

Examine the skill set of the instructor.

Avoid attending classes with your team on technical subjects.

Send an entire team to class at the same time.

Reinforce training as soon as possible.

Keep records.

Choose training based on adult learning theories.

Use the training hexagon.   In Chapter 6, I presented the hexagon in Figure 14–2 as a way of organizing a personalized development program. The same figure can be used to identify the training needed in the team by organizing the skills needed for success. Here are the steps.

1. Add the specific skills required by your project in the second layer of the hexagon. Suppose your current implementation language is FORTRAN and you are in the process of planning the move to C. Place both FORTRAN and C in the second layer of the technical sextant, as you have to make certain you have enough developers skilled in both languages to manage the transition.

2. Determine if the items listed in the second layer are required by all members of the team or just a subset. This helps you pick one of the training approaches described above. If everyone needs it, you have a need for breadth and depth. If only a few people need it, you probably are dealing most directly with a depth issue. In this case, the move to C requires that the entire staff be trained in C, so breadth is required. In addition, it is usually helpful to have a few "gurus" on the staff, so it would be beneficial to identify at least two to four individuals for advanced training. Your training vendor or internal training organization should be able to provide assistance in mapping skills. If they can't, find a new vendor!

Repeating this process for each sextant provides an easy mechanism for organizing the training plan. The bonus is that when finished, you will also have a much deeper understanding of the requisite variety needed for success in the project. This approach can also be used when planning, as it can document the current skill sets of the team and define where additional requisite variety is needed.

I originally developed this hexagon to help provide a structure identifying the overall skills I needed in one project. By making these skills explicit, I realized an unexpected

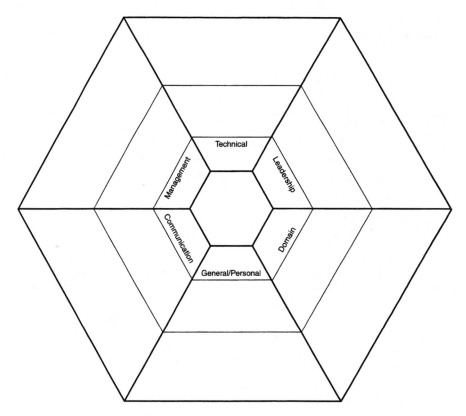

Figure 14–2   Organizing the Requisite Variety Needed for Success

benefit. The diagram identified those areas where the team needed general skills shared by all team members (broad knowledge) and specific skills in a given area (deep knowledge). From there, organizing a training plan and looking for the right team members was a snap.

Support architectural roles with explicit training.   Section 12.4 listed the skills associated with common architectural layers. Make certain your training plan provides the skills identified in Tables 12–3 through 12–8.

Plan—and budget—for training.   Educational opportunities don't suddenly materialize from thin air. Instead, they require planning and budgeting, just like every other aspect of the project.

Budgeting for training can be especially difficult in a large organization, as corporate bean counters find it very easy to slash training budgets at the end of the fiscal year. Find a way to get around this. Send one of your best people to class and have them share the techniques they've learned with others. Of course, don't be stupid. Don't photocopy or otherwise illegally distribute copyrighted material.

Search the Web for on-line courses providing a conceptual introduction to specific concepts before your developers take the class. I firmly believe in the power of traditional Lecture-Style Instruction (LSI). I doubt any computer program will soon manage a student struggling to learn a difficult concept as effectively as I can. However, I also believe in the power of Computer-Based Training (CBT) as a precursor to LSI.

Make friends with an instructor in the corporate training department and have them teach a special class for your team at nights or on weekends. The very first class I ever taught in C programming was organized by a former manager of mine when I was working on another assignment. He didn't have the money in his budget to send his team to a formal class, so he instead asked me to develop a special course just for his team. It sounded like fun, so I secured permission from my current manager to help out, and we had the class. As you can guess, the class was not quite as complete as the class developed by the corporate training department—it was, after all, my first one! However, the class was a success and provided his team with a sound introduction into C programming.

Avoid thinking of training as a bonus or perk.   If the training is required as part of their job, it isn't a bonus. If you pick the training, it isn't a bonus. If *they* pick the training, it *might* be a bonus. The real point, of course, is *not* who "picks" the training. It is developing the attitude that says "I value my people."

Remain aware of the impact training has on overall compensation.   As you invest time and energy in developing your people, they will become more valuable to both you and your competitors. In the long run, a developer who continually improves their skills without a corresponding increase in compensation will be tempted to pursue other job offers.

There are two ways you can respond to this. First, you simply avoid training your people in any way. This is a solution I do *not* recommend. Second, you can give employees who have completed relevant training programs and can demonstrate enhanced job skills compensation commensurate with these skills. If your employee is more valuable to your competitor, why not you?

Examine the skill set of the instructor.   Before sending the team to an entire class, take some time to examine the skill sets of the instructor. Ask for a resume. The single most important quality of an instructor is competence. Do they know the material? Of much less importance is the sheer number of years they have been teaching or whether or not they have a good sense of humor. Certainly humor helps to create a comfortable learning environment, but ultimately you want substance over style. Consider briefly assessing the value system of the instructor, or sharing your own value system with the instructor. The goal is to make certain you are using the very best instructor possible.

Avoid attending classes with your team on technical subjects.
No matter how good your relationship is with your team, attending a class with them

is likely to strain it. Suppose you are clearly more expert in the subject material. Will your subordinates be motivated to ask as many questions? Will they feel completely free to "look stupid" in front of their manager? What about the other extreme? Suppose you don't have any experience in the topic area? Are you willing to ask "dumb" questions in front of your subordinates?

I don't want to dissuade you from taking a technical class with your team. If you have a supportive, open culture where individuals can freely and openly discuss the things they know as well as the things the don't, then great! Attend the class. However, unless you are *certain* you know the disposition of *each* developer toward learning (which increases our vulnerability because we must operate in new and unknown territory), I don't recommend it.

> *An experienced manager attending a technical class can be a real recipe for disaster. I recently taught an introductory Smalltalk class to 18 developers, all from the same company. The manager of a different department attended. It was obvious he was clearly the most capable programmer in the class. Unfortunately, he was a jerk. He had to prove it. He jumped on every question, dominated design teams, and asked countless detailed (and oftentimes irrelevant) questions. I did my best to encourage other members of the class to respond, but it was clear they felt uncomfortable responding while he was in the room. I ended up going to lunch with several students and staying late to make certain they could ask questions in a safe manner.*

Send an entire team to class at the same time.   Not only will it reinforce teamwork, but they will also hear the same thing from the same instructor, improving consistency. This can be an especially good team-building exercise, especially if the team is young.

Reinforce training as soon as possible.   As shown in Figure 6–2, skills decrease very rapidly in lower levels of expertise unless they are quickly reinforced. And, the best possible reinforcement is an assignment requiring the newly learned skills.

Keep records.   Both the SEI-CMM and ISO 9000 quality standards require organizations to track the amount and kind of training provided to students. Even if your organization is not actively pursuing either of these initiatives, keeping accurate records is beneficial for at least four reasons. First, records are required from a practical perspective to ensure everyone has been provided with the necessary training. Second, records facilitate career planning. By knowing what training a developer has taken, you can help them prepare for the future more effectively. Third, records can be converted to visible progress indicators, showing how much of the team has attended the recommended sequence of training. This can provide added motivation to continue training, especially when the training is part of a long-term strategy. Fourth, records can be used when recruiting to show your commitment to the career development of every employee.

Choose training based on adult learning theories.   Not all adult education programs are created equal. Techniques that work effectively for children fail when applied to adults. Simplified training experiences, in which students simply follow the leader, are also ineffective. Adult learning theories address how adults learn most effectively. Here are some of the most important aspects of adult learning theory you should consider when selecting training [Knowles 1984].

- ◆ The training should be based on objective, measurable performance criteria that relate directly to job requirements. Learning objectives should be clearly presented to students so they have the ability to frame the learning in the context of their current knowledge. Students should be given as much flexibility as possible in tailoring the course to meet their perceived needs.

- ◆ A positive, supportive environment is needed so that students do not feel anxious or "exposed" as they learn new skills. This goes far beyond a beautiful classroom with cookies after lunch (although these are nice). The proper environment focuses on all aspects of the learning experience to create physical, emotional, and intellectual comfort.

- ◆ Hands-on, project-based exercises that enable students to apply the learning objectives should form the core of the course. This is also referred to as "Learning By Doing," and for good reason. Unless students apply their new-found knowledge, they are not likely to retain it. At the end of each exercise, positive but thorough and complete feedback is given to the student. Without such feedback students are left to wonder if their performance in the classroom would be appropriate at work. Note how dramatically this changes the primary role of the instructor. Instead of being a lecturer, he is now a resource, facilitator, or coach.

Taking time the time to evaluate a training program with respect to adult learning theory will help ensure your training budget is spent wisely.

ADVICE TO DEVELOPERS

There are a wide variety of training options offered by companies. Pursuing as many as possible enhances your long-term growth.

> Take advantage of "soft skill" training.
> Use your allotted training time.

Take advantage of "soft skill" training.   As discussed in Chapter 6, developers often concentrate their training on technical subjects, failing to develop their skills in other areas. I have witnessed a similar phenomenon with respect to training in the organization. Many times developers take only the classes relating to their current jobs and fail to take classes offered in the values, business, and/or goals of the company. This is a mistake, for such training exists to support the explicit needs of the company.

For example, let's assume your company has decided to pursue ISO 9000 certification. As part of the certification process, a series of four informal lectures are to be held each Tuesday, from 4:30 P.M. to 5:30 P.M. The purpose of these lectures is to explain why the company has decided to pursue certification and provide an overview of how senior management intends to integrate ISO 9000 compliant development practices into the organization. Failing to attend these classes is a big mistake, as they offer as much of an opportunity to learn about ISO 9000 (and how it will impact your job) as they offer a chance to learn more about the values and goals of the organization.

Use your allotted training time.   Many organizations view training like vacation: You have a certain number of days or weeks per year, use it or lose it. Use it.

Part Five

The final part of this book addresses issues related to context. Chapter 15 begins by elaborating on what it means to be a professional.

It is difficult to determine if a given working environment is good or bad during the interview process, especially if you are an external candidate to the organization. The courtship between a developer and the potential hiring organization goes two ways. Both you and the organization are "putting your best foot forward" in the hopes of attracting the other. Developing software is full of activities whose final outcome is uncertain. The hiring process is just one more. Specifically, you cannot really determine how "good" an organization is until after you have worked in it for six months to a year. More importantly, you almost certainly cannot determine the total quality of the development environment via conversations with the management team during an interview. Yet, given the importance of finding a good development environment, there must be some strategies for finding the right one for you. There is, and you will find them in Chapter 16.

In Chapter 16, advice is given about how to detect (and avoid!) poor working environments. This is easier than it sounds, and try as you may, it is easy to find yourself in a poor working environment. Don't despair! Read Chapter 17, which will help sustain you until the current job improves or you can find a new one.

15

WORKING AS A PROFESSIONAL

Webster's defines a professional as "an individual who engages in an occupation for pay." It is obvious a professional is more than this. A professional cares deeply about their client and works to ensure his or her needs are fairly and accurately met—whoever the client may be. A professional is someone who strives to practice Guy Kawasaki's [1990] admonition to do the right thing the right way. A professional not only knows how to lead, they know how to follow. This chapter extends the ideas presented in earlier parts of this book and moves toward increasing our understanding of "professional."

Chapter Overview

Section 15.1 discuses job mobility—making yourself valuable without making yourself *too* valuable. There is a lot written about effective leaders, but without followers there are no leaders. Section 15.2 discusses what it means to be an effective follower. Section 15.3 discusses ways to help colleagues while Section 15.4 addresses the negative aspects of office politics. Working so as not to unnecessarily disturb others is discussed in Section 15.5. The final two sections, 15.6 and 15.7, address your career from the long-term perspective. Section 15.6 addresses taking care of yourself. Section 15.7 addresses taking care of others.

15.1 JOB MOBILITY

Randy is a developer at SuperSoftware who works on SuperSpreadsheet. Over time, he has quickly established himself as one of the most valued members of the team. His knowledge of the system is immense, and whenever there is a error, even in code he did not write, he manages to make the correction quickly and efficiently. Management praises his talents, his ego grows, and he becomes ever more deeply entrenched in the system.

Everyone is happy with this situation until Randy decides to pursue a new opportunity. Suddenly, the world comes crashing down. Randy is told he can't leave because he has become indispensable. Randy's feelings of elation turn to despair and frustration (and his management begins to feel worried). If some form of solution is not reached, Randy's feelings will continue to intensify, perhaps to the point he becomes motivated to leave the company. The problem is not that Randy isn't valuable. He's *too* valuable.

To fix this problem, don't become a Randy. That is, don't allow yourself to become indispensable in your current job unless you plan on keeping it for a very long time. This, of course, is not nearly as easy as it sounds. On one hand, you want to establish yourself as a valuable contributor. On the other hand, you don't want to be viewed as indispensable, as this will limit your options to pursue other opportunities.

The goal is to create a balance. Be valuable but not indispensable. One way to think about the difference between these two conflicting demands is to skew your efforts slightly in the direction of indispensability while you want to pursue advancement in your current job, and toward dispensability when you think you might want to pursue a new opportunity. Making yourself dispensable enables job mobility. Dispensability makes it easier to pursue other options, and, when you do leave, it helps to make certain your old team can continue to operate effectively in your absence.

How can you work to make yourself dispensable yet still be viewed as an essential, valuable member of the team? First, adhere to the structures defined in your job as well as you can. This means following standards, documenting your work clearly, and otherwise making it easier for others to know what you are doing. Second, make certain other members of the team are aware of the essential aspects of your current work assignment. Third, and perhaps most importantly, prepare high quality outcomes. Write clear, straightforward, easily understood source code. Create models communicating essential information about the problem using the appropriate notation.

15.2 BE A GOOD FOLLOWER

Although there is substantial literature on what it takes to be a good leader, there is little published about what it means to be a good follower. Yet, as Kelley points out, without good followers good leaders are of little value [1991]. Donnithorne [1993] echoes this point of view from the perspective of how leadership is developed at the United States Military Academy at West Point. The first phase of learning how to be a leader at West Point is *learning how to be a good follower*, because to be a good leader you must be a good follower! If you think about it, being a good follower is practical. Most of our working lives (even as a manager) are spent following, not leading. Integrating and summarizing the work of Kelley and Donnithorne, good followership is based on the following characteristics.

- ◆ *Self-managing.* A good follower knows how to manage their time well, spending it on the right activities. When given an ill-defined task, they know how to organize themselves (first) and others (second, as needed) in order to get the job done.
- ◆ *Competent and capable.* A good follower is competent in their job and focused in their work. They know the structures, processes, and outcomes associated with their job. They are able to engage in processes to create appropriate outcomes.
- ◆ *Proactive.* Rather than sitting on their heels waiting to be told what to do, a good follower takes the initiative.
- ◆ *Self-worth.* A good follower's sense of self-worth is internally generated and not externally given.
- ◆ *Hungry for success.* A good follower makes a habit out of success. They *hunger* for it and work persistently to obtain it. They know their leaders don't want to hear about why they *couldn't* do the job. And, they derive enjoyment from a job well done.
- ◆ *Underpromises and overdelivers.* A good follower knows their limits and does not commit to more than what they can deliver. A good follower does not merely take an order but knows when (and how) to question them when needed. A good follower will even say "no" to a superior when needed.
- ◆ *Loyalty.* A good follower identifies with their team and actively supports them. This, in turn, increases mutual trust and loyalty.
- ◆ *Courageous, honest, and honorable.* Perhaps the most important point made by Kelley is that good followers are

credible, honest, and courageous. They establish themselves as independent, critical thinkers whose knowledge and judgment can be trusted. They give credit where credit is due, admitting mistakes and sharing successes. They form their own views and ethical standards and stand up for what they believe in. [Kelley 1991].

West Point cadets are explicitly taught these skills as they learn ethics in a series of increasingly complex ethical problems.

Certainly, this is not an exhaustive list. A good follower possesses a myriad of desirable qualities. Nor do I mean to imply being a good follower is checking off a majority of the items on this list. Instead, as good followers and their leaders know, being a good follower is a style, an approach, an attitude framing how we work as a professional.

15.3 HELPING COLLEAGUES

Find ways to help your colleagues. It doesn't take much. Take a few extra seconds to write a meaningful comment or pick a descriptive variable name. Make a fresh pot of coffee after you drink the last cup. Use assertions in your C code. Would you seriously consider using a C library that did not contain assertions? If not, why should another member of your team seriously consider using your code if you didn't add assertions?

Of course, all of this requires a little more work on your part—a good assertion takes a bit of time to write and needs to be maintained like any other aspect of the code. In each case you help other members of the team. The long-term net effect of such an approach is quite literally incalculable: Each time we work to make someone else's job a bit easier, the overall efficiency and effectiveness of the organization increases.

> *It can be easy to forget or ignore this advice, because we sometimes think being more helpful is harder than it really is. When I started teaching classes I was very sloppy: As I removed transparencies from the overhead, I would simply place them on the table in any order, safe in the knowledge that our secretary who cleaned up the room would put the slides back in proper order while she was cleaning them. One day, she commented on how messy I was, but I didn't take the time to listen carefully to what she was saying. More importantly, I didn't take the time to listen past her surface comment to understand what she was really saying, which was: "Luke, leaving slides in a disordered mess makes my job extremely difficult."*

> *I managed to catch on to this problem, and a way to solve it, after another instructor was hired. Our secretary commented on how much easier it was to clean up the room after this new person primarily because even though he wrote on the slides, he maintained them in proper order. I got the point and now take the time to keep the slides in sorted order. And, it really isn't much work on my part. As students work on assignments, I simply take a few moments of otherwise idle time to make certain the transparencies of the previous lecture are in order. Basic algorithmic knowledge confirms the final outcome: Lots of little sorting is easier and quicker than one big sort! More importantly, a few minutes of my idle time makes someone else's job much easier.*

15.4 AVOID OFFICE POLITICS

In any environment, good or bad, there will always be a group of individuals who gravitate to rumors, hearsay, and general gossip. While there are some situations where office gossip is acceptable, such as sharing good news in an informal manner, more often than not these discussions focus on the negative aspects of the working environment. It is easy to find negative aspects of *any* environment. It can be even easier to magnify them, making small problems appear much worse.

Avoid participation in such conversations. Invest the time in improving your performance as a professional. I'm not suggesting you cut yourself completely from the office grapevine—you may miss valuable information, and you certainly want to know when others are talking about you. The best way to handle this is participate in conversations until they turn to rumors or useless gossip. When this happens, simply excuse yourself and get back to your work.

15.5 OFFICE ETIQUETTE

While most authors who write about "peopleware" issues (including myself) advocate individual offices for software developers, the fact of the matter is most of us are going to be working in cubicles.[1] As such, there are some basic rules of cubicle etiquette that make work significantly more enjoyable for everyone.

- ◆ Talk at a whisper level, loud enough to be heard in conversation, but quiet enough so as to minimize disturbing others. Be especially cognizant of this fact when talking on the phone. Avoid the use of speaker phones.
- ◆ Avoid walking through cubicle hallways, where you can easily disturb other people. Instead, walk around them. This is also known as weight-lifter's etiquette: Never walk in front of a person while they are lifting, as this can disturb their concentration. Instead, walk behind them, so they can concentrate on their form.
- ◆ Hold meetings in the cafeteria.

Suppose others are rude. What can you do?

- ◆ Buy a good computer and ask if you can work at home.
- ◆ Confront them in a nonthreatening manner (refer to Section 9.2 for the details).
- ◆ Shift your working hours, by coming into the office a little earlier or staying a little later.

15.6 TAKE CARE OF YOURSELF

Peak mental performance is based on more than the depth and breadth of your cognitive library. It is also based on our physical health. Being a professional means attending to both *physical* and *mental* needs.

---

[1] Sometimes I think more copies of *Peopleware* by DeMarco and Lister [1987] were purchased to try and convince upper management of the need for individual offices than for any other reason! For every attempt that found success, bravo! For every attempt that found failure, keep trying.

15.6.1 Eat in Moderation

Many of us can recall happy memories of an impressive dinner.[2] In honor of one occasion or another, the family gathers around a table laden with food, and you happily enjoy all you can possibly eat in one sitting. When finished, you lethargically find your way to the couch, where you proceed to rest for several hours.

The sleepy feeling you experience is caused by many factors. Chief among these factors is the stomach requires more blood to digest the food. This leaves less blood available to the brain, resulting in a slightly reduced oxygen supply and a "sleepy" feeling. Depending on the type of food consumed, you may also be feeling tired because of the chemicals released by the food. For example, chocolate desserts will release endorphins in the brain, which have an overall sedative effect.

Did you have the same experience at lunch last Wednesday? A group of your colleagues decided to go to lunch, and you joined them. Stopping at your favorite Mexican restaurant, you proceeded to eat four baskets of chips! By the time you made it back to the office, there was no way you could effectively engage in the development process: All you wanted to do was take a nap! In the long run, such behavior is counterproductive, and many companies have realized the days of the three-martini lunch are long gone.

Eating properly does have an impact on performance. Research has consistently shown breakfast is one of the most important meals of the day. Eating a small, but nutritious, breakfast prepares the body for work in the morning, and provides the energy (i.e., a consistent level of blood sugar) needed to work through the morning until lunch. A good breakfast doesn't have to be big and fancy—a piece of fruit and a sports bar or a plain bagel are among the many good choices available.

During lunch, keep your overall consumption of food to a reasonable amount. Be especially careful with fast foods, as most are not designed with optimal levels of nutrition. Most, especially the prototypical cheeseburger, has far too much fat. Of course, this by design: Fat tastes good, and by making foods high in fat, fast food companies lure you into purchasing their product.

15.6.2 Exercise Regularly

Most software developers and other knowledge workers do not get enough exercise. Quite simply sitting at your desk all day long does not provide you with the exercise you need to stay healthy. Sadly, while many developers feel exercise is important, they just don't make the effort to get it. And they should, for several reasons directly impacting performance.

First, exercise provides a safe and effective outlet for the stress. People who exercise regularly have lower levels of stress.

---

[2] The examples of overeating described in this section are somewhat culturally biased. In many non-Western cultures, overeating—and all the problems that are associated with it—is significantly less common than in typical Western cultures. The examples are presented for illustration purposes only.

Second, exercise has been proven to play a role in keeping our mental skills fresh as we age. Quite specifically, individuals who are more physically fit "think" more effectively. The reasons for this aren't entirely known, but many researchers believe exercise improves mental performance by increasing the amount of oxygenated blood flowing to the brain (the brain accounts for 20 percent to 25 percent of the body's demand for oxygen). Exercises involving complex motor skills (e.g., racquetball or aerobics) may improve the mental processes even further as such exercise appears to generate new synapses. (Synapses are the connections between neurons in the brain; improving them can help the brain process information faster and more efficiently.)

Third, complicated physical exercise helps develop spatial relationships and visualization abilities, key components in software development, as most developers reason about data structures *visually*.

Fourth, exercise contributes to overall health, reducing general incidence of illness.

One of the biggest reasons most people fail to get enough exercise is an erroneous belief that creating an exercise program is difficult. This is simply not true. It is rather easy to create a physical fitness program maintaining good levels of physical fitness. Current recommendations from the American College of Sports Medicine (ACSM) [1991] for apparently healthy individuals include the following.[3]

- ◆ *Modality.* Any aerobic exercise involving the major muscle groups which is rhythmic in nature. Examples include walking, swimming, cycling, running, and so forth.
- ◆ *Intensity.* Exercise should be conducted at 55 percent to 90 percent of maximal heart rate. Since determining this accurately can be problematic, a much simpler, but equally effective system called the Rating of Perceived Exertion (RPE) can be used. RPE measures perceived exercise intensity on a scale of one to ten. A rating of one is being completely sedentary (e.g., laying down on a couch). A rating of ten equates to maximal effort (e.g., a full-out sprint). Use the RPE to rate exercise intensity. The goal is to achieve an intensity of between 6 and 8. The advantages of the RPE are twofold. First, although it is simple, it has been rigorously and scientifically validated. Quite simply, the RPE works. Second, it is appropriate for anyone at any fitness level.
- ◆ *Frequency and duration.* The exercise must be engaged for at least 15 to 60 minutes, three to five days per week.

As a fitness professional, I know firsthand the benefits of regular physical activity. As a software professional and husband, I know how difficult it can be to find the time to exercise. Make the time. Thirty minutes spent walking is far, far better for you than watching the news.

---

[3] These recommendations are appropriate for *apparently* healthy adults. As always, before undertaking or significantly changing any exercise program, you should consult your physician.

15.6.3 Work as Comfortably as Possible

Each of us has a different set of preferences in our working environment. You like country music. Your colleague to the left prefers classical, while your colleague to the right enjoys silence. The rest of the team is messy. You are neat. As discussed in Chapter 4, some of these variations stem from our basic personality, and there appear to be some basic differences in how different personality types organize their working environment. The question is: How can you create a comfortable working environment for yourself while remaining considerate of your fellow workers? The answer lies in controlling what is in your sphere of influence and concentrating on good ergonomics.

It is beyond the scope of this book to discuss all of the ergonomic issues associated with working comfortably and effectively. For a comprehensive discussion of these issues, I recommend the book *Zap! How Your Computer Can Hurt You—and What You Can Do about It* by Don Sellers [1994]. That said, here are a few things I have found to be especially important.

- Get a good chair and sit with proper posture. Sitting with appropriate posture actually uses less total energy than slouching, is much better for your back, and helps you maintain alertness throughout the day.
- Take breaks, about 15 minutes for every two hours of work. *Get up and walk around.*
- Keep eye drops handy. I keep a bottle in my briefcase and one in my desk drawer.
- Get an ergonomic keyboard (there are several). Type lightly—the keys are not your enemy! Keep relaxed and position your wrists so they float above the keyboard.

15.6.4 Take Vacations

A vacation is a chance to recharge our batteries and gain new perspectives on our work. Unfortunately, many developers skip vacations, especially when working on a large project. Don't do it. Go no longer than two years, and preferably no longer than one, between vacations.

15.6.5 Get a Reasonable Amount of Sleep

Many of us have experienced the need to work extra hours to complete a difficult project. We have stayed up late, foregoing sleep to get the job done. While this may achieve a short-term goal, over a long period of time a chronic lack of sleep will cause a significant drop in performance. In general, most humans need between $7^1/_2$ and $8^1/_2$ hours of sleep per night, some more, others less.

Edwin Moses, the famed 100-meter hurdler, partially attributed his astounding string of victories to one key element: He slept more than his competitors, as much as 12–14 hours per day! The large amount of sleep enabled his body to better withstand his rigorous training schedule and helped make certain he was completely rested (and prepared) for each race.

15.6.6 Know When to Say No

It is the middle of a "killer" project, and you find yourself personally motivated to work the extra hours needed to get the job done. The feeling is exciting, almost as if you were flying. The team just passed the first integration test without a hitch. Spirits and morale are high, and there is an intense desire among everyone to continue working at a feverish pace until the system is finished. I don't know about you, but I relish these experiences, and in general look back upon and forward to them with fondness. Indeed, my closest friends know that I have a special term for working lots of hours: MPM, or *Massive Programming Mode*.

However, there are times when I worked extremely hard and *did not* feel good about the final result. Reflecting on these experiences, I find when I worked hard but was not *internally* motivated to do so I ended up feeling my manager had taken unfair advantage of my desire to do a good job. Sometimes I was simply following a command I had every right to refuse—and should have. The worst experience I've ever had was being promised a bonus for completing a project on time, working extremely hard to do so, and *not* receiving the bonus as promised when finished!

I am *not* going to tell you that you shouldn't work extra hard for small stretches of time (two to four weeks is about right). Indeed, there are times when working this hard feels almost purative. You focus your entire *self* on solving a problem. What I am going to tell you is that in order to gain satisfaction from intense work, you must be internally motivated to do so because in most organizations you *won't* be recognized for it in any significant manner. Anything less and you will end up feeling disappointed.

15.7 TAKE CARE OF YOUR RELATIONSHIPS

Creating great systems takes time and energy. So does creating a great relationship. Unfortunately, the time and energy needed for each are not mutually supportive. Learning how to manage these competing demands is uniquely difficult but supremely important.

I find it helpful to think of my relationship with my wife Noura as my permanent, highest priority process that sometimes generates nonmaskable interrupts. When I am at work, this process is in background mode. All it takes is a phone call (an interrupt) to switch it to the foreground!

♦ Be honest and up-front with your significant other. If you think you are going to be working on a project intensely for the next few weeks, tell them. This is not a license for neglect. Just because you have told them you are busy does not give you the right to perpetual 80-hour work weeks.

♦ Get your significant other an e-mail account on a system compatible with your own and use it to stay in close contact. This can be especially beneficial if one or both of you travel.

♦ Handle phone calls in the following manner. First, ascertain its importance. If it is something important, handle it immediately. If not, decide how long you can speak. If you are currently busy, tell them so and arrange for a time to call them back. If you are not currently busy, tell them about how much time you have for the call. In all cases, *devote your full attention to the call!* I find it helpful to turn away from my monitor or turn on the screen saver. *Never* type while your significant other is on the phone. They can hear it and sense your distraction. You wouldn't type with a customer on the other end of the line, so don't do it when it is your significant other.

♦ Don't always talk about computers. Yes, I know you are excited about the endless innovations in our field and that even though your manager stinks your current project is using a cool new technology. However, your significant other may not share your enthusiasm about technology and may instead prefer to discuss something *other* than computers. Show them you are a real human, and not just a geek!

To make certain I always have at least one noncomputer related topic to talk about with Noura, I try to listen to National Public Radio on the way home from work and remember one noncomputer related story to discuss with her.

♦ Travel, an inevitable part of our business, can be especially demanding on your significant other. Do the following to make things easier on them. Before you leave make certain they have a *complete* copy of your itinerary. Call them when you arrive. Call them at least once per day while away. Call them from the plane on the way home. It's worth it.

Above all, find ways to let your significant other know you care for them.

16

AVOIDING BAD WORKING ENVIRONMENTS

Is every software development organization the same? Of course not! Some are really terrific places to work. Good managers keep volatile requirements under control. Developers support and trust each other. Other teams work with the developers in a mutually supportive manner. Unfortunately, some environments are just plain horrid. The most basic structures and processes needed for effective development are neither in place nor are they practiced. Schedules are completely unreasonable, deadlines and feature sets are arbitrary, and there is no concept of a method. By flagrantly abusing the most rudimentary software development practices, such places create abominable software.

You may be thinking "Yeah, right. Such organizations used to exist in the past, when not a lot was known about software engineering and effective management practices. These organizations don't exist today." I wish this were true, but it's not. There is much anecdotal evidence, and a fair amount of empirical evidence, to believe most organizations do not practice any form of controlled development (a partial list of references discussing this include Yourdon [1992], Maguire [1994], and McConnell [1993].

One company I worked for had a sales organization regularly making special promises to customers in order to obtain their business. In and of itself, this is not uncommon. Specialized processing rules (e.g., if this customer has done more than $10,000 in business this month, take an extra 10 percent off the final price) are common in business, and the development techniques needed to handle such rules properly are well known (especially to object-oriented developers). The problem in this case was that the salespeople were making these promises without any input whatsoever from the development *group. Developers were never asked how long it would take to solve the problem properly. They were only given the deadlines promised to the customer!*

When the developers requested more time to solve the problem properly, they were told to "hard code" the result. I mean this literally, not figuratively. The code in the system was nothing more than a poorly designed sequence of modules containing specific rules for specific customers in a haphazard manner. Much of the code was repeated, and as new customers came on board the system continued to bloat. Over time the system had become filled with such modifications. Each such modification made future modifications more difficult, creating a negative spiral of productivity.

The developers realized the folly of this approach. Most came on board eager to do things correctly. Over time, they realized senior management didn't care about doing things correctly—if doing things correctly were important, senior management would not support the behavior of the sales organization. Usually one of two things happens. First, developers stay only a few months. This is pretty common and the turnover rate is phenomenal. Second, developers stay with the organization but become completely apathetic. Over time, they just don't care anymore. This is less common but is even more damaging in its own way.

Of course, one does not wish to unduly constrain the sales organization. If they must be given the ability to provide exception processing based on a single customer, then provide for this requirement in the basic design of the system. If not known up front, then modify the system to support a general mechanism for handling exceptional business rules. The point is that this is an organization to avoid for they refuse to let the developers build the system the right way.

It is difficult to determine if a given working environment is bad during the interview process, especially if you are an external candidate. The courtship between a developer and the hiring organization goes two ways. Both you and they are "putting your best foot forward" in the hopes of attracting the other. Developing software is full of activities whose final outcome is uncertain, and herein lies another: You cannot really determine the quality of the working environment until you have worked in it for several months to one year. More importantly, you almost certainly cannot determine the quality of the development environment during an interview. Yet, given the importance of finding a good environment, it is important to try.

Rather than trying to give you information on how to find the perfect working environment—which I can't—the purpose of this chapter is to provide strategies on how to avoid obviously bad ones. You might be happy working in a development organization failing any one of the "tests" posed in the following sections, but I doubt that you will be satisfied if you were to work for an organization failing three or more.

Chapter Overview

Each section in this chapter concentrates on specific aspects of the working environment you can ascertain through the interview process. Section 16.1 discusses why and how the hiring organization should evaluate your skills. Examining the product release strategy provides important clues about the overall development process; Section 16.2 tells you why. Section 16.4 discusses why you should have a defined role while Section 16.4 addresses turnover from the perspective of the developer.

There are *many* structures, processes, and outcomes associated with world-class software development. The *minimal* set is discussed in Section 16.6. Closely associated with these are the outstanding bug reports. Reviewing these provides important insights into the working environment as described in Section 16.7.

Your direct manager has a substantial influence on your career. Assessing their ability as a leader is discussed in Section 16.8. Of course, your potential colleagues also have an important influence. Assess them while you assess the overall environment as described in Section 16.9.

16.1 DEMONSTRATE YOUR SKILLS

Be careful of any organization failing to directly evaluate your skills. Why? If they don't ask to review your work or evaluate your ability *before* they hire you, then they probably haven't taken the time to evaluate your potential colleagues' ability *before* hiring them. Part of building a great team is selecting the best people. How can you be certain you are selecting the best people if you aren't evaluating them? Is there a way they can realistically evaluate your skills? Certainly! It is described in detail in Chapter 13.

Suppose you interview with a team and they don't evaluate your skills as described in Chapter 13. Does this mean they are incompetent? That depends on the circumstances. Maybe each member of the team knows each other from prior successful projects. Because they didn't need to formally evaluate each other's skills, they may not think to evaluate yours. Or, maybe you are a referral from an existing member of the team. That person may be so well trusted they may decide to forego skill evaluation and simply make a hiring offer based on the strength of the recommendation. In general, I would very rarely recommend taking a job without some demonstration of your skills. If they don't ask, *offer* to bring in source code for their review and suggest they give you a hands-on design problem.

> *I've always tried to follow this advice as a manager, and usually it produced good results. However, I didn't realize how much fun it could be on the receiving end until I had my first interview with ObjectSpace. After a few minutes of introductions, two people asked me to design a solution to a simplified version of the game of Monopoly, actively questioning and challenging my design decisions every step of the way.*

> *After 30 minutes, I was exhausted, but excited, for I felt this was a working environment I would enjoy. This scenario was repeated two more times before a hiring offer was made. In total I had three interviews and was asked to solve a different problem in each interview. The entire process was invaluable, because it gave me a real opportunity to examine how my potential colleagues interact. It also gave them the opportunity to examine*

my problem-solving ability as well as my style (i.e., would I be a good fit for the Object-Space culture?).

16.2 EVALUATE THE PRODUCT RELEASE STRATEGY

Be careful of development teams who release products too quickly or too slowly. The trend appears to be releasing product too quickly, which is very costly to both the company and the customer. Products released too quickly are often poorly tested. As a result, support costs increase. In the long run, revenues decrease as customers defect and overall market share decreases.

Even if the product is well tested, customers can become confused. A short release cycle implies instability in the feature set of the product. The reasonable response is to delay purchasing the current release and instead wait for the next one. This results in lost revenue (no customers are purchasing the new product) and increased support costs (new customers will obtain the new release, but now there are multiple releases to support).

Releasing a product too slowly, on the other hand, introduces a different set of problems. Customers and support staff must manage an ever-increasing set of fixes and small modifications to the product. Market share is lost as customers seek newer products from other vendors promising superior features. While a very short release cycle causes many problems, a very slow cycle indicates the presence of problems. A long cycle could be caused by any number of factors, including high turnover, unstable requirements, lack of market focus, and poor development practices (i.e., waterfall), each of which are undesirable.

What constitutes a reasonable product release strategy? There is no easy answer to this question, because it depends on the size and complexity of the product, the size and capabilities of the development staff, and a host of other factors. In general, a normal cycle is between four and twelve months for a major release. Of course, minor releases and bug fixes are often required between major releases to incorporate critical corrections or enhancements.

> *I once worked for a manager who mandated a monthly product release! Yes, you read the previous sentence correctly. Every month there was to be a completely new product. At first, my teams and others tried to meet this request even though everyone knew how shortsighted this mandate was. No time was spent in improving the basic architecture which had some serious problems. New features continued to be added based on the existing architecture, making a bad situation worse. Testing was done minimally, if at all. If it compiled, it shipped!*

> *The development team was not the only team who suffered. The schedule was even harder on the product support team, who had to maintain extensive product knowledge of what version had what feature (or bug!). The documentation and shipping departments also suffered, and many times the rate of change was greater than the system could handle. More than once the wrong documentation or system was shipped to a new customer.*

The person most detrimentally affected, however, was the customer. Customers with older versions of the software had to come to us to get a new release. I tried to stop the madness by calculating the economic impact of a monthly release (i.e., the cost of preparing new diskettes and manuals and shipping this to several thousand customers). When I told my manager of the financial cost, he told me to ship the new product release only to new customers or to customers renewing their service agreement. The problem kept getting worse until one month when I had no choice but to tell him the current release would be missed. No new features or bug fixes had been tested sufficiently to warrant a new release. I thought by being firm I could fix the problem once and for all. Incredibly, I was wrong. He simply replied: "Give the current release a new version and ship it."

Before writing off a company seeming to release products too quickly or too slowly, try to understand their motivation. There are many good reasons for a faster than expected (or scheduled) product release. Perhaps a competitor released a new version of a competing product, and the organization must respond. If so, then ask what was changed in the development schedule in order to meet the new deadline. The government may have made a regulatory change, and the company may be simply responding to the change. There may have been changes in tax laws, inventory management practices, or a whole host of other factors. Use the product release strategy as data to motivate obtaining additional information about the company.

16.3 HAVE A DEFINED ROLE

This advice was given to me by a friend who has worked for several different companies over the last ten years. He noted, "If they can't tell you what they think you will be doing, they probably haven't thought about it much." This small piece of advice has important implications.

First, it illustrates a very basic human need. Each of us likes to know what contributions we are expected to make, how we are to "fit" into the current team. Second, your potential colleagues probably know the kind of person needed by the team. They have quite likely already formed expectations of your role, and you have a right to know what others expect from you. Third, an inability to define your role implies they haven't thought about it. Do they need people because the turnover rate is so high you are just another "warm body" to fill the place of someone else when they leave? Are they basing their hiring decisions on the architecture of the system and complexity of the problem? If not, why not?

Of course, this does not mean the job you interview for must be the same job you eventually take. Many companies, with good reason, simply look for bright, motivated, and talented people, safe in the knowledge their internal training program can mold the person as needed for the job they will eventually hold. Sometimes, a company is growing so fast they can't really tell you what job you will be doing! This happened to me when I joined ObjectSpace. During the interview I was hired for one job. Once hired, I started working on a complete different assignment because of the incredible growth of the company. Again, balance is needed. A precisely detailed specification of your role is not required, but not having any idea of what you are being hired for, no matter how loosely defined, is a cause for concern.

16.4 EXAMINE THE TURNOVER RATE

In the ideal world, a development team, once established, would remain together for the duration of the project. The ideal world doesn't exist, and most development projects will experience some amount of turnover over the life of the project. In general, a normal turnover rate is considered to be somewhere between 10 percent and 30 percent. Smaller development teams, those with less than 25 developers, tend to be on the lower end of the scale, while larger development teams, those with more than 50 developers, tend to be on the higher end of the scale.

Regardless of the size of the team, turnover has more of a negative effect on productivity than people realize. Losing a member of the team usually means losing valuable domain knowledge, experience, and skill. Training a replacement requires time, energy, and money and puts a burden on the existing team. Productivity often suffers during the transition, as it generally takes a completely new team member between two to six months (sometimes longer) to become fully productive.

Thus, when looking for a job, try to determine the turnover rate. A high turnover rate means something is wrong. *What* may be wrong may not be known. In many ways the actual cause doesn't matter (and you probably won't be able to find out during the interview process). There are numerous reasons why organizations experience abnormally high rates of turnover, and none of them are good.

16.5 EXAMINE THE OPPORTUNITY FOR ADVANCEMENT

When looking for a new job, try to find one matching your personal goals for career advancement. Is there a formal training plan or policy? Will they support people hiring into one role (e.g., maintenance) and moving to another (e.g., design or teaching)? Is there a tuition reimbursement program? Does the company promote from within? What is the track record for doing so?

16.6 ARE THE BIG THREE PRACTICED?

The three most important practices of software engineering are

1. the use of a method, even if they use it poorly, making an attempt to use it well is far better than not trying at all (see Section 3.4 for a description of the minimum models that should be prepared using the method).
2. outcome reviews; and,
3. source code configuration management.

Run, don't walk, from organizations failing to engage in these *minimal* practices.

16.7 REVIEW OUTSTANDING BUG REPORTS

A sure sign of a poor working environment is an excessively high number of bug reports. One environment I knew of had logged more than 10,000 specific errors with the current system. To rectify the situation, they simply deleted the database and started over!

If you gain access to the bug reports, examine them carefully. Do the same bugs keep reappearing over and over again? Are customers continually reporting the same problems? If so, why? What explanations can be provided for any trends? Are these explanations reasonable?

16.8 INTERVIEW YOUR DIRECT MANAGER

Your direct manager has a huge impact on your career. He or she should be a vital resource, helping you shape, grow, and enhance it. While there is no shortage of books or articles describing the attributes of a good manager (e.g., trustworthiness, mutual respect, and so forth), one critically important attribute is often overlooked: technical competence.

First-line managers must be technically competent, and *should make every effort to stay that way!* If your manager does not understand your work, they cannot establish realistic schedules, control the progress of work, or be certain of the quality of the outcomes produced. Most importantly, they fail in their most important duty: Creating structures to help *you* be effective.

This point is eloquently made by C.A. Hoare [1981] in his 1980 Turing Award Lecture, which describes a project that failed under his direction, because (in the words of his superior) "you let your programmers do things which you yourself do not understand." After some reflection, Mr. Hoare agreed with his managers and was able to bring the project back to an acceptable level of performance by requiring "the project leader to convince *me* . . . that the design of the new feature was appropriate, and that the plans and schedules for implementation were realistic. Above all, I did not allow anything to be done which I did not myself understand. It worked!"

This does not mean your manager should be as technically competent as you. They certainly don't have to perform every job better than you. As managers move higher in the corporate hierarchy, different skills become increasingly important. Learning these new skills requires others to decrease, and technical skills decrease rapidly unless they are practiced. This view is also prevalent in the military, in which first-line commanding officers are expected to know every detail of their subordinates' work, while senior officers are expected to have broader based skills built on top of the details. What remains most important to me, however, is technically competent first-line managers.

Sadly, some organizations actually encourage technical incompetence by doing such silly things as refusing to let managers write source code, take classes in technical areas, or other things. While this is rare, it does happen. Alternatively, and much more commonly, first-line managers fail to expend the energy in remaining technically competent. Once they become a manager, all of their energy is directed to moving up the corporate ladder. Finally, I've known first-line managers who were just content to remain the same for their entire career. One of the most incompetent managers of all time I've ever met was a 26-year veteran who was asked to lead a client-server project and thought C++ was written using the Visual Basic programming environment!

> *One day, my direct manager called me into his office and announced he was going to pursue a new position. This is not a cause for concern, and moving to a new job is common. What he said next was quite uncommon: "You should start looking for a new job. I know my replacement, and while he is a good leader, his technical skills are lacking. Because I know you are concentrating on building your technical skills at this stage of your career, you will find yourself extremely unhappy working for this man, because he cannot contribute to your growth. I suggest you look for a new job as quickly as possible, and I'll be happy to help you in your search." At first, I was somewhat shocked to hear this, because it sounded like (at best) an inappropriate thing to say. I decided to stay put and see for myself. What a mistake! Within a month I realized everything my former manager said was true. My new manager was a good leader (trustworthy, consistent, and so forth), but a technical nincompoop. Two months later I had a new job.*

> *Following your own advice can be hard, but you should still do it. Later in my career I was promoted to be the manager of a mixed platform, mixed language development environment. The languages included C, COBOL, Visual Basic, and a few others. The platforms included Tandems, PCs, and a few other special hardware devices, each with their own languages. Until then, I had worked in and/or managed development only on personal computers (Macintosh and PC) or workstations (Sun, Apollo, and HP). I knew nothing about the mainframe, except for an assembly language class in college.*

> *In the meeting announcing my arrival, I practically boasted about how little I knew of mainframe development. Big mistake number one: alienating half of the development staff, who suddenly thought:*

> a. *"My job is in jeopardy because the new manager doesn't know about mainframes, and therefore is going to transition development to the PC";*
> b. *"If I want to, I can fool him on every phase of development. How will he know the difference?"*
> c. *"Even if I didn't want to fool him, it doesn't matter. I can't discuss problems with him because he won't even know what I'm talking about."*

> *While (b) is pretty uncommon, the fear caused by (a) negatively impacted the team. Over time, I realized not knowing anything about the mainframe was inhibiting my ability to lead the team. Unfortunately, my manager explicitly forbade me from concentrating on technical areas, especially any form of programming. Big mistake number two: following poor advice. What I should have done was learn the basics of COBOL and the mainframe operating environment. I should have ignored his advice. The bottom line is this: Direct managers owe it to themselves and their teams to remain technically competent.*

16.9 TALK WITH OTHER DEVELOPERS

Who can give you the best information about the potential working environment? The people who are currently working in it! During the interview process, ask if you can talk directly with members of the current team without any managers or human resources people. Your goal is to try to determine if you are a good match for this job. How should you do this? The best way is to ask specific, but nonthreatening questions. If necessary, ask them to be as candid as possible and assure them all answers will be held in strict confidence. Of course, obtaining a straight answer may be nearly impossible in a poor environment, for answering a question directly ("Don't take a job here. This place stinks.") could put someone in "danger" should you refuse an offer.

What you are looking for is a general feeling saying, "This place is a good place to work." In a good environment you will find lots of enthusiasm, enjoyment in the job, and a general "can-do" attitude. A good environment just feels different—better—than a bad environment. I know this is a vague statement, but it is true.

Of course, there are other reasons why you want to interview your potential colleagues. You want to get a feel for their skills, interests, and abilities. Are you being hired as a mentor because of your vast experience? If so you should probably assess their raw intelligence. Are you going to enjoy working with these people? If your passion is golf, but membership in the team bowling league is mandatory, this may be the sign of deeper, more fundamental differences. Are you an extreme KAI-innovative interviewing with a team of extreme KAI-adaptives? These differences are going to cause friction. Can you handle it? Can they?

In addition to the topics listed above you may wish to discuss the following items.

- What are the relations between the development staff and upper-level management? Does the senior management of the company think of the Information Systems (IS) department as a strategic advantage or a nuisance? The ideal company recognizes IS as a key resource to business competitiveness.
- What is the average tenure of upper-level management, especially the CIO (Chief Information Officer)? Far too often CIOs are asked to make sweeping changes, but the only sweeping change made is their replacement after a few months.
- Do they have a cool Web page?
- What is the training program like? Do they have a library? What magazines are available to developers? Do they send you to conferences?
- What tools are used? Why were these selected? I know of many developers who have an (unhealthy) attachment to certain vendors' tools. Why cause yourself unnecessary stress? If you are attached to *your* tools, try to find a job using them!
- How much travel is really expected? Are meetings held late in the evening, or on weekends? Do they pay for 40 hours per week and expect you to work 60?

- ◆ Do they have any stated values? If not stated, do they have any values they feel are important? Are these consistent with your own values?
- ◆ Try to determine if the social environment is one you would enjoy. Some development teams are very social, regularly sharing many events. Others are not very social at all—but are still wonderful places to work! Are you a social person? Do you often create special relationships with colleagues outside of work? Do you like the same kinds of social events as the rest of the team? What if they play golf every Saturday, but you prefer bowling on Friday night? Both are social events, but they may be incompatible.

17

WORKING IN A POOR ENVIRONMENT

Avoiding poor working environments is harder than it seems. Try as you may, it is easy to find yourself working in one. Everything may have looked good before taking the job, but once there it turned out to be terrible. There are other good reasons why people find themselves working in a poor environment. Your old manager, whom you liked and respected a great deal, may have decided to take a new job, and the new manager is creating a real nightmare. In rare circumstances you may even *choose* to work in a poor environment because it is closer to day care, closer to home, or offers great benefits. Regardless of the reason, how can you survive on grubs and water? This chapter gives some ideas.

Chapter Overview

It doesn't make sense to worry *too* much about a bad environment if what is "bad" is temporary. Section 17.1 tells why. Suppose the environment really is terrible. What can you do? Section 17.2 provides some positive suggestions for working for change.

If the environment is poor, you will eventually want to look for a new home. Your network, as described in Section 17.3, can help. While you are looking, Section 17.4 discusses keeping what you *can* control under control.

When the environment is really poor, it is often helpful to focus inward instead of outward. See Section 17.5 for the details. Finally, Section 17.6 and Section 17.7 provide a plan for documenting problems and a warning on going too far when you leave.

17.1 IS IT REALLY THAT BAD?

Before you despair about your current environment, consider this. What is considered a "bad environment" is quite subjective. What I consider to be intense, you may consider oppressive. What you consider essential qualities of a good manager, I may consider irrelevant. And so the list goes.

My point is this. Before you decide on the quality of the environment, try to work in it for two to three months. Are you angry because your last pay raise was smaller than expected? Is there a short-term influence producing unusual amounts of stress among you, your colleagues, or your management? Will the working conditions improve when the stress is removed? If, after a reasonable evaluation, you decide you are indeed working in a poor environment, then read on. If not, hang tough until whatever is causing the problem is fixed.

17.2 WORK TO IMPROVE

So, you think you are in a poor working environment? What are you going to do to improve it? What? You think there is *nothing* you can do? Ah, but you are wrong. You can make suggestions (properly documented via e-mail or on paper) on specific actions to improve the working environment.

You can work informally to make small changes in the working environment that have big impacts. Suppose your environment doesn't practice formal design reviews. Instead of suggesting an elaborate design review process, why not simply ask a colleague to review your design informally. As someone walks by, invite them to join the review. You have a minireview and plant a seed that can be grown into a more comprehensive program. Change always occurs through the efforts of people who work to make the change happen. Be that person.

17.3 MAINTAIN YOUR NETWORK

Your network is all the people with whom you can share information in a productive manner. The list includes friends, fellow developers, people you've met in school, current and former managers, people you've met at social events, and so forth. A good network provides a set of relationships helping to expand you career and a means whereby you can find a path out of a poor working environment. How? Use your network to locate other opportunities both within and outside your company. Most jobs are found through networking. By keeping yours current, you substantially increase your chances of finding a new job.

Unfortunately, our natural tendency when placed in a poor environment is to hide. Instead of working to maintain or expand our network, we become more reclusive. While this is natural, fight it. No matter how good—or bad—the environment is, work to maintain a current network.

One final word. Unless your are confident you can trust another person, be discrete in pursuing new opportunities. Avoid sounding too negative, as this can come back to haunt you. Finally, don't view your network as something you should use only in times of need. Instead, keep your network informed of your career; keep them involved. And, be ready to help others.

17.4 CONTROL WHAT YOU CAN CONTROL

When working in a poor environment, you are likely to find you have a very limited span of control. You can't control the behavior of your managers, you can't prepare realistic project deadlines, your suggestions for improvement are ignored, and your co-workers may be creating poorly written code. The requirements may be poorly written, the analysis and design may be terrible, and you are stuck with the job of coding the solution!

You begin to despair and feel there is *nothing* you can do. But there is. Instead of worrying about what you can't control, take positive action about what you *can* control: Any outcome you produce. Consider source code. Even if the design is terrible you can write high-quality source code in the constraints of any environment. You can write source code whose variable names are well written and whose logical structure is clearly understood. Ultimately, you are the person writing the source code. Write it as cleanly as possible. If your team has a coding standard, follow it. If not, invent your own.

While this is difficult, try not to let your values be compromised. If you know about a bug, try and fix it. If you can't fix it, inform your management. (A working environment or manager is certainly not *bad* if they ship a product with a known defect. No sufficiently complex software is completely bug free.)

Avoid becoming apathetic in the production of outcomes. Other people creating poorly written source code do not give you license to do the same. And, creating poorly written source code will come back to haunt you in unexpected ways. Suppose you are interviewing for a new job and the new manager asks your current manager for a copy of your source code for evaluation. You may claim the poorly written source code was not your problem, but I don't think that will be a convincing argument to your new manager. The *last* thing you need is a reputation for creating poorly written source code.

17.5 IMPROVE YOUR SKILLS

Regardless of your current working environment, maintaining your skills is your responsibility. As Chapter 6 is devoted to this topic, I'll concentrate on the special opportunities (yes, opportunities) a poor environment presents.

First, maintain an awareness of your surroundings. Purchase a special project notebook to record these observations. Reflect on your experiences, and those of your fellow developers. Learn what *not* to do by examining the actions of your current management and recording how you would have done things differently (and why). Should you decide to become a manager, this notebook will be a valuable, long-term asset.

Second, see if you can discover, through direct questioning or other indirect observation, the motivations behind the decisions made by your management. Perhaps your manager is operating under exceptional conditions and is trying to respond as best he can. By recording this data in your notebook, you can compare and contrast how your manager handles both normal and exceptional operating conditions.

Third, you can always control some aspect of your personal development. Spend the money to subscribe to *at least* one magazine related to software development. Use it to improve your skills.

17.6 USE A BOMB FILE

A *bomb file* contains a copy of all the important events in your current work environment you can use it to justify your behavior while recording the behavior of others. Kept privately and securely, it is your record of the state of the environment. To illustrate how a bomb file could be used, consider the following situation. You are working with Marty, the ultimate incompetent developer. He consistently writes code full of errors, refuses to follow coding standards, rejects the results of code reviews, and is highly disruptive in meetings, just to name a few of his more common behaviors.

Start a bomb file and document all this behavior. When you have amassed enough evidence, schedule a private meeting with a superior who can do something to improve the situation (this may not be your current manager) and present your observations. I cannot guarantee you will like the results of this meeting, in that the outcome may not be exactly what you hoped for. However, using evidence, as opposed to feelings, will significantly bolster your position.

> *If you suspect your manager is engaging in illegal activity, a bomb file is absolutely essential. One close friend had to leave a job because of sexual harassment. Sadly, she never documented any of the abuse. Had she started and maintained a bomb file, she would have had the evidence necessary to sue the schmuck.*

17.7 BURN BRIDGES CAREFULLY

I have burned a few bridges over the years. Sometimes this was the right thing to do, and I'm glad I did it. Sometimes, it was the wrong thing to do, and in retrospect I shouldn't have done it. In general, burning a bridge is not necessary. It may feel good in the short run, but burning bridges will almost always have intense, long-term repercussions you cannot foresee. I can appreciate an intense desire to slam the door in the face of your manager and thumb your nose at your colleagues as you walk out the door, but I urge you to reconsider. As a former manager once told me, "Don't burn bridges when you leave. You never know who you might be working for in the future."

GLOSSARY

accidental complexity unnecessary complexity introduced as an artifact of the problem-solving process based on human frailty (i.e., bounded rationality).

adaptability the ability to self-correct for perceived problems in the environment.

adaptor a person who prefers problem solving using existing and/or mutually agreed upon structures.

ambiguity something that can be understood in two or more ways.

behavioral discretion the ability of a team to select their most effective manner of working free from external influence.

bounded rationality information and perceptual processing limits preventing humans from always acting in a completely rational manner.

careful communication the effort the sender puts into the creation of a message conveying information accurately, correctly, and unambiguously.

change something perceived as new or different.

change agents individuals who advocate the adoption of an innovation.

clarity the degree to which the receiver can understand the semantic meaning of the message in an unambiguous and unequivocal manner.

coalition a small group of developers formed from a larger team.

cognitive library used to describe the mental location of plans associated with problem solving.

cognitive model a description of the mental processes associated with problem solving.

cognitive style the amount of structure each of us prefers during problem solving. See *adaptor* and *innovator.*

cohesion how closely the activities within a single component or among a group of components are related to each other.

collective mind a separate transactional memory system created among a team working together.

communication channels the structures by which messages are transmitted. These include everything from e-mail to voice mail, meeting rooms to whiteboards.

competency framework a structure organizing multidimensional skills. Used in the development of a training plan.

corporate knowledge the skills and abilities members of the larger organization have that are made available to the team.

coupling the degree of interdependence among different components in a system.

crisis a severe threat to the existence of the organization.

culture the way we do things around here.

education a sequence of planned activities focused on building critical thinking skills.

equifinal meaning a collective understanding of what is to be achieved.

equivocality the degree of certainty over the meaning of an outcome.

essential complexity the complexity needed to solve the problem correctly.

formality the degree to which a message adheres to the lexical and syntactic rules describing the message.

functional values values guiding us in our daily actions with respect to how we perform our job duties.

future perfect thinking a problem-solving technique whereby a future event is imagined as having already occurred. Instead of asking, "What *should* the system do?" future perfect thinking instead directs us to ask, "What *will* the system have done?"

goal an outcome guiding and controlling long-term behavior.

ground rules explicit structures establishing acceptable and unacceptable behaviors with respect to specific communication contexts.

groupthink a breakdown in group processes in which individuals fail to critically evaluate outcomes and instead look for ways to support them.

guideline a formal specification of desired lexical, syntactic, and semantic features of the outcomes routinely shared among developers.

heterophily the degree to within individuals differ in attributes such as beliefs, education, social status, and the like.

homophily the degree to which individuals share attributes, such as beliefs, education, social status, and the like.

information hiding a design technique that emphasizes hiding the inner working of a component.

innovations tools, techniques, and/or outcomes perceived as new.

innovators a person who prefers problem solving using little external or mutually agreed upon structures.

interpersonal values values associated with how team members interact.

irrationality arbitrary motivations for decision making.

Java an object-oriented programming language developed by Sun Microsystems.

law of diminishing returns the idea that you should stop trying to understand a problem when spending more time on understanding will not substantially increase understanding.

learning style individual differences in learning. See *reckless explorer* and *plodder.*

leveling the movement between different kinds of thought and mental processes during problem solving.

linguistic determinism the idea that language structures thought. Derived from the Sapir-Whorf hypothesis.

linguistic determinism the idea that people who speak different languages perceive and think about the world differently. Derived from the Sapir-Whorf hypothesis.

mental model an internal representation of the problem.

mental set the implicit expectations or beliefs we bring to a problem-solving task.

message an exchange of information between two entities.

method "a disciplined process for generating a set of models that describe various aspects of a software system under development, using some well-defined notation." [Booch 1994]

norms social conventions established by a team serving to guide, control, and regulate behavior.

notation a specific *language* created to communicate specific kinds of information.

optimism the belief "things" will go well.

organizational engineering the ongoing activity of creating, optimizing, and changing with economy, elegance, and aesthetics the structures, processes, values, culture, and goals that enable a software development team to be maximally effective in the creation of desired outcomes.

outcome things produced through mental or physical processes.

pattern a generalized and externalized plan that can be taught to others.

performance gap failure to meet one or more established objectives.

personal space the amount of distance separating us when talking (or otherwise interacting) with others.

personality a complex set of relatively stable behavioral and emotional characteristics that can be used to uniquely identify a person.

pessimism the belief "things" will go poorly.

plan a stereotypic solution to a problem.

plodder a person who prefers to avoid mistakes in learning a computer system by reading manuals and other supporting documentation carefully.

power the ability to directly influence or control others to doing what you want.

process the mental and physical activities we use to produce outcomes.

rationality making decisions based on the best available knowledge.

reasonable person theory the idea that people act in a reasonable manner for any given situation according to the structures of the environment, their cognitive library of plans, cognitive style and personality, values, goals, and constraints of their environment.

reckless explorer a person who prefers to learn a computer system through experimentation. They tend to make many mistakes during the learning process.

reinventions slight modifications to innovations often required for successful adoption.

reorganizations changes in and among members of the team over time.

rituals semiformal or formal repeated patterns of behavior among members of the team often associated with specific actions and behaviors or providing stable frameworks for such actions and behaviors.

role a set of formal and/or informal expectations held by an individual and other members of the team about how that individual should act in a given situation and the implicit and/or explicit responsibilities that individual has been given with respect to the proper functioning of the team

role ambiguity when an individual is unsure about the role they have been explicitly given or have implicitly assumed.

role conflict when expected roles require contradictory actions and/or behaviors.

rules of discourse guidelines for the implementation of programs shared among developers.

self-efficacy a person's beliefs about their capacity to continually engage in problem-solving processes.

shared goal working together in a harmonious manner to achieve an equifinal meaning using an agreed upon set of structures and processes.

skill-based competency a specific identifiable skill that can be assessed in terms of performance (i.e., there is a way to measure proficiency in exhibiting the skill).

standard a formal specification of required lexical, syntactic, and semantic features of the outcomes routinely shared among developers. Outcomes prepared in violation of a standard should be rejected.

strategy a set of mutually supportive SPO frameworks designed to accomplish the major objectives of the organization.

structure the definition of the form and content of outcomes; the prescription and support of the processes needed to create outcomes.

semantic knowledge general strategies we have learned about problem solving and programming paradigms.

stepwise refinement a top-down problem-solving technique whereby solutions to a problem are constructed from a high-level specification through a series of refinement steps.

strategic-contingency theory the idea that power accrues to those individuals and teams dealing most directly and effectively with organizational problems

syntactic knowledge knowledge of a specific programming language or development environment.

task-relevant maturity (TRM) the ability, desire, and motivation to take on the responsibility of an explicit role. TRM is based on many factors, including education, training, and experience and is usually specific to a particular kind of role.

team a group of between two and twelve developers.

techniques process innovations.

tools structural innovations.

training a sequence of planned activities focused on building a specific set of operational skills to accomplish a well-defined task.

trust an assured reliance on the character, ability, strength, and truthfulness of another person and the feeling we are free to say or do things without fear or misgiving.

value a concept deemed worthy or important.

workflow diagram a model showing all of the entities and process steps associated with the production of an outcome.

BIBLIOGRAPHY

ABDEL-HAMID, T. K., AND MADNICK, S. E. "The Elusive Silver Lining: How We Fail to Learn from Software Development Failures." *Sloan Management Review,* Vol. 32, No. 1 pp. 39–48 (Fall 1990).

ABDEL-HAMID, T. K., AND MADNICK, S. E. *Software Project Dynamics: An Integrated Approach.* Englewood Cliffs, NJ: Prentice Hall, 1991.

ADELSON, B. "When Novices Surpass Experts: The Difficulty of a Task May Increase with Expertise." *Journal of Experimental Psychology: Learning, Memory, and Cognition,* Vol. 10, No. 3, pp. 483–495 (1984).

ADELSON, B., AND SOLOWAY, E. "The Role of Domain Experience in Software Design." *IEEE Transactions on Software Engineering,* Vol. SE-11, No. 11, pp. 1351–1360 (Nov. 1985).

ALLEN, T. J. "Organizational Structure, Information Technology, and R&D Productivity." *IEEE Transactions on Engineering Management,* Vol. EM-33, No. 4, pp. 212–217 (Nov. 1986).

AMERICAN COLLEGE OF SPORTS MEDICINE. *Guidelines for Exercise Testing and Prescription,* 4th ed. Malvern, PA: Lea & Febiger, 1991.

ASTLEY, W. G., AND VAN DE VEN, A. H. "Central Perspectives and Debates in Organization Theory." *Administrative Science Quarterly,* Vol. 28, pp. 245–273 (1983).

BABICH, W. *Software Configuration Management.* Reading, MA: Addison-Wesley, 1986.

BARNES, L. B. "Managing the Paradox of Organizational Trust." *Harvard Business Review,* pp. 107–116 (March–April 1981).

BARNEY, J. B. "Organizational Culture: Can It Be a Source of Sustained Competitive Advantage?" *Academy of Management Review,* Vol. 11, No. 3, pp. 656–665 (1986).

BARR, A., AND FEIGENBAUM, E. *The Handbook of Artificial Intelligence, Vol. 1.* Reading, MA: Addison-Wesley, 1981.

BASHSHUR, N. *Personal Communication* (1995).

BASILI, V., BAILEY, A., AND YOUSSEFI, F. "Optimizing the Utilization of Human Resources: a Framework for Research." in *Software Engineering: Practice and Experience. Proceedings of the 2nd Software Engineering Conference,* Nice, France (June 1984).

BASTEIN, D. T., AND HOSTAGER, T. J. "Jazz Concert." *Communication Studies,* Vol. 43, No. 2 (Summer 1992).

BAVELAS, J. B. "Effects of the Temporal Context of Information." *Psychological Reports,* Vol. 31, pp. 695–698 (1973).

BECKER, F.D. "Technological Innovation and Organizational Ecology." *Handbook of Human-Computer Interaction.* M. Helander (ed.) New York: Elsevier Science Publishers B.V., New York.

BELADY, L.A., AND LEHMAN, M. M. "A Model of Large Program Development." *IBM Systems Journal,* Vol.15, No. 3, pp. 225–252 (1976).

BENNIS, W. *On Becoming a Leader.* Reading, MA: Addison-Wesley, 1989.

BENTLY, J., AND KNUTH, D. "Literate Programming." *Comm. of the ACM,* Vol. 29, No. 5, pp. 364–369 (May 1986).

BERARD, E. V. "Selecting and Using Consultants for Object-Oriented Technology." *Journal of Object-Oriented Programming,* Vol. 6, No. 5, pp. 48–53 (Sept. 1993).

BERSOFF, E. H., AND DAVIS, A. M. "Impacts of Life Cycle Models on Software Configuration Management." *Comm. of the ACM,* Vol. 34, No. 8, pp. 104–118 (August 1991).

BERTELS, K., VANNESTE, P., AND DE BACKER, C. "A Cognitive Model of Programming Knowledge for Procedural Languages." *Computer Assisted Learning,* Springer-Verlag, New York. 4th International Conference, ICCAL, 1992.

BLUM, B. "A Taxonomy of Software Development Methods." *Comm. of the ACM,* Vol. 37, No. 11, pp. 82–94 (November 1994).

BOEHM, B.W. "Software and Its Impact: A Quantitative Assessment." *Datamation,* Vol. 19, No. 5 (May 1973).

BOEHM, B. W. *Software Engineering Economics.* Englewood Cliffs, NJ: Prentice Hall, 1981.

BOEHM, B.W. "Verifying and Validating Software Requirements and Design Specifications." *IEEE Software,* Vol. 1, No. 1, pp. 75–88 (Jan. 1984).

BOEHM, B. W., GARY, T. E., AND SEEWALDT, T. "Prototyping versus Specifying a Multi-Project Experiment." *IEEE Trans Soft Eng,* Vol. 10, No. 3, pp. 290–303 (1984).

BOOCH, G. *Object-Oriented Analysis and Design with Applications.* 2d ed. Redwood City, CA: Benjamin/Cummings, 1994.

BOOCH, G., AND RUMBAUGH, J. *Unified Method for Object-Oriented Development Version 0.8.* Santa Clara, CA: Rational Software Corporation, 1995.

BOTT, H. S. "The Personnel Crunch." *Perspectives on Information Mangement,* J.B. Rochester (ed.). New York: John Wiley & Sons, 1982.

BOUGON, M.G. "Congregate Cognitive Maps: A Unified Dynamic Theory of Organization and Strategy." *Journal of Management Review,* Vol. 29, No. 4, pp. 369–389 (May 1992).

BOYATZIS, R. E., AND SKELLY, F. E. "The Impact of Changing Values on Organizational Life." In Kolb, J., Rubin I. M., and Osland, J. S. (eds) *The Organizational Reader.* Englewood Cliffs, NJ: Prentice Hall, 1991.

BRADFORD, D., AND COHEN, A. "Overarching Goals." In *Managing for Excellence.* New York: John Wiley and Sons, Inc., 1984.

BRANSFORD, J. D., AND JOHNSON, M. K. "Contextual Prerequisites for Understanding: Some Investigations of Comprehension and Recall." *Journal of Verbal Learning and Verbal Behavior*, Vol. 11, pp. 717–726 (1972).

BROOKS, F. P., JR. *The Mythical Man-Month: Essays on Software Engineering.* Reading, MA: Addison-Wesley, 1975.

BROOKS, F. P., JR. *The Mythical Man-Month: Essays on Software Engineering.* Anniversary ed. Reading, MA: Addison-Wesley, 1995.

BROWN, K. A., KLASTORIN, T. D., AND VALLUZZI, J. L. "Project Performance and the Liability of Group Harmony." *IEEE Transactions on Engineering Management,* Vol. 37, No. 2, pp. 117–125 (May 1990).

CARD, S. K., MORAN, T. P., AND NEWELL, A. *The Psychology of Human-Computer Interaction.* Hillsdale, NJ: Lawrence Erlbaum Associates, 1983.

CARGILL, T. *C++ Programming Style.* Reading, MA: Addison-Wesley, 1992.

CARROLL, J., AND CARRITHERS, C. "Training Wheels in a User Interface." *Comm. of the ACM,* Vol. 27, No. 8 (August 1984).

CARROLL J., AND AARONSON, A. "Learning by Doing with Simulated Intelligent Help." *Comm. of the ACM,* Vol. 31, No. 9 (September 1988).

CHANDLER, D. C. "The Sapir-Whorf Hypothesis" http://www.aber.ac.uk/~dgc/whorf.html (1994).

CHASE, W. G., AND SIMON, H. "Perception in Chess." *Cognitive Psychology,* Vol. 4, pp. 55–81 (1973).

CHRISTIANSEN, D. "On Good Designers." *IEEE Spectrum,* Vol. 24, No. 5 (May 1987).

COAD, P., NORTH, D., AND MAYFIELD, M. *Object Models: Strategies, Patterns, and Applications.* Englewood Cliffs, NJ: Prentice Hall, 1995.

COLEMAN, D., ARNOLD, P., BODOFF, S., DOLLIN, C., GILCHRIST, H., HAYES, F., AND JEREMAES, P. *Object-Oriented Development: The Fusion Method.* Englewood Cliffs, NJ: Prentice Hall, 1994.

CONWAY, M. E. "How Do Committees Invent." *Datamation,* Vol. 14, No. 10, pp. 28–31 (Oct. 1968).

CONSTANTINE, L. "Teamwork Paradigms and the Structured Open Team." In *Proceedings of Software Development '90.* San Francisco: CA, Miller Freeman Publishing, 1990.

CONSTANTINE, L. "Work Organization: Paradigms for Project Management and Organization." *Comm. of the ACM,* Vol. 36, No. 10, pp. 34–43 (Oct. 1993).

CONSTANTINE, L. *Constantine of Peopleware.* Englewood Cliffs, NJ: Prentice Hall, 1995.

COPLIEN, J., AND SCHMIDT, D. C. *Pattern Languages of Program Design.* Reading, MA: Addison-Wesley, 1995.

CORTES-COMERER, N. "Organizing the Design Team—Motto for Specialists: Give some, Get Some." *IEEE Spectrum,* pp. 41–46 (May 1987).

CROUCH, C. J., AND CROUCH, D. B. "The Impact of External Factors on Productivity in an Engineering Support Organization." *IEEE Transactions on Engineering Management,* Vol. 35, No. 3, pp. 147–157 (Aug 1988).

CUFF, D. *Architecture: The Story of Practice.* Cambridge, MA: MIT Press, 1992.

CURTIS, B. "Substantiating Programmer Variability." *Proceedings of the IEEE,* Vol. 69, No. 7 (1981).

CURTIS, B., GUINDON, R., KRASNER, H., WALZ, D., ELAM, J., AND ISCOE, N. "Empirical Studies of the Design Process: Papers for the Second Workshop on Empirical Studies of Programmers." MCC Technical Report STP-260-87 (Sept. 1987).

CURTIS, B., KRASNER, H., AND ISCOE, N. "A Field Study of the Software Design Process for Large Systems." *Comm. of the ACM,* Vol. 31, No. 11 (Nov. 1988).

DEMARCO, T., AND LISTER, T. *Peopleware: Productive People and Teams.* New York: Dorset House, 1987.

DEMARCO, T. *Controlling Software Projects.* Englewood Cliffs, NJ: Prentice Hall, 1982.

DEMING, W. E. *Out of the Crisis.* Cambridge, MA: MIT, Center for Advanced Engineering Study, 1986.

DENIS, H. "Matrix Structures, Quality of Working Life, and Engineering Productivity." *IEEE Transactions on Engineering Management,* Vol. EM-33, No. 3, pp. 148–156 (Aug. 1986).

DIJSKTRA, E.W. "The Structure of the 'THE'-multiprogramming System." *Comm. of the ACM,* Vol. 11, No. 5, pp. 341–346 (May 1968).

DIJKSTRA, E. W. "The Humble Programmer."(1972) in *ACM Turing Award Lectures.* New York: ACM Press, 1987.

DONABEDIAN, A. *The Definition of Quality and Approaches to Its Assessment.* Ann Arbor, MI: Health Administration Press, 1981.

DONNELLON, A., GRAY, B., AND BOUGON, M. G. "Communication, Meaning, and Organized Action." *Administrative Science Quaterly,* Vol. 31, pp. 43–55 (1986).

DONNITHORNE, L. *The West Point Way of Leadership: From Learning Principled Leadership to Practicing It.* New York: Doubleday, 1993.

DRISCOLL, J. W. "Trust and Participation in Organizational Decision Making as Predictors of Satisfaction." *Academy of Management Journal,* Vol. 21, No. 1, pp. 44–56 (1978).

ENRIGHT, J. *Change and Resiliance.* Eden Prairie, MN: Wilson Learning Corp., 1984.

FAFCHAMPS, D. "Organizational Factors and Reuse." *IEEE Software,* Vol. 11, No. 5, pp. 31–41 (Sep. 1994).

FAGAN, M.E. "Design and Code Inspections to Reduce Errors in Program Development." *IBM Systems Journal*, Vol. 15, No. 3, pp. 182–211 (Feb. 1976).

FAIRLEY, R. *Software Engineering Concepts.* New York: McGraw-Hill, 1985.

FOXALL, G. R. "Consumer Initiators: Both Innovators and Adaptors." In Kirton, M. (ed.), *Adapters and Innovators*, New York: Routledge, 1994.

FREEDMAN, D., AND WEINBERG, G. *Handbook of Walkthroughs, Inspections, and Technical Reviews.* New York: Dorset House, 1990.

FREEMAN-BELL, G., AND BALKWILL, J. *Management in Engineering: Principles and Practice.* Hertfordshire, UK: Prentice Hall International, 1993.

GALBRAITH, J. *Designing Complex Organizations.* Reading, MA: Addison-Wesley, 1979.

GAMMA, E., HELM, R., JOHNSON, R., AND VLISSIDES, J. *Design Patterns: Elements of Reusable Object-Oriented Software.* Reading, MA: Addison-Wesley, 1995.

GAUSE G., AND WEINBERG, G. *Are Your Lights On?* New York: Dorset House, 1990.

GAUSE G., AND G. WEINBERG. *Exploring Requirements Quality Before Design.* New York: Dorset House, 1989.

GELLERMAN, S. W. "In Organizations, as in Architecture, Form Follows Function." *Organizational Dynamics,* Vol. 18, No. 3, pp. 57–68 (Winter 1990).

GILB, T. *Principles of Software Engineering Management.* Avon, UK: The Bath Press, 1988.

GLASS, R. L., AND NOISEUX, R. A. *Software Maintenance Guidebook.* Englewood Cliffs, NJ: Prentice Hall, 1981.

GLASS, R. L. *Software Creativity.* Englewood Cliffs, NJ: Prentice Hall, 1995.

GLEICK, J. *Chaos: Making a New Science.* New York: Penguin Books, 1987.

GOLDBERG, A., AND RUBIN, K. *Succeeding With Objects: Decision Frameworks for Project Management.* Reading, MA: Addison-Wesley, 1995.

GOLDSMITH, R. E. "Creative Style and Personality Theory." In Kirton, M. (ed.), *Adapters and Innovators.* New York: Routledge, 1994.

GOLSON, H. L. "The Technically-Oriented Personality in Management." *IEEE Transactions on Engineering Management,* Vol. EM-32, No. 1, pp. 105–110 (Feb. 1985).

GOULD, J. D. "How to Design Usable Systems." In Helander, M. (ed.), *Handbook of Human-Computer Interaction.* Elsevier Science Publishers B.V., New York, 1988.

GRISS, M. L. "Software Reuse: From Library to Factory." *IBM Systems Journal,* Vol. 32, No. 4, pp. 548–566 (1993).

GROVE, A. *High Output Management.* United Kingdom: Random House and Souvenir Press, 1983.

GROVE, A. "Management: Task-Relevant Maturity." *Modern Office Technology,* Vol. 29, No. 8, pp. 16–20 (Aug 1984).

GUZDIAL, M. *Emile: Software-Realized Scaffolding for Science Learners Programming in Mixed Media.* PhD Thesis. Ann Arbor, MI: University of Michigan, 1993.

HALEY, U. C. V., AND STUMPF, S. A. "Cognitive Trails in Strategic Decision-Making: Linking Theories of Personalities and Cognitions." *Journal of Management Studies,* Vol. 26, No. 5, pp. 477–497 (Sept. 1989).

HALL, J. "Communication Revisited." *California Management Review,* Vol. 15, No. 3 (1973).

HAMMER, M., AND CHAMPY, J. *Reengineering the Corporation: A Manifesto For Business Revolution.* New York: HarperCollins Publishers, Inc., 1993.

HANKS, K., AND PARRY, J. *Wake Up Your Creative Genius.* Los Altos, CA: Crisp Publications, Inc., 1991.

HAREL, D. *Algorithmics: The Spirit of Computing.* Wokingham, UK: Addison-Wesley, 1987.

HAREL, D. "Biting the Silver Bullet: Toward a Brighter Future for System Development." *Computer,* pp. 8–20 (Jan. 1992).

HARRIS, R. J., AND BREWER, W. F. "Deixis in Memory for Verb Tense." *Journal of Verbal Learning and Verbal Behavior,* Vol. 12, pp. 590–597 (1973).

HATCH, M. J. "The Dynamics of Organizational Culture." *Academy of Management Review,* Vol. 18, No. 4, pp. 657–693 (1993).

HATCHL, B. *Maps and More: Your Guide to Census Bureau Geography.* Washington, DC: U.S. Bureau of the Census, 1992.

HAYWORD, G., AND EVERETT, C. "Adapters and Innovators: Data From The Kirton Adaption-Innovation Inventory in a Local Authority Setting." *Journal of Occupational Psychology,* Vol. 56, pp. 339–342 (1983).

HENDERSON, J. C., AND NUTT, P. C. "The Influence of Decision Style on Decision Making Behavior." *Management Science,* Vol. 26, No. 4, pp. 371–386 (April 1980).

HENDERSON-SELLERS, B. "The Economics of Reusing Library Classes." *Journal of Object-Oriented Programming,* Vol. 6, No. 4 (July–Aug 1993).

HOARE, C. "The Emperors Old Clothes." (1981). In *ACM Turing Award Lectures.* New York: ACM Press, 1987.

HOARE, C. "An Overview of Some Formal Methods for Program Design." *IEEE Computer,* Vol. 20, No. 9, pp. 85–91 (Sept. 1987).

HOFSTEDE, G. "Motivation, Leadership, and Organization: Do American Theories Apply Abroad?" *Organizational Dynamics,* Vol. 9, No. 1, pp. 42–63 (Summer 1980).

HOHMANN, L. "An Object-Oriented Data Model of Programming Plans." Software Engineering Research Paper, University of Michigan unpublished.

HOHMANN, L., GUZDIAL, M., AND SOLOWAY, E. "SODA: A Computer-Aided Design Environment for the Doing and Learning of Software Design." In *Computer Assisted Learning.* New York: Springer-Verlag, 4th International Conference on Computers and Learning (1992).

HOLDSWORTH, J. *Software Process Design.* UK: McGraw-Hill International, 1994.

HOPKINS, T. *How to Master the Art of Selling.* New York: Warner Books, 1982.

HOWLEY, E., AND FRANKS, D.B. *Health Fitness Instructor's Handbook.* Champaign, IL: Human Kinetic Books, 1992.

HUMPHREY, W. S. "Characterizing the Software Process: A Maturity Framework." *IEEE Software,* Vol. 5, No. 2, pp. 73–79 (March 1988).

HUMPHREY, W. S. *A Discipline for Software Engineering.* Reading, MA: Addison-Wesley, 1995.

HUNT, J. W. *The Restless Organization.* Sydney: Wiley and Sons, Australia Pty. Ltd., 1972.

IDEA FOUNDATION. *Aerobic Dance-Exercise Instructor Manual.* San Diego, CA: IDEA Foundation, 1987.

IEEE Standard Glossary of Software Engineering Terminology, IEEE Standard, pp. 729, 1983.

IOOSS, W. *RareAir: Michael on Michael.* New York: HarperCollins Publishers.

JAY, A. "How to Run a Meeting." *Harvard Business Review.*

Jacobson, I., Christerson, M., Jonsson, P., and Övergaard, G. *Object-Oriented Software Engineering: A Use Case Driven Approach.* Reading, MA: Addison-Wesley, 1992.

Janis, I. L. "Groupthink." *Psychology Today* (Nov. 1971).

JENNER, M. G. *Software Quality Management and ISO 9001.* New York: John Wiley & Sons, 1995.

JOHNSON, J., SKOGLUND, R., AND WISNIEWSKI, J. *Program Smarter, Not Harder.* New York: McGraw-Hill, Inc., 1995.

JOHNSON, P. *Personal Communication* (1995).

JONES, C. "How Software Personnel Learn New Skills." *IEEE Computer,* Vol. 28, No. 12, pp. 88–89 (Dec. 1995).

JURAN, J. M. *Out of the Crisis.* Cambridge, MA: MIT, Center for Advanced Engineering Study, 1986.

KAHN, J. A. *Failure Construction in Organizations: Exploring the Effects of Failure Norms.* PhD Thesis. Ann Arbor, MI: University of Michigan, 1994.

KANTER, R. M. *The Changemasters.* New York: Simon and Schuster, 1983.

KAWASAKI, G. *The Macintosh Way.* San Francisco: HarperCollins Publishers, 1990.

KEIRSEY, D., AND BATES, M.. *Please Understand Me: Character and Temperament Types.* Del Mar, CA: Prometheus Nemesis Book Company, 1984.

KELLEY, R. E. "In Praise of Followers." In Gabarro, J. *Managing People and Organizations.* Boston, MA: Harvard Business School Publications, 1992.

KERNAGHAN, J. A., AND COOKE, R. A. "The Contribution of the Group Process to Successful Project Planning in R&D Settings." *IEEE Transactions on Engineering Management,* Vol. EM-33, No. 3, pp. 134–140 (Aug. 1986).

KIRTON, M. *Adapters and Innovators,* New York: NY. Routledge, 1994.

KNOWLES, M. *The Adult Learner: A Neglected Species,* 3d ed. Houston, TX: Gulf Publishing, 1984.

LAMMERS, S. *Programmers at Work.* Redmond, WA: Microsoft Press, 1989.

LAMPSON, B. "Hints for Computer System Design." *IEEE Software,* pp. 11–30 (Jan. 1984).

LIEBLEIN, E. "The Department of Defense Software Initiative—A Status Report." *Comm. of the ACM,* Vol. 29, No. 8 (Aug. 1986).

LINN, M.C., AND CLANCY, M. J. "The Case for Case Studies of Programming Problems." *Comm. of ACM,* Vol. 35, No. 3 (Mar. 1992).

LITTMAN, D. C., PINTO, J., LETOVSKY, S., AND SOLOWAY, E. "Mental Models and Software Maintenance." *Jrnl. of Systems and Software,* Vol. 7, No. 4, pp. 341–355 (Dec. 1987).

LORENZ, M. "A Return on Your Consulting Investment: How to Hire an Outside Consultant." *Journal of Object-Oriented Programming,* Vol. 6, No. 5 (Sept. 1993).

MACKIE, R. R., AND WYLIE, C. D. "Factors Influencing Acceptance of Computer-Based Innovations." In Helander, M. (ed.), *Handbook of Human-Computer Interaction.* New York: Elsevier Science Publishers B.V., 1988.

MAGUIRE, S. *Writing Solid Code.* Redmond, WA: Microsoft Press, 1993.

MAGUIRE, S. *Debugging the Development Process.* Redmond, WA: Microsoft Press, 1994.

MARTIN, J., AND TSAI, W. T. "N-Fold Inspection: A Requirements Analysis Technique." *Comm. of the ACM,* Vol. 32, No. 2 (Feb. 1990).

MARTIN, R. M. *The Meaning of Language.* Cambridge, MA: MIT Press, 1989.

MATHIS, R. F. "The Last 10 Percent." *IEEE Transactions on Software Engineering,* Vol. SE-12, No. 6, pp. 705–712 (June 1986).

MCCABE, T. J. "A Complexity Measure." *IEEE Trans. on Soft. Eng.,* Vol. 2, No. 6 (Dec. 1976).

MCCASKEY, M. B. "A Framework for Analyzing Work Groups." In Gabarro, J. *Managing People and Organizations.* Boston, MA: Harvard Business School Publications, 1992.

MCCONNELL, S. *Code Complete.* Redmond, WA: Microsoft Press, 1993.

MCCARTHY, S. *Dynamics of Software Development.* Redmond, WA: Microsoft Press, 1995.

MCCOLLUM, J. K., AND SHERMAN, J. D. "The Effects of Matrix Organization Size and Number of Project Assignments on Performance." *IEEE Transactions on Engineering Management,* Vol. 38, No. 1, pp. 75–78 (Feb. 1991).

MEYER, B. *Object-Oriented Software Construction.* Englewood Cliffs, NJ: Prentice Hall, 1988.

MEYERS, S. *Effective C++.* Reading, MA: Addison-Wesley, 1992.

MILLER, M. L. "A Structured Planning and Debugging Environment for Elementary Programming." In *Intelligent Tutoring Systems*. San Diego, CA: Academic Press, 1982.

MINTZBERG, H., AND QUINN, J. B. *The Strategy Process—Concepts and Contexts*. Englewood Cliffs, NJ: Prentice Hall, 1992.

MORROW, D. G. "Prepositions and Verb Aspect in Narrative Understanding." *Journal of Memory and Language,* Vol. 24, pp. 390–404 (1985).

NADLER, D. A., ET AL. *Organizational Architecture: Designs for Changing Organizations.* San Francisco: Jossey-Bass, 1992.

NEWELL, A., AND SIMON, H. A. "Computer Science as Empirical Inquiry: Symbols and Search." In *ACM Turing Award Lectures*. New York: ACM Press, 1987.

NIELSEN, J. *Usability Engineering.* New York: Harcourt Brace & Company, Publishers, 1993.

NOE, J. R. *Peak Performance Principles for High Achievers.* New York: Frederick Fell Publishers, 1984.

NORDEN, P. "Curve Fitting for a Model of Applied Research and Development Scheduling." *IBM J. Rsch. Dev.,* Vol. 2, No. 3 (1958).

NUTT, P. C. "Influence of Decision Styles on Use of Decision Models." *Technological Forecasting and Social Change,* Vol 14, pp. 77–93 (1979).

O'CONNELL, F. *How to Run Successful Projects.* Hertfordshire, UK: Prentice Hall, 1994.

ORPEN, C. "Individual Needs, Organizational Rewards, and Job Satisfaction Among Professional Engineers." *IEEE Trans. on Eng. Mgt.,* Vol. EM-32, No. 4 (Nov. 1985).

ORTON, J. D., AND WEICK, K. E. "Loosely Coupled Systems: a Reconceptualization." *Acadamy of Management Review,* Vol. 15, No. 2, pp 203–223 (1990).

OZ, EZZY "When Professional Standards are Lax: The CONFIRM Failure and Its Lessons." *Comm. of the ACM,* Vol. 37, No. 10, pp. 29–36 (Oct. 1994).

PAGE-JONES, M. *Practical Project Management.* New York: Dorset House, 1985.

PAGE-JONES, M. *The Practical Guide to Structured Systems Design, 2d ed.* Englewood Cliffs, NJ: Prentice Hall, 1988.

PAGE-JONES, M. "The Seven Stages in Software Engineering." *American Programmer,* (July–Aug., 1990).

[PARNAS 1972A] PARNAS, D. L. "A Technique for Software Module Specification with Examples." *Comm. of the ACM,* Vol. 15, No. 5, pp. 330–336 (May. 1972).

[PARNAS 1972B] PARNAS, D. L. "On the Criteria to Be Used in Decomposing Systems into Modules." *Comm. of the ACM,* Vol. 15, No. 12, pp. 1053–1058 (Dec. 1972).

PARNAS, D. L. "On the Design and Development of Program Families." *IEEE Trans. On Soft. Eng.,* Vol. SE-2, No. 1, pp. 1–9 (March 1976).

PARNAS, D. L. "Designing Software For Ease of Extension and Contraction." *IEEE Trans. on Soft. Eng.,* Vol. SE-5, No. 2, pp. 128–138 (March 1979).

PARNAS, D. L., AND CLEMENTS, P. C. "A Rational Design Process: How and Why to Fake It." *IEEE Trans. on Soft. Eng.,* Vol. SE-12, No. 2, pp. 251–257 (Feb. 1986).

PASCALE, R. T., AND ATHOS, A. G. "Great Companies Make Meaning." in Williamson, J. N. (ed.) *The Leader Manager.* New York: John Wiley and Sons, 1981.

PERRY, D. E., STAUDENMAYER, N. A., AND VOTTA, L. G. "People, Organizations, and Process Improvement." *IEEE Software,* pp. 36–45 (July 1994).

PETERS, T., AND WATERMAN, R. *In Search of Excellence.* New York: Harper and Row, 1982.

PETROSKI, H. *To Engineer is Human: The Role of Failure in Successful Design.* New York: St. Martin's Press, 1985.

PHILLIPS, J. R., AND KENNEDY, A. A. "Shaping and Managing Shared Values." in Williamson, J. N. (ed.) *The Leader Manager.* New York: John Wiley and Sons, 1981.

PIRSIG, R. M. *Zen and the Art of Motorcycle Maintenance.* New York: Bantam Books, 1975.

PIRSIG, R. M. *Lila.* New York: Bantam Books, 1991.

PITTMAN, M. "Lessons Learned in Managing Object-Oriented Development." *IEEE Software* (Jan. 1993).

PORTER, M. E. *Competitive Strategy.* Macmillan, Inc.

POYLA, G. *How to Solve It: A New Aspect of Mathematical Method,* 2d ed. Princeton, NJ: Princeton University Press, 1957.

PRATT, J. H. "Socio-Issues Related to Home-Based Work." In Helander, M. (ed.), *Handbook of Human-Computer Interaction.* New York: Elsevier Science Publishers, 1988.

PRESSMAN, R. *A Manager's Guide to Software Engineering.* McGraw-Hill, 1993.

PUTNAM, L. "A Macro-Estimating Methodology for Software Development." *Proc. IEEE COMPCON '76* (Sept. 1976).

PUTNAM, L. "A General Empirical Solution to the Macro Software Sizing and Estimating Problem." *IEEE Trans. on Soft. Eng.,* Vol. SE-4, No. 4, pp. 345–361 (July 1978).

QUINN, J. B. "Managing Innovation: Controlled Chaos." *Harvard Business Review* (July–Aug. 1975).

QUINN, R. S. *Beyond Rational Management.* San Francisco, CA: Jossey-Bass, 1988.

QUINN, R. S., FAERMAN, M., THOMPSON, AND MCGRATH, M. *Becoming a Master Manager: A Competency Framework.* New York : John Wiley and Sons, 1990.

RITTEL, H., AND WEBBER, M. "Dilemmas in a General Theory of Planning." *Policy Sciences,* Vol. 4, pp. 155–169 (1973).

ROGERS, E. M. *Diffusion of Innovations* 3d ed. New York: The Free Press, 1983.

ROWEN, R. B. "Software Project Management Under Incomplete and Ambiguous Specifications." *IEEE Tran. on Eng. Mgt.,* Vol. 37, No. 1, pp. 10–21 (Feb. 1990).

RUMBAUGH, J., BLAHA, M., PREMERLANI, W., EDDY, F., AND LORENSEN, W. *Object-Oriented Modeling and Design.* Englewood Cliffs, NJ: Prentice Hall, 1991.

SACKMAN, H., ERIKSON, W. J., AND GRANT, E. E. "Exploratory Experimental Studies Comparing Online and Offline Programming Performance." *Comm. of the ACM,* Vol. 11, No. 1, pp. 3–11 (Jan. 1968).

SALANCIK, G. R., AND PFEFFER, J. "Who Gets Power—And How They Hold On To It: A Strategic Contigency Model of Power." *Organizational Dynamics* (Winter, 1977).

SCHEIN, E. H. "Coming to a New Awareness of Organizational Culture." *Sloan Management Review,* Vol. 25, No. 2, pp. 3–16 (Winter 1984).

SCHNEIDER, G. M, MARTIN, J., AND TSAI, W. T. "An Experimental Study of Fault Detection in User Requirements Documents." *ACM Trans. on Soft. Eng. and Methodology,* Vol. 1, No. 2 (April 1992).

SCHNEIDEWIND, N. F. "The State of Software Maintenance." *IEEE Trans. on Soft. Eng.,* Vol. SE-13, No. 3, pp. 303–310 (Mar. 1987).

SCHOLTES, P. R. *The Team Handbook.* Madison, WI: Joiner Associates, 1988.

SCHON, D. A. "Deutero-Learning in Organizations: Learning for Increased Effectiveness." in Williamson, J. N. (ed.) *The Leader Manager.* New York: John Wiley and Sons, 1986.

SCHULTZ, R. *Object-Oriented Project Management.* OOPSLA-95 Austin: TX, 1995.

SECMM-94-04. *A Systems Engineering Capability Maturity Model, Version 1.0.* Software Engineering Institute (Dec. 1994).

SHNEIDERMAN, B. *Software Psychology.* Cambridge, MA: Winthrop Press, 1980.

SMITH, D. H. "A Parsimonious Definition of 'Group': Toward Conceptual Clarity and Scientific Utility." *Sociological Inquiry,* Vol. 37, No. 2 (Spring 1967).

SILVERMAN, B. G. "Expert Intuition and Ill-Structured Problem Solving." *IEEE Trans. on Eng. Mgt.,* Vol. EM-32, No. 1 (Feb. 1985).

SIMON, H. A. *Administrative Behavior.* New York: Free Press, 1957.

SIMON, H. A. *The Sciences of the Artificial* 2d ed. Cambridge, MA: MIT Press, 1981.

SELLERS, D. *Zap! How Your Computer Can Hurt You—And What You Can Do About It.* Berkeley, CA: Peachpit Press, 1994.

SOLOWAY, E., BONAR, J., AND EHRLICH, K. "Cognitive Strategies and Looping Constructs." *Comm. of the ACM,* Vol. 26, No. 11 (1983).

SOLOWAY, E., AND EHRLICH, K. "Empirical Studies of Programming Knowledge." *IEEE Trans. on Soft. Eng.,* Vol. 10, No. 5, pp. 595–609 (Sept. 1984).

SOLOWAY, E., PINTO, L., LETOVSKY, S., LITTMAN, D., AND LAMPERT, R. "Designing Documentation to Compensate for Delocalized Plans." *Comm. of the ACM,* Vol. 31, No. 11 (Nov. 1988).

SPANGENBERG, G. *Personal Communication* (1995).

STARBUCK, W. H. "Keeping a Butterfly and an Elephant in a House of Cards: The Elements of Exceptional Success." *Journal of Management Studies,* Vol. 30, No. 6, pp. 885–921 (Nov. 1993).

STEVENS, W., MYERS, G., AND CONSTANTINE, L. "Structured Design." *IBM Systems Journal,* Vol. 13, No. 2 (1974).

STROUSTRUP B. *The C++ Programming Language, 2d Edition.* Reading, MA: Addison-Wesley, 1991

STROUSTRUP B. *The Design and Evolution of C++.* Reading, MA: Addison-Wesley, 1994.

SWARTOUT, W., AND BALZER, R. "On the Inevitable Intertwining of Specification and Implementation." *Comm. of the ACM* (July 1982).

SZILAGYI, A. D., AND J. M. IVANCEVICH. *Organizational Behavior and Performance.* Santa Monica, CA: Goodyear Publishing Company,

TANNIRU, M. R. "Causes of Turnover Among DP Professionals." *Proceedings of the 8th Annual Computer Personnel Research Conference,* Miami, FL, (June 1981).

THAMHAIN, H. J., AND WILEMON, D. L. "Building High Performance Engineering Project Teams." *IEEE Transactions on Engineering Management,* Vol. EM-34, No. 3, pp. 130–137 (Aug. 1987).

THIELEN, D. *No Bugs.* Santa Monica, CA: Addison-Wesley.

THOMPSON, K. "Refelections on Trusting Trust." *Comm. of the ACM,* Vol. 27, No. 9, pp. 761–764 (1984).

THOMSETT, R. *Third Wave Project Management: A Handbook for Managing the Complex Information Systems of the 1990s.* Englewood Cliffs, NJ: Prentice Hall, .

TROPMAN, J. E., AND MORNINGTAR, G. *Entrepreneurial Systems for the 90's: Their Creation, Structure, and Management.* New York: Quorum Books, 1989.

TUCKMAN, B. W. "Developmental Sequence in Small Groups." *Psychological Bulletin* 63, pp. 384–399 (1965).

VINTON, D. E. "A New Look At Time, Speed, and the Manager." *Acadamy of Management Executive,* Vol. 6, No. 4, pp. 7–16 (Nov. 1992).

WALTON, M. *The Deming Management Method.* New York: Perigree Books.

WARE, J. "How To Run a Meeting" *Harvard Business Review.*

WATERMAN, R. H., JR., PETERS, T. J., AND PHILLIPS, J. R. "Structure is Not Organization." *Business Horizons,* Vol. 23, No. 3, pp. 14–26 (June 1980).

WATERS, R. C. "KBEmacs: A Step Toward the Programmer's Apprentice." *MIT Technical Report AI-TR 753* (1985).

WEGNER, D. M. "Transactive Memory: A Contemporary Analysis of the Group Mind." in Mullen, B., and Goethals, G. R. (eds.), *Theories of Group Behavior,* pp 185–208, New York: Springer-Verlag,

WEICK, K. *The Social Psychology of Organizing,* 2d ed. New York: Random House, 1979.

WEICK, K. E. "Educational Organizations as Loosely Coupled Systems." *Administrative Science Quarterly,* Vol. 21, No. 1, pp. 1–19 (March 1976).

WEICK, K. E. "Organized Improvization: 20 Years of Organizing." *Communication Studies,* Vol. 40, No. 4 (Winter 1989).

WEICK, K. E. "Organizational Culture as a Source of High Reliability." *California Management Review,* Vol. 29, No. 2, pp. 112–127 (Winter 1987).

[WEICK 1993A] WEICK, K. E., AND ROBERTS, K. H. "Collective Mind in Organizations: Heedful Interrelating on Flight Decks." *Administrative Science Quarterly,* Vol. 38, No. 3, pp. 357–381 (June 1993).

[WEICK 1993B] WEICK, K. E. "The Collapse of Sensemaking in Organizations: The Mann Gulch Disaster." *Administrative Science Quarterly,* Vol. 38, No. 4, pp. 628–652 (Dec. 1993).

WEINBERG, G. M. *The Psychology of Computer Programming.* New York: Van Nostrand Reinhold, 1971.

WEINBERG, G. M., AND SCHULMAN, E. L. "Goals and Performance in Computer Programming." *Human Factors,* Vol. 16, No. 1, pp. 70–77 (1974).

WEINBERG, G. M. "Overstructured Management of Software Engineering." *Proceedings of the Sixth International Conference on Software Engineering,* Sept. 13–16, pp. 2–8, Tokyo, Japan (1982).

WEINBERG, G. M. *Quality Software Management Volume 1: Systems Thinking.* New York: Dorset House, 1992.

WEINBERG, G. M. *Quality Software Management Volume 2: First-Order Measurement.* New York: Dorset House, 1993.

WEINBERG, G. M. *Quality Software Management Volume 3: Congruent Action.* New York: Dorset House, 1994.

WEISBAND, S. P., AND REINIG, B. A. "Managing User Perceptions of E-mail Privacy." *Comm. of the ACM,* pp. 40–47 (Dec. 1995).

WHITESIDE, J. "Usability Engineering: Our Experience and Evolution." In Helander, M. (ed.), *Handbook of Human-Computer Interaction.* New York: Elsevier Science Publishers, 1988.

WHITMAN, R. F., AND BOASE, P. H. *Speech Communication.* New York: Macmillan Publishing Co., Inc., 1983.

WHORF, B. L. *Language, Thought, and Reality.* Carroll, J. B. (ed.), Cambridge, MA: MIT, 1956.

WILF, H. S. *Algorithms and Complexity.* Englewood Cliffs, NJ: Prentice Hall, 1986.

WILLIAMS, C. L. "Managing People, Process, and Place in High-Technology Industries." In *Managing and Designing for High-Technology Workplaces.* New York: Van Nostrand Reinhold, 1989.

WINOGRAD, T. "Beyond Programming Languages." *Comm. of the ACM,* Vol. 22, No. 7 (July 1979).

WIRTH, N. "Program Development by Stepwise Refinement." *Comm. of the ACM,* Vol. 14, No. 4, pp. 221–227 (April 1971).

WOOD, R. E., AND LOCKE, E. A. "Goal Setting and Strategy Effects on Complex Tasks." *Research in Organizational Behavior,* Vol. 12, pp. 73–109 (1990).

YOURDON, E., AND CONSTANTINE, L. *Structured Design.* Englewood Cliffs, NJ: Prentice Hall, 1979.

YOURDON, E. *Decline and Fall of the American Programmer.* Englewood Cliffs, NJ: Prentice Hall, 1992.

AUTHOR INDEX

SUBJECT INDEX

About the Author

Luke Hohmann graduated from the University of Michigan in 1992 with an M.S.E. in Computer Science and Engineering. He is a member of the IEEE and ACM. A former competitive figure skater, Luke garnered numerous honors and awards in his fourteen-year career. In 1985, he and his partner won the United States National Junior Pairs Championship and represented the United States in international competition. Luke was a two-time competitor at the United States Olympic Festival. At present, Luke maintains an active lifestyle as an American College of Sports Medicine (ACSM-HFI) certified aerobics instructor, teaching between three and five aerobics classes per week. His experience as an athlete have provided valuable inspiration for improving his abilities as a software professional and have served to illustrate several key concepts in this book. He lives in Dallas, Texas with his beautiful wife and best friend, Noura. Luke and Noura have a lot of fun playing with their two dogs, Zoa and Austin.